Transforming the Language Teaching Experience in the Age of AI

Galip Kartal
Necmettin Erbakan University, Turkey

A volume in the Advances in Educational Technologies and Instructional Design (AETID) Book Series

IGI Global
PUBLISHER of TIMELY KNOWLEDGE

Published in the United States of America by
IGI Global
Information Science Reference (an imprint of IGI Global)
701 E. Chocolate Avenue
Hershey PA, USA 17033
Tel: 717-533-8845
Fax: 717-533-8661
E-mail: cust@igi-global.com
Web site: http://www.igi-global.com

Library of Congress Cataloging-in-Publication Data

Names: Kartal, Galip, 1986- editor.
Title: Transforming the language teaching experience in the age of AI / edited by Galip Kartal.
Description: Hershey, PA : Information Science Reference, 2024. | Includes bibliographical references and index. | Summary: "The objective of this book is to provide a comprehensive, in-depth analysis of the role of artificial intelligence (AI) in language education, elucidating its potential for reshaping pedagogical practices and enhancing learning outcomes"-- Provided by publisher.
Identifiers: LCCN 2023034634 (print) | LCCN 2023034635 (ebook) | ISBN 9781668498934 (hardcover) | ISBN 9781668498941 (ebook)
Subjects: LCSH: Languages, Modern--Study and teaching--Technological innovations. | English language--Study and teaching--Technological innovations. | English language--Study and teaching--Foreign speakers. | Artificial intelligence--Educational applications.
Classification: LCC PB36 .T73 2024 (print) | LCC PB36 (ebook) | DDC 418.0078/5--dc23/eng/20230906
LC record available at https://lccn.loc.gov/2023034634
LC ebook record available at https://lccn.loc.gov/2023034635

This book is published in the IGI Global book series Advances in Educational Technologies and Instructional Design (AETID) (ISSN: 2326-8905; eISSN: 2326-8913)

British Cataloguing in Publication Data
A Cataloguing in Publication record for this book is available from the British Library.

Advances in Educational Technologies and Instructional Design (AETID) Book Series

ISSN:2326-8905
EISSN:2326-8913

MISSION

Education has undergone, and continues to undergo, immense changes in the way it is enacted and distributed to both child and adult learners. In modern education, the traditional classroom learning experience has evolved to include technological resources and to provide online classroom opportunities to students of all ages regardless of their geographical locations. From distance education, Massive-Open-Online-Courses (MOOCs), and electronic tablets in the classroom, technology is now an integral part of learning and is also affecting the way educators communicate information to students.

The **Advances in Educational Technologies & Instructional Design (AETID) Book Series** explores new research and theories for facilitating learning and improving educational performance utilizing technological processes and resources. The series examines technologies that can be integrated into K-12 classrooms to improve skills and learning abilities in all subjects including STEM education and language learning. Additionally, it studies the emergence of fully online classrooms for young and adult learners alike, and the communication and accountability challenges that can arise. Trending topics that are covered include adaptive learning, game-based learning, virtual school environments, and social media effects. School administrators, educators, academicians, researchers, and students will find this series to be an excellent resource for the effective design and implementation of learning technologies in their classes.

COVERAGE

- Collaboration Tools
- Adaptive Learning
- Online Media in Classrooms
- Bring-Your-Own-Device
- Instructional Design
- Digital Divide in Education
- E-Learning
- Virtual School Environments
- Curriculum Development
- Educational Telecommunications

The Advances in Educational Technologies and Instructional Design (AETID) Book Series (ISSN 2326-8905) is published by IGI Global, 701 E. Chocolate Avenue, Hershey, PA 17033-1240, USA, www.igi-global.com. This series is composed of titles available for purchase individually; each title is edited to be contextually exclusive from any other title within the series. For pricing and ordering information please visit http://www.igi-global.com/book-series/advances-educational-technologies-instructional-design/73678. Postmaster: Send all address changes to above address.

Titles in this Series

For a list of additional titles in this series, please visit:
http://www.igi-global.com/book-series/advances-educational-technologies-instructional-design/73678

Developing Skills and Competencies for Digital and Green Transitions
Patricia Ordóñez de Pablos (The University of Oviedo, Spain) Mohammad Nabil Almunawar (School of Business and Economics, University of Brunei Darussalam, Brunei) and Muhammad Anshari (School of Business and Economics, University of Brunei Darussalam, Brunei)
Business Science Reference • copyright 2023 • 367pp • H/C (ISBN: 9781668490891) • US $250.00 (our price)

Artificial Intelligence Applications Using ChatGPT in Education Case Studies and Practices
Muhammad Shahzad Aslam (School of Traditional Chinese Medicine, Xiamen University Malaysia, Malaysia) and Saima Nisar (School of Computing, UUM College of Arts and Sciences, University Utara Malaysia, Sintok, Malaysia)
Information Science Reference • copyright 2023 • 234pp • H/C (ISBN: 9781668493007) • US $215.00 (our price)

Using Assistive Technology for Inclusive Learning in K-12 Classrooms
Jeremy Bell (University of Louisiana, Monroe, USA) and Timothy Gifford (Movia Robotics Inc., USA)
Information Science Reference • copyright 2023 • 280pp • H/C (ISBN: 9781668464243) • US $215.00 (our price)

The Impact and Importance of Instructional Design in the Educational Landscape
Christie F. Calhoun (Jacksonville State University, USA)
Information Science Reference • copyright 2023 • 295pp • H/C (ISBN: 9781668482087) • US $215.00 (our price)

Global Perspectives on Effective Assessment in English Language Teaching
Miguel Fernández Álvarez (Universidad Politécnica de Madrid, Spain) and Amanda Lira Gordenstein Montes (Northeastern Illinois University, USA)
Information Science Reference • copyright 2023 • 287pp • H/C (ISBN: 9781668482131) • US $215.00 (our price)

For an entire list of titles in this series, please visit:
http://www.igi-global.com/book-series/advances-educational-technologies-instructional-design/73678

IGI Global
PUBLISHER of TIMELY KNOWLEDGE

701 East Chocolate Avenue, Hershey, PA 17033, USA
Tel: 717-533-8845 x100 • Fax: 717-533-8661
E-Mail: cust@igi-global.com • www.igi-global.com

Table of Contents

Detailed Table of Contents

While AI technology has advanced, research on ChatGPT's role in language teaching is quite limited. No study yet has explored its impact among Turkish English educators. This study engaged English teachers from primary to higher education. 110 teachers, 49.1% from K-12 schools and 50.9% from universities, responded to an online survey in March 2023. ChatGPT's potential emerged in supplying authentic texts, fostering skills, and personalizing content. Concerns arose about ethics, plagiarism, and content quality. Some found ChatGPT inadequate without human validation. It also raised worries about curbing student creativity and critical thinking. The study suggested teachers need digital competencies—tech skills, pedagogical alignment, and ethical awareness—to improve teaching practices, assessment methods, and engagement. Teachers need guidance on ChatGPT use and ethical awareness, and training on integrating higher order thinking into lessons.

This chapter examines the integration of artificial intelligence (AI) in language learning assessment and feedback. It highlights limitations of traditional models before exploring AI-driven innovations in automated scoring, speech recognition, multimodal analytics and adaptive testing. The ensuing pedagogical transformation is discussed. AI feedback mechanisms including automated writing evaluation, intelligent tutoring systems, conversational agents, affective computing and learning analytics dashboards are analyzed. Benefits are presented alongside

is to propose an application in which language teaching professionals and language learners will engage in English-speaking practice through a multidimensional (MD) environment incorporating cubic images and bilateral sound perception (hearing and speaking). The AI application will assign tasks to multidimensional characters using realistic sound effects to create a highly immersive and interactive environment for language teaching professionals.

Generative artificial intelligence systems are disruptive technologies that have been found useful in various domains, including academia and education. Being one of these technologies, ChatGPT can have smart conversations with its human users, answer questions and produce content virtually on any topic. Like other conversational agents, ChatGPT has advanced text processing capabilities, such as writing paragraphs, essays, research reports and paraphrasing texts. The use of this technology in academic writing classes and scholarly publications necessitates a discussion of possible problems and challenges that might undermine ethical and responsible use. This is because the ability of this new technology to produce content that sounds like human output has wider ethical implications not only for academic writing and publishing but also for learning and instruction. The issues of concern are related to transparency and credibility of the content, ownership of the text produced and integrity.

When the trendsetting 'buzz word' in technology came forth in recent years, some educators became a little wary of the term "artificial intelligence." Why is that? Perhaps the idea that something existing other than the human brain to make calculated decisions regarding the creation of exams, or the ability to plan a lesson without hours of research seemed too 'foreign' or 'unnatural' to them. However, for some, the realization of yet another branch of technology to assist practitioners in the ever-evolving pedagogical fields seems quite natural as well as massively time-saving. This chapter will attempt to lightheartedly decipher a few points of artificial intelligence and its implications for greatly improving the future of teaching and learning, plus a few wise words of caution… both for the teacher and the learner.

Artificial intelligence is the simulation of human intelligence processes by machines, especially computer systems. Specific applications of AI include expert systems, natural language processing, and speech recognition and machine vision. Learning is the core feature that is connected to education. Actually, with AI, we are trying to force machines to imitate human behavior. Education increases the power of visualization and to differentiate between right and wrong. Education these days has become costly for the poor guardians. Education helps realize the real values in relation to social and cultural behavior so that one can become a decent person in nature and in society. The role of technology in modern education helps to look at the current trends and to solve the problems using artificial intelligence in education.

The overarching goal of this chapter is to provide language educators and researchers with valuable insights and practical guidance for navigating the rapidly changing landscape of AI in education. This chapter investigates the transition from digital literacy to AI literacy in language teaching, a shift necessitated by the rapid evolution of AI-assisted technologies. Beginning with a comprehensive overview of digital literacy in the context of language teaching, the chapter explores the associated pedagogical practices, benefits, and challenges. The discussion then moves to the concept of AI literacy, an emerging necessity in education. The chapter delves into the implications of integrating AI technologies into language teaching and learning, stressing the potential of AI to revolutionize language education. The chapter encourages further research on the long-term impacts of AI literacy on language learning outcomes and the effectiveness of different strategies for AI literacy integration.

In recent years, there has been an increasing development in promoting newer ways to integrate artificial intelligence (AI) into various digital tools, applications, and platforms. On the other hand, machine translation (MT), which is processed through AI, has already been in use for translation purposes for about three decades. Additionally, it has been a software frequently resorted for language learning purposes through free online platforms. The association between MT use and language learning tends to bring about several related issues such as ethical concerns. Diving into depths of these issues, this chapter presents a literature review on the key concepts related to MT use in language learning, which is supported by research findings and implications.

This chapter presents an in-depth analysis of chatbots and the integration of ChatGPT into vocabulary acquisition. The chapter begins with an introduction to artificial intelligence (AI) and continues with a definition of chatbots to highlight their role as computer programs designed to mimic human interaction. It subsequently focuses on the use of chatbots in language education. The potential benefits associated with the integration of chatbots into language learning environments are further explored. However, special attention is dedicated to the use of chatbots in vocabulary teaching, which is a fundamental aspect of language acquisition. The chapter also explores the use of ChatGPT, an AI-powered language model, particularly in the context of teaching vocabulary. The chapter ends with highlighting how ChatGPT can help learners master word form, meaning and usage, based on Nation's multidimensional aspects of vocabulary knowledge.

The advancement of technology over the past two decades has provided various tools and platforms that facilitate and optimize the language-teaching-learning process using diverse teaching methods that help learners to acquire and understand new knowledge interactively. Despite extensive research highlighting the intersection between education and artificial intelligence technologies, many language teachers are unaware of innovative learning approaches at their disposal. As a result, the potential to transform classroom learning is yet to be realized. The chapter aims to close this gap by providing an overview of the transformation of language teaching experiences in the artificial intelligence age and exploring the opportunities and

Preface

In a dynamic world where the realms of education and technology are rapidly converging, the significance of research cannot be overstated. As educators, researchers, and practitioners, we stand at the precipice of an extraordinary transformation in language education—one fueled by the profound influence of artificial intelligence (AI). This edited reference book, *Transforming the Language Teaching Experience in the Age of AI*, serves as a beacon guiding us through this uncharted terrain, illuminating how research will play a pivotal role in addressing challenges and shaping solutions.

The problems that educators and learners face in the realm of language education are multifaceted and ever-evolving. As our global society grows more interconnected, the need for effective communication across languages becomes increasingly urgent. Language educators strive to cater to a diverse range of learner needs and preferences, while researchers grapple with understanding the ethical, social, and cultural implications of integrating AI into language education. Policy makers and administrators, on their part, endeavor to chart the most judicious path forward amidst the potential pitfalls and opportunities of this AI-enabled landscape.

It is within this intricate web of challenges that the importance of research emerges as an indispensable guide. This book embarks on a journey of discovery—a journey fueled by rigorous exploration and evidence-based insights. Each chapter is a testament to the power of inquiry, revealing novel methodologies that redefine language teaching, unearthing the potential of AI to provide personalized and engaging learning experiences, and uncovering the myriad ways in which natural language processing and conversational agents can be harnessed to enhance language skills.

As the editor of this volume, I envision the research within these pages not merely as academic exercises, but as catalysts for practical change. The innovative methodologies and strategies presented herein empower educators to adapt their teaching approaches to accommodate the diverse needs of their learners. By examining the ethical, social, and cultural dimensions of AI integration, researchers lay the groundwork for informed decision-making and responsible implementation. The case studies of successful AI applications serve as blueprints for designing effective tools and platforms that resonate with learners, while the overarching interdisciplinary dialogue forges a common vision among stakeholders.

The solutions to the challenges outlined in this volume are embedded in the research presented. Each insight, each empirical finding, and each innovative idea contributes to a mosaic of potential solutions that can reshape the landscape of language education. It is our hope that the research gathered here transcends the confines of these pages and permeates into classrooms, research institutions, and policy discussions around the world.

The fusion of research and practice is where true transformation takes root. By embracing the wealth of knowledge contained within this book, educators can adapt their teaching methods to harness AI's potential, researchers can uncover new avenues for exploration, and technologists can design tools that revolutionize learning experiences. Policy makers and administrators can navigate the complexities of AI implementation armed with insights that foster responsible and inclusive education practices. Ultimately, the learners themselves stand to benefit the most, as they embark on a journey of language acquisition enriched by the best of what AI and research have to offer.

"Transforming the Language Teaching Experience in the Age of AI" is a testament to the indomitable spirit of inquiry and innovation. As we traverse the frontier of AI-assisted language education, we invite our audience of educators, researchers, practitioners, and policymakers to journey with us. Let research be our compass, guiding us towards a future where language education is not only transformed, but elevated to new heights of effectiveness and inclusivity.

CHAPTER OVERVIEW

Chapter 1: Examining the Use of ChatGPT in Language Teaching: Teachers' Experiences and Perceptions

In this chapter, Sibel Özdemir-Çagatay from Middle East Technical University, Turkey, sheds light on the underexplored realm of AI technology, specifically ChatGPT, in language teaching. The study focuses on Turkish English educators and their experiences with ChatGPT. Through a comprehensive online survey, the author engages 110 English teachers from various education levels. The chapter unveils ChatGPT's potential in enhancing language education by providing authentic content and personalizing learning experiences. It also delves into educators' concerns about ethics, plagiarism, content quality, and the role of human validation. Furthermore, the chapter emphasizes the need for educators to develop digital competencies to effectively integrate AI into teaching practices while maintaining ethical awareness and pedagogical alignment.

Chapter 2: AI-Enabled Assessment and Feedback Mechanisms for Language Learning: Transforming Pedagogy and Learner Experience

Yusuf Emre Yesilyurt, from Burdur Mehmet Akif Ersoy University, Turkey, presents a comprehensive exploration of AI integration into language learning assessment and feedback. This chapter critically evaluates traditional models, uncovering their limitations, and then delves into the transformative potential of AI-driven innovations in automated scoring, speech recognition, multimodal analytics, and adaptive testing. The pedagogical transformation ushered in by AI feedback mechanisms is discussed, including automated writing evaluation, intelligent tutoring systems, conversational agents, affective computing, and learning analytics dashboards. Ethical considerations, challenges, and case studies offer a balanced perspective on the opportunities and limitations of this approach.

Chapter 3: Personalized Learning Through Gamification: A ChatGBT Approach to English Language Learning

Sabahattin Yesilçinar, from Mus Alparslan University, Turkey, introduces the concept of gamification as a tool for enhancing engagement and motivation in English language learning. The chapter explores how ChatGBT, an AI-powered language model, can be integrated into gamified learning environments. By capitalizing on ChatGBT's interactive and personalized capabilities, educators can create immersive experiences that facilitate vocabulary acquisition, grammar practice, and reading comprehension. The chapter also addresses challenges and limitations while emphasizing the potential of gamification to enhance language skills and keep learners motivated and engaged.

Chapter 4: Corpus Assisted Multidimensional AI Applications in Language Teaching and Intelligent Virtual Speaker

Ali Özbay, Aysenur Hosoglu, Buse Uzuner, and Ercüment Öztürk, hailing from various Turkish universities, propose an evidence-based virtual AI application for language learners and educators. The chapter advocates for interdisciplinary collaboration between corpus linguists, language educators, and computer engineers. The authors introduce a multidimensional AI application that engages learners in English-speaking practice through cubic images and bilateral sound perception. The immersive and interactive environment is designed to enhance language learning through realistic sound effects and innovative multidimensional characters.

Chapter 5: ChatGPT in Academic Writing and Publishing: An Overview of Ethical Issues

Arif Bakla, from Ankara Yildirim Beyazit University, Turkey, delves into the ethical implications of utilizing ChatGPT for academic writing and publishing. The chapter discusses how the capabilities of generative AI, such as ChatGPT, raise concerns about content transparency, credibility, ownership, and integrity. The author highlights the potential challenges posed by AI-generated content, particularly in the context of academic writing, scholarly publications, and education. By addressing these ethical issues, the chapter contributes to a broader understanding of responsible AI integration in language education.

Chapter 6: Artificial Intelligence's Contribution to English Language Teaching: Are we Asking AI the Right Questions?

Zoe Marlowe, from TC Biruni University, Turkey, tackles the paradigm shift brought by artificial intelligence to education. This chapter playfully engages with the apprehensions some educators hold regarding AI in language teaching. By lightheartedly exploring the advantages and potential pitfalls, the chapter aims to reconcile these concerns and underline the ways in which AI can significantly enhance teaching and learning outcomes. It offers a reflective examination of AI's role in language education and urges educators to embrace this innovative toolset.

Chapter 7: Transforming the Language Teaching Experience in the Age of AI: Ethical, Social and Cultural Considerations in Implementing AI in Language Education

Reena Satpute, from Datta Meghe Institute of Higher Education & Research, India, provides an insightful exploration of AI's role in language education. The chapter acknowledges AI's transformative impact on language teaching while underscoring its ethical, social, and cultural implications. By delving into the ethical dimensions of AI integration, the chapter encourages a comprehensive understanding of the technology's potential in reshaping education practices while addressing ethical challenges.

Chapter 8: From Digital Literacy to AI Literacy in Language Teaching: Embracing the Artificial Intelligence Age

Galip Kartal, from Necmettin Erbakan University, Turkey, delves into the transition from digital literacy to AI literacy in language teaching. This chapter emphasizes the importance of adapting teaching methodologies in response to the evolving AI landscape. The author discusses the implications of integrating AI technologies into language education, highlighting its potential to revolutionize pedagogy. The chapter advocates for the development of AI literacy among educators and learners to effectively harness AI's transformative potential while maintaining ethical awareness and responsible use.

Chapter 9: Machine Translation Use in Language Learning: Learner Characteristics, Beliefs and Ethical Concerns

Ümran Üstünbas, from Zonguldak Bülent Ecevit University, Turkey, investigates the intersection of machine translation (MT) and language learning. The chapter presents an in-depth analysis of the use of MT in language education, addressing both its benefits and ethical concerns. By examining learners' characteristics, beliefs, and perceptions, the chapter offers insights into the implications of MT use for language learners and educators. The author underscores the importance of considering ethical dimensions when incorporating MT into language learning environments.

Chapter 10: Exploring the Potential of Chatbots and ChatGPT in Enhancing Vocabulary Knowledge

Mustafa Yildiz, from Samsun University, Turkey, offers an extensive exploration of chatbots and the integration of ChatGPT into vocabulary acquisition. The chapter outlines the role of AI chatbots in language learning and highlights how ChatGPT can enhance vocabulary knowledge by assisting learners with word forms, meanings, and usage. The author discusses practical applications of ChatGPT in vocabulary teaching and examines its potential to foster language proficiency through personalized and interactive experiences.

Chapter 11: Innovative Language Learning Approaches: Immersive Technologies and Gamification

Mavis Chamboko-Mpotaringa and Blandina Manditereza, from universities in South Africa, present a comprehensive analysis of innovative learning approaches using immersive technologies and gamification. The chapter explores the opportunities and challenges associated with incorporating immersive and gamification technologies into language teaching. By emphasizing the transformative potential of innovative technologies, the authors offer insight into how educators can create engaging and effective language learning experiences for their students.

Chapter 12: Breaking Down Barriers with Artificial Intelligence (AI): Cross-Cultural Communication in Foreign Language Education

Ali Karakas, from Mehmet Akif Ersoy University, Turkey, delves into the role of AI in facilitating cross-cultural communication in foreign language education. The chapter emphasizes how AI technology, through its language exchange platforms, can foster intercultural dialogue and enhance learners' cross-cultural competence. By presenting the benefits and potential challenges, the chapter provides educators with tools to leverage AI for creating cross-cultural learning experiences.

Chapter 13: Enhancing Outcomes, Fostering Values, and Shaping Pedagogy with ChatGPT in English Learning Courses: AI in Two Value-Oriented English Language Courses

Chad Davidson, from University of Delaware, United States, introduces a value-oriented framework for leveraging ChatGPT in English learning courses. The chapter highlights how AI can enhance learning outcomes and align with individual student values. Through practitioner research in two courses, the chapter offers practical insights into how ChatGPT can be used to foster both educational and personal values, thus contributing to evidence-based practices in AI-assisted language education.

Chapter 14: Opinions of ESL Preservice Teachers on Using Artificial Intelligence Language Models in Language Education

Matti Ibrahim and Mohamed Ibrahim, from Arkansas Tech University, United States, delve into the opinions of ESL preservice teachers regarding the use of AI language models in language education. The chapter examines participants' views on the potential role of AI in teaching and learning English. By addressing ethical, social, and cultural concerns, the chapter emphasizes the need for comprehensive training to navigate AI integration responsibly and effectively in language education contexts.

IN SUMMARY

As we conclude this journey through the pages of *Transforming the Language Teaching Experience in the Age of AI,* we find ourselves at the crossroads of a future brimming with possibilities. This edited reference book stands as a testament to the collective efforts of scholars, educators, and researchers who have dared to explore the uncharted territories where artificial intelligence intersects with language education.

The chapters within this volume have illuminated the transformative potential of AI in language teaching, shedding light on innovative methodologies, tools, and practices that redefine the landscape of education. From examining the impact of ChatGPT on language educators' perceptions to delving into the ethical dimensions of AI integration, from harnessing gamification to enhance vocabulary acquisition to embracing cross-cultural communication facilitated by AI, each chapter contributes a distinct facet to the multifaceted canvas of AI-assisted language learning.

It is evident from the insights presented that AI has evolved from a nascent concept into a dynamic force capable of revolutionizing language education. As editors, we are heartened by the enthusiastic engagement of language educators, researchers, practitioners, and policymakers with this transformative potential. The chapters underscore the intricate balance between embracing technological innovation and nurturing ethical considerations, ensuring that AI's integration aligns with values of responsible and equitable education.

This book does not mark an endpoint; rather, it stands as a catalyst for ongoing exploration and collaboration. The research shared herein opens doors to new avenues of inquiry and experimentation, beckoning educators and researchers to join hands and forge a collective path towards an AI-enriched future of education. The chapters reveal that AI is not here to replace the human touch in education, but to amplify it—to empower educators, students, and learners on a global scale.

In the coming years, we anticipate that AI will continue to evolve, offering educators evermore sophisticated tools to enhance teaching and learning experiences. While the book has endeavored to address numerous facets of AI in language education, we acknowledge that this field is dynamic and ever-changing. As new innovations emerge and AI's potential continues to unfold, this book serves as a starting point—an invitation for continued research, experimentation, and reflection.

We extend our heartfelt gratitude to the authors who have contributed their expertise and insights to this collective endeavor. Your dedication to advancing the field of AI-assisted language learning is truly commendable. We also express our gratitude to the readers—educators, researchers, practitioners, and learners—who will engage with this volume and carry its lessons into their classrooms, research projects, and policy discussions.

As the editor, I am inspired by the dialogue this book has initiated and the conversations it will spark. The transformative power of AI in language education is within our grasp, and the future beckons us to shape it responsibly, ethically, and with a profound commitment to nurturing the full potential of every learner. Together, let us chart a future where the age of AI becomes synonymous with an age of inclusive, effective, and inspiring language education.

Galip Kartal
Necmettin Erbakan University, Turkey

Chapter 1
Examining the Use of ChatGPT in Language Teaching:
Teachers' Experiences and Perceptions

Sibel Özdemir-Çağatay
https://orcid.org/0000-0002-0202-2081
Middle East Technical University, Turkey

ABSTRACT

While AI technology has advanced, research on ChatGPT's role in language teaching is quite limited. No study yet has explored its impact among Turkish English educators. This study engaged English teachers from primary to higher education. 110 teachers, 49.1% from K-12 schools and 50.9% from universities, responded to an online survey in March 2023. ChatGPT's potential emerged in supplying authentic texts, fostering skills, and personalizing content. Concerns arose about ethics, plagiarism, and content quality. Some found ChatGPT inadequate without human validation. It also raised worries about curbing student creativity and critical thinking. The study suggested teachers need digital competencies—tech skills, pedagogical alignment, and ethical awareness—to improve teaching practices, assessment methods, and engagement. Teachers need guidance on ChatGPT use and ethical awareness, and training on integrating higher order thinking into lessons.

INTRODUCTION

With the introduction of new technologies and their incorporation into the learning process, the educational milieu has undergone substantial changes in recent years. Artificial intelligence (AI) and natural language processing, in particular, have

DOI: 10.4018/978-1-6684-9893-4.ch001

emerged as significant technologies for improving educational effectiveness. One notable AI chatbot, ChatGPT, which was released in November 2022, has garnered widespread attention due to its free accessibility and availability to all users (Yu, 2023). This has attracted the interest of language educators, who are intrigued by its underlying language processing mechanism. ChatGPT can generate highly coherent and relevant responses to a wide range of inquiries and topics after being trained on a large corpus of different text data (Deng & Lin, 2022). This feature streamlines the lives of language learners and teachers by providing a broad spectrum of opportunities in the language learning process. However, because it is a brand-new paradigm shift in education, it also comes with certain drawbacks. In order to shed light onto this new technology, this study aims to evaluate the potentials of ChatGPT in the advantages and disadvantages for both students and teachers in language acquisition. Hence, the present research could make a modest contribution to the ongoing research on AI in education from the perspective of English teachers in Turkey.

LITERATURE REVIEW

Several studies have emphasized the advantages of AI in language acquisition. One of the most notable features of ChatGPT is its ability to generate a diverse range of content (Bayne et al., 2015; Chen et al., 2022). This content generation can foster various activities, such as creating innumerable content or providing a great deal of input to students. Many AI tools, including ChatGPT, have been found to effectively enhance learners' language skills (Mohamed, 2023). One of these assets could be seen in reading skills, specifically. AI holds promise for differentiating between low and high-achieving students in reading performance, enabling tailored approaches to reading texts (Xiao & Hu, 2019). Additionally, the AI-based approach supports the improvement and instruction of writing skills (Barrot, 2023; Chen et al., 2022; Kartal, 2023; Mohamed, 2023). This advantage manifests in various forms, such as pre-writing brainstorming sessions and immediate, detailed AI-assisted feedback on written work (Baidoo-Anu & Owusu Ansah, 2023; Bayne et al., 2015; Chen et al., 2022; Ekoç-Özçelik & Ergun-Gündüz, 2023; Fitria, 2023; Jeon, 2021; Kohnke et al., 2023; Mohamed, 2023; Yan, 2023). This ChatGPT feature expedites error correction and skill enhancement, benefiting both students and teachers. Moreover, ChatGPT's ability to provide feedback on multiple aspects of writing can contribute to personalized feedback, reducing teachers' workload (Ekoç-Özçelik & Ergun-Gündüz, 2023; Mohamed, 2023; Kasneci et al., 2023). Learners can also benefit from peer feedback on AI tools like ChatGPT, fostering language skill improvement and critical thinking (Ekoç-Özçelik & Ergun-Gündüz, 2023).

In terms of oral skill development, ChatGPT addresses a challenge for language learners in EFL contexts by offering practice opportunities at their convenience (Ekoç-Özçelik & Ergun-Gündüz, 2023; Kohnke et al., 2023). Students can engage in simulated conversations, enabling authentic interactions and pronunciation improvement (Kartal, 2023). ChatGPT's role in vocabulary learning is also valuable (Kartal, 2023; Kohnke et al., 2023; Koraishi, 2023), as it not only provides definitions but also contextualizes terms, enhancing language comprehension. This contributes to comprehensive understanding of language usage, especially for unclear terms in texts as Kartal (2023) points out in his study.

In addition to its distinct contributions to the enhancement of language proficiency, ChatGPT additionally presents specific affordances that contribute to the broader spectrum of the learning process. One advantage is that ChatGPT facilitates individualized instruction by responding to learners' various interactions (Kartal, 2023). This interactive learning approach prepares students for exams and interviews, enhancing academic success and accessibility (Adıgüzel et al., 2023; Mohamed, 2023). Moreover, ChatGPT addresses affective needs, boosting motivation and engagement while reducing anxiety (Adıgüzel et al., 2023; Bao, 2019; Chen et al., 2022; Kohnke et al., 2023; Mohamed, 2023; Sumakul et al, 2022). Enhanced motivation can lead to increased autonomy and active participation in learning (Ali et al., 2023; Ekoç-Özçelik & Ergun- Gündüz, 2023).

ChatGPT provides advantages not solely confined to learners; it also confers benefits upon educators and instructors. For educators, ChatGPT aids in creating individualized lesson plans (Baskara, 2023; Ekoç-Özçelik & Ergun-Gündüz, 2023), providing additional resources, explanations, and methodologies (Kasneci et al., 2023). Teachers can swiftly prepare materials and design tests (Kohnke et al., 2023; Raina & Gales, 2022; Rodriguez-Torrealba et al., 2022) tailored to their classroom needs (Ekoç-Özçelik & Ergun-Gundis, 2023; Koraishi, 2023). Additionally, ChatGPT assists in administrative tasks, such as tracking student progress and managing portfolios, relieving teachers' workload (Adıgüzel et al., 2023). In such a way, ChatGPT serves as a teaching assistant (Li, 2019; Saharadgah & Sadi 2022), freeing up time for personalized attention to students' requirements (Ekoç-Özçelik & Ergun-Gündüz, 2023; Kasneci et al., 2023; Mohamed, 2023).

While AI, particularly ChatGPT, offers numerous advantages for both teachers and students, concerns exist among researchers and educators regarding its use in learning. Despite claims of promoting interaction, ChatGPT does not replace human interaction (Baidoo-Anu & Owusu Ansah, 2023; Kartal, 2023; Mohamed, 2023). It possesses limited comprehension, missing nuances in human speech and context. Similarly, the mechanistic nature of some responses indicates a lack of authentic human interaction.

Researchers have identified misinformation as another concern, as AI tools may produce inaccuracies due to AI hallucination (Ekoç-Özçelik & Ergun-Gündüz, 2023; Kartal, 2023; Mohamed, 2023). This poses a risk of students accessing incorrect information and potentially encountering unlearning difficulties. Furthermore, students may become overly-reliant on ChatGPT, potentially diminishing their critical thinking and problem-solving skills (Ekoç-Özçelik & Ergun-Gündüz, 2023; García-Peñalvo, 2023; Hong, 2023). Easier access to information might also lead to issues like plagiarism due to the rapid generation of responses (Baskara & Mukarto, 2023; Kartal, 2023; Kasneci et al., 2023; Koraishi, 2023). Ethical challenges such as plagiarism and cheating are also notable concerns associated with ChatGPT (Cotton et al., 2023; Mhlanga, 2023).

Another drawback involves ChatGPT's lack of sensitivity to cultural differences or nuances, posing challenges for English as a Lingua Franca (ELF) contexts (Sakai, 2023). ChatGPT's inability to produce non-native English limits its cultural sensitivity in written data (Kohnke et al., 2023). This issue is tied to data input and training, suggesting potential improvements with increased inclusion of non-native speakers in the system. Bias in the current algorithm is also highlighted as a significant challenge by researchers (Adıgüzel et al., 2023; Baidoo-Anu & Owusu Ansah, 2023; Baskara & Mukarto, 2023; Kartal, 2023). In addition to all these challenges, a striking concern derived from the teachers' responses in the literature seem that ChatGPT can take their own role as a teacher and they could become unemployed or redundant in the future (Ausat et al., 2023).

While researchers have increasingly explored the prospects and challenges of ChatGPT in the field of education (Adıgüzel et al., 2023; Baidoo-Anu & Owusu Ansah, 2023; Garcia-Ponolvo, 2023; Kasneci et al., 2023; Opara et al., 2023), limited research has focused on its applications in language teaching. Some studies have examined ChatGPT's use in teaching writing (Baidoo-Anu & Owusu Ansah, 2023; Barrot, 2023; Bayne et al., 2015; Chen et al., 2022; Ekoç-Özçelik & Ergun-Gündüz, 2023; Fitria, 2023; Jeon, 2021; Kohnke et al., 2023; Mohamed, 2023; Yan, 2023), personalized learning (Sakai, 2023), or material preparation in English Language Teaching (ELT) (Koraishi, 2023).Top of Form While the potential of the ChatGPT language model to enhance language learning is acknowledged in these studies, its application in English as a Foreign Language (EFL) instruction and educators' experiences with it remain unclear. This study aims to explore the potential of ChatGPT in EFL teaching, identifying both prospects and challenges associated with integrating chatbots in language teaching. The outcomes of this investigation could shape the utilization of AI-driven educational technologies, leading to more effective and efficient EFL instruction by addressing teachers' positive attitudes and apprehensions regarding ChatGPT.

With this objective in mind, the study endeavors to examine how EFL teachers perceive the usefulness of ChatGPT and shed light on the merits and drawbacks of incorporating ChatGPT into EFL lessons. The research aims to address the following inquiries:

1. To what degree are English teachers familiar with the applications of ChatGPT in language instruction?
   1a. Is there a statistically significant difference between the perception levels of K-12 English teachers and tertiary-level English instructors concerning their awareness and utilization of ChatGPT?
2. What are the primary benefits of utilizing ChatGPT in language learning and instructional processes, as observed by both K-12 and university-level EFL educators?
3. What are the disadvantages of integrating ChatGPT into language learning and teaching, as perceived by English instructors teaching students at both K-12 and university levels?

METHODOLOGY

Participants

Using a survey research approach, this study investigated English teachers' perceptions of ChatGPT as an aid for language acquisition. The survey was sent to English teachers by an online survey platform in March-April, 2023. In order to shed light on this recently introduced technology, English language teachers and instructors from primary (K12 schools) to higher education levels were recruited as participants for this study. A convenient and snowball sampling method was employed. The number of the respondents is 110 and the teachers work at different levels of teaching. The details of their work are shown as below:

As shown in the Figure above, almost half of the participants teach at K-12 level (49.1%) and a little more than half of them (50.9%) work at tertiary level to teach English.

The demographic questions also asked how long the participants teach English. The findings are as below:

Most of the participant teachers have worked in this profession for about 11-15 years (31.8%) or 16-20 years and the lowest respondent rate came from the teachers who have 26 years or more (4.5%). The lowest rate in the experienced teachers might be they could have got retired or they did not willingly take part in a very recent trend in AI.

Figure 1. At what level participants teach English

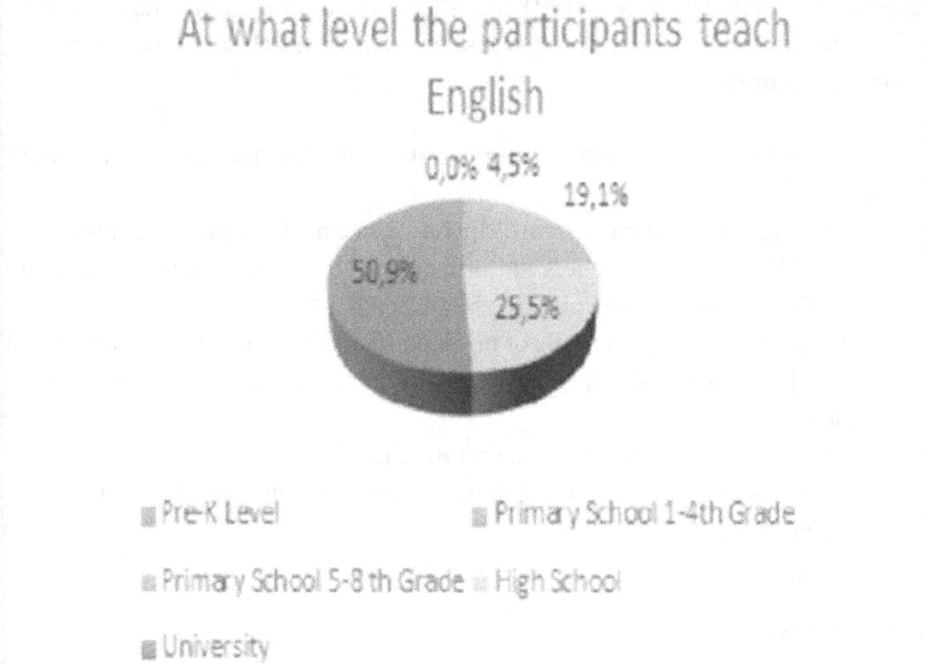

Figure 2. How long the participant teachers have worked

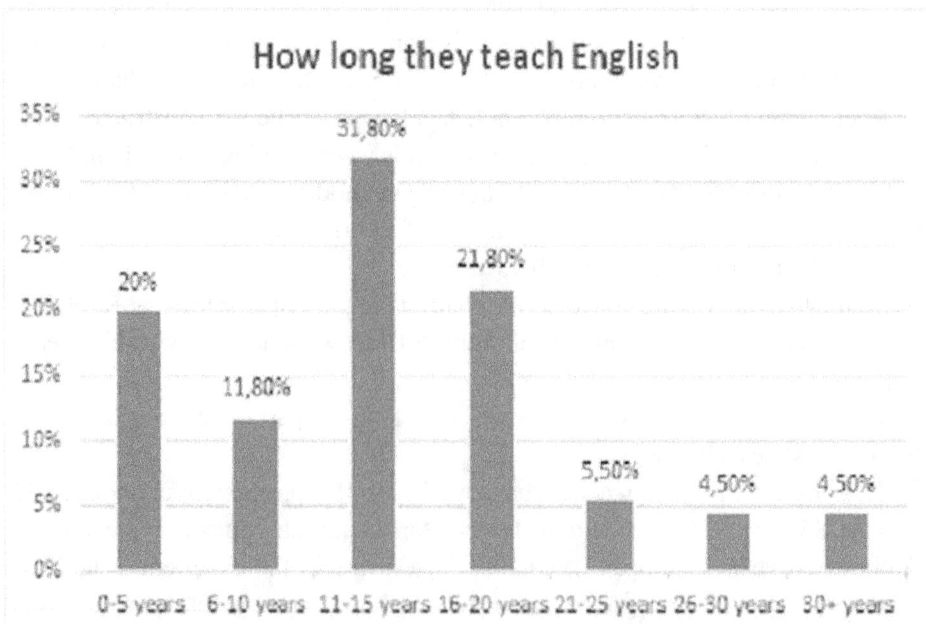

In the second part of the questionnaire, to what extent the participants have knowledge about the ChatGPT was asked, and 31.8% of them (N=35) stated that they have no idea of it, 33.6% of them (N=37) find themselves as novice user, 31.8 of them (N=35) find themselves as somehow knowledgeable and only 2.7% of them (N=3) consider themselves as experts in this AI tool. This shows that most of the participant teachers are in the learning process.

Instrument

A questionnaire consisting of 5 Likert-scale and 5 open-ended items was prepared by the researcher. The content validity of the survey was reviewed by experts in digital tools in education. The questionnaire has three main sections. The questionnaire's first section included demographic questions concerning the professional experience of the participants. The second section focused on general knowledge about ChatGPT, covering questions about the participants' proficiency levels, awareness of ChatGPT, previous training on its usage, and the range of tasks the chatbot can perform. The last part, which is the scope of the present research is on the professional uses of ChatGPT; the advantages and the challenges of using it.

Data Collection and Data Analysis Procedures

Following the development and testing of the survey questions, they were delivered to English teachers by e-mail, social networking sites, or with the assistance of the researcher's colleagues.

It took around two weeks to collect all data. It was distributed to approximately 400 instructors, and 110 of them answered. The analysis of the data was performed based on descriptive statistics and frequency analysis for the close items on SPSS 25 and deductive and inductive qualitative analyses were conducted on the qualitative analysis software Atlas.ti. To determine whether there is a significant difference in the English instructors' competency level between K-12 level and tertiary level for the first research question, the mean scores for their competence level were calculated. The histogram and skewness of the data were also used to determine whether it was regularly distributed or not. For this question, the independent samples t test was used after establishing that the distribution was normal. As for the second and third research questions, the open-ended questions were analyzed using content analysis in relation to the benefits and drawbacks. Both inductive and deductive analyses were employed depending upon the literature and also the emerging data of the respondents.

FINDINGS

The Participants' Level of Knowledge on ChatGPT

In order to shed light onto the participants' level of awareness in ChatGPT, they were asked to rate whether they have no idea (1), or they feel novice (2), somewhat knowledgeable (3) or expert (4) on this chatbot.

To be able to identify the difference between the English teachers at K-12 schools and the universities on their awareness of ChatGPT, a normality test was conducted and the data was found normally-distributed. An independent samples t test was used to evaluate this and as shown in Table 1, there is a statistically significant difference between teachers at university (*M*= 2.38, *SD*=.75) and the ones at K-12 schools (*M*= 1.72, *SD*=.85) with a large effect size. (*d*=.8). The findings are illustrated in the table below:

Table 1. The difference between the level of knowledge among English teachers at K12 schools and universities

Teaching Level		N	M	SD	t	df	p	Cohen's d
K-12		54	1.72	.85	4.253	108	.000	.8
University		56	2.38	.75				

Note. N= The number of the participants; M= Mean score; SD= Standard Deviation

Figure 3. The percentages of ChatGPT use for language teaching

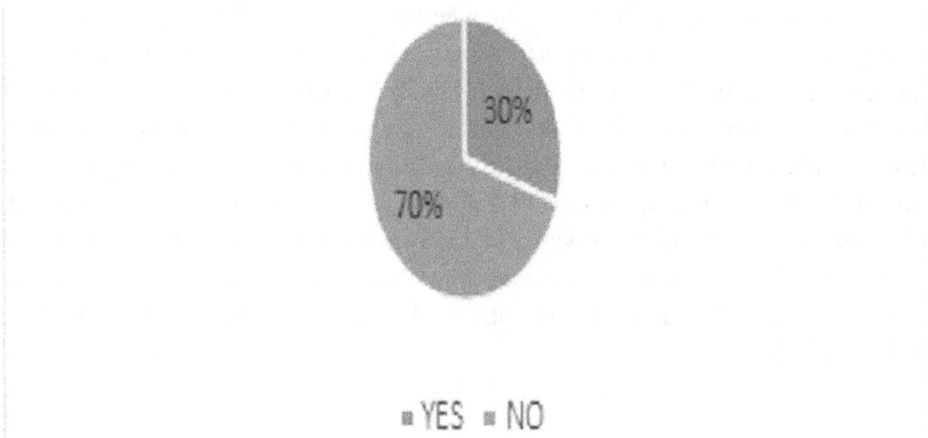

To understand the overall trend in using ChatGPT, the participants were addressed a question on whether they have used ChatGPT for their profession before. The distribution of the responses is shown as below:

Most of the English teachers (*N*= 77; 70%) in the present study stated that they did not use ChatGPT for their profession. The findings from the Likert-scale questions also revealed that the majority of participants had not received any formal or informal training on the use of AI.

Related to their knowledge level in the specific advantages and disadvantages, some striking findings have been found. As the instructions in the survey lead the participants to skip the advantages or disadvantages if they have no idea about these details, the blank responses were considered as "no idea". However, some of them clearly wrote down the fact that they do not know about these pros and cons. Both responses have been considered as the lack of knowledge on the part of the participants. On the other hand, if they mention that they have an idea about ChatGPT and they do not think that it brings about any advantage or disadvantage, they write "no advantage" or "no disadvantage" as indicated in the instructions.

The findings show that more than a quarter of the participants (N=27) revealed that they did not know any of the advantages, so they have not written down any comment in the open-ended question. Almost a third (N=29) of the participant teachers express that they have no idea about the disadvantages of the tool as they are not familiar. Seven of them maintain that there is no challenge of ChatGPT.

The Advantages of ChatGPT

As for the second research question, the participants of the study were asked about what kind of advantages ChatGPT could offer in English language teaching. The researcher initially coded and then collated the codes under the themes (or advantages) with the help of another researcher. Finally, they categorized these positive sides of ChatGPT for teachers and the students separately; however, some of them were noted for both parties. The frequencies of the advantages will be presented in the table and then the quotations for the most common ones will appear in this section with an abbreviation of the participant teacher number as "T No". The frequencies of these affordances are indicated below in the table and the positive sides of this chatbot are added to the sections of both parties in the table.

Looking into the frequencies in the table, participants state certain advantages for the teachers. According to them, the greatest perceived advantage falls on the time-saving feature of ChatGPT (*f*=28). The participants also report that providing immediate feedback (*f*=8), material design (*f*=8), the preparation for the assessment process (*f*= 5), lesson planning (*f*=5), collaboration with the other colleagues (*f*=1), content delivery (*f*=5),), doing preliminary research (f= 2), improving writing skills

Table 2. Advantages of ChatGPT for language teaching

Advantages for the Teachers	Frequency	Advantages for the Students	Frequency
Time-saving	28	Individualized/personalized learning	8
Providing immediate/ quick feedback	8	Speaking &Interaction	5
Material preparation	8	Motivation	4
Assessment preparation	5	Doing practice	3
Lesson Planning	5	Doing assignments	2
Content delivery	5	Brainstorming	2
Preliminary research facility	2	Finding resources	2
Collaboration with the other colleagues	1	Interactive learning	2
Improving writing skills	1	Improving writing skills	2
Teaching vocabulary in context	1	Autonomy	1
Practicality		4	
No need for outdated books		1	

(*f*=1) and teaching vocabulary in context (*f*=1) become much easier with the help of the ChatGPT.

The mostly cited affordance of ChatGPT for the English teachers is that it saves a great deal of time, thus, it reduces the workload of them. Some of the relevant quotations are as below:

T10: I think it is a very suitable technology in terms of being time saving.

T36: Saving time is very important for every field today, and I think this will be its main contribution to my profession.

T95: I think it will save time on material/exam preparation.

T8: It can save time while planning the lesson

Teachers frequently associate another commonly-cited benefit "material preparation" with the effective conservation of time and the mitigation of their workload, as exemplified in the subsequent instances. They also highlight the ease in preparing the materials addressing the needs of the learners.

T 56: It saves time on material preparation.

T101: It can reduce the workload of teachers, especially in materials, preparing exam questions and written feedback.

T39: It can save time in the production and follow-up of additional English materials to the school and ...

T10: ChatGPT can assist in preparing material for students' needs and characteristics.

The provision of instant feedback is similarly highlighted by educators as a notable advantage.

T3: Giving feedback on the writing pieces

T66: It provides instant feedback

T70: It can help the student to give feedback

In terms of lesson planning, ChatGPT could enable the English teachers to find sample lesson plans and organize their classes accordingly. Sample quotations related to this point are:

T3: Lesson planning

T81: It can help me find sample lesson plans.

According to the teachers, the preparation process while designing assessment tools also becomes easier. This is expressed in the quotations as:

T37: Preparing alternative measurement and evaluation items

T133: It could be helpful for text hunting for exams and in task materials

T65: It will save time in designing test questions.

As to the content delivery, teachers find ChatGPT quite useful in creating content for the profession such as:

T2: It can help with finding sample text. For reading, it can be for writing or even a sample listening or speaking text. Question and answer practice can be done, or sample texts can be found. Comprehensive texts can be found when we are looking for an answer to a question. The student can be taught where to find a good text.

T16: It can act as an assistant in lesson planning and content development when time crunch and mental fatigue are experienced.

The participant teachers also express some other positive sides with a low frequency. They think that they can collaborate with their colleagues around the world through ChatGPT. Two of the participant teachers are of the opinion that they can have an overall idea about a topic with the help of a preliminary research that ChatGPT offers.

When it comes to the advantages for the students, the participant teachers underline individualized or personalized learning as the number-one asset for the language learners. Here are some quotations on this point:

T10: It can assist in preparing material for students' needs and characteristics.

T71: I believe it will be beneficial in terms of individualizing education.

In addition to individualized learning opportunity, ChatGPT was also found to promote students' motivation as such different ways:

T 5: It can encourage more active participation of students in the lesson because it was first designed as a chat engine and inevitably offers us the opportunity to chat emotionally. For example, ChatGPT can approach a student who is feeling down today, saying what should I do, like a normal teacher or family member, and make him/her feel better.

T 46: The use of new technologies can attract students' attention and increase motivation in the lessons.

T18: I hope that it will increase the interest and motivation of my students.

As to the improvement in the learners' speaking skills or interaction, some of the participants' statements are as below:

T29: It can make a positive contribution to speaking skills by enabling students to practice at their own level.

T34: It provides more comprehensive communication

Concerning the other advantages of ChatGPT which are not reported as much as the above-mentioned ones, some instructors suggest that learners could get help from ChatGPT while doing their assignments. They also add that they can do some brainstorming before they start their projects or assignments, which could save time on the students' parts. They can find different ways to practice the language while using ChatGPT and they can also improve their writing by looking at the paraphrased version or a sample version of their writing and/or by getting feedback from the chatbot. According to the teachers in the present study, English learners can also do some research using the tool and interact with the AI. As they can do all these with the help of ChatGPT, students can also have more autonomy in this process.

The Disadvantages of ChatGPT

The third research question asked study participants what kind of pitfalls ChatGPT may cause in English language instruction. With the assistance of another researcher, the researcher originally coded and then collated the codes under the themes (or disadvantages). Finally, the coders separated the negative aspects of ChatGPT for teachers and students. Additionally, another section for the disadvantages were called as "disadvantages with the tool itself" in the table. For, some of the indicated problems stem from the technical AI problems of ChatGPT. The frequency of the disadvantages will be displayed, followed by quotations for the most popular ones in this section. The frequency of these affordances is noted in the table below, and the negative aspects of this chatbot are added to the sections of both parties.

As to the disadvantages related to the teachers, the most frequent one is that some participants have developed some concerns over the fact that ChatGPT can take over their roles as teachers.

T 66: unemployment

T 72: It can cause questioning the necessity of the teaching profession.

Another significant drawback for educators is that the use of ChatGPT might potentially induce a sense of apathy towards generating original content. Sample quotations are as follows:

Table 3. Disadvantages of ChatGPT for language teaching

Disadvantages for the Teachers	f	Disadvantages for the Students	f	Disadvantages with the tool itself	f
Taking the role of the teachers	7	Ethical issues	37	Misinformation	4
Causing laziness on the teachers	5	Inhibiting creativity	6	No human interaction	2
Difficult to set assignments	3	No effort in getting information	6	Lack of contextual understanding	1
Difficult to detect plagiarism	3	Hindering critical thinking	3	Lack of originality	1
Testing reliability	3	Overdependence on the tool	2		
Difficulty to integrate into the curriculum	1	Hindering research skills	2		
Need to adapt the materials	1	Negative effects on students' development	2		
		Distractive for the students	1		
		Inequality between the users of it and non-users	1		
		Loss in motivation	1		

T4: I believe it will breed laziness in the teaching profession and lead to less attention to their work.

T6: It causes ease and laziness. Teachers may not be as original, creative and efficient as they used to be. We can stop trying and try to avoid the preparation for the lessons and that is a bad example for students.

When examining Table 3, it is clearly seen that a great majority of the respondents (N=37 out of 74) underscored the fact that there are certain ethical issues related to the use of ChatGPT. The codes under this common theme are illustrated as it is the most outstanding disadvantage of the present study:

Some of the quotations related to each code will be presented below in brackets. The first one is that ChatGPT leads to plagiarism.

T15: I am concerned about authenticity and ethics. (Ethical Issues)

Figure 4. The codes and the theme of ethical issues

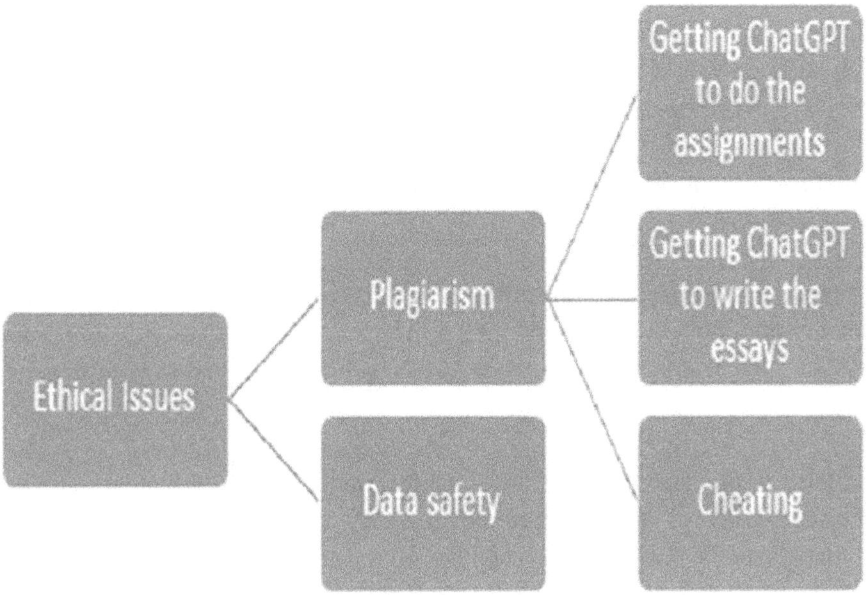

T42: I think it leads students to plagiarism. (Plagiarism)

Some of the teachers are quite concerned that instead of students doing their assignments or written pieces, they could have ChatGPT produce the output. This can be seen in the following statements:

T69: The student may cause the given work not to reach its purpose by doing their homework and studies here (Getting ChatGPT to do the assignments)

T33: It is a big problem for students to use it while writing an article. I am also worried that, like all conveniences, this will lead to laziness in thinking. (Getting ChatGPT to write the essays).

T66: Data sharing with the third parties (Data safety)

T19: Cheatin' will be easy (Cheating)

Teachers seem to be worried that it is difficult to set assignments for their students as the learners could plagiarize or it is difficult to detect if they resort to it, afterwards.

Ensuring testing reliability for this reason and also having some problems while integrating it into the curriculum were noted as some other challenges for the teachers.

Looking into the disadvantages for the students, one negative impact of ChatGPT is that students would not expend much effort in getting information, which also causes laziness or devlaues information.

T46: Students' use of ChatGPT while preparing homework may reduce their individual efforts.

T90: Instead of looking for information, students can get information more readily, which devalues information. There will be no student effort in exams or homework ... when we ask you to write an article on the subject, you can do your homework quickly,

Related to the decrease in effort to get information, the other most remarkable disadvantage seems to fall on inhibiting creativity. The participant teachers hold the idea that ChatGPT poses some challenges on the creativity of the students.

T 7: The student can bring homework as if he wrote it himself. This can stifle their creativity.

T63: Non-recourse to individual creativity

T25: Creativity may decrease

In relation to getting information without making much effort, some other disadvantages as overdependence on the tool, being distractive for the learners, hindering their critical thinking and research skills were indicated with lower frequencies. One teacher emphasized the inequality between the learners when they do not access or when they do not use ChatGPT in their studies as it is difficult to identify such students. Two instructors stated overall negative effect of ChatGPT on the students' development without referring to the details.

DISCUSSION

Familiarity With ChatGPT

As AI technology, including ChatGPT, becomes more prevalent, scholars have started investigating its role in education, particularly in language learning. However, like any digital tool, ChatGPT has its advantages and challenges in educational contexts. This study aims to understand how English teachers in Türkiye perceive and use ChatGPT, considering its pros and cons.

Before diving into their opinions about ChatGPT, participants were asked about their familiarity with it. The results showed that most teachers, regardless of their level, had some awareness of the tool, allowing for a more in-depth exploration of their views. Despite ChatGPT being a recent release, 30% of English teachers reported having used it in their profession, which shows promising potential for integrating AI into their teaching practices; however, this finding also implies that the majority of the teachers need to be encouraged more to use the tool in their profession for the advantages to take. Interestingly, K-12 teachers seemed less familiar with ChatGPT compared to university English instructors. Some K-12 teachers even encountered the term for the first time in the survey. This could be because adult learners, like university students, might be more accustomed to using such technology for learning.

The higher awareness among university instructors might be due to their students' increased exposure to online education and digital tools like ChatGPT. University students, who often have more writing assignments, may have turned to AI tools for help, which could explain the discrepancy.

In light of these findings, there is a potential need to provide more support and training to K-12 English teachers. Offering workshops or training sessions could help them better understand and use ChatGPT, allowing them to keep up with the evolving educational landscape and the needs of their students.

The Advantages of ChatGPT in Language Teaching and Learning

The teachers who participated in the study emphasized a notable advantage of ChatGPT: its time-saving feature. This advantage is closely intertwined with other benefits mentioned, such as efficient preparation of materials and lesson plans, designing tailored tests and assessment tools, meeting student needs, and providing immediate feedback. These advantages become particularly significant given the demanding pace of the modern world, where administrative tasks often consume substantial time. These highlighted benefits, such as crafting lesson plans (Baskara, 2023; Ekoç-Özçelik & Ergun-Gündüz, 2023) or formulating tests (Kohnke et al., 2023; Raina & Gales, 2022; Rodriguez-Torrealba et al., 2022), have also been underscored by earlier researchers.

Diverging from prior studies, the participating teachers illuminated additional advantages of ChatGPT, including enhanced collaboration among colleagues. While collaborative learning among students was advocated in the study of Ekoç-Özçelik and Ergun-Gündüz (2023), the engagement of English teachers in collaborative efforts emerges as a distinct positive facet of ChatGPT in the present study. Although this aspect was not elaborated upon by the teachers, the potential for collaboration could be facilitated through accessible responses. This could involve analyzing disparities and commonalities in ChatGPT responses to similar prompts, such as lesson planning. Sharing outputs and guiding students in ethical tool usage might be enabled as a future action.

While a minority of participants expressed skepticism, suggesting that increased and effective usage of ChatGPT could render it redundant, this perspective appears marginal. However, considering the evolving landscape of English teaching materials alongside digital advancements, this notion could gain credence over time. Currently, ChatGPT might not offer entirely cohesive, comprehensive, or culturally-neutral materials. This shortcoming could arise from a lack of consideration for contextual or linguistic differences (Adıgüzel et al., 2023; Baidoo-Anu & Owusu Ansah, 2023; Baskara & Mukarto, 2023; Kartal, 2023), and a possible oversight of the growing importance of English as a Lingua Franca. While ChatGPT's responses are primarily derived from native English speakers, its Natural Language Processing could evolve as more non-native speaker data is integrated.

Another noteworthy advantage derived from the data pertains to teachers' own skill development. They highlighted the potential to enhance their writing skills by receiving feedback from the system or conducting preliminary research on topics. However, the latter approach requires caution due to the persistence of misinformation (Ekoç-Özçelik & Ergun-Gündüz, 2023; Kartal, 2023; Mohamed, 2023).

Regarding student benefits, the advantages pinpointed by teachers align with existing literature. Specifically, the teachers referred to personalized learning (Kartal, 2023; Kasneci et al., 2023). Given ChatGPT's capacity to generate tailored responses, educators believe learners can adapt their learning experiences. This versatility allows students to engage in language practice through writing, speaking, and reading, with the chatbot adjusting materials to their proficiency levels. The ease of access and flexibility afforded by this tool is particularly advantageous. Notably, the most significant benefit appears to be the opportunity for enhanced interaction and practice of oral language skills, a crucial aspect for English as a Foreign Language (EFL) learners who often lack platforms for oral practice.

Disadvantages

Most of the concerns raised by the participating teachers align with prior research findings. In line with existing literature (Ausat et al., 2023), there appears to be apprehension about the potential for ChatGPT and other AI tools to replace the teaching profession, potentially leading to future unemployment for teachers. This concern holds merit, as failure to adapt to these new technological advancements could indeed pose challenges in effectively catering to the needs of the evolving generation and the dynamic tools shaping the global educational landscape. Consequently, the role of teachers necessitates a redefinition. For instance, as echoed by certain teachers and previous scholars (Ekoç-Özçelik & Ergun-Gündüz, 2023; García-Peñalvo, 2023; Hong, 2023), it becomes evident that ChatGPT might impede students' development of critical thinking and problem-solving abilities. This observation paves the way for the conceptualization of new responsibilities in crafting instructional materials that foster these skills while leveraging the assistance of ChatGPT or other AI tools. However, this should not be misunderstood as a diminishment of teachers' involvement in the decision-making processes related to activity design, as it is educators who possess the keenest insight into their students' needs.

A recurring point noted by both the teachers and earlier researchers (Baidoo-Anu & Owusu Ansah, 2023; Baskara & Mukarto, 2023; Mohamed, 2023) is the deficiency of human nuances and interpersonal interactions in ChatGPT. Despite its capabilities, the chatbot falls short in replicating the subtleties and depth of human engagement. Teachers must guide the learning process, whereas ChatGPT should primarily serve as a tool to aid in this process. This means that teachers should be actively involved in supporting and directing the learning experience, whereas ChatGPT is intended to supplement rather than replace teachers in the classroom.

Another major issue that was addressed by the participant teachers was the ethical issues. This theme is relevant to the plagiarism problem as students tend to retrieve the content that ChatGPT prepares while they do their assignments or do some online activities such as online tests. This apparent problem has been incorporated in several studies (Cotton et al., 2023; (Ekoç-Özçelik & Ergun-Gündüz, 2023; Kılıçkaya & Kıc-Drgas, 2023). It seems quite difficult to detect the texts that was produced by ChatGPT although many detectors of AI have been released and used. For the time being, the best way to address plagiarism and cheating problems would be to assign projects or written work where students need to write their own understanding and reflection. Alternatively, academic integrity could be ensured through a contract with the students as Kılıçkaya and Kıc-Drgas (2023) suggest in their studies. García-Peñalvo (2023) also inform in her article that European Union is working on a proposal of a law which regulates its use in education and job applications. This legal action could also ensure some sanctions on the misuse of it in the future. As Kasneci et al (2023) suggest in their study, teachers can also inform the learners about the threats of getting incorrect information and teach them how to crosscheck the responses with the more valuable and reliable data sources.

CONCLUSION

Educational institutions should not reject or ignore the potential of using advanced tools in teaching. Instead, they should understand how these tools can assist in activities like analyzing information, comparing sources, and creating relevant topics for discussion. Similar to how calculators are controlled in certain math levels, these tools should be used carefully for specific skills in education (García-Peñalvo, 2023).

These tools can create practice questions and tests, helping students better understand and remember their subjects. They can also improve problem-solving skills by providing explanations, detailed solutions, and follow-up questions. This approach helps students grasp the reasoning behind solutions and promotes creative thinking (Kasneci et al., 2023).

Through the utilization of webinars, in-service training, and other streamlined resources, educators at all levels are encouraged to modify their instructional methodologies and evaluative practices to effectively integrate the expanding influence of technology. Once the initial concerns fade, instructors will likely recognize the benefits of these changes and embrace the opportunities presented by new technology (Hong, 2023).

Overall, the benefits and drawbacks of ChatGPT in language instruction and many other domains are still being debated. Integrating it as a tool rather than an assistant may be the best line of action for saving time on the major tasks of the teacher and ensuring better individualized learning environments for the students' needs.

REFERENCES

Adiguzel, T., Kaya, M. H., & Cansu, F. K. (2023). Revolutionizing education with AI: Exploring the transformative potential of ChatGPT. *Contemporary Educational Technology*, *15*(3), 1–13. doi:10.30935/cedtech/13152

Ali, J. K. M., Shamsan, M. A. A., Hezam, T. A., & Mohammed, A. A. (2023). Impact of ChatGPT on learning motivation: Teachers and students' voices. *Journal of English Studies in Arabia Felix*, *2*(1), 41–49. doi:10.56540/jesaf.v2i1.51

Ausat, A. M. A., Massang, B., Efendi, M., Nofirman, N., & Riady, Y. (2023). Can chat GPT replace the role of the teacher in the classroom: A fundamental analysis. *Journal of Education*, *5*(4), 16100–16106. doi:10.31004/joe.v5i4.2745

Baidoo-Anu, D., & Owusu Ansah, L. (2023). Education in the era of generative artificial intelligence (AI): Understanding the potential benefits of ChatGPT in promoting teaching and learning. http://dx.doi.org/ doi:10.2139/ssrn.4337484

Bao, M. (2019). Can home use of speech-enabled artificial intelligence mitigate foreign language anxiety–Investigation of a concept. *Arab World English Journal (AWEJ). SSRN*, (5). Advance online publication. doi:10.2139srn.3431734

Barrot, J. S. (2023). Using ChatGPT for second language writing: Pitfalls and potentials. *Assessing Writing*, *57*, 100745. doi:10.1016/j.asw.2023.100745

Baskara, F. R., & Mukarto, F. X. (2023). Exploring the Implications of ChatGPT for Language Learning in Higher Education. *Indonesian Journal of English Language Teaching and Applied Linguistics*, *7*(2), 343–358. doi:10.210 93/ijeltal.v7i2.1387

Bayne, S. (2015). Teacherbot: Interventions in automated teaching. *Teaching in Higher Education*, *20*(4), 455–467. doi:10.1080/13562517.2015.1020783

Chen, X., Zou, D., Xie, H., Cheng, G., & Liu, C. (2022). Two Decades of Artificial Intelligence in Education: Contributors, Collaborations, Research Topics, Challenges, and Future Directions. *Journal of Educational Technology & Society*, *25*(1), 28–47. https://www.jstor.org/stable/48647028

Cotton, D. R., Cotton, P. A., & Shipway, J. R. (2023). Chatting and cheating: Ensuring academic integrity in the era of ChatGPT. *Innovations in Education and Teaching International*, 1–12. doi:10.1080/14703297.2023.2190148

Deng, J., & Lin, Y. (2022). The benefits and challenges of ChatGPT: An overview. *Frontiers in Computing and Intelligent Systems*, *2*(2), 81–83. doi:10.54097/fcis.v2i2.4465

Ekoç-Özçelik & Ergun-Gündüz. (2023). Embracing ChatGPT in foreign language writing classes: potentials and challenges. In Ferdig, R.E., Hartshorne, R., Baumgartner, E., Kaplan-Rakowski, R. & Mouza, C. (Eds.), what prek-12 teachers should know about educational technology in 2023: A research-to-practice anthology, (1st ed., pp. 133-143). AACE2023.

Fitria, T. N. (2023, March). Artificial intelligence (AI) technology in OpenAI ChatGPT application: A review of ChatGPT in writing English essay. *ELT Forum: Journal of English Language Teaching, 12*(1), 44-58. 10.15294/elt.v12i1.64069

García-Peñalvo, F. J. (2023). The perception of Artificial Intelligence in educational contexts after the launch of ChatGPT: Disruption or Panic? *Education in the Knowledge Society*, *24*. doi:10.14201/eks.31279

Hong, W. C. H. (2023). The impact of ChatGPT on foreign language teaching and learning: Opportunities in education and research. *Journal of Educational Technology and Innovation*, *5*(1), 37–45. https://jeti.thewsu.org/index.php/cieti/article/view/103

Jeon, J. (2021). Chatbot-assisted dynamic assessment (CA-DA) for L2 vocabulary learning and diagnosis. *Computer Assisted Language Learning*, 1–27. doi:10.1080/09588221.2021.1987272

Kartal, G. (2023). Contemporary Language Teaching and Learning with ChatGPT. *Contemporary Research in Language and Linguistics, 1*(1). 59-70. http://crlljournal.org/index.php/crll/article/view/10/9

Kasneci, E., Seßler, K., Küchemann, S., Bannert, M., Dementieva, D., Fischer, F., Gasser, U., Groh, G., Günnemann, S., Hüllermeier, E., Krusche, S., Kutyniok, G., Michaeli, T., Nerdel, C., Pfeffer, J., Poquet, O., Sailer, M., Schmidt, A., Seidel, T., & Kasneci, G. (2023). ChatGPT for good? On opportunities and challenges of large language models for education. *Learning and Individual Differences*, *103*, 102274. doi:10.1016/j.lindif.2023.102274

Kılıçkaya, F. & Kıc-Drgas, J. (2023). *Misuse of AI (Artificial Intelligence) in assignments.*

Kohnke, L., Moorhouse, B. L., & Zou, D. (2023). ChatGPT for Language Teaching and Learning. *RELC Journal*. Advance online publication. doi:10.1177/00336882231162868

Koraishi, O. (2023). Teaching English in the age of AI: Embracing ChatGPT to optimize EFL materials and assessment. *Language Education and Technology, 3*(1). 55-72. https://langedutech.com/letjournal/index.php/let/article/view/48

Li, X. (2019). The application and feasibility of artificial intelligence in college English teaching. In *Proceedings of the 9th International Conference on Education and Social Science* (pp. 1627–1631). Francis Academic Press. https://webofproceedings.org/proceedings_series/ESSP/ICESS%202019/ICESS19312.pd

MhlangaD. (2023). Open AI in education, the responsible and ethical use of ChatGPT towards lifelong learning. *Education, the Responsible and Ethical Use of ChatGPT Towards Lifelong Learning,* doi:10.2139/ssrn.4354422

Mohamed, A. M. (2023). Exploring the potential of an AI-based Chatbot (ChatGPT) in enhancing English as a Foreign Language (EFL) teaching: Perceptions of EFL Faculty Members. *Education and Information Technologies*, 1–23. doi:10.100710639-023-11917-z

OparaE.Mfon-Ette TheresaA.AdukeT. C. (2023). ChatGPT for teaching, learning and research: Prospects and challenges. *Global Academy Journal of Humanities and Social Sciences, 5 (2)*. 33-40. https://ssrn.com/abstract=4375470

Raina, V., & Gales, M. (2022). Multiple-Choice Question Generation: Towards an Automated Assessment Framework. *arXiv preprint arXiv:2209.11830*. https://doi.org//arXiv.2209.11830 doi:10.48550

Rodriguez-Torrealba, R., Garcia-Lopez, E., & Garcia-Cabot, A. (2022). End-to-End generation of Multiple-Choice questions using Text-to-Text transfer Transformer models. *Expert Systems with Applications*, *208*, 118258. doi:10.1016/j.eswa.2022.118258

Sakai, N. (2023). *Investigating the Feasibility of ChatGPT for Personalized English Language Learning: A Case Study on its Applicability to Japanese Students*. https://osf.io/cv9f2/download

Sharadgah, T. A., & Sa'di, R. A. (2022). A Systematic Review of Research on the Use of Artificial Intelligence in English Language Teaching and Learning (2015-2021): What are the Current Effects? *Journal of Information Technology Education*, *21*, 333–377. doi:10.28945/4999

Sumakul, D. T. Y., Hamied, F. A., & Sukyadi, D. (2022). Artificial intelligence in EFL classrooms: Friend or foe? *LEARN Journal: Language Education and Acquisition Research Network, 15*(1), 232-256. https://files.eric.ed.gov/fulltext/EJ1336138.pdf

Xiao, Y., & Hu, J. (2019). Assessment of optimal pedagogical factors for Canadian ESL learners' reading literacy through artificial intelligence algorithms. *International Journal of English Linguistics*, *9*(4), 1–14. doi:10.5539/ijel.v9n4p1

Yan, D. (2023). Impact of ChatGPT on learners in a L2 writing practicum: An exploratory investigation. *Education and Information Technologies*, 1–25. doi:10.100710639-023-11742-4

Yu, H. (2023). Reflection on whether Chat GPT should be banned by academia from the perspective of education and teaching. *Frontiers in Psychology*, *14*, 1181712. doi:10.3389/fpsyg.2023.1181712 PMID:37325766

KEY TERMS AND DEFINITIONS

AI-Assisted Learning (AIAL): AIAL refers to an adaptable learning experience that supplements our natural learning style with machine intelligence. Artificial intelligence can see patterns and make decisions that benefit people. There are a variety of diverse patterns in human learning.

Artificial Intelligence (AI): Artificial intelligence is the simulation of human cognitive and linguistic processes by computer systems. AI tools as well as applications are based on natural language processing, speech or voice recognition, and machine vision.

Chatbot: A chatbot is a computer software that analyses customer inquiries and automates responses to mimic human dialogue. Chatbots can assist users in finding the information they require by responding to their queries and requests via text, speech, or both, without requiring human intervention.

ChatGPT: The ChatGPT application was created by OpenAI. It can create responses to your questions, write or copy different contexts, create content, explain code using different programming languages, translate and transform natural language to code depending on the prompts offered to it

EFL: English as a Foreign Language (EFL) is the study and practise of English as a second language in a country that does not speak English.

Generative AI: A type of artificial intelligence known as "generative AI" is able to create a variety of content, including text, images, audio, and made-up data. The user-friendly interfaces of cutting-edge tools, which enable users to quickly create excellent text, graphics, and films in only a few seconds, are the source of the current excitement around generative AI.

Natural Language Processing: Natural language processing (NLP) is a branch of artificial intelligence (AI) that enables computers to comprehend written and spoken words as in the same way that people do.

Open AI: OpenAI is an AI research and development company. Their stated goal is to ensure that artificial general intelligence serves mankind as a whole.

Chapter 2
AI-Enabled Assessment and Feedback Mechanisms for Language Learning:
Transforming Pedagogy and Learner Experience

Yusuf Emre Yesilyurt
Burdur Mehmet Akif Ersoy University, Turkey

ABSTRACT

This chapter examines the integration of artificial intelligence (AI) in language learning assessment and feedback. It highlights limitations of traditional models before exploring AI-driven innovations in automated scoring, speech recognition, multimodal analytics and adaptive testing. The ensuing pedagogical transformation is discussed. AI feedback mechanisms including automated writing evaluation, intelligent tutoring systems, conversational agents, affective computing and learning analytics dashboards are analyzed. Benefits are presented alongside challenges regarding ethics, overreliance on technology and transparency. Case studies provide examples across educational contexts. The future outlook considers emerging innovations, increased accessibility, research gaps, policies and human-AI partnerships. The conclusion emphasizes responsible, human-centric integration of AI to enhance pedagogy and learner experience.

DOI: 10.4018/978-1-6684-9893-4.ch002

INTRODUCTION

The advent of artificial intelligence (AI) has spurred a paradigm shift in various fields, including language education. The confluence of AI technologies with traditional teaching methods has opened new vistas for personalized and automated assessment and feedback mechanisms. The application of AI in language learning is not a novel phenomenon, yet its integration in assessment and feedback is an emerging and transformative area (Liu, 2023).

This chapter delves into the intricacies of AI-enabled assessment and feedback in language learning, bridging the gap between technological advancements and pedagogical practices. It explores the limitations of traditional assessment models and highlights AI-driven innovations, pedagogical transformation, feedback mechanisms, case studies, benefits, challenges, evolving roles of educators, and future outlook. The chapter complements the broader theme of the book, "Transforming the Language Teaching Experience in the Age of AI," by focusing on the transformation of assessment and feedback through AI.

The scope of this chapter encompasses the intersection of AI, assessment, and feedback in language learning. It aims to provide educators, researchers, and practitioners with insights into the transformative potential of AI in enhancing pedagogy and learner experience. The objectives include an in-depth examination of AI-enabled assessment techniques, the exploration of ethical considerations, and a critical evaluation of the impact on learners and educators. This chapter contributes to the academic discourse by presenting a comprehensive and innovative perspective on AI's role in transforming language learning assessment.

LIMITATIONS OF TRADITIONAL ASSESSMENT MODELS IN LANGUAGE LEARNING

Traditional language learning assessment models predominantly emphasize summative assessments, which often occur at the end of an instructional period. This approach primarily aims to evaluate learners' overall proficiency rather than the learning process itself. While summative assessments are essential for gauging performance, they can lead to a narrow view of language competence, overlooking the nuances of ongoing learning and development (Shohamy, 2020).

In traditional assessment models, personalized and timely feedback is often constrained by various logistical and practical barriers. Teachers' time and resources are limited, making it challenging to provide individualized and immediate feedback that addresses each learner's unique needs. This lack of personalized feedback can hinder learners' engagement and motivation, reducing the effectiveness of the learning process (Hattie & Timperley, 2007; Nicol & Macfarlane-Dick, 2006).

Human assessors, while invaluable for providing qualitative insights, are often constrained by their capabilities and resources. The labor-intensive nature of manual grading, coupled with potential subjectivity and inconsistency, can affect the reliability and validity of assessments. These limitations can result in a lack of diverse and frequent assessment opportunities, which are crucial for continuous improvement in language learning (Bachman & Adrian, 2022).

Traditional assessment models often fall short in providing ample opportunities for formative assessment, which focuses on ongoing feedback to facilitate learning and improvement. Formative assessments are essential for understanding learners' strengths and weaknesses, but they are often underutilized or implemented superficially in conventional language education settings. This inadequacy limits the potential for dynamic and responsive teaching strategies that cater to individual learning trajectories (Heritage, 2021).

AI-DRIVEN INNOVATIONS IN LANGUAGE ASSESSMENT

Natural language processing (NLP) has revolutionized the field of automated essay scoring (AES). Utilizing machine learning algorithms and linguistic analysis, NLP enables the objective evaluation of essays based on various criteria such as grammar, coherence, and argumentation. This innovation not only enhances efficiency but also provides consistent and unbiased scoring, making it a powerful tool for language assessment (Hussein, Hassan, & Nassef, 2019; Sethi & Singh, 2022; Shermis & Burstein, 2013; Valenti, Neri, & Cucchiarelli, 2003).

Speech recognition technology has brought transformative changes to speaking and pronunciation assessment in language learning. It allows for real-time analysis of speech patterns, intonation, and pronunciation, offering personalized feedback and assessment. This technology fosters an interactive and responsive learning environment that caters to individual needs and facilitates targeted improvement in speaking skills (Witt, 2012; Xi, 2010).

Multimodal analytics, integrating computer vision and sensor data, has opened new frontiers in language assessment. By analyzing facial expressions, gestures, and physiological responses, these analytics provide a nuanced understanding of learners' engagement and emotions during assessments. This multidimensional approach offers a more comprehensive evaluation of language competence, bridging the gap between cognitive and affective aspects of learning (D'Mello & Graesser, 2012; Blikstein & Worsley, 2016).

Adaptive testing and personalized item generation through AI offer a tailored assessment experience for learners. These innovations use algorithms to dynamically adjust the difficulty and content of assessment items based on individual performance and learning profiles. Such adaptivity enhances the validity and relevance of assessments, promoting a learner-centered approach that aligns with diverse needs and abilities (Cawthon et al., 2013; Heitmann et al., 2018).

Stealth assessment and embedded analytics are emerging trends in AI-driven language assessment. These techniques seamlessly integrate assessment within learning activities, providing continuous and unobtrusive evaluation. Stealth assessment captures complex problem-solving and critical thinking skills, while embedded analytics offer actionable insights to guide instruction. These innovations foster a holistic learning experience that transcends traditional assessment boundaries (Shute & Ventura, 2013; Spector et al., 2016).

PEDAGOGICAL TRANSFORMATION THROUGH AI-ENABLED ASSESSMENT

The integration of AI in language assessment signifies a shift from traditional to modern practices. This transformation is characterized by the use of intelligent algorithms and adaptive testing platforms, allowing for a more nuanced and individualized understanding of learners' abilities. Unlike traditional methods, AI-enabled assessment emphasizes continuous, dynamic evaluation, fostering a learning environment that is more responsive to individual needs and progress (Mallik & Gangopadhyay, 2023; Van der Kleij, Feskens, & Eggen, 2015).

AI-enabled assessment offers opportunities to enhance cultural inclusiveness and sensitivity in language learning. By leveraging data-driven insights and personalized algorithms, assessments can be tailored to reflect diverse cultural contexts and linguistic nuances. This approach fosters an inclusive learning environment that recognizes and values cultural diversity, promoting equity and fairness in language assessment (Mayfield et al., 2019)

The rise of AI-assisted language learning encourages interdisciplinary collaboration among educators, technologists, linguists, and researchers. This synergy fosters the development of innovative assessment tools and pedagogical strategies that draw from various disciplines. Such collaboration enhances the quality and effectiveness of AI-enabled assessment, bridging the gap between technological innovation and educational practice, and nurturing a holistic approach to language education (Sottilare et al., 2018).

AI FEEDBACK MECHANISMS TO ENHANCE LEARNING

Automated writing evaluation (AWE) programs leverage AI algorithms to assess written text, providing immediate, objective, and detailed feedback on grammar, syntax, and rhetorical structure. These programs support learners in identifying their strengths and weaknesses, encouraging iterative refinement and self-directed learning. AWE offers a scalable solution that transcends the limitations of human evaluators, fostering enhanced writing proficiency (Warschauer & Ware, 2006; Shermis & Burstein, 2013).

Intelligent tutoring systems (ITS) represent a significant advancement in personalized learning. Utilizing AI-driven analytics, ITS provide real-time, adaptive feedback tailored to individual learners' needs. These systems promote active learning by adjusting instructional content and providing scaffolded support, aligning closely with learners' abilities and goals. Research has shown that ITS can significantly enhance learning outcomes by facilitating targeted, personalized instruction (Koedinger et al., 1997; VanLehn, 2011).

Conversational agents and chatbots offer innovative avenues for interactive feedback in language learning. These AI-driven tools engage learners in dialogues, simulating human-like interactions and providing instant responses. This interactive feedback mechanism fosters a more engaging and responsive learning experience, allowing learners to practice and refine language skills in a safe and supportive environment (Chae et al., 2023).

Affective computing and sentiment analysis utilize AI to analyze learners' emotions and attitudes, adding a new dimension to feedback personalization. These technologies detect subtle cues in learners' expressions and language use, enabling feedback that resonates with their emotional states. This emotionally aware feedback can enhance motivation and engagement, contributing to a more empathetic and effective learning experience (Calvo & D'Mello, 2010; D'Mello & Graesser, 2012).

Learning analytics dashboards, powered by AI, offer actionable insights into learners' progress and performance. These dashboards visualize data in an accessible manner, providing educators and learners with an overview of key metrics and trends. By translating complex data into understandable insights, these tools empower educators to make informed decisions and learners to take charge of their learning trajectories (Siemens & Long, 2011; Verbert et al., 2014).

CASE STUDIES AND EXAMPLES OF AI IMPLEMENTATION

Personalized Writing Feedback in School Systems

Writing is a complex skill, requiring mastery in areas like grammar, vocabulary, and style. Educators find providing feedback time-consuming, especially in large-scale settings. AI technologies, through automated writing evaluation (AWE) programs, can offer solutions by analyzing and scoring learners' texts.

Criterion, developed by ETS, is an AWE program that gives instant feedback on essays based on six traits (Quinlan, Higgins, & Wolff, 201). It provides holistic scores using ETS's e-rater engine, utilizing natural language processing (NLP). It's used by educators for assigning tasks and monitoring progress and by learners to practice and improve skills.

WriteToLearn, by Pearson, is a web-based AWE tool that integrates reading and writing activities with automated feedback (Shermis & Burstein, 2013) It offers tasks in summary and essay writing and provides feedback on various aspects of the text. The scoring based on Pearson's Knowledge Analysis Technologies engine.

The use of AWE programs offers benefits for educators and learners. Educators are afforded the opportunity to significantly reduce their workload through the utilization of automated systems, which saves time for other pedagogical activities (Donova et al., 2021). Concurrently, learners benefit from receiving personalized feedback, allowing for the identification of individual strengths and weaknesses. This not only fosters a more tailored learning experience but also serves to enhance motivation and promote continuous development in writing skills. The integration of AI support in this context further amplifies these benefits by introducing a level of efficiency and adaptability that represents a substantial improvement in the educational process. However, challenges exist, including ethical concerns about data privacy, the risk of overreliance on automation, and the need for transparency in feedback and scoring. Ensuring data protection, fostering critical thinking, and providing clear explanations of feedback criteria are essential for responsible use of AWE programs in schools.

Automated Speech Recognition for Pronunciation Practice

Pronunciation practice is vital in language learning, and providing feedback is challenging for educators. AI technologies can address this through automated speech recognition (ASR) systems that analyze and evaluate learners' speech. Rosetta Stone is an ASR system used in language learning, assessing pronunciation and giving immediate feedback (Nielson, 2011). It compares learners' speech with native speakers and provides visual feedback, allowing learners to adjust the difficulty level. Duolingo, another ASR system, uses technology to enhance speaking and listening skills, offering various exercises and gamified feedback, including points and badges (Settles & Meeder, 2016).

ASR systems offer several benefits for educators and learners. Educators receive objective and consistent feedback without human intervention, saving time. Learners receive personalized and immediate feedback, boosting confidence and engagement and offering authentic speaking opportunities.

However, challenges include the technical limitations and error rate of ASR technology, the pedagogical appropriateness of feedback, and learners' perceptions and attitudes toward ASR feedback. Ensuring robust and adaptable ASR systems, aligning feedback with learning objectives, and fostering positive learner attitudes are essential for effective pronunciation practice.

Adaptive Language Learning Apps and Platforms

Language learning requires individualized acquisition of diverse skills, and AI technologies can provide adaptive apps and platforms to customize learning according to students' needs. Research has shown that adaptive learning platforms offer effective and flexible learning pathways, accommodating diverse learners' needs and preferences (Heift & Schulze, 2007).

Adaptive language learning platforms such as Duolingo use algorithms to adjust the difficulty and content of lessons according to individual performance, enhancing engagement and retention (Settles & Meeder, 2016). Babbel, offering courses in 14 languages, uses AI to personalize learning experiences based on level, interests, and goals, adapting content and using spaced repetition techniques (Godwin-Jones 2019). Knewton, an AI-powered platform, creates personalized paths for learners in subjects like English, adjusting content based on responses and providing real-time feedback (Knewton, 2020).

Adaptive language learning platforms benefit educators by providing data-driven instruction, enhancing teaching efficiency, and learners by offering personalized experiences, increasing motivation and flexibility in learning.

Challenges include ethical concerns about data privacy and consent, ensuring pedagogical quality and validity, and managing learner perception and attitude. Addressing these issues is vital for the effective and responsible use of adaptive language learning apps and platforms.

Stealth Assessment in Immersive Games

Stealth assessment, embedded within immersive games provides unobtrusive evaluation of learners' problem-solving skills. These assessments are woven into the gameplay, allowing for continuous monitoring of learning progress without interrupting the flow of engagement. Case studies have demonstrated the potential of stealth assessment in promoting critical thinking and creativity in an interactive and enjoyable learning environment (Shute & Ventura, 2013;)

Immersive games provide rich contexts for language learning, but traditional assessments are intrusive and limited. AI technologies, using stealth assessment techniques, can embed assessments within games and offer ongoing feedback. Eco is a multiplayer game simulating a virtual ecosystem (Strange Loop Games, 2023). It assesses players' language, cognitive, and social skills, providing feedback through features like quests and reports. Trace Effects is a 3D game teaching American English and culture (Freepik, 2023). It measures language skills and intercultural competence, providing support through dialogues, quizzes, and comics.

Analytics-Driven Intervention and Support Systems

Analytics-driven intervention systems, such as those implemented in higher education institutions, utilize AI to monitor students' performance and provide targeted support. By analyzing data on attendance, engagement, and grades, these systems identify at-risk students and trigger timely interventions. Case studies have highlighted the success of these systems in enhancing retention and academic achievement through personalized support and early intervention (Arnold & Pistilli, 2012; Dietz-Uhler & Hurn, 2013).

i-Ntervene integrates a learning management system with automatic code grading, using analytics to analyze students' learning behaviors, offering personalized feedback, and providing teachers with diagnostic reports (Utamachant, Anutariya, & Pongnumkul, 2023). Knewton Alta is a web-based adaptive courseware platform (Knewton, 2020). It collects data on students' learning outcomes and preferences, offering personalized learning paths and providing teachers with actionable insights. These tools illustrate how AI can enhance both the gaming experience in language learning and the analytics-driven support system, making the process more dynamic and efficient.

BENEFITS OF AI-ENABLED ASSESSMENT AND FEEDBACK

AI-enabled assessment tools facilitate more frequent and granular data collection, providing insights into learners' progress at a micro-level. The continuous tracking and detailed analysis of performance enable educators to identify specific areas of strength and weakness, allowing for targeted interventions. This enhancement in data precision contributes to more informed and effective educational decision-making (Baker & Siemens, 2014; Sclater, Peasgood, & Mullan, 2016).

Through automation, AI-enabled assessment allows for the delivery of personalized and timely feedback at scale. Unlike manual assessment, which can be time-consuming and inconsistent, AI algorithms provide immediate, customized feedback that aligns with individual learners' needs and abilities. This personalization fosters a more responsive learning experience, enhancing motivation and engagement (Van der Kleij et al., 2015).

AI-enabled assessment empowers learners with greater control over their learning process. By providing instant and detailed feedback, these tools encourage metacognition and self-regulation, enabling learners to reflect on their performance and devise strategies for improvement. This enhanced learner agency fosters a more proactive and autonomous approach to learning, contributing to long-term success (Zimmerman, 2008; Azevedo & Hadwin, 2005).

The automation of assessment tasks through AI reduces the workload for educators, freeing them to focus on more complex and nuanced aspects of teaching. Automation streamlines grading and feedback processes, enhancing efficiency without compromising quality. This shift in responsibilities allows educators to dedicate more time to individualized instruction and relationship-building, enriching the overall educational experience (Dietz-Uhler & Hurn, 2013; Eynon, 2013).

AI-enabled assessment ensures greater reliability and consistency in evaluation. Unlike human assessors, who may be influenced by biases or fatigue, AI algorithms provide uniform and objective scoring. This consistency ensures fairness and transparency in assessment, building trust and confidence in the evaluation process. The improved reliability of AI-enabled assessment contributes to more accurate and fair educational outcomes (Shermis & Burstein, 2013).

CHALLENGES AND CONSIDERATIONS

AI-enabled assessment and feedback systems inherently rely on the collection and analysis of vast amounts of personal data. This raises significant ethical concerns about data privacy and the potential for algorithmic bias. Ensuring that sensitive information is handled with care, maintaining transparency in data use, and scrutinizing algorithms for inherent biases are crucial challenges that must be addressed (Zou & Schiebinger, 2018; Zeide, 2017).

The automation brought by AI in assessment and feedback may lead to an overreliance on technology, potentially diminishing the human touch in education. While AI can provide efficiency and scalability, the risk of losing nuanced, empathetic feedback and the vital interpersonal connection between educators and learners cannot be ignored. Striking a balance between automation and human interaction is a complex challenge that warrants careful consideration (Selwyn, 2019).

The impersonal nature of AI-driven feedback might lead to learner distrust or disengagement. The absence of human connection and the potential for misunderstanding contextually nuanced language can create barriers to acceptance. Building trust in AI systems and ensuring that they resonate with learners' needs and expectations is an ongoing challenge that requires attention to design, communication, and user experience (Wang et al., 2023; Xu, 2023).

AI algorithms often operate as "black boxes," where the decision-making process is obscured. This lack of transparency and explainability can hinder understanding and acceptance among both educators and learners. Developing interpretable models and providing clear explanations of how decisions are made is essential to foster trust and to ensure that AI-enabled assessment aligns with educational goals and ethical standards (Doshi-Velez & Kim, 2017; Guidotti et al., 2018).

THE EVOLVING ROLE OF EDUCATORS

The integration of AI in education necessitates that educators evolve in their role as designers of assessments. This includes crafting assessments that are not only meaningful but are also meticulously aligned with learning objectives. Leveraging AI, educators can create adaptive and personalized assessments that resonate with individual learning paths while maintaining alignment with broader educational goals (Mislevy, Almond, & Lukas, 2003; Shute & Rahimi, 2017).

While AI can provide instantaneous and quantitative feedback, the role of educators in offering nuanced qualitative feedback remains paramount. Educators possess the human understanding needed to interpret contextual subtleties, emotions, and motivations, ensuring that feedback is empathetic and resonant. The synergy of AI-generated feedback with human insight creates a comprehensive feedback loop that fosters deeper learning and engagement (Duijnhouwer, Prins, & Stokking, 2012).

AI-enabled analytics provide educators with powerful insights into learner progress. However, the interpretation and application of these analytics require human expertise. Educators must analyze the data, discern meaningful patterns, and translate them into actionable insights to guide instruction. This evolving role emphasizes the importance of data literacy among educators to leverage AI-driven analytics effectively (Sclater, Peasgood, & Mullan, 2016; Siemens, 2013).

The burgeoning field of educational AI offers a plethora of tools, and the onus of selecting and integrating the most appropriate ones falls on educators. This requires an understanding of the unique needs of learners, the objectives of the curriculum, and the capabilities and limitations of various AI tools. This facet of the evolving educator role underscores the importance of technological proficiency and discerning judgment (Passey, 2019; Herodotou et al., 2019).

Despite the advancement of AI, human oversight and responsibility remain indispensable. Educators must ensure that ethical considerations are upheld, and that human values and judgment guide the deployment of AI. The role of educators in maintaining clear human oversight ensures that education remains a human-centric endeavor, where technology serves to enhance rather than replace human interaction and wisdom (Greene, Hoffman, & Stark, 2019; Selwyn, 2019).

FUTURE OUTLOOK AND OPPORTUNITIES

Emerging Innovations in Multilingual AI Assessment

The future of AI in education is set to witness remarkable innovations in multilingual assessment. AI's ability to understand and process multiple languages can revolutionize language learning and assessment, fostering global connectivity and cultural understanding. This paves the way for more inclusive and adaptive language education, accommodating the diversity of learners' linguistic backgrounds (Salas-Pilco, Xiao, & Oshima, 2022).

Potential for Increased Accessibility and Inclusion

AI holds tremendous potential to increase accessibility and inclusion in education. By leveraging assistive technologies such as speech-to-text, personalized learning paths, and adaptive content, AI can cater to diverse learning needs, including those of learners with disabilities. This opens doors for more equitable and universal access to quality education, transcending physical, cognitive, and socio-economic barriers (Alper & Goggin, 2017; Hernández-Leo et al., 2019).

Research Priorities and Gaps

As AI continues to reshape education, it is crucial to identify and address research priorities and gaps. Future research must focus on ethical considerations, interpretability of algorithms, human-AI collaboration, and contextualized implementation. Exploring these areas will contribute to a more robust, responsible, and relevant integration of AI in education, aligning with societal values and educational objectives (Holstein, McLaren, & Aleven, 2019).

Role of Policy and Regulations

The integration of AI in education necessitates clear and thoughtful policy and regulations. Governments and educational institutions must develop frameworks that ensure ethical use, data privacy, quality standards, and accountability. Collaborative efforts between policymakers, researchers, and practitioners are vital to create a regulatory environment that fosters innovation while protecting the interests of all stakeholders (Daly et al., 2019).

Partnerships Between Educators and Technology Leaders

The future of AI in education will likely be shaped by dynamic partnerships between educators and technology leaders. Such collaborations can drive the co-creation of AI tools that are pedagogically sound, user-centered, and ethically aligned. These partnerships can bridge the gap between technological innovation and educational practice, ensuring that AI serves the real needs of learners and educators (Reich & Ruipérez-Valiente, 2019; Selwyn & Jandrić, 2020).

CONCLUSION

The chapter has explored the multifaceted landscape of AI-enabled assessment and feedback in language learning. Through an examination of traditional limitations, innovative applications, pedagogical transformations, challenges, and future opportunities, it has provided a comprehensive view of the current state and potential of AI in reshaping educational practices. The central theme emphasizes the synergy between technology and human insight to create more personalized, inclusive, and effective learning experiences (Baker & Siemens, 2014; Selwyn, 2019).

The integration of AI within language learning assessment and feedback has the potential to enact a transformative impact on both pedagogy and the learner experience. By enabling more precise assessments, timely feedback, and personalized learning paths, AI supports a shift towards learner-centered education. It enhances accessibility and inclusion, redefines the role of educators, and opens new horizons for collaboration and innovation. This transformation, though filled with promise, requires careful navigation, ethical consideration, and a sustained focus on human values and educational goals (Kooli, 2023).

The journey towards fully realizing the potential of AI in language learning is complex and evolving. It invites educators, technologists, policymakers, and researchers to engage in continuous dialogue, exploration, and critical reflection. The future calls for responsible innovation, where technology is harnessed not as an end in itself but as a means to enhance education in a manner that resonates with human dignity, equity, and excellence. It's a call to action for a collaborative, informed, and purpose-driven approach to AI in education, ensuring that it serves the best interests of learners and society at large (Reich & Ruipérez-Valiente, 2019).

REFERENCES

Alper, M., & Goggin, G. (2017). Digital technology and rights in the lives of children with disabilities. *New Media & Society*, *19*(5), 726–740. doi:10.1177/1461444816686323

Arnold, K. E., & Pistilli, M. D. (2012, April). Course signals at Purdue: Using learning analytics to increase student success. In *Proceedings of the 2nd International Conference on Learning Analytics and Knowledge* (pp. 267-270). IEEE. 10.1145/2330601.2330666

Azevedo, R., & Hadwin, A. F. (2005). Scaffolding self-regulated learning and metacognition–Implications for the design of computer-based scaffolds. *Instructional Science*, *33*(5/6), 367–379. doi:10.100711251-005-1272-9

Bachman, L., & Adrian, P. (2022). *Language assessment in practice: Developing language assessments and justifying their use in the real world*. Oxford University Press.

Baker, R. S., & Siemens, G. (2014). Educational data mining and learning analytics. In R. K. Sawyer (Ed.), *The Cambridge Handbook of the Learning Sciences* (2nd ed., pp. 253–274). Cambridge University Press. doi:10.1017/CBO9781139519526.016

Blikstein, P., & Worsley, M. (2016). Multimodal learning analytics and education data mining: Using computational technologies to measure complex learning tasks. *Journal of Learning Analytics*, *3*(2), 220–238. doi:10.18608/jla.2016.32.11

Calvo, R. A., & D'Mello, S. (2010). Affect detection: An interdisciplinary review of models, methods, and their applications. *IEEE Transactions on Affective Computing*, *1*(1), 18–37. doi:10.1109/T-AFFC.2010.1

Cawthon, S., Leppo, R., Carr, T., & Kopriva, R. (2013). Toward accessible assessments: The promises and limitations of test item adaptations for students with disabilities and English Language Learners. *Educational Assessment*, *18*(2), 73–98. doi:10.1080/10627197.2013.789294

Chae, H., Kim, M., Kim, C., Jeong, W., Kim, H., Lee, J., & Yeo, J. (2023). TUTORING: Instruction-Grounded Conversational Agent for Language Learners. arXiv preprint arXiv:2302.12623.

D'Mello, S., & Graesser, A. (2012). Dynamics of affective states during complex learning. *Learning and Instruction*, *22*(2), 145–157. doi:10.1016/j.learninstruc.2011.10.001

Daly, A., Hagendorff, T., Hui, L., Mann, M., Marda, V., Wagner, B., & Witteborn, S. (2019). Artificial intelligence governance and ethics: global perspectives. arXiv preprint arXiv:1907.03848.

Dietz-Uhler, B., & Hurn, J. E. (2013). Using learning analytics to predict (and improve) student success: A faculty perspective. *Journal of Interactive Online Learning*, *12*(1), 17–26.

Donova, M., Kiselev, V., Veretennikova, E., Lozina, E. N., & Shcherbakov, S. (2021). *Automation of Tutor's Activities in Higher Education Institutions.*

Doshi-Velez, F., & Kim, B. (2017). Towards a rigorous science of interpretable machine learning. arXiv preprint arXiv:1702.08608.

Duijnhouwer, H., Prins, F. J., & Stokking, K. M. (2012). Feedback providing improvement strategies and reflection on feedback use: Effects on students' writing motivation, process, and performance. *Learning and Instruction*, *22*(3), 171–184. doi:10.1016/j.learninstruc.2011.10.003

Eynon, R. (2013). The rise of Big Data: What does it mean for education, technology, and media research? *Learning, Media and Technology*, *38*(3), 237–240. doi:10.1080/17439884.2013.771783

Freepik. (2023, April 15). *Trace effect PSD*. Freepik. https://www.freepik.com/psd/trace-effect

Godwin-Jones, R. (2019). In a world of SMART technology, why learn another language? *Journal of Educational Technology & Society*, *22*(2), 4–13.

Greene, D., Hoffmann, A. L., & Stark, L. (2019). Better, nicer, clearer, fairer: A critical assessment of the movement for ethical artificial intelligence and machine learning. In *Proceedings of the 52nd Hawaii International Conference on System Sciences.* 10.24251/HICSS.2019.258

Guidotti, R., Monreale, A., Ruggieri, S., Turini, F., Giannotti, F., & Pedreschi, D. (2018). A survey of methods for explaining black box models. *ACM Computing Surveys*, *51*(5), 1–42. doi:10.1145/3236009

Hattie, J., & Timperley, H. (2007). The power of feedback. *Review of Educational Research, 77*(1), 81–112. doi:10.3102/003465430298487

Heift, T., & Schulze, M. (2007). *Errors and intelligence in computer-assisted language learning: Parsers and pedagogues*. Routledge. doi:10.4324/9780203012215

Heitmann, S., Grund, A., Berthold, K., Fries, S., & Roelle, J. (2018). Testing is more desirable when it is adaptive and still desirable when compared to note-taking. *Frontiers in Psychology, 9*, 2596. doi:10.3389/fpsyg.2018.02596 PMID:30619005

Heritage, M. (2021). *Formative assessment: Making it happen in the classroom.* Corwin Press.

Hernández-Leo, D., Martinez-Maldonado, R., Pardo, A., Muñoz-Cristóbal, J. A., & Rodríguez-Triana, M. J. (2019). Analytics for learning design: A layered framework and tools. *British Journal of Educational Technology, 50*(1), 139–152. doi:10.1111/bjet.12645

Herodotou, C., Rienties, B., Boroowa, A., Zdrahal, Z., & Hlosta, M. (2019). A large-scale implementation of predictive learning analytics in higher education: Lessons learned and challenges ahead. *Educational Technology Research and Development, 67*(5), 1273–1302. doi:10.100711423-019-09685-0

Holstein, K., McLaren, B. M., & Aleven, V. (2019). Intelligent tutors as teachers' aides: Exploring teacher needs for real-time analytics in blended classrooms. In *Proceedings of the Seventh International Learning Analytics & Knowledge Conference* (pp. 257-266).

Hussein, M. A., Hassan, H., & Nassef, M. (2019). Automated language essay scoring systems: A literature review. *PeerJ. Computer Science, 5*, e208. doi:10.7717/peerj-cs.208 PMID:33816861

Knewton. (n.d.). Adaptive learning for all. Retrieved from https://www.knewton.com/

Koedinger, K. R., Anderson, J. R., Hadley, W. H., & Mark, M. A. (1997). Intelligent tutoring goes to school in the big city. *International Journal of Artificial Intelligence in Education, 8*(1), 30–43.

Kooli, C. (2023). Chatbots in education and research: A critical examination of ethical implications and solutions. *Sustainability (Basel), 15*(7), 5614. doi:10.3390u15075614

Liu, M. (2023). Exploring the Application of Artificial Intelligence in Foreign Language Teaching: Challenges and Future Development. In *SHS Web of Conferences* (*Vol. 168*). EDP Sciences.

Mallik, S., & Gangopadhyay, A. (2023). Proactive and reactive engagement of artificial intelligence methods for education: A review. *Frontiers in Artificial Intelligence*, *6*, 1151391. doi:10.3389/frai.2023.1151391 PMID:37215064

Mayfield, E., Madaio, M., Prabhumoye, S., Gerritsen, D., McLaughlin, B., Dixon-Román, E., & Black, A. W. (2019, August). Equity beyond bias in language technologies for education. In *Proceedings of the Fourteenth Workshop on Innovative Use of NLP for Building Educational Applications* (pp. 444-460). 10.18653/v1/W19-4446

Mislevy, R. J., Almond, R. G., & Lukas, J. F. (2003). *A Brief Introduction to Evidence-Centered Design*. Educational Testing Service. doi:10.1002/j.2333-8504.2003.tb01908.x

Nicol, D. J., & Macfarlane-Dick, D. (2006). Formative assessment and self-regulated learning: A model and seven principles of good feedback practice. *Studies in Higher Education*, *31*(2), 199–218. doi:10.1080/03075070600572090

Nielson, K. B. (2011). Self-study with language learning software in the workplace: What happens? Passey, D. (2019). Computer science (CS) or information and communication technologies (ICT): The curriculum needs both. *Education and Information Technologies*, *24*(2), 1039–1058.

Quinlan, T., Higgins, D., & Wolff, S. (2012). Evaluating the construct coverage of the e-rater® scoring engine. *ETS Research Report Series*, *2012*(1), 1–21.

Reich, J., & Ruipérez-Valiente, J. A. (2019). The MOOC pivot. *Science*, *363*(6423), 130–131. doi:10.1126cience.aav7958 PMID:30630920

Salas-Pilco, S. Z., Xiao, K., & Oshima, J. (2022). Artificial intelligence and new technologies in inclusive education for minority students: A systematic review. *Sustainability (Basel)*, *14*(20), 13572. doi:10.3390u142013572

Sclater, N., Peasgood, A., & Mullan, J. (2016). *Learning Analytics in Higher Education: A Review of UK and International Practice*. Jisc.

Selwyn, N. (2019). *Should Robots Replace Teachers?* AI and the Future of Education. Polity.

Selwyn, N., & Jandrić, P. (2020). Postdigital living in the age of Covid-19: Unsettling what we see as possible. *Postdigital Science and Education*, *2*(3), 233–238. doi:10.100742438-020-00166-9

Sethi, A., & Singh, K. (2022, March). Natural language processing based automated essay scoring with parameter-efficient transformer approach. In *2022 6th International Conference on Computing Methodologies and Communication (ICCMC)* (pp. 749-756). IEEE. 10.1109/ICCMC53470.2022.9753760

Settles, B., & Meeder, B. (2016). A trainable spaced repetition model for language learning. In *Proceedings of the 54th Annual Meeting of the Association for Computational Linguistics* (Volume 1: Long Papers) (pp. 1848–1858). Berlin, Germany: Association for Computational Linguistics. 10.18653/v1/P16-1174

Shermis, M. D., & Burstein, J. (Eds.). (2013). *Handbook of Automated Essay Evaluation: Current Applications and New Directions.* Routledge. doi:10.4324/9780203122761

Shohamy, E. (2020). *The power of tests: A critical perspective on the uses of language tests*. Routledge. doi:10.4324/9781003062318

Shute, V., & Rahimi, S. (2017). Review of computer-based assessment for learning in elementary and secondary education. *Journal of Computer Assisted Learning, 33*(1), 1–19. doi:10.1111/jcal.12172

Shute, V. J., & Ventura, M. (2013). *Stealth Assessment: Measuring and Supporting Learning in Video Games.* MIT Press. doi:10.7551/mitpress/9589.001.0001

Siemens, G. (2013). Learning analytics: The emergence of a discipline. *The American Behavioral Scientist, 57*(10), 1380–1400. doi:10.1177/0002764213498851

Siemens, G., & Long, P. (2011). Penetrating the fog: Analytics in learning and education. *EDUCAUSE Review, 46*(5), 30.

Sottilare, R. A., Graesser, A. C., Hu, X., & Sinatra, A. M. (2018). Design recommendations for intelligent tutoring systems: Volume 6 - affect and learning. US Army Research Laboratory. https://doi.org/ doi:10.21236/ada600864

Spector, J. M., Lockee, B. B., Childress, M. D., & Magliaro, S. G. (Eds.). (2016). *Learning, Design, and Technology*. Springer.

Strange Loop Games. (n.d.). *Eco*. Strange Loop Games. https://play.eco/

Utamachant, P., Anutariya, C., & Pongnumkul, S. (2023). i-Ntervene: Applying an evidence-based learning analytics intervention to support computer programming instruction. *Smart Learning Environments, 10*(1), 37. doi:10.118640561-023-00257-7

Valenti, S., Neri, F., & Cucchiarelli, A. (2003). An Overview of Current Research on Automated Essay Grading. *Journal of Information Technology Education*, *2*(1), 319–330. doi:10.28945/331

Van der Kleij, F. M., Feskens, R. C., & Eggen, T. J. (2015). Effects of feedback in a computer-based learning environment on students' learning outcomes: A meta-analysis. *Review of Educational Research*, *85*(4), 475–511. doi:10.3102/0034654314564881

VanLehn, K. (2011). The relative effectiveness of human tutoring, intelligent tutoring systems, and other tutoring systems. *Educational Psychologist*, *46*(4), 197–221. doi:10.1080/00461520.2011.611369

Verbert, K., Duval, E., Klerkx, J., Govaerts, S., & Santos, J. L. (2013). Learning analytics dashboard applications. *The American Behavioral Scientist*, *57*(10), 1500–1509. doi:10.1177/0002764213479363

Wang, Q., Madaio, M., Kane, S., Kapania, S., Terry, M., & Wilcox, L. (2023). Designing Responsible AI: Adaptations of UX Practice to Meet Responsible AI Challenges. In *Proceedings of the 2023 CHI Conference on Human Factors in Computing Systems* (pp. 1-16). 10.1145/3544548.3581278

Warschauer, M., & Ware, P. (2006). Automated writing evaluation: Defining the classroom research agenda. *Language Teaching Research*, *10*(2), 157–180. doi:10.1191/1362168806lr190oa

Witt, S. M. (2012, June). Automatic error detection in pronunciation training: Where we are and where we need to go. In *International Symposium on Automatic Detection on Errors in Pronunciation Training* (Vol. 1).

Xi, X. (2010). Automated scoring and feedback systems: Where are we and where are we heading? *Language Testing*, *27*(3), 291–300. doi:10.1177/0265532210364643

Xu, W. (2023). AI in HCI Design and User Experience. arXiv preprint arXiv:2301.00987.

Zeide, E. (2017). The structural consequences of big data-driven education. *Big Data*, *5*(2), 164–172. doi:10.1089/big.2016.0061

Zimmerman, B. J. (2008). Investigating self-regulation and motivation: Historical background, methodological developments, and future prospects. *American Educational Research Journal*, *45*(1), 166–183. doi:10.3102/0002831207312909

Zou, J., & Schiebinger, L. (2018). AI can be sexist and racist — It's time to make it fair. [Shermis]. *Nature*, *559*(7714), 324–326. doi:10.1038/d41586-018-05707-8 PMID:30018439

KEY TERMS AND DEFINITIONS

Adaptive Testing: A type of testing that adjusts the difficulty of questions based on the learner's performance, enabled through AI algorithms for personalized assessment.

Affective Computing: The study and development of systems that can recognize and interpret human emotions, applied in language learning to understand and respond to learners' emotional states.

Artificial Intelligence (AI) in Language Learning Assessment: The integration of artificial intelligence (AI) technologies with traditional teaching methods to enable personalized and automated assessment and feedback mechanisms in language learning.

Automated Essay Scoring: A process that uses AI-driven algorithms to grade and evaluate written essays, allowing for consistent and unbiased scoring.

Automated Writing Evaluation (AWE): AWE programs use AI algorithms to assess written text, providing immediate feedback on grammar, syntax, and structure. They support learners in refining their writing skills while offering educators a scalable and efficient solution for evaluating writing proficiency.

Learning Analytics Dashboards: Tools that collect and analyze data on students' learning outcomes and preferences, offering personalized learning paths and providing educators with actionable insights.

Multimodal Analytics: The analysis of multiple types of data, such as text, speech, and visual information, to provide comprehensive insights and assessment in language learning.

Speech Recognition: The application of AI to transcribe and interpret human speech, used in language learning for pronunciation practice and assessment.

Chapter 3
Personalized Learning Through Gamification:
A ChatGPT Approach to English Language Learning

Sabahattin Yeşilçınar
https://orcid.org/0000-0001-6457-0211
Muş Alparslan University, Turkey

ABSTRACT

Gamification has emerged as an effective method for enhancing student engagement and motivation. This approach can be especially useful for English language learning, where learners may face challenges in staying motivated and engaged with the material. By utilizing ChatGBT, learning can be gamified to improve the learning experience. This chapter explores the benefits of gamification for English language learning and outlines how ChatGBT can be used as a gamification tool. ChatGBT's interactive and personalized capabilities can be utilized to create a gamified learning environment. Furthermore, this chapter provides practical examples of how ChatGBT can be used to gamify various aspects of English language learning, including vocabulary acquisition, grammar practice, and reading comprehension. The chapter also discusses challenges and limitations of ChatGBT. Overall, this chapter emphasizes the potential of gamifying English language learning through ChatGBT to enhance learners' motivation and engagement, as well as to improve their language skills in a fun and interactive way.

DOI: 10.4018/978-1-6684-9893-4.ch003

INTRODUCTION

Gamification has emerged as an influential educational approach that integrates game elements and mechanics into traditional learning environments. It has gained significant attention in recent years due to its potential to enhance student engagement, motivation, and learning outcomes. In the context of English language learning, where learners often face challenges in maintaining motivation and engagement, gamification offers a promising solution. By incorporating game elements into the language learning process, learners can immerse themselves in an interactive and enjoyable experience that stimulates their enthusiasm for mastering English. Research studies have indicated the benefits of gamification in education, with findings supporting its positive impact on student engagement and motivation (Dicheva et al., 2015; Landers, 2014). Moreover, gamified learning environments provide opportunities for learners to develop critical thinking and problem-solving skills as they navigate through language-based challenges and puzzles. By engaging in these activities, learners can enhance their cognitive abilities and apply their language knowledge in practical contexts.

Gamified learning environments, through elements such as challenges, rewards, and progress tracking, create a sense of purpose, achievement, and excitement among learners. These elements tap into intrinsic motivation and foster a sense of autonomy, competence, and relatedness, as proposed by Self-Determination Theory (Ryan & Deci, 2000). Consequently, learners become actively involved in their language learning journey and develop a stronger commitment to the process.

Recent research has demonstrated the positive impact of gamification on language learning. A meta-analysis by Hamari et al. (2014a) revealed that gamification has a positive effect on knowledge retention, problem-solving skills, and information recall. This finding underscores the potential of gamified learning environments to enhance the learning experience and outcomes. The interactive and immersive nature of gamified experiences promotes active learning, critical thinking, and the application of acquired language skills. Learners are encouraged to explore and experiment within a safe and supportive environment, leading to a deeper understanding and improved language proficiency (Kapp, 2012). In parallel with the rise of gamification, advancements in artificial intelligence (AI) have opened up new possibilities for innovative approaches to language learning. Among these models, ChatGPT has garnered attention for its potential in enhancing language teaching and learning. The study by Kohnke, Moorhouse, and Zou (2023) in the RELC Journal explores the use of ChatGPT for language teaching and learning, shedding light on its benefits. This research showcases how the integration of AI technologies, such as ChatGPT, can revolutionize language learning experiences by providing personalized and interactive interactions.

Furthermore, research by Lai et al. (2023) delves into the comprehensive evaluation of ChatGPT in multilingual learning, showcasing its versatility. The findings highlight how ChatGPT facilitates language learning across different languages, enabling learners to overcome language barriers and expand their linguistic repertoire. The adaptability and versatility of ChatGPT make it a powerful tool in the hands of language learners seeking to acquire proficiency in multiple languages.

The impact of ChatGPT on learning motivation is emphasized in the study by Ali et al. (2023), highlighting positive experiences from both teachers and students. This research underscores how ChatGPT's interactive and responsive nature fosters engagement and motivation among learners, creating a dynamic and supportive learning atmosphere. Teachers and students alike report positive experiences with ChatGPT, as it provides personalized interactions and real-time feedback that enhance the language learning process and inspire learners to persist in their language learning journey. By combining the benefits of gamification with the capabilities of AI, learners can experience a comprehensive and effective language learning approach that sparks their enthusiasm, nurtures their autonomy, and empowers them to become proficient language users.

Not limited to English language learning alone, ChatGPT exhibits promising applications in various subjects. Wardat et al. (2023) discuss its revolutionary impact in mathematics education. Fitria (2023) reviews the use of ChatGPT in writing English essays, focusing on its contribution to skill development. Additionally, researchers such as Baskara and Mukarto (2023) explore the implications of ChatGPT in higher education language learning. These studies highlight the wide-ranging potential of ChatGPT in transforming education across different disciplines, demonstrating its adaptability and effectiveness in supporting learners' academic growth and skill acquisition.

In the realm of foreign language teaching and learning, ChatGPT provides opportunities for optimization. Hong (2023) discusses the potential impact of ChatGPT on foreign language instruction, shedding light on the ways in which the technology can revolutionize the traditional classroom setting. By providing interactive and personalized language learning experiences, ChatGPT can offer learners individualized guidance, practice, and feedback, catering to their specific language needs and preferences. While Hong focuses on foreign language instruction, Koraishi (2023) highlights the role of ChatGPT in enhancing materials and assessment. With its language generation capabilities, ChatGPT offers valuable contributions to the creation of diverse and interactive learning materials. These materials cover various language skills such as listening, speaking, reading, and writing, providing learners with comprehensive opportunities to enhance their language proficiency. Moreover, ChatGPT's automated evaluation features enable teachers to efficiently monitor learners' progress and identify areas for improvement through timely and detailed feedback. As the potential of ChatGPT in language learning is explored, it is essential to address the ethical considerations and challenges that emerge when deploying large language models in educational contexts. The study conducted by Kasneci et al. (2023) delves into these matters, addressing concerns related to data privacy, potential biases in algorithms, and responsible AI usage in educational settings. These discussions underscore the significance of maintaining transparency, fairness, and equality during the implementation of ChatGPT, ensuring the safeguarding of learners' data and employing the technology as an empowering tool that mitigates educational disparities. To facilitate the responsible integration of ChatGPT into education, Halaweh (2023) proposes a range of strategies for its implementation. These strategies encompass the establishment of clear guidelines for ethical usage, providing teacher training and professional development opportunities, and continuously evaluating and enhancing the technology's effectiveness. By adopting a framework that ensures responsible implementation, educators can harness the full potential of ChatGPT while effectively managing risks and maximizing its advantages in language teaching and learning.

Considering the aforementioned studies, integrating ChatGPT into gamified English language learning offers a personalized and transformative experience. ChatGBT's interactive and personalized capabilities offer learners a unique opportunity to engage in conversational exchanges that adapt to their individual proficiency levels, learning preferences, and progress. Learners receive immediate feedback, personalized guidance, and support, which are crucial elements for effective language acquisition. Through this personalized approach, learners can develop their language skills in a manner that aligns with their specific needs and preferences.

This chapter aims to explore the benefits of gamification for English language learning and outline how ChatGBT can be utilized as a powerful tool to gamify the learning process. Practical examples will be provided to demonstrate how ChatGBT can be integrated into various aspects of English language learning, including vocabulary acquisition, grammar practice, and reading comprehension. Additionally, the chapter will address the challenges and limitations of using ChatGBT as a gamification tool, ensuring a comprehensive understanding of its potential and applicability in the English language learning context. In conclusion, the combination of gamification and AI language models, such as ChatGBT, offers exciting possibilities to enhance learners' motivation, engagement, and language skills. By leveraging the engaging elements of gamification and the interactive capabilities of AI, learners can embark on an immersive and personalized learning journey that fosters their English language proficiency in an enjoyable and meaningful manner.

BENEFITS OF GAMIFICATION IN ENGLISH LANGUAGE LEARNING

Gamification has emerged as a highly influential approach in education, offering significant advantages for English language learning. By incorporating game elements and mechanics into traditional learning environments, gamification has the potential to enhance student engagement, motivation, and learning outcomes. Extensive research studies have examined the benefits of gamification in various educational contexts, including English language learning. By incorporating gamification into English language learning, educators can harness the benefits of enhanced engagement, motivation, collaboration, and communication. Additionally, the use of AI language models like ChatGBT further amplifies the advantages, offering a personalized and interactive learning experience. This comprehensive approach fosters learners' English language proficiency effectively and ensures an engaging and enjoyable learning journey.

Enhanced Engagement and Motivation

Gamified learning environments, featuring elements such as challenges, rewards, and progress tracking, create a sense of purpose, achievement, and excitement among learners (Landers, 2014; Dicheva et al., 2015). Moreover, the introduction of gamification in language learning has been shown to have a significant impact on learners' motivation and engagement levels (Landers, 2014). These elements tap into intrinsic motivation, aligning with the principles of Self-Determination Theory (Ryan & Deci, 2000). When learners are actively engaged and motivated, they are more likely to persist in their language learning journey and achieve better learning outcomes (Dicheva et al., 2015). The interactive nature of gamified learning environments promotes active participation as students are motivated to explore and experiment within a supportive environment. Through the incorporation of interactive game elements, learners are encouraged to actively engage with the language learning content, fostering a sense of autonomy and control over their learning experience (Landers, 2014). As learners progress through the challenges and earn rewards, they experience a sense of accomplishment, which further fuels their motivation and drives their continued participation (Dicheva et al., 2015). These elements instill a sense of purpose, accomplishment, and excitement among learners. In other words, learners actively participate in their language learning journey, maintaining high levels of motivation and engagement (Dicheva et al., 2015; Landers, 2014). By employing a gamified learning environment that is rich in interactivity and immersion, learners become proactive agents in their individual learning process, assuming responsibility for their language learning objectives and propelling their advancement (Dicheva et al., 2015). The integration of challenges, rewards, and progress tracking ensures that learners sustain their motivation and involvement throughout their language learning journey, yielding improved learning outcomes and a more profound grasp of the language (Landers, 2014).

Gamification harnesses learners' intrinsic motivation, nurturing autonomy, competence, and relatedness (Deci & Ryan, 2000; Zichermann & Cunningham, 2011). By integrating game elements aligned with learners' interests and preferences, gamified language learning experiences provide a meaningful context for language acquisition. This encourages learners to engage in self-directed learning and develop a strong commitment to the language learning process.

Overall, gamified learning environments present a potent instrument for heightening learner engagement and motivation in language learning. Through the adept utilization of gamification principles, educators can shape vibrant and immersive encounters that nurture intrinsic motivation, autonomy, and a sense of accomplishment among learners (Dicheva et al., 2015; Landers, 2014). These environments empower learners to actively participate, explore, and experiment within a supportive framework, ultimately culminating in more purposeful and efficacious language learning experiences.

Improved Learning Outcomes

Research indicates that gamification positively impacts learning outcomes. In fact, studies have shown that learners who engage in gamified experiences demonstrate higher levels of knowledge acquisition and retention. The interactive and immersive nature of gamified experiences fosters active learning, critical thinking, and the practical application of language skills (Hamari et al., 2014b; Sailer et al., 2017). Learners are motivated to practice and apply their knowledge in real-world scenarios, leading to a deeper understanding and improved language proficiency. Engaging in gamified activities provides learners with practical contexts to reinforce their comprehension and facilitate knowledge transfer. This active participation promotes a comprehensive grasp of the language, empowering learners to communicate effectively and confidently in real-life situations.

Gamification promotes knowledge retention by creating memorable learning experiences. Elements like challenges, quizzes, and rewards reinforce learners' understanding and memory of English language concepts (Hamari et al., 2014b; Landers, 2014). The repetitive nature of gamified activities enhances learners' ability to retain and recall information, facilitating long-term language acquisition. By engaging in gamified experiences, learners encounter opportunities for repetition and reinforcement, solidifying their language skills and ensuring the retention of essential language knowledge.

A comprehensive meta-analysis by Hamari et al. (2014a) demonstrated the benefits of gamification in terms of knowledge retention, problem-solving skills, and information recall. The findings from this meta-analysis underscore the positive impact of gamification on learning outcomes, highlighting its potential to foster a deep understanding of the language and improve language proficiency. The interactive and immersive nature of gamified experiences promotes active learning, critical thinking, and the practical application of acquired language skills. Learners are encouraged to explore and experiment within a supportive environment, leading to a deeper understanding and improved language proficiency (Kapp, 2012). Through the incorporation of gamification into language learning, educators can harness its potential to enhance learning outcomes, facilitate knowledge retention, and encourage the practical application of language skills. By designing engaging and interactive gamified experiences, learners can develop a comprehensive understanding of the language, enhancing their communication skills and overall language proficiency.

Personalized Learning Experience

The integration of gamification with AI language models, such as ChatGBT, enables a personalized learning experience. By combining gamification with AI language models, learners can benefit from a highly tailored and individualized approach to language learning. ChatGBT's interactive and adaptive capabilities facilitate conversational exchanges tailored to individual proficiency levels, learning preferences, and progress. AI models provide personalized guidance, feedback, and support tailored to individual learner needs and preferences (Zawacki-Richter et al., 2019). Through interactive conversations with AI language models, learners can engage in real-time interactions, receiving immediate feedback and ample opportunities to practice their language skills within a conversational context. This personalized feedback and guidance play a vital role in effective language acquisition, as learners can address their specific areas of improvement and make progress at their own pace (Kohnke et al., 2023). By leveraging the integration of gamification and AI language models, learners can access a truly personalized language learning experience. The combination of interactive gamified elements and AI-driven personalization provides learners with tailored support, engaging activities, and real-time feedback, promoting effective language acquisition and proficiency development. This personalized approach acknowledges and caters to learners' unique learning needs and preferences, fostering a more engaging and effective language learning journey.

Promotion of Collaboration and Communication

Gamification in English language learning often integrates social and collaborative elements. These social and collaborative aspects of gamified language learning create opportunities for learners to engage in team-based activities, competitions, or cooperative learning experiences, fostering peer interaction and communication in English. Learners engage in team-based activities, competitions, or cooperative learning experiences, facilitating peer interaction and communication in English. Collaborative gamified tasks encourage language practice, negotiation, and cooperation, ultimately enhancing learners' communicative competence (Kohnke et al., 2023).

The inclusion of collaboration and communication within gamified language learning environments enhances learners' language proficiency by providing authentic contexts for language usage. By actively engaging in interactive and socially-driven gamified activities, learners are afforded opportunities to apply their language skills in real-life scenarios, which contributes to the development of fluency, accuracy, and confidence in English communication. This collaborative approach not only improves learners' linguistic abilities but also cultivates essential skills that are beneficial for their future academic and professional pursuits.

In conclusion, the integration of social and collaborative elements within gamified English language learning fosters the growth of learners' communication and collaboration skills. Through the implementation of team-based activities, competitions, and cooperative tasks, learners are motivated to practice their language skills, negotiate meaning, and collaborate effectively, leading to an enhanced communicative competence (Kohnke et al., 2023). These gamified experiences provide learners with genuine opportunities for language usage, thereby nurturing their language proficiency and empowering them to communicate and collaborate with confidence in English-speaking environments.

USING CHATGBT FOR GAMIFIED ENGLISH LANGUAGE LEARNING

ChatGBT, as explored in the study conducted by Kohnke, Moorhouse, and Zou (2023), exhibits interactive and personalized features that position it as a valuable tool for implementing gamification in English language learning. The study emphasizes the interactive and personalized nature of ChatGBT, enabling learners to engage in conversational exchanges tailored to their specific language proficiency level, learning preferences, and progress. Through interactive conversations with ChatGBT, learners can actively practice their language skills and receive customized and individualized responses that cater to their unique needs and requirements.

The personalized approach offered by ChatGBT, as supported by the research conducted by Ali et al. (2023) and Hong (2023), significantly contributes to enhancing the learning experience. Learners can benefit from tailored support, guidance, and motivation provided by ChatGBT, which effectively addresses their individual challenges and areas of improvement. By receiving personalized responses and feedback, learners can focus on their specific language learning goals, receive targeted guidance, and maintain motivation throughout their language learning journey.

The integration of ChatGBT within gamified language learning environments presents learners with an interactive and personalized learning experience, fostering meaningful and dynamic conversations. Learners can take advantage of ChatGBT's instant and customized feedback, enabling them to effectively enhance their language skills. By leveraging the interactive and personalized capabilities of ChatGBT, educators can optimize the gamification process and provide learners with a more engaging and personalized language learning experience.

In a nutshell, ChatGBT, as highlighted in the study conducted by Kohnke, Moorhouse, and Zou (2023), boasts interactive and personalized capabilities that make it an ideal tool for gamifying English language learning. Through tailored conversational exchanges, ChatGBT facilitates learners with personalized support, guidance, and motivation. The findings from the research conducted by Ali et al. (2023) and Hong (2023) further corroborate the effectiveness of the personalized approach in augmenting the learning experience. By integrating ChatGBT into gamified language learning, educators can establish an interactive and personalized environment that promotes effective language practice and offers individualized support to learners.

To gamify English language learning with ChatGBT, let's explore practical examples in three key areas: vocabulary acquisition, grammar practice, and reading comprehension.

Vocabulary Acquisition

Vocabulary Challenges and Quests (Baskara & Mukarto (2023))

Learners can participate in interactive challenges and quests where they collect and master new words. For example, ChatGBT can provide word puzzles, word association games, or even virtual scavenger hunts where learners need to find and remember specific vocabulary items.

Rewards and Leveling Systems (Wardat et al., 2023)

Implementing rewards and leveling systems can motivate learners to achieve milestones and unlock new vocabulary content. Learners earn points or badges as they progress, providing a sense of accomplishment and encouraging them to continue expanding their vocabulary.

Progress Tracking and Feedback Mechanisms (Fitria, 2023)

Integrating progress tracking and feedback mechanisms allows learners to monitor their vocabulary growth and receive feedback on their performance. ChatGBT can provide regular progress reports, offer suggestions for improvement, and highlight areas where learners excel.

By incorporating these strategies, learners can actively engage in vocabulary acquisition within a gamified language learning environment. The inclusion of interactive challenges and quests offers an enjoyable and immersive approach to acquiring and retaining new words, adding dynamism and engagement to the vocabulary learning process. Rewards and leveling systems provide a sense of achievement and progression, motivating learners to continue expanding their vocabulary skills. Additionally, progress tracking and feedback mechanisms empower learners to monitor their own progress, receive valuable guidance, and make informed decisions about their vocabulary learning.

Grammar Practice

Interactive Grammar Quizzes and Exercises (Kohnke et al., 2023)

Learners can engage in interactive quizzes and exercises to practice grammar rules. ChatGBT can present multiple-choice questions, fill-in-the-blank exercises, or even interactive dialogues where learners need to choose the correct grammatical structures.

Immediate Feedback and Explanations (Ali et al., 2023)

ChatGBT can provide instant feedback and explanations to help learners understand grammar concepts effectively. Learners receive clarification on grammar rules, examples of correct usage, and guidance on common mistakes, fostering a deeper understanding of the language.

Progression-Based Challenges (Kohnke et al., 2023)

Designing progression-based challenges allows learners to gradually increase the difficulty level of their grammar practice. ChatGBT can offer increasingly complex grammar tasks or provide more advanced language structures as learners demonstrate proficiency, ensuring continuous improvement in their grammar skills.

By incorporating these strategies, learners can actively engage in vocabulary acquisition within a gamified language learning environment. The inclusion of interactive challenges and quests offers an enjoyable and immersive approach to acquiring and retaining new words, adding dynamism and engagement to the vocabulary learning process. Rewards and leveling systems provide a sense of achievement and progression, motivating learners to continue expanding their vocabulary skills. Additionally, progress tracking and feedback mechanisms empower learners to monitor their own progress, receive valuable guidance, and make informed decisions about their vocabulary learning.

Reading Comprehension

Interactive Reading Activities and Comprehension Questions (Kasneci et al., 2023)

Learners can engage in interactive reading activities with ChatGBT, such as interactive stories or news articles. Following the reading, learners can answer comprehension questions or participate in discussions with ChatGBT to enhance their reading comprehension skills.

Customizable Reading Adventures and Storylines (Hong, 2023)

ChatGBT can provide customizable reading adventures and storylines, where learners become active participants in the narrative. Learners make choices and interact with the characters, requiring them to actively comprehend and respond to the text.

Tracking Reading Achievements and Skill Development (Wardat et al., 2023)

ChatGBT can track learners' reading achievements, such as the number of books read or the complexity of texts tackled. Learners can set personal reading goals, monitor their progress, and receive recommendations for further reading materials based on their interests and reading level.

By incorporating these strategies, learners can actively engage in reading comprehension activities within a gamified language learning environment. Interactive reading activities and comprehension questions provide learners with opportunities to practice and improve their reading comprehension skills. Engaging with ChatGBT in customizable reading adventures and storylines promotes an immersive reading experience that encourages active comprehension and response to the text. Tracking reading achievements and skill development allows learners to set goals, monitor progress, and receive personalized recommendations, fostering a sense of accomplishment and continuous growth in reading comprehension abilities.

In summary, the integration of interactive reading activities and comprehension questions, customizable reading adventures and storylines, and tracking reading achievements and skill development significantly contributes to reading comprehension within a gamified language learning environment. These strategies provide learners with dynamic and interactive reading experiences that enhance their comprehension skills. By utilizing ChatGBT, learners can actively engage with the text, make choices, and receive personalized recommendations based on their progress and interests. By implementing these strategies, learners can effectively develop and improve their reading comprehension skills in an engaging and gamified manner.

CHALLENGES AND LIMITATIONS

Implementing gamification in English language learning comes with its fair share of challenges and limitations that need to be considered for successful integration. These factors require careful attention to ensure the effectiveness and appropriateness of gamification strategies within language learning contexts. The following aspects highlight the key challenges and limitations:

Technical Considerations

The successful implementation of gamification relies on digital platforms and technologies, which may pose challenges related to accessibility, device availability, and internet connectivity (Kohnke et al., 2023). In resource-limited educational settings, these technical requirements may hinder the effective adoption of gamification. Ensuring adequate technical infrastructure and support is essential for a seamless gamified learning experience.

To address the challenges in resource-limited environments, innovative approaches are emerging. Mobile technologies, such as smartphones and tablets, are increasingly prevalent even in remote areas. This enables educators to design gamified learning experiences accessible through mobile devices, extending their reach to a wider audience of learners. Additionally, the development of lightweight gamification frameworks can alleviate technical barriers. These frameworks prioritize simplicity and low resource usage, making them suitable for environments with limited technological capabilities. By reducing computational requirements, educators can deliver gamified content even on older devices or with limited internet connectivity.

Integration with existing learning management systems (LMS) is another important consideration. Seamlessly incorporating gamification features into established LMS platforms allows educators to leverage existing technical infrastructure and support mechanisms. This integration enhances the user experience and minimizes the need for additional technical setup or maintenance. Cloud-based solutions provide scalability and flexibility in resource-limited settings. By utilizing cloud computing, gamified learning platforms can offload the computational burden from individual devices. This approach enables learners to access gamified content and activities without necessitating powerful hardware or extensive storage capabilities on their own devices.

Design and Implementation Complexity

Designing and implementing gamified learning experiences require careful planning, instructional design expertise, and understanding of pedagogical principles. In addition, it is essential to consider the target audience's age, interests, and learning preferences during the design process. Striking the right balance between game elements and language learning objectives is crucial (Kasneci et al., 2023). This delicate balance ensures that learners remain motivated and engaged while progressing toward their language learning goals.

Poorly designed gamification strategies may result in superficial engagement or divert learners' attention from the core learning goals. To avoid these issues, it is necessary to conduct thorough testing and iterate on the design. Valuable insights can be gained by conducting pilot studies and obtaining feedback from learners, which can then be used to make necessary adjustments. Additionally, involving language educators and experts in the design process can provide further guidance and ensure the alignment of game elements with the intended learning outcomes.

It is crucial to ensure that the gamified elements align with the intended learning outcomes. Achieving this alignment requires careful mapping of game mechanics, rewards, and challenges to the specific language learning objectives. By incorporating language-related tasks, quizzes, or simulations into the gamified experience, learners are able to actively practice and reinforce their language skills in an interactive and enjoyable manner.

Furthermore, effective implementation of gamified learning experiences necessitates comprehensive training and support for educators. Offering professional development opportunities that focus on integrating gamification into language teaching can significantly enhance educators' confidence and competence in utilizing gamified approaches. Equipping educators with the necessary skills and knowledge empowers them to effectively guide learners through the gamified activities, monitor their progress, and provide timely feedback.

Individual Variations

Learners exhibit diverse preferences, learning styles, and digital literacy levels. Not all learners may respond equally well to gamified approaches, and certain game elements may be less engaging or motivating for some individuals. Considering learners' individual needs and preferences is essential when designing gamified activities (Ali et al., 2023). Tailoring the gamified experience to accommodate individual variations can create a more inclusive learning environment.

Personalization and adaptivity in gamification can help address these individual variations and create a more inclusive learning environment. By incorporating personalized learning paths and adaptive features, educators can cater to the specific needs and preferences of each learner. Furthermore, incorporating options for learners to choose from different game elements can enhance engagement and motivation. Providing learners with a range of game options allows them to select activities that align with their learning preferences. This flexibility empowers learners to take ownership of their learning journey.

Assessment and Feedback Challenges

Evaluating learners' progress and providing meaningful feedback in gamified learning environments can be challenging. Traditional assessment methods may not fully capture the learning outcomes achieved through gamification. Educators need to explore innovative assessment strategies that align with the gamified context and effectively evaluate learners' language proficiency (Koraishi, 2023). Ensuring accurate assessment and timely feedback is crucial to support learners' progress and growth.

To overcome these challenges, educators can explore alternative assessment methods that are suitable for gamified learning environments. These methods should be designed to measure the diverse skills and competencies developed through gamification. By incorporating performance-based assessments, portfolio assessments, or self-assessment activities, educators can gain a comprehensive understanding of learners' language proficiency. These innovative assessment strategies allow educators to capture a more holistic view of learners' progress.

Technology-enabled assessment tools and platforms can play a crucial role in providing accurate assessment and timely feedback in gamified learning environments.

These tools can track learners' performance, identify areas for improvement, and offer immediate feedback. By utilizing such tools, educators can provide learners with valuable insights and guidance for their language development. In addition, fostering peer assessment and collaborative learning activities within gamified environments can contribute to the assessment process. Peer assessment allows learners to provide feedback to their peers, encouraging active participation and creating a supportive learning community. This collaborative approach enhances the accuracy and richness of feedback, benefiting both the learners and the assessors.

By embracing a comprehensive approach to assessment and feedback in gamified learning environments, educators can ensure a robust evaluation process and support learners' progress. Regular formative assessments, technology-enabled tools, alternative assessment methods, and peer collaboration all contribute to a more effective assessment and feedback system. This system enables educators to adapt their instructional strategies based on learners' individual needs and promote continuous improvement.

Sustaining Engagement

While gamification initially enhances motivation and engagement, maintaining learners' enthusiasm over time can be a hurdle. Learners may become accustomed to game elements, requiring educators to continuously update and innovate gamified activities to sustain interest (Hong, 2023). To address this challenge, educators need to focus on strategies to sustain learners' interest and prevent disengagement. One approach is to introduce progressive challenges and unlockable content. Gradually increasing the difficulty level and providing new content as learners progress can keep them motivated and engaged.

Regularly refreshing and introducing new elements can help prevent learners from losing interest and ensure ongoing engagement in the language learning process. Educators can periodically incorporate new game mechanics, themes, or storylines to add variety and excitement to the gamified activities. Furthermore, incorporating social elements into gamified learning environments can contribute to sustained engagement. Integrating collaborative activities, competitions, or leaderboards allows learners to interact with peers and engage in friendly competition, fostering a sense of community.

Ethical Considerations

The utilization of AI language models like ChatGBT raises ethical concerns surrounding data privacy, security, and algorithmic biases. Responsible use of these technologies is essential to safeguard learners' personal information and address potential issues related to biased language generation (Halaweh, 2023). Ensuring data protection, informed consent, and addressing biases is crucial when incorporating AI-powered language models in gamified learning environments.

To ensure data privacy and security, robust measures should be implemented. Stringent security protocols should be employed to safeguard learner data, including anonymization and encryption techniques. Obtaining informed consent from learners and their guardians is essential to ensure transparency and respect for privacy regulations.

Addressing algorithmic biases is another critical aspect. Ongoing evaluation and mitigation efforts should be undertaken to identify and rectify any biases that may arise from AI language models. Regular monitoring, feedback collection, and the use of bias detection algorithms can aid in detecting and addressing biases effectively.

To foster inclusivity, incorporating diverse perspectives is important. Involving language educators, experts, and stakeholders from diverse cultural backgrounds can help mitigate biases and ensure a more inclusive gamified learning environment. By considering multiple viewpoints, educators can make informed decisions regarding the use of AI language models and promote fairness and equity.

Training and Support

Educators may require training and professional development to effectively implement gamified language learning approaches. Additionally, learners may need guidance and support in navigating the gamified environment and maximizing their learning experience (Fitria, 2023). Providing adequate training and support to both educators and learners is essential for successful implementation and utilization of gamification in language learning.

To address these needs, training programs can be designed to equip educators with the necessary knowledge and skills to leverage gamification in their teaching practices. These programs can include workshops, seminars, or online courses that cover instructional design principles, gamification strategies, and the integration of technology tools. Furthermore, educators should ensure that learners receive clear instructions and orientations to familiarize them with the gamified platform and its features. This initial guidance can help learners understand how to navigate through the activities, track their progress, and access resources. Ongoing support should be available to address any questions or concerns that learners may have. Timely feedback and guidance can help learners stay on track, identify strengths, and areas for improvement. Additionally, fostering a collaborative and supportive learning community can enhance the gamified language learning experience.

By acknowledging and addressing these challenges and limitations, educators can mitigate potential obstacles and create a more effective and inclusive gamified language learning environment. Strategic planning, continuous evaluation, and ongoing improvement efforts are key to harnessing the benefits of gamification while managing its associated challenges.

CONCLUSION

Drawing upon the information and studies presented, it is evident that incorporating gamification into English language learning yields a wide range of benefits. The integration of game elements and mechanics enhances student engagement, motivation, and learning outcomes. Research studies (Dicheva et al., 2015; Landers, 2014) provide evidence supporting the positive impact of gamified learning environments on student engagement and motivation, fostering a sense of purpose, achievement, and excitement. These elements tap into intrinsic motivation and foster autonomy, competence, and relatedness, as proposed by Self-Determination Theory (Ryan & Deci, 2000), leading to active involvement and a stronger commitment to the language learning process.

Furthermore, gamification has been found to improve learning outcomes. A meta-analysis conducted by Hamari et al. (2014a) reveals the positive effect of gamification on knowledge retention, problem-solving skills, and information recall. The interactive and immersive nature of gamified experiences promotes active learning, critical thinking, and the application of language skills, resulting in a deeper understanding and improved language proficiency (Kapp, 2012). The incorporation of gamified elements offers learners engaging and interactive experiences that facilitate their understanding and retention of language concepts. These elements encourage learners to actively participate, make decisions, and solve problems within the gamified environment. As a result, learners develop a deeper understanding of the language and improve their language skills. Furthermore, the use of gamification provides immediate feedback and personalized challenges, enabling learners to receive timely guidance and reinforcement. This feedback helps learners identify areas for improvement and further develop their language skills.

In parallel, advancements in artificial intelligence (AI) have introduced new possibilities for enhancing English language learning. AI language models, such as ChatGBT, leverage natural language processing and machine learning algorithms to generate contextually relevant and interactive responses, simulating conversations and facilitating language practice. The integration of AI language models in gamified learning environments offers opportunities for interactive language exercises and simulations. Learners can engage in conversations and receive feedback, enabling authentic language practice and skill development. Moreover, AI language models provide a safe and supportive environment for learners to experiment with language structures and vocabulary. They can build confidence and fluency at their own pace, with AI-powered feedback and support. Additionally, AI language models can personalize the learning experience based on learners' individual needs and progress. Adaptive algorithms can adjust the difficulty level of language exercises to match learners' proficiency, ensuring appropriate challenges and support.

Integrating AI language models like ChatGBT into gamified English language learning further enhances the learning experience. ChatGBT's interactive and personalized capabilities provide learners with individualized conversational exchanges that adapt to their proficiency levels, learning preferences, and progress. Learners receive immediate feedback, personalized guidance, and support, crucial elements for effective language acquisition. This personalized approach enables learners to develop their language skills according to their specific needs and preferences. However, it is important to acknowledge and address the challenges and limitations associated with implementing gamification in English language learning. Technical considerations, design complexity, individual variations, assessment and feedback challenges, sustaining engagement, ethical considerations, and the need for training and support require careful attention to ensure successful integration (Kohnke, Moorhouse, & Zou, 2023).

In conclusion, the combination of gamification and AI language models, such as ChatGBT, presents exciting possibilities for enhancing learners' motivation, engagement, and language skills in an enjoyable and meaningful manner. By leveraging the engaging elements of gamification and the interactive capabilities of AI, educators can create immersive and personalized learning environments that foster English language proficiency (Kohnke et al., 2023). To ensure successful integration, strategic planning is necessary to align gamified activities with specific language learning objectives. Educators should carefully consider the design of game elements, incorporating language-related tasks, quizzes, or simulations that reinforce targeted language skills and promote active learning (Lai et al., 2023). Continuous evaluation of gamified learning experiences is essential to identify areas of improvement and optimize their effectiveness. By collecting feedback from learners and monitoring their progress, educators can make data-driven decisions to refine the gamification strategies and enhance the overall learning experience (Ali et al., 2023; Wardat et al., 2023). It is important to acknowledge and address the challenges and limitations associated with gamification in English language learning. Factors such as individual variations, technical considerations, assessment and feedback challenges, sustaining engagement, ethical considerations, and the need for training and support for educators should be taken into account (Hong, 2023; Baskara & Mukarto, 2023; Fitria, 2023; Koraishi, 2023; Kasneci et al., 2023; Halaweh, 2023). By understanding these challenges and implementing strategies to overcome them, educators can maximize the potential of gamification in English language learning.

With careful planning, evaluation, and addressing the limitations, the integration of gamification and AI language models can pave the way for a dynamic and effective approach to language acquisition (Kapp, 2012; Hamari et al., 2014a).

By implementing gamification effectively and improving its application over time, English language learning can be transformed, empowering learners to become proficient and confident users of the language (Kohnke et al., 2023). The benefits of gamification, coupled with the advancements in AI language models, present promising opportunities for the future of English language learning, offering a more engaging, personalized, and effective approach to language acquisition. Furthermore, the combination of gamification and AI language models has the potential to enhance language learning by providing learners with interactive experiences. Through gamification, learners can participate in various language-related activities that are enriched by AI language models. AI language models can analyze learners' performance and customize the learning experience to suit their individual needs and preferences. These models can adapt to learners' proficiency levels, strengths, and areas for improvement, delivering personalized content and feedback. Learners can receive targeted guidance and support, facilitating a more efficient language learning journey. Moreover, the integration of AI language models in gamified environments enables learners to engage in dynamic language interactions. Virtual characters or language tutors powered by AI can simulate realistic communication scenarios, allowing learners to practice their speaking, listening, and comprehension skills within a simulated real-world context.

REFERENCES

Ali, J. K. M., Shamsan, M. A. A., Hezam, T. A., & Mohammed, A. A. (2023). Impact of ChatGPT on learning motivation: Teachers and students' voices. *Journal of English Studies in Arabia Felix*, *2*(1), 41–49. doi:10.56540/jesaf.v2i1.51

Baskara, F. R., & Mukarto, F. X. (2023). Exploring the Implications of ChatGPT for Language Learning in Higher Education. *Indonesian Journal of English Language Teaching and Applied Linguistics, IJELTAL*, *7*(2), 343–358.

Deci, E. L., & Ryan, R. M. (2000). The "what" and "why" of goal pursuits: Human needs and the self-determination of behavior. *Psychological Inquiry*, *11*(4), 227–268. doi:10.1207/S15327965PLI1104_01

Dicheva, D., Dichev, C., Agre, G., & Angelova, G. (2015). Gamification in education: A systematic mapping study. *Journal of Educational Technology & Society*, *18*(3), 75–88.

Fitria, T. N. (2023, March). Artificial intelligence (AI) technology in OpenAI ChatGPT application: A review of ChatGPT in writing English essay. *ELT Forum: Journal of English Language Teaching, 12*(1), 44-58. https://doi.org/10.15294/elt.v12i1.64069

Halaweh, M. (2023). ChatGPT in education: Strategies for responsible implementation. *Contemporary Educational Technology*, *15*(2), ep421. doi:10.30935/cedtech/13036

Hamari, J., Koivisto, J., & Sarsa, H. (2014a). Does gamification work?–a literature review of empirical studies on gamification. In *2014 47th Hawaii international conference on system sciences (HICSS)* (pp. 3025–3034). IEEE.

Hamari, J., Shernoff, D. J., Rowe, E., Coller, B., Asbell-Clarke, J., & Edwards, T. (2014b). Challenging games help students learn: An empirical study on engagement, flow, and immersion in game-based learning. *Computers in Human Behavior*, *54*, 170–179. doi:10.1016/j.chb.2015.07.045

Hong, W. C. H. (2023). The impact of ChatGPT on foreign language teaching and learning: Opportunities in education and research. *Journal of Educational Technology and Innovation*, *5*(1).

Kapp, K. M. (2012). *The gamification of learning and instruction: Game-based methods and strategies for training and education*. John Wiley & Sons.

Kasneci, E., Seßler, K., Küchemann, S., Bannert, M., Dementieva, D., Fischer, F., Gasser, U., Groh, G., Günnemann, S., Hüllermeier, E., Krusche, S., Kutyniok, G., Michaeli, T., Nerdel, C., Pfeffer, J., Poquet, O., Sailer, M., Schmidt, A., Seidel, T., & Kasneci, G. (2023). ChatGPT for good? On opportunities and challenges of large language models for education. *Learning and Individual Differences*, *103*, 102274. . doi:10.1016/j.lindif.2023.102274

Kohnke, L., Moorhouse, B. L., & Zou, D. (2023). ChatGPT for language teaching and learning. *RELC Journal*, 00336882231162868.

Koraishi, O. (2023). Teaching English in the age of AI: Embracing ChatGPT to optimize EFL materials and assessment. [LET Journal]. *Language Education & Technology*, *3*(1), 55–72.

Lai, V. D., Ngo, N. T., Veyseh, A. P. B., Man, H., Dernoncourt, F., Bui, T., & Nguyen, T. H. (2023). Chatgpt beyond english: Towards a comprehensive evaluation of large language models in multilingual learning. *arXiv preprint arXiv:2304.05613*.

Landers, R. N. (2014). Developing a theory of gamified learning: Linking serious games and gamification of learning. *Simulation & Gaming*, *45*(6), 752–768. doi:10.1177/1046878114563660

Ryan, R. M., & Deci, E. L. (2000). Intrinsic and extrinsic motivations: Classic definitions and new directions. *Contemporary Educational Psychology*, *25*(1), 54–67. doi:10.1006/ceps.1999.1020 PMID:10620381

Sailer, M., Hense, J. U., Mayr, S. K., & Mandl, H. (2017). How gamification motivates: An experimental study of the effects of specific game design elements on psychological need satisfaction. *Computers in Human Behavior*, *69*, 371–380. doi:10.1016/j.chb.2016.12.033

Wardat, Y., Tashtoush, M. A., AlAli, R., & Jarrah, A. M. (2023). ChatGPT: A revolutionary tool for teaching and learning mathematics. *Eurasia Journal of Mathematics, Science and Technology Education*, *19*(7), em2286. doi:10.29333/ejmste/13272

Zawacki-Richter, O., Marín, V. I., Bond, M., & Gouverneur, F. (2019). Systematic review of research on artificial intelligence applications in higher education–where are the educators? *International Journal of Educational Technology in Higher Education*, *16*(1), 1–27. doi:10.118641239-019-0171-0

Zichermann, G., & Cunningham, C. (2011). *Gamification by design: Implementing game mechanics in web and mobile apps*. O'Reilly Media.

Chapter 4
Corpus-Assisted Multidimensional AI Applications in Language Teaching and an Intelligent Virtual Speaker

Ali Şükrü Özbay
https://orcid.org/0000-0002-3421-0650
Karadeniz Technical University, Turkey

Buse Uzuner
https://orcid.org/0000-0002-9661-3164
Bahçeşehir University, Turkey

Ayşenur Hoşoğlu
https://orcid.org/0000-0003-3369-6406
Avrasya University, Turkey

Ercüment Öztürk
https://orcid.org/0000-0001-9623-6955
Artvin Çoruh University, Turkey

ABSTRACT

The authors propose an evidence-based virtual AI application geared to using a successful implementation of AI for language learners and language teaching professionals and a virtual speaking tool that will serve as a foundation for further research and experimentation. The study promotes interdisciplinary collaboration among corpus linguists, language educators, and computer engineers for fostering the skills and the competences and the exchange of ideas and a shared vision for the future of AI-assisted language learning. The main objective of this action plan is to propose an application in which language teaching professionals and language learners will engage in English-speaking practice through a multidimensional (MD) environment incorporating cubic images and bilateral sound perception (hearing and speaking). The AI application will assign tasks to multidimensional characters using realistic sound effects to create a highly immersive and interactive environment for language teaching professionals.

DOI: 10.4018/978-1-6684-9893-4.ch004

1. INTRODUCTION

The affordances and benefits of artificial intelligence in education are widely recognized in recent years. Thanks to artificial intelligence (AI, henceforth), it is now possible to create an awareness of knowledge-gap which may aid language learners and language teaching professionals learning and teaching effectively and efficiently by applicable instructions (Chen et al., 2022). Artificial intelligence can not only enhance and personalise the learning environment but also provide language teaching professionals opportunity to regulate the curriculum and assess their students effectively (Chen et al., 2020; Vázquez-Cano, 2021) as well as these professionals have many chances to benefit from artificial intelligence such as making oral assessments, grading in reading, or network for writing. It can also be seen that the use of artificial intelligence plays an important role in improving automation as well as the depth of students in the learning process (Yanhua, 2020).

The popularity of virtual reality (VR) and artificial intelligence (AI) is rising. Despite the differences between the two new technologies, they complement one another to strengthen ties between people and the digital world. Virtual reality is a method of computer-human interaction where a genuine or made-up environment is simulated. Users continuously engage in interaction and manipulation with this reality. Our study, therefore, particularly promotes interdisciplinary collaboration among corpus linguists, language educators and computer engineers for fostering the skills and the competences as well as the exchange of ideas and a shared vision for the future of AI-assisted language learning.

From a theoretical framework, natural language processing (NLP) is a branch of computer science and artificial intelligence (AI) giving computers ability to comprehend texts and spoken language and produce it in the same way as humans to understand human language better (Torfi et al., 2020). Virtual reality, on the other hand, is generally described as the technology that allows 5-dimensional pictures and animations transformed into the computer environment to help people feel and imagine the presence of a natural environment aided by the latest technology and tools for interaction. We aim to question the potential effects of multidimensional (henceforth MD) virtual reality applications on foreign language teaching and how animations are used effectively in the classroom and web-based distance education processes. The active and effective employment of multidimensional virtual reality in language teaching brings about successful results from various dimensions such as motivation, involvement, task-engagement, and appropriateness for various other intelligence types. The role of virtual speaker agents in enhancing language skills and language learning processes is investigated in this study with a specific focus on the role and function of intelligent virtual speakers on pre-assigned task patterns that ranges from daily conversation to academic discussion in and outside the classroom setting.

Different technological resources are used in today's education and training practices. The wide availability and use of the internet is a significant factor for the development of the significance of these technological resources. Among them are web technologies and programs such as social networking sites, web-based encyclopaedias, weblogs, 5-dimensional multi-user virtual environments, games, and simulations. These technologies provide users with suitable environments for the development of various activities in education and training environments, by allowing multiple uses, containing different types of information at the same time, providing the opportunity to learn and share this information with their communities, all applied in virtual environment. The concept of student-centred electronic learning directs curriculum design to a learning environment that emphasizes reality and interaction. Online virtual reality technology offers a combination of the virtual world and reality in this respect. This reality encourages autonomy, a self-directed and controlled learning method, and provides a representative living process by enabling students to learn and interact. Virtual reality technology in the language curriculum does not only provide real-world-like audio-visual simulations but also combines a virtual and real learning environment for mutual interaction which, in turn, increases students' interest and motivation for learning.

The main objective of our action plan for virtual speaker is to propose an application in which language teaching professionals and language learners will engage in English-speaking practice through a multidimensional (MD) environment incorporating cubic images and bilateral sound perception (hearing and speaking). In other words, we propose a scheme or an AI application that assigns tasks to multidimensional characters using realistic sound effects to create a highly immersive and interactive environment for language teaching professionals to provide the users or learners with authentic and focused communication opportunities in English. This study is essential in terms of contributing to the language learners' acquisition and development of their language skills in this environment as it presents the language structures and common multiword combinations in a predictable sequence. Considering that no study has been conducted so far in Turkey on the proposed application through artificial intelligence, the creation of virtual environment in the form of virtual speaker application is planned to include the following features.

a. The target student group will be provided with the opportunity to practise the language with real-time characters in a MD environment.
b. The virtual characters will be designed to use meaningful, situational, and natural language structures to be obtained and levelled through target corpora.

c. The target learner group will immerse in an affordable and interactive audio-visual environment to practice their language skills without going abroad or taking further actions to do so.
d. The authentic MD environment will present the students with comparable tasks at various proficiency levels, which will control, guide and facilitate the language learning process with the use of pre-arranged pedagogical tasks and activities.
e. The application will also aim to assess the students' language proficiency through audio and visually levelled dialogues.
f. The visual stimuli to be provided with the students will closely correspond to real-world visuals, ensuring a realistic and meaningful learning experience.
g. The application offers a distinctive contribution by providing students with varying educational and language proficiency levels, an opportunity to improve their speaking skills through one-to-one interactions in a virtual reality environment.
h. Students will be required to spend effort and enthusiasm to reach the visual and verbal communication goals that they need to fulfil, based on different situated and meaningful tasks.
i. This proposed application will make an important contribution in terms of having information about the communication strategies students use in AI environment while fulfilling the required tasks and revealing the language structure and functions to be followed in teaching these strategies.
j. Learners may have difficulties in terms of fulfilling task-oriented communicative language functions and this proposed scheme will aid the language learners at all levels who want to practice English language in a meaningful and task-oriented atmosphere.
k. Although the learners respond to the language data given to them in the functional dimension, it is seen that they experience some problems in terms of the appropriateness of the language samples they use in terms of natural and authentic language structures, and the proposed virtual speaker environment will have a distinctive value in terms of providing a holistic approach for language practice.
l. The expected target population who will benefit from this application will primarily be the Erasmus Student Exchange Programme candidates who are entitled to do the mobility. Since a great number of these candidates will have study-abroad experience for the first time, they will be able to practice speaking English with the sample corpus-based scenario contents prepared in the multidimensional virtual speaking environments to be created within the scope of the proposed action plan.

m. Corpora of spoken language to be used in this application involves transcriptions of spontaneous or planned speech and there are several spoken corpora such as British Academic Spoken Corpus (BASE) containing 1 million words, British National Corpus 2014 (BNC2014) containing 10 million words and Open American National Corpus containing 3 million words. BNC2014 will be used in this study as a source for spoken corpora to create the conversational tasks in the virtual MD environment.
n. In line with the aims of the study, twenty-four scenarios consisting of four different levels will be used as content data. Pronunciation, word stress, word choice and pause time will be used as predictors of successful language proficiency. The criteria and the content determined for language practice will be applied to 20 students as a pilot and the scenarios will be reconstructed following the validity analysis.
s. Each scenario will consist of four different levels, and the level of the scenario will vary within the given four levels according to the responses by the users. These scenarios will be based on task-based situations that students will encounter or experience in daily lives abroad.
o. Pronunciation, pause time, intonation, word stress and choice and sentence length and content relevancy will be considered as significant criteria for proficiency assessment.

Finally, considering several dimensions together, the language learners will be provided support in terms of speaking and practice. This proposed AI based virtual speaker application is also expected to provide several pedagogical benefits and conclusive evidence related to the integration of AI technology into language teaching and learning. Initially, it will be determined whether the users (teachers and learners) comprehend and successfully execute verbal instructions provided to them in specific scenarios, utilizing several criteria stated above as a means of evaluation. Secondly, the study will assess whether students effectively employ stressed and unstressed expressions in response to scenario-based questions. The accuracy of the students' pronunciations and adherence to standard pronunciation will also be evaluated in the overall proficiency assessment of the users. Additionally, the study will assess the appropriateness of word choices made by students at varying levels, as pre-determined and arranged by the system, for the given context. Moreover, the study will also evaluate whether the students are able to continue the dialogues in communicatively effective and meaningful ways and continue conversation successfully.

2. REVIEW

2.1. Virtual Reality and Language Learning

Language education is among the fields which benefit from technological innovations. In parallel to these developments, Virtual Reality has gained popularity in the past years. In fact, Lee (1999) defined VR as a way of bridging "the gap between reality and abstract knowledge by the discovery method" (p. 72). Similarly, Machover and Tice (1994) indicated that VR is "a fresh look at human interaction" (p. 15). With this respect, creating an environment close to reality is a key element of VR technology. Lan (2020a) pointed out that particularly in language education, EFL teachers should provide an environment for their students in order to actively interact with each other in meaningful contexts. The main reason why VR can be effective and significant for language education is that it enables visual experiences, entertainment, social networking, operation, and creation (Lan, 2020b). Similarly, Radianti et al. (2020) also emphasized the topic of experience and active engagement in VR methods which integrate students into the learning process effectively.

To create such interactive environments, systems often include full integration of artificial intelligence and a wide range of social communication tools. Therefore, VR is rapidly being used to foster authentic and immersive education environments due to its several features (Lin & Lan, 2015). Furthermore, Lan (2020a) highlighted that the application of VR in a classroom setting increased students' performance as well as their motivations. The visual experience is one of the effective parts of VR. Regarding this, Lan (2020) shared an example which is when students engaged in a visual experience with VR, they feel like being there, experiencing almost a similar environment in real-like characters and natural content. Dhimolea et al. (2022) also noted that the growing interest in VR technology and its implementations of it in language education "facilitate students' second or foreign language learning by offering authentic communicative opportunities, improving language learning outcomes, and strengthening cultural competence" (p. 810).

2.2. The Authentic Environment in Language Learning

The authentic environment is one of the key components of effective learning process. Learners experience real-life situational, task-based, and conversational content aided by native speakers of the language. Herrington and Oliver (2000) stated that authentic contexts, activities, and assessment in language learning environment provides real-life relevant and meaningful situations so that learners can increase their knowledge in the best way possible. Real life language is only provided through authentic materials; thus, new dimensions of language can be interpreted by learners

(Nikitina, 2011). Also, teachers can easily guide their students with low proficiency levels by providing authentic language instructions (Huang & Chuang, 2016). Authentic environments in language learning enable learners to use their previous knowledge in real life situations and share their experiences with others. It also can be used outside the classroom to improve language skills of learners. Previous literature shows that using mobile tools have an impact on enhancing learner interest based on grammar and writing (Li & Hegelheimer, 2013) and reading skills (Lan et al., 2007). These mobile tools are also seen as effective tools and promote real life experiences that increases the learner awareness (Shadiev et al., 2017). As a result, increasing authentic environment in language learning can motivate learners and contribute to their proficiency in language through exposure to real-life situations.

2.3. Revolutionizing Language Teaching: The Power of Artificial Intelligence

Artificial Intelligence (AI), which dates to the 1940s, was introduced as a concept by McCarthy in the 1950s. Due to the inability to meet the system requirements and storage costs, it could not progress much until the 1980s. Today, these problems have been solved and access to data sets has become easier. As a natural result of this outcome, it has recently become a phenomenon in scientific studies again. In addition to these developments, AI (Russell, 2010) has become a specific one that is making great progress in parallel with rapidly changing and developing technology. It is clear from today that the application of AI-based systems will likely to be more common and prevalent. This will naturally enable more efficient, safe, and innovative solutions to emerge in many sectors including education and business.

Figure 1. Artificial intelligence

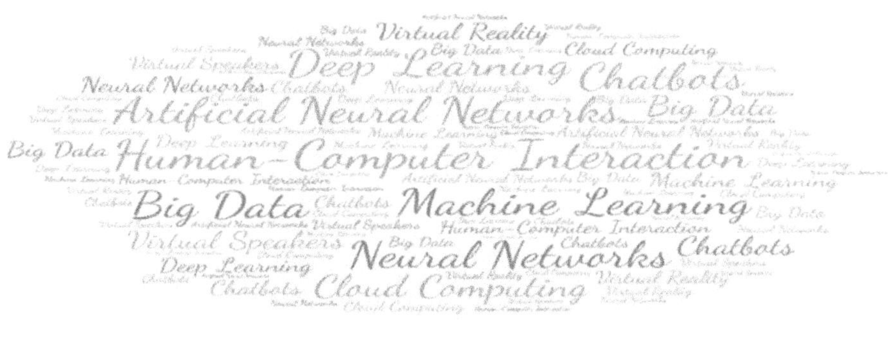

AI is the systems that make it possible for machines to perform human-like tasks, learn from experience, adapt to new inputs, and are distinguished from other technologies in this respect. In other words, AI is a computer program that has the capacity to mimic human intelligence to perform specific tasks and can improve themselves by repeating the information they collect. AI works on the basis of combining large-scale data with various algorithms and iterative computing. In this process, the features of the processed data allow the artificial intelligence to learn automatically. Artificial intelligence is a general concept and has approaches such as machine learning (ML) (Zhou, 2021a), artificial neural networks (ANN) (Zhou, 2021b), deep learning (DL) (LeCun, Bengio, & Hinton, 2015), natural language processing (NLP) (Chowdhary, 2020) and cognitive computing (Modha, et al., 2011). The most important issue to be considered in AI studies is to formulate the problem. There are three different types of learning in ML, which forms the basis of this proposed AI application. These are "Reinforcement Learning", "Supervised Learning" and "Unsupervised Learning".

Figure 2. Learning types in machine learning
(Kim & Tagkopoulos, 2019)

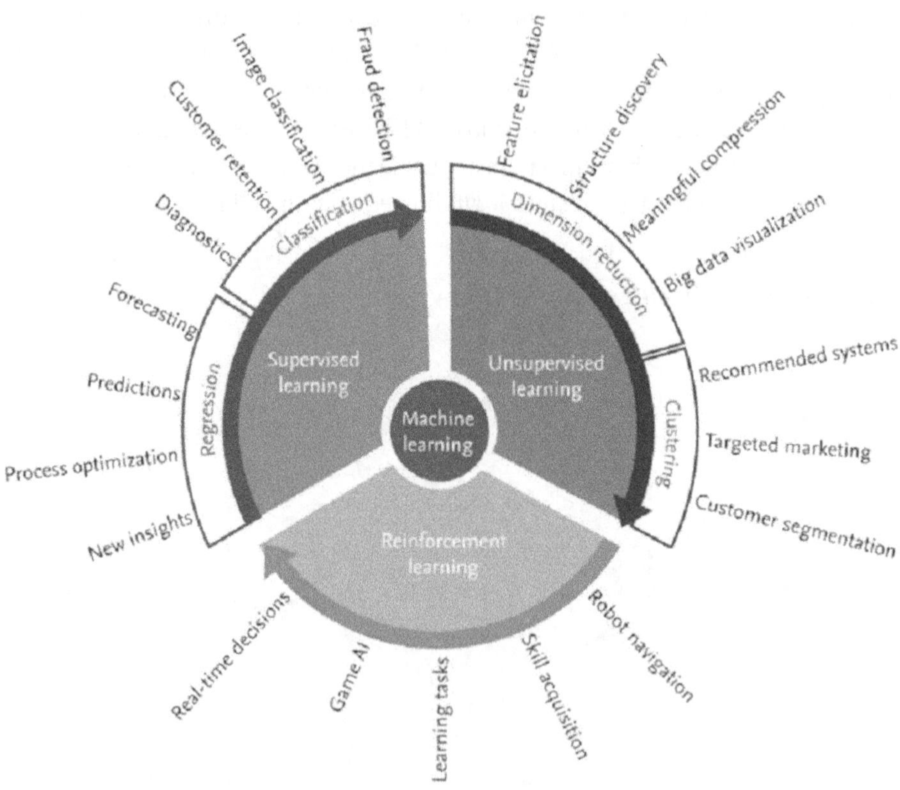

Unlike all other machine learning models, reinforcement learning (learn from errors) has a dynamic structure and is based on the reward-punishment method in interaction with the environment. For this reason, it is preferred when the data set is limited and not fixed (Sutton & Barto, 2018). In supervised learning (task-driven) method, labelled data is used to make predictions based on what they have learned. Instructional learning requires datasets that contain meaningful features. The number of classes and the class belonging to a group of samples are calculated using probability approaches (Buluz & Kızrak, n.d.). Unsupervised learning (data-driven) is generally used in problems of extracting relations between inputs. In unsupervised learning, target outputs are not given and the model is expected to create a template from the inputs given in itself. The approaches that make clustering by calculating different information such as the proximity of the data whose properties we do not know, which class and group it belongs to, are called "learning without an instructor". Thus, it becomes possible that unlabelled hidden similarities in the data are detected (Buluz & Kızrak, n.d.).

2.4.1. Human-Computer Interaction

The first issue to be addressed when examining the use of artificial intelligence in language education is Human Computer Interaction (HCI hereafter) (Rogers, Sharp, & Preece, 2011). HCI plays a pivotal role in the design and development of computer systems. The interaction between humans and computers has become increasingly important with the widespread use of digital interfaces in everyday life. HCI focuses on improving the usability and user experience of computer systems by studying users' behaviours and cognitive processes. HCI employs various research methods to gather data and evaluate the effectiveness of computer interfaces. These include user surveys, interviews, observational studies, and controlled experiments. By employing a combination of qualitative and quantitative methods, HCI researchers can gain insights into users' needs, preferences, and behaviours (Nielsen, 1994).

Artificial intelligence has made a significant impact in the field of language education, as in all other fields, in recent years. A number of artificial intelligence-based tools have been developed to support and enrich language teaching. These tools are used to improve students' language skills and optimize the learning process.

Artificial intelligence-based mobile applications are widely used to provide language learning experiences to learners. These applications help learners improve their vocabulary, learn grammar rules, and improve the practical use of language (The Impact of AI on Language Learning and Teaching, n.d.). AI is used in interactive language teaching programs, also known as virtual language teachers. These programs provide learners with audio and written feedback, helping them develop correct pronunciation and grammar skills (Stickler & Hampel, 2015). AI is used in automatic assessment systems used to evaluate students' written and oral language skills. These systems are an effective tool for providing immediate feedback to students and monitoring the development of their language skills (de Wet, Van der Walt, & Niesler, 2009).

There are many scenarios or solution methods in which AI can be used in language education. However, for an effective learning process, the following three steps should be considered.

2.4.1.1. Individualized Learning

AI can assess the language level and goals of the individuals involved. In this way, customized learning materials can be offered according to the needs of the individuals concerned (Grant and Basye, 2014).

2.4.1.2. Automatic Feedback

It can provide immediate feedback by assessing the speaking, writing or pronunciation skills of the individuals involved. In this way, individuals who want to learn or improve a language will have the opportunity to correct their mistakes and learn the correct version (Pinherio et al., 2021)

2.4.1.3. Speaking Practice

AI can offer students the opportunity to practice in virtual speaking environments. This is where VR technology comes into play. Although they look like essentially different structures, VR is part of AI. For this reason, VR systems are built on AI technology and are powered by AI ("AI in Virtual Reality," 2022).

2.4.2. Virtual Reality (VR)

Virtual Reality (VR) (Zheng, Chan, & Gibson, 1998) technology can enhance the learning process by providing an interactive and tactile experience with its potential to be a harmonious human-machine environment. Some benefits of using VR in language education can be given as follows: First, VR is generated by modern technology through computer technology as the core and provides the opportunity to animate real-life scenarios with 3D visuals, game platforms or videos. VR platforms also provide the opportunity to practice speaking and pronunciation skills. It can simulate real-life situations by interacting with the characters in the virtual environment. Finally, VR can be combined with gamification elements to provide a more fun and motivating learning experience. Developing language skills with interactive games can also become fun. As a matter of fact, the type of learning with fun activities is one of the most permanent ones in the minds majority who are engaged in educating themselves regardless of age, education, and gender.

2.4.3. Chatbots

Language education requires interaction and interactive experiences to develop learners' language skills. Using artificial intelligence and natural language processing capabilities, chatbots can provide students with real-time language practice and an individualized instruction. The role of chatbots in language education can be given as follows:

First, they can offer personalized language instruction tailored to learners' language needs and abilities. It assesses learners' language level and offers customized lesson plans and activities accordingly (Huang, Hew, & Fryer, 2022). Secondly, chatbots offer students the opportunity to practice the language in real time. Students can access language learning materials, practice speaking and get feedback through chatbots (Kim, Cha, & Kim, 2019). Finally, they provide students with broad support in grammar and vocabulary. Through chatbots, students can ask grammar questions, learn word meanings and usages, and reinforce grammar rules with practice (Frąckiewicz, n.d.). In summary, chatbots have an important role in language education. Personalized language learning experiences, language practices, and grammar/vocabulary support provide students with a more effective language learning experience, and it is expected that language education will develop further with chatbot technology.

2.5. NLP and Language Learning/Teaching

Technological developments have a noticeable impact on human life which also provide improvements to language learning and teaching through Natural Language Processing (NLP). As a sub-field of Artificial Intelligence (AI), NLP is building a bridge between human language and machine understanding of authentic language produced by humans. The distinctive feature of NLP is the understanding and processing of human language and translating it into machine-readable text; on the other hand, Machine Learning (ML) learns from the data supported by NLP and develops algorithms to solve problems (Mkansi & Mkalipi, 2023). Regarding the language learning perspective, NLP applications can be divided into two main sections: the analysis of learner language and the analysis of native language. NLP can be applied to computational linguistics, to examine the language produced by learners; moreover, it is also used to analyse native language to provide reading materials to learners (Meurers, 2020). The pedagogical potential of NLP is defined as "an area that combined AI and linguistics in general and is concerned with the automated processing of human language" (Schmidt & Strasser, 2022, p. 167).

The applications of NLP such as tokenization, POS-tagging and lemmatization provide basis for learner errors, which also proves the learners' needs through demonstrating the nature of learner language (Granger et al., 2007; Meurers, 2015). While tokenization is a process through which the targeted data is substituted with unique symbols known as a token, POS-tagging and lemmatization are the labelling the words in a corpus as belonging to a certain part of speech and grouping together different inflected forms of the same word. Corpus annotation and NLP tools are used together to analyse learners' competence in language focusing on the complexity, accuracy, and fluency (Meurers & Dickinson, 2017). Dodigovic (2005) highlighted the importance of NLP-based tools as "a tireless language model, interlocutor and error correction or grading authority" (p. 97). For the reasons stated above, NLP can be used to detect linguistics errors, and language teachers can design new classroom materials to increase learners' awareness. The application of NLP provides an immense environment for both learners and teachers to improve their competence in the language. NLP has the potential to extract linguistic patterns and provide learners with authentic data to extend their knowledge (Alexopoulou et al., 2017). As the language education environment embraces the innovations provided by digital worlds such as NLP tools, the capabilities of NLP will provide inclusive dimensions to the efforts for successful language learning/teaching.

2.6. Spoken Corpora as a Source for Authentic Conversation: The Spoken BNC2014

With the growth in technology, the use of corpora in education has been steadily growing in recent years. Researchers and teachers have been willing to integrate corpus into their works. The basic definition of the corpus is that it is the electronic storage of authentic texts which have representative features of the language. Most of the time, written corpora have been used by researchers and teachers in classroom settings for various purposes. However, there has been a growing interest in the use of spoken corpora as well, particularly, in terms of the need for language users and professionals to communicate in English. Generally defined, spoken corpus is a recording of the speakers' speeches and then transcribing the records into the texts which should be representative for a certain genre or feature (Aijmer, 2020). Corpus linguistics consists of authentic texts which enable researchers to analyse language-in-use. With this respect, Mauranen (2004) pointed out that "spoken corpora score high in authenticity and classroom usability, and that they offer direct access to characteristics of speech, so often inadequately described in textbooks"

(p. 89). Furthermore, Mauranen (2004) highlighted that spoken corpus is a king of "freeze real speech for observation" by providing a great number of language use examples (p. 92). Regarding this, it can be claimed that being representative of the real-life language, spoken corpora provides a high level of authenticity to the language. Similarly, Adolphs and Knight (2010) also stated that spoken corpus enable users to access "a unique resource for the exploration of naturally occurring discourse" (p. 38).

The Spoken British National Corpus 2014 (The Spoken BNC2014) is among the leading corpus which consists of British spoken data. The Spoken BNC2014 was developed by the ESRC Centre for Corpus Approaches to Social Science (CASS) at Lancaster University and Cambridge University Press as a kind of subcorpus of the original British National Corpus which was completed in 1994 (Love et al., 2017). The Spoken BNC2014 consisted of present-day spoken British English which was collected through informal, casual, and daily contexts. The data were gathered between 2012 to 2016 and it consisted of 11.5 million words which were transcribed from 668 speakers in 1,251 recordings.

3. PROPOSED APPLICATION DESIGN STAGES

In this study, we aimed to highlight the general design features of a fast and effective learning application by designing a virtual speaker platform with the ML method. With the words, phrases, sentences, and pronunciation forms included in the application, the system should start working with fewer errors and higher accuracy and precision. Therefore, the AI based learning process continues cumulatively during future processes after a first step. The system consists of two stages: Speech detection and text reading.

In the speech detection stage, it is checked whether the speech is perceived, the words are separated, and the pronunciations are made correctly with NLP. The text-to-speech process, on the other hand, has a less complex process than the speech detection method. There is less complexity to combine existing metrics and to ensure they are pronounced correctly. While performing these operations, 3-dimensional (3D) images or videos can be used. In this way, the learning process is carried out more effectively and it is ensured that it is more permanent. In order to carry out these operations, a word/sentence pool must be created. This pool is the database of the designed system. All algorithmic operations are done through this database and a scoring database is also created for the score. In artificial intelligence studies, a database is also called a data set. For this reason, the words database or dataset are used in the texts, and both have the same meaning.

Figure 3. Text vocalization
(Adalı, 2012)

Algorithm 1. Text vocalization psuedocode

```
from gtts import gTTS
from playsound import playsound
text = input(from database)
tts = gTTS(text=text, lang='tr')
tts.save(“”)
playsound(“”)
```

Figure 4. Speech detection
(Adalı, 2012)

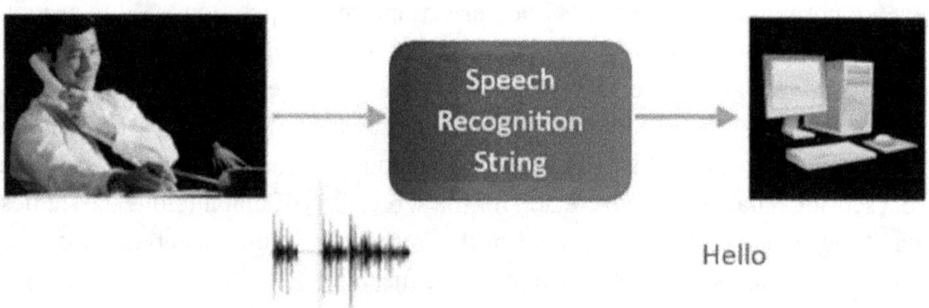

In the first stage of the platform, the text read through the existing database is correctly pronounced and voiced, and this vocalization process is visualized with 3D visuals or videos and the teaching process is provided.

In the second stage of the platform, the texts voiced by the students are evaluated and an accuracy coefficient is obtained. For this to happen, two different evaluations are required, either separately or simultaneously. Therefore, the same text should be taken from more than one reader. Thus, the degree of intelligibility of a text is obtained and the accuracy rate, including pronunciations, can be deduced. In this way, it can be determined at what level the speaking skill is proportionally.

$$AD = 1 - \frac{YS_1 + YS_2 + \ldots + YS_N}{M_1 + M_2 + \ldots + M_N}$$

In this equation;

AD: Degree of intelligibility

YS: Incorrect number

M: Number of words in the text

N: Represents the number of participants (students).

In order to perform this operation, the code written in the Python programming language performs the following operations: It divides the entered text into sentences, sentences into words and words into letters and checks whether the pronunciation is done correctly. A short example of the source code used is in the following;

Algorithm 2. Psuedocode of splitting

```
import nltk
from nltk.tokenize import word_tokenize
text = input("")
sentences = nltk.sent_tokenize(text)
tokens = [word_tokenize(sentence) for sentence in sentences]
normalized_tokens = [word.lower() for sentence in tokens for
word in sentence if word.isalpha()]
word_freq = nltk.FreqDist(normalized_tokens)
most_common_words = word_freq.most_common(5)
print("MostCommonWords")
for word, frequency in most_common_words:
print(f"{word}: {frequency}")
```

Algorithm 3. Sample code used for graphic design to be viewed in VR

```
import numpy as np
import matplotlib.pyplot as plt
from mpl_toolkits.mplot3d import axes3d
x = np.linspace(-5, 5, 100)
y = np.linspace(-5, 5, 100)
X, Y = np.meshgrid(x, y)
Z = np.sin(np.sqrt(X**2 + Y**2))
fig = plt.figure()
ax = fig.add_subplot(111, projection='3d')
ax.plot_surface(X, Y, Z)
ax.set_xlabel('X-axis)
ax.set_ylabel('Y-axis')
ax.set_zlabel('Z-axis')
plt.show()
```

In Algorithm 3, numpy, matplotlib.pyplot and mpl_toolkits.mplot3d libraries are used. Data is created with numpy. Then, necessary actions are taken to draw the 3D graph with matplotlib.pyplot. At the beginning of the code, the x and y ranges and resolution are determined. The 2D coordinate plane is created using the np.meshgrid() function. Next, the z sequence is defined to be used when working on the values of the Z axis. The figure is created with fig=plt.figure() and the axes to which the 3D graphic will be added are specified with add_subplot(). A 3D graph is drawn with ax.plot_surface(). Finally, the label of each axis is determined by the functions ax.set_xlabel(), ax.set_ylabel(), and ax.set_zlabel(). The graph is displayed with plt.show().

4. GRAPHICAL REPRESENTATION OF APPLICATION BACKGROUND

In this part, we describe the virtual speaker application background through graphical representation. The proposed application consists of several background processes. In the researching phase, for example, the conceptual content of the proposed application is detailed with specific reference to the related theoretical framework. Natural language processing (NLP) as a sub-field of artificial intelligence (AI) plays a pivotal role in the design, make-up, and implementation of the application. The theoretical framework follows a holistic approach and is extended to include multidimensional array of technology concepts such as artificial neural networks (ANN), deep learning (DL), cognitive computing (CC), machine learning (ML), human-computer interaction (HCI), and virtual reality (VR).

Figure 5. Application background

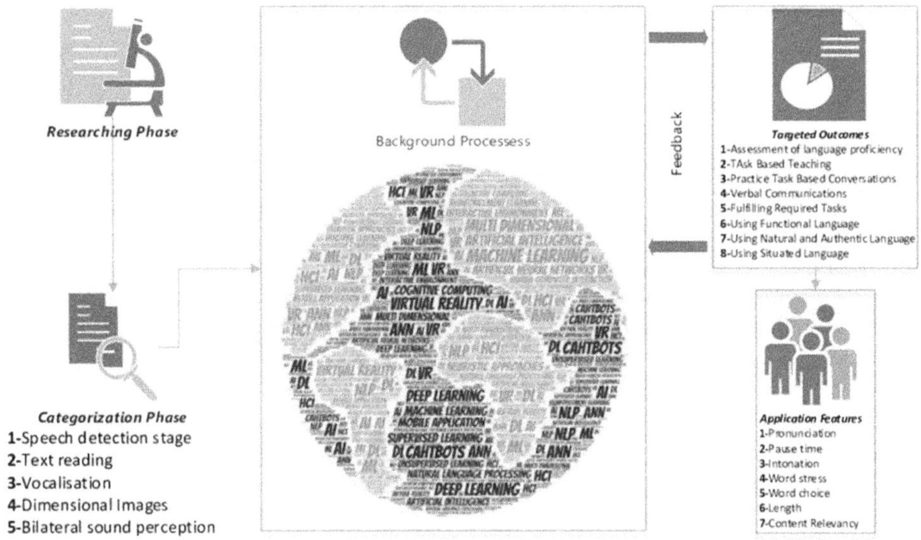

The categorisation phase includes several technical aspects of multidimensional AI application such as speech detection stage, text reading, vocalisation, the creation of dimensional images, and the bilateral sound perception. The speech detection stage in AI is activated by transforming spoken language into digital signals that can be analysed and interpreted by AI technology by taking several stages such as signal processing, feature extraction, acoustic modelling, language modelling, and decoding. As part of the background processes, several theoretical concept frameworks are created with reference to targeted aims and functions from the application. This follows the targeted outcomes phrase. In this phase, the assessment of linguistic performance in the form of task-based conversations and situated dialogues will be used as means of verbal communications. The successful fulfilment of the required tasks based on a functional language use criteria using authentic and natural linguistics forms will be evaluated by AI based virtual speaker application. The AI based virtual speaker application will work on the basis of several pre-determined criteria such as appropriate pronunciation, pause time, intonation, word stress and choice and sentence length and content relevancy. We propose the effective use of AI based virtual speaker application with reference to above-mentioned application features. All these features outlined so far call for a close cooperation and involvement of a multi-disciplinary group of researchers from corpus linguistics, computer programming, AI experts and language teaching professionals.

Figure 6. Application interface

5. GRAPHICAL REPRESENTATION OF APPLICATION INTERFACE

Interface is one of the essential elements of the application. No need to mention that it should be clear, smooth, and user-friendly. In our proposed application, the interface is demonstrated in Figure 6. The proposed application interface consists of several stages. First, prospective users will choose their profiles as language teacher, language learner or exchange program candidate. Then, the prospective users will decide the level with which they want to be tested or given a task-based conversation practice. Then, the users will need to choose the task-based conversation contents by selecting one scenario among 24 others adapted to 4 language levels. These scenarios are comprised of events that can be experienced in real-life situations such as giving orders in restaurants, checking-in airports, dormitory, and conversations with foreign people. Thanks to these real-life experiences, users will have a chance to experience different scenarios according to their language levels. They can even re-experience the same scenario at different levels. Once they respond to the dialogues, their speech will be assessed on the basis of pre-determined criteria such as pronunciation, pause time, intonation, word stress and choice and sentence length and content relevancy and scored automatically by the proposed Intelligent Virtual Speaker. This process will give the prospective users to self-evaluate their language proficiency as well as an opportunity to speaking practice.

6. CONCLUSION

Artificial intelligence, when used in the field of foreign language education (teaching and learning), has the potential to improve students' language skills and optimize the learning process as well as aid language teaching professionals to use the most up-to-date technology in and outside the classroom. Considering the fact that artificial intelligence-based tools are widely used in areas such as language learning applications, virtual language teachers, and automated assessment systems, the future development of this field will be possible with the further improvement of artificial intelligence technology and its increased integration into language education.

Language education has a great importance in today's world. Language learning, along with the numerous opportunities it offers, also provides communication in and with various cultures. In our proposed scheme of AI application, the benefits of using VR and AI technologies in language education has been examined and evaluated and the possibility of a virtual platform that could be used in language education has been discussed and a draft framework has been presented as a viable option. It is aimed to realize the learning process more effectively on the platform designed by supporting VR technology, 3D graphics and videos. We said earlier that VR enables people to interact with 5D pictures and animations that are designed in the computer environment, as well as giving them the sense of being in a natural environment in their minds with technological tools. Therefore, the role of virtual speaker agents in improving language skills and language learning processes is explored in this study by focusing on the role and function of smart virtual speakers in predetermined task models in the classroom environment.

In conclusion, successful language teaching and effective learning is aimed with the help of NLP algorithms using a pre-created data set. In addition, the design and integration of a scoring system is offered by evaluating the language skills of the speakers and the degree of resulting success level is determined by a score. Depending on whether the speaker pronounces the words correctly or not, word-based scoring is performed to ensure maximum acceptability and word usage patterns to eliminate possible divergences. However, by using computer graphics in the vocalization of existing texts, the learning process is ensured to be permanent. This chapter has been presented as a draft version of a larger project that is currently under development by a large multidisciplinary team of researchers and language experts who are recruited in various universities and research institutes in and outside of Turkey from diverse fields including corpus linguistics, computer programming, software engineering, instructional and ELT curriculum designers, and language assessment experts. More detailed technical and pedagogical information will be available soon.

REFERENCES

Adolphs, S., & Knight, D. (2010). Building a spoken corpus: What are the basics? In A. O'Keeffe & M. McCarthy (Eds.), *The Routledge handbook of corpus linguistics* (pp. 38–52). Routledge. doi:10.4324/9780203856949.ch4

AI in Virtual Reality. (2022). *IEEE Digital Reality*. IEEE. https://digitalreality.ieee.org/publications/ai-in-virtual-reality

Aijmer, K. (2020). Spoken corpora. In S. Adolphs & D. Knight (Eds.), *The Routledge handbook of English language and digital humanities* (pp. 5–25). Routledge. doi:10.4324/9781003031758-2

Alexoloulou, T., Michel, M., Murakami, A., & Meurers, D. (2017). Task effects on linguistic complexity and accuracy: A large-scale learner corpus analysis employing natural language processing techniques. *Language Learning*, *67*(1), 180–208. doi:10.1111/lang.12232

Amidi, A., & Amidi, S. (n.d.). *Gözetimli öğrenme el kitabı. Shervine Amidi*. Stanford. https://stanford.edu/~shervine/l/tr/teaching/cs-229/cheatsheet-supervised-learning

Chen, L., Chen, P., & Lin, Z. (2020). Artificial intelligence in education: A review. *IEEE Access : Practical Innovations, Open Solutions*, *8*, 75264–75278. doi:10.1109/ACCESS.2020.2988510

Chen, X., Zou, D., Xie, H., Cheng, G., & Liu, C. (2022). Two decades of artificial intelligence in education: Contributors, collaborations, research topics, challenges, and future directions. *Journal of Educational Technology & Society*, *25*(1), 28–47.

Chowdhary, K. R. (2020). Natural language processing. *Fundamentals of artificial intelligence,* 603-649.

de Wet, F., Van der Walt, C., & Niesler, T. R. (2009). Automatic assessment of oral language proficiency and listening comprehension. *Speech Communication*, *51*(10), 864–874. doi:10.1016/j.specom.2009.03.002

Dhimolea, T. K., Kaplan-Rakowski, R., & Lin, L. (2022). A systematic review of research on high-immersion virtual reality for language learning. *TechTrends*, *66*(5), 810–824. doi:10.100711528-022-00717-w

Dodigovic, M. (2005). *Artificial intelligence in second language learning: Raising error awareness*. Multilingual Matters., doi:10.21832/9781853598319

Frąckiewicz, M. (2023, April 17). *The impact of chatbots on language learning and teaching*. Ts2 Space. https://ts2.space/en/the-impact-of-chatbots-on-language-learning-and-teaching/

Granger, S., Kraif, O., Ponton, C., Antoniadis, G., & Zampa, V. (2007). Integrating learner corpora and natural language processing: A crucial step towards reconciling technological sophistication and pedagogical effectiveness. *ReCALL, 19*(3), 252–268. doi:10.1017/S0958344007000237

Grant, P., & Basye, D. (2014). *Personalized learning: A guide for engaging students with technology*. International Society for Technology in Education.

Hampel, R. (2015). *Developing online language teaching: Research-based pedagogies and reflective practices*. Springer. doi:10.1057/9781137412263

Herrington, J., & Oliver, R. (2000). An instructional design framework for authentic learning environments. *Educational Technology Research and Development, 48*(3), 23–48. doi:10.1007/BF02319856

Huang, W., Hew, K. F., & Fryer, L. K. (2022). Chatbots for language learning—Are they really useful? A systematic review of chatbot-supported language learning. *Journal of Computer Assisted Learning, 38*(1), 237–257. doi:10.1111/jcal.12610

Huang, Y.-H., & Chuang, T.-Y. (2016). Technology-assisted sheltered instruction: Instructional streaming video in an EFL multi-purpose computer course. *Computer Assisted Language Learning, 29*(3), 618–637. doi:10.1080/09588221.2014.1000933

Kim, N. Y., Cha, Y., & Kim, H. S. (2019). Future English learning: Chatbots and artificial intelligence. *Multimedia-Assisted Language Learning, 22*(3).

Krogh, A. (2008). What are artificial neural networks? *Nature Biotechnology, 26*(2), 195–197. doi:10.1038/nbt1386 PMID:18259176

Lan, Y. J. (2020a). Immersion into virtual reality for language learning. *Psychology of Learning and Motivation, 72*, 1–26. doi:10.1016/bs.plm.2020.03.001

Lan, Y. J. (2020b). Immersion, interaction and experience-oriented learning: Bringing VR into FL learning. *Language Learning & Technology, 24*(1), 1–15.

Lan, Y. J., Sung, Y. T., & Chang, K. E. (2007). A mobile-device-supported peer-assisted learning system for collaborative early EFL reading. *Language Learning & Technology, 11*(3), 130–151.

LeCun, Y., Bengio, Y., & Hinton, G. (2015). Deep learning. *Nature, 521*(7553), 436–444. doi:10.1038/nature14539 PMID:26017442

Lee, J. (1999). Effectiveness of computer-based instructional simulation: A Meta-analysis. *International Journal of Instructional Media*, *26*(1), 71–85.

Li, Z., & Hegelheimer, V. (2013). Mobile-assisted grammar exercises: Effects on self-editing in L2 writing. *Language Learning & Technology*, *17*(3), 135–156.

Lin, T. J., & Lan, Y. J. (2015). Language learning in virtual reality environments: Past, present, and future. *Journal of Educational Technology & Society*, *18*(4), 486–497.

Love, R., Dembry, C., Hardie, A., Brezina, V., & McEnery, T. (2017). The Spoken BNC2014: And building a spoken corpus of everyday conversations. *International Journal of Corpus Linguistics*, *22*(3), 319–344. doi:10.1075/ijcl.22.3.02lov

Machover, C., & Tice, S. E. (1994). Virtual reality. *IEEE Computer Graphics and Applications*, *14*(1), 15–16. doi:10.1109/38.250913

Mauranen, A. (2004). Spoken corpus for an ordinary learner. In J. Sinclair (Ed.), *How to use corpora in language teaching* (pp. 89–105). John Benjamins Publishing Company. doi:10.1075cl.12.09mau

Meurers, D. (2015). Learner corpora and natural language processing. In S. Granger, G. Gilquin, & F. Meunier (Eds.), *The Cambridge handbook of learner corpus research* (pp. 537–566). Cambridge University Press., doi:10.1017/CBO9781139649414.024

Meurers, D. (2020). Natural language processing and language learning. In C. A. Chapelle (Ed.), *The Concise Encyclopedia of Applied Linguistics* (pp. 817–831). John Wiley & Sons Inc.

Meurers, D., & Dickinson, M. (2017). Evidence and interpretation in language learning research: Opportunities for collaboration with computational linguistics. *Language Learning*, *67*(1), 66–95. doi:10.1111/lang.12233

Mkansi, M., & Mkalipi, N. (2023). Natural language processing and machine learning approach to teaching and learning research philosophies and paradigms. *Electronic Journal of Business Research Methods*, *21*(1), 14–30. doi:10.34190/ejbrm.21.1.2627

Modha, D. S., Ananthanarayanan, R., Esser, S. K., Ndirango, A., Sherbondy, A. J., & Singh, R. (2011). Cognitive computing. *Communications of the ACM*, *54*(8), 62–71. https://doi.acm.org/10.1145/1978542.1978559. doi:10.1145/1978542.1978559

Nesi, H., & Thompson, P. (2006). *The British academic spoken English corpus manual*. University of Warwick.

Nielsen, J. (1994). *Usability engineering*. Morgan Kaufmann.

Nikitina, L. (2001). Creating an authentic learning environment in the foreign language classroom. *International Journal of Instruction*, *4*(1), 33–46.

Pinherio, A., Barbosa, A., Carvalho, R., Freitas, F., Tsai, Y. S., Gasevic, D., & Ferreira, R. (2021). Automatic feedback in online learning environments: A systematic literature review. *Computers and Education Artificial Intelligence*, *2*, 1–17. doi:10.1016/j.caeai.2021.100027

Radianti, J., Majchrzak, T. A., Fromm, J., & Wohlgenannt, I. (2020). A systematic review of immersive virtual reality applications for higher education: Design elements, lessons learned, and research agenda. *Computers & Education*, *147*, 1–29. doi:10.1016/j.compedu.2019.103778

Rogers, Y., Sharp, H., & Preece, J. (2011). *Interaction design: Beyond human-computer interaction* (3rd ed.). John Wiley & Sons.

Russell, S. J. (2010). *Artificial intelligence a modern approach.* Pearson Education, Inc.

Schmidt, T., & Strasser, T. (2022). Artificial intelligence in foreign language learning and teaching. Anglistik. *International Journal of English Studies*, *33*(1), 165–184. doi:10.33675/ANGL/2022/1/14

Shadiev, R., Hwang, W. Y., & Huang, Y. M. (2017). Review of research on mobile language learning in authentic environments. *Computer Assisted Language Learning*, *30*(3–4), 284–303. doi:10.1080/09588221.2017.1308383

Sutton, R. S., & Barto, A. G. (2018). *Reinforcement learning: An introduction.* MIT Press.

The impact of AI on language learning and teaching. (n.d.). *TalkPal AI.* https://talkpal.ai/the-impact-of-ai-on-language-learning-and-teaching/

Thompson, P., & Nesi, H. (2001). The British Academic Spoken English (BASE) Corpus Project. *Language Teaching Research*, *5*(3), 263–264. doi:10.1177/136216880100500305

Torfi, A., Shirvani, R. A., Keneshloo, Y., Tavaf, N., & Fox, E. A. (2020). Natural language processing advancements by deep learning. *Survey (London, England).* Advance online publication. doi:10.48550/arXiv.2003.01200

Vázquez-Cano, E. (2021). Artificial intelligence and education: A pedagogical challenge for the 21st century. *Educational Process: international journal*, *10*(3), 7-12.

Yanhua, Z. (2020). The application of artificial intelligence in foreign language teaching. *ICAIE*, *40-42*, 40–42. doi:10.1109/ICAIE50891.2020.00017

Zheng, J. M., Chan, K. W., & Gibson, I. (1998). Virtual reality. *IEEE Potentials*, *17*(2), 20–23. doi:10.1109/45.666641 PMID:9699075

Zhou, Y. (2021b). Artificial neural network-based smart aerogel glazing in low-energy buildings: A state-of-the-art review. *iScience*, *24*(12), 103420. doi:10.1016/j.isci.2021.103420 PMID:34849473

Zhou, Z. H. (2021a). *Machine learning*. Springer Nature. doi:10.1007/978-981-15-1967-3

Chapter 5
ChatGPT in Academic Writing and Publishing:
An Overview of Ethical Issues

Arif Bakla
Ankara Yıldırım Beyazıt University, Turkey

ABSTRACT

Generative artificial intelligence systems are disruptive technologies that have been found useful in various domains, including academia and education. Being one of these technologies, ChatGPT can have smart conversations with its human users, answer questions and produce content virtually on any topic. Like other conversational agents, ChatGPT has advanced text processing capabilities, such as writing paragraphs, essays, research reports and paraphrasing texts. The use of this technology in academic writing classes and scholarly publications necessitates a discussion of possible problems and challenges that might undermine ethical and responsible use. This is because the ability of this new technology to produce content that sounds like human output has wider ethical implications not only for academic writing and publishing but also for learning and instruction. The issues of concern are related to transparency and credibility of the content, ownership of the text produced and integrity.

INTRODUCTION

Being a disruptive technology, Open AI's generative pre-trained transformer (ChatGPT) is deeply rooted in research into artificial intelligence (AI), natural language processing (NLP) and large language models (LLMs). It has been a hot

DOI: 10.4018/978-1-6684-9893-4.ch005

topic among researchers, educators, educational administrators, students and other relevant people in academia and educational contexts. It provides its users with a range of functionalities that have exerted a discernible impact on how research is carried out and written up, along with how students learn and teachers teach. Teubner et al. (2023) describe this innovative tool as "the latest pinnacle of the steady development of AI-powered chatbots" (p. 95). It acquired a surprising number of users soon after its release in late 2022. Regardless of what publishers, editors, researchers, educators and students think about it, it seems to have the power to shape research, writing and instruction around the world and open up new avenues of discussion and research.

Therefore, as Eke (2023) recommends, educational institutions have to prepare their students for the new world that is being deeply changed and reshaped by generative AI systems. The academic community has a similar responsibility: integrating new technological advancements into the process of doing and writing scholarly research in an ethical way. Both academic researchers and educators have to consider the ins and outs of using ChatGPT and similar tools, incorporating the latest advancements for research and educational purposes. There is a pressing need for scholarly discussions about the use of ChatGPT to develop a thorough understanding of this issue. Therefore, this chapter aims to fill this need by discussing the key ethical issues related with the use of ChatGPT in academic research and writing. Globally considered, it aims to help academics and students to use this new tool in an ethical and responsible way. Major issues to be discussed include authorship of ChatGPT-generated content, issues of integrity (particularly those of plagiarism) and transparency. The chapter also provides some guidelines on ethical, legitimate and responsible use of this innovative tool.

Authorship

Authorship is not only related with claiming the intellectual property rights of a paper or a similar output that is the product of human mind, but also related with taking the responsibility of a scholarly paper and its content; authorship brings both rights and responsibilities. Recently, there have been several instances of crediting ChatGPT with co-authorship in scientific publications (Aljanabi et al., 2023; O'Connor, 2022); it was even listed as the first author in a paper (Zhavoronkov, 2022). However, these publications have justifiably faced a negative attitude from the scientific community (Stokel-Walker, 2023). Some researchers have already revealed their stance (e.g., Teixeira da Silva, 2023; Thorp, 2023) by saying that ChatGPT or (similar text-to-text AI tools) may be useful to some extent, but they cannot be considered the author of a scientific paper, nor any component of a scholarly paper (e.g., figures, images) can be created by such tools. Lending support to these perspectives, Lee (2023) reports that many legal authorities and copyright experts voiced their objections to the acknowledgement of AI authorship in scholarly papers.

While some publishing houses and journals have announced their policies regarding authorship issues (e.g., Nature, Science), a great majority of them have remained silent about such policies or principles that might guide how AI could be used in academic writing in a way to ensure integrity. However, Anderson et al. (2023) note that although most of them do not directly refer to the use of AI in academic papers in the policy statements, they implicitly disapprove the use of text generation tools for such purposes. The policy announcements clearly reveal that ChatGPT cannot be credited with authorship (at least in its current form). This is mainly because the most significant aspect of authorship is producing some kind of intellectual output, which can hardly be achieved by ChatGPT or other similar large language models. Even if ChatGPT is used during research and write-up processes, how it is used should be clearly disclosed. As providing such information is critical, it is included in the policy draft proposed in the editorial by Hosseini et al. (2023) to be adopted to guide practice and to clarify issues pertaining to the use of natural language processing in the research studies submitted to *Accountability in Research*, a scholarly journal that aims to promote integrity in academic research.

All authors submitting manuscripts to Accountability in Research must **disclose** *and describe the use of any NLP systems in writing the manuscript text or generating ideas used in the text and* **accept full responsibility** *for the text's factual and citation accuracy; mathematical, logical, and commonsense reasoning; and originality (italics in the original) (p. 6).*

Siegerink et al. (2023) highlight two aspects of authorship that Committee on Publication Ethics (COPE) and International Committee of Medical Journal Editors (ICMJE) deem critical: credit for contribution and accountability. The ICMJE put forward the following commonly cited four criteria: (1) significant contribution to the design of research, along with contribution to the collection, analysis and interpretation of data, (2) preparing drafts of the study and revising its intellectual content, (3) approving the final version of the paper before publication and (4) being accountable for every aspect of the research output and ensuring accuracy and integrity of it (ICMJE, n.d.). Challenging the issue of authorship in O'Connor's (2022) article, in which ChatGPT was listed as the second author, Teixeira da Silva (2023) claims that the five paragraphs written by ChatGPT in the aforementioned study, were plagiarized from the databases on the Internet, and much worse, the target audience of the paper was not informed about this. Teixeira da Silva concludes that authorship was a significant issue in this paper as ChatGPT predominantly failed to meet the ICMJE's criteria.

ChatGPT can successfully respond to queries thanks to AI and machine learning after it is trained on supplied content. This implies that what it produces a type of output that is hardly intellectual. This obviously leads to some ethical implications and concerns. If the information produced by ChatGPT is not the intellectual output produced by the software itself, it must have been produced by others, or at least it is based on previously supplied information; it is not something that is fully original. This is particularly so even if ChatGPT-generated content passes originality tests in plagiarism detection software.

For these reasons, the contribution of ChatGPT does not give the software the right to be credited with authorship as the function of the software is hardly substantial if intellectually considered. The software makes little intellectual contribution to the paper, if any at all. Giving support to this, Yeo-Teh and Tang (2023) note that ChatGPT mostly fails to meet authorship criteria; it can by no means put forward something intellectual, nor can it be held accountable. Similarly, Springer Nature (2023b) rightly announced that "..an attribution of authorship carries with its accountability for the work, which cannot be effectively applied to LLMs" (Online, para. 1). Inclusion of ChatGPT as an author of a paper, despite the fact that it mostly fails to meet authorship criteria discussed above, leads to the problem of guest authorship, which refers to the practice of listing someone as as the author/co-author of a paper although they basically fail to meet the "substantial contribution" criteria, or they have no contribution at all.

There are also concerns about who owns the intellectual property of the text produced by ChatGPT (Çerası & Balcıoğlu, 2023). While the work produced by ChatGPT does not directly belong to a third-party author, the fact that it learns to produce responses based on earlier work apparently gives serious cause for concern. A student author or a scholar can claim authorship only if all the content they produced belongs to them. The content produced by ChatGPT clearly does not belong to them, so they cannot use it, nor can they cite ChatGPT as the source of the information. This is because citing a source means acknowledging that the intellectual property of the idea belongs to that source, which is not the case in IA output. It is not clear whom the AI-generated text belongs to. A software tool cannot claim ownership of what it produces, nor can the owner of the software claim the intellectual property rights of what an AI tool generates. In short, there is a grey area in terms of the ownership of the content created by ChatGPT (Eke, 2023).

As a rule of thumb, just as authors are expected to declare the use of language editing services (particularly if such services make significant changes in the paper) or how other key contributors improved the quality of the paper (Teixeira da Silva, 2023), the use of an AI tool in research and academic writing (not as a co-author but as an aid) should be clearly disclosed and acknowledged. In the policy draft they proposed, Hosseini et al. (2023) recommend that if the authors of a paper used NLP tools (e.g., ChatGPT) in their paper, they should clearly disclose this (particularly in the methods section of the paper and in the references); they should provide sufficient information about who used the tool, when they used it, what prompts were supplied, and they should specify the texts (or ideas) that were the result of tool use. Revealing the ideas produced by ChatGPT, according to Teixeira da Silva (2023), could help decide if the software is a guest author or not (if it has made a substantial contribution). However, even if the portions of texts produced by the software are clearly disclosed, as one can never be sure of the nature of the content created by ChatGPT, there is always a possibility of (unintentional) plagiarism. Therefore, researchers and students should be aware of this. In short, software cannot be held accountable for the research process and its written version (Yeo-Teh & Tang, 2023) because, as Stokel-Walker's (2023) says, it cannot assume any ethical and legal responsibilities.

Credibility

Another aspect of the issue is that what is presented by ChatGPT could well be incorrect. It is possible that AI-generated output could include information that conflicts with or runs counter to general facts. For instance, Haman and Školník (2023) conducted a small test, in which they prompted ChatGPT to list ten seminal articles with their digital object identifier numbers in the field of medicine; they did this five times. ChatGPT provided 48 unique results, but 66% of these articles were fake; they did not exist at all. The authors concluded that this software cannot even be recommended as a tool to facilitate literature review. Using AI-generated output in a research study would make the scientific bases of that study questionable. In this respect, as one of the authorial or scholarly responsibilities is to present accurate and useful information, using output from ChatGPT is not legitimate. Moreover, as Teubner et al. (2023) note, inaccurate ChatGPT responses could prove "particularly dangerous for uninformed and naïve use" (p. 97). In this respect, researchers, teachers, and students should exercise caution when they intend to use information from ChatGPT queries; it is worth cross checking any information provided by ChatGPT. Printed materials, search engine results, scientific data bases, scholarly journal articles and other potential sources could be used for cross checking such information.

Academic Integrity

There appears to be a growing concern about the possibility of students' and researchers' outsourcing their writing tasks to ChatGPT (Eke, 2023; Springer Nature, 2023a). This concern is deepened not only by the free availability of ChatGPT, but also by the lack of reliable software tools to detect the use of this chatbot (Eke, 2023). Research on educators' and students' ability to distinguish between AI-generated versus human-generated writing seems to justify such concerns about academic integrity. For instance, Avila-Chauvet and Mejía (2023) carried out an experimental study to investigate whether students and professors could successfully distinguish between essays written by students and ChatGPT and to compare essays in terms of their quality. The results indicated that both the students and professors assigned higher quality scores to the essays written by ChatGPT; neither of the groups could successfully distinguish between ChatGPT-generated essays and those written by the students. Likewise, in a pilot study, Landa-Blanco et al. (2023) provided AI-generated texts (three poems and a short story) to the participants in the experimental and control groups. Although all the creative writing texts were written by ChatGPT, the participants in the control group were told that the texts were written by a human writer, while those in the experimental group were told the truth. The participants were asked to rate the level of creativity and originality of the text, along with how much they enjoyed these creative writing texts. The results indicated that the groups did not differ significantly in terms of their ratings of creativity, originality, how much enjoyment they got out of reading these texts, and whether they could recommend these stories to others. Finally, in another study, researchers prompted ChatGPT to generate 50 abstracts. These abstracts were checked using ChatGPT output detectors and plagiarism software. ChatGPT-generated abstracts were accurately detected using output detectors, but the abstracts were considered %100 original by plagiarism detection software. Although the human reviewers correctly identified 68% of the fabricated abstracts, they incorrectly labelled the 14% of the genuine abstracts as fabricated. Moreover, human raters reported that it proved difficult for them to distinguish fabricated abstracts from human-generated ones.

Such preliminary search results signal two major problems. First, because people, particularly professors, may not be able to distinguish between AI- and human-generated content, they may fail to detect AI-generated content which is passed off as original writing by their students, unless they use software as an aid to decide whether a piece of writing is AI-generated or written by a human. Probably due to this possibility, some researchers note that the future of essays as a form of evaluation might be in danger (Eke, 2023; Stokel-Walker, 2022).

Owners of plagiarism detection software have announced that they have been undertaking serious work to accurately distinguish AI content from human-generated text. Turnitin, for example, already provides an AI index, along with its usual similarity index, yet this feature is in its infancy and needs further development. There are also other tools on the Internet that help detect ChatGPT-generated content. However, my personal experience from an academic writing course tells me that such tools (e.g., Zerogpt.net, 2023) are sometimes likely to present faulty results although they claim to offer relatively higher levels of accuracy. Besides using AI-generated content detection software, it is possible for journal editors in academia and professors at schools to study the distinguishing characteristics of AI-generated texts. In this way, they can more successfully identify such texts. However, this task might still be challenging, particularly when AI-generated writing does not seem to possess discernible characteristics that could reveal its identity. Moreover, while plagiarism software (e.g., Turnitin) struggle to come up with solutions to detect ChatGPT output, there are also tools that supposedly alter ChatGPT-generated content to by-pass AI content detection tools. In other words, there seems to be a 'war' between people who apparently intend to misuse AI and those who want to take countermeasures to help reduce such misuse in academic research and writing.

In short, from the perspectives of editors and university professors submitting AI content as original work or inserting portions of AI-generated texts in an original essay or research paper is much more serious than copying content from the Internet or printed sources because plagiarism detection software (e.g., Turnitin, Ithenticate, PlagScan, etc.) presently do not offer sophisticated methods to detect AI content, although it can successfully identify texts plagiarised from online sources.

Transparency

The issue of transparency is related with two aspects of using ChatGPT for academic research and writing. On the one hand, publishing houses, journals, and journal editors should introduce and follow clear policies on authorship issues, along with revealing their principles related with legitimate/illegitimate use(s) of ChatGPT and provide guidance on how to use it appropriately. An example of this is Nature journal which clearly announced that AI cannot be credited with authorship. Making reference to Nature's policy announcement, Anderson et al. (2023) predict that other publishing houses and editorial boards could soon make similar decisions. Similarly, arXiv, an open-access platform on which scholars share their research, states that while it is legitimate to use both simple and very sophisticated tools to do research and to prepare the research report by using them, the use of AI-powered language tools may lead to inaccurate and misleading results, so disclosing what tools were used is critical to help the audience of a research study evaluate and interpret the results (arXiv.org, January, 2023). arXiv clearly requires authors to report the use of generative AI in a research paper and goes on to warn that it is the author who would be responsible for any mistake committed by the AI tool, such as plagiarism, missing references, content errors and so forth. On the other hand, to ensure transparency, it would be wise to acknowledge the legitimate uses of ChatGPT in research and academic writing (e.g., using it as a search engine, getting feedback from it, asking it to do some mechanical tasks such checking grammar, spelling or punctuation) and to avoid submitting content created by ChatGPT as original work. Anderson et al. (2023) state that transparency in disclosing AI tool use in writing could be an alternative approach, yet it should be noted that this is only reserved for legitimate uses of AI tools.

ChatGPT as a Legitimate Research and Writing Tool

Academic researchers and authors use various software tools and applications to help them collect and analyse data and write up the results of their research. The examples of such software tools include, but are not limited to, word processors, statistical packages (e.g., SPSS, Matlab), qualitative data analysis software (e.g., NVivo, Atlas.ti, MAXQDA) grammar and spell check software, plagiarism software and various other tools that serve for more specific purposes. These software tools assist researchers while doing their research studies and write up; none of them claim to replace the researcher who is responsible for designing the research, collecting and analysing the data and writing the research report as each of these tasks involve some kind of intellectual activity.

ChatGPT is not different from the software mentioned above. There are of course numerous legitimate and recommendable uses of ChatGPT in academic research and writing. It can be used to facilitate research and learning. Lee (2023) states that "today's most advanced AI chatbot seems to be able to play the role of a research assistant in much the same way as a search engine" (p. 4). One of my colleagues talked about his plan to use ChatGPT to fulfil some mechanical tasks, such as checking spelling or punctuation and comparing the list of references with intext citations to ensure that all the intext citations are listed in the references section, and vice versa. This appears to be a legitimate use of this new technology, yet it would be safe to acknowledge such uses in a research paper, just as you report that you used a statistical package to analyse quantitative data or computer-assisted qualitative data analysis software to analyse textual data or to review the literature.

In an instructional context, ChatGPT can assume various instructional roles. First of all, it could function as a search engine that provides organised answers to specific queries related with academic writing. For example, it could function as a comprehensible source for an intermediate student who wants to learn the basics of writing a topic sentence. It could provide a reading material that could function as input before students undertake a writing task. It could be used as a brainstorming tool to get more ideas on a specific topic. It may also help students to prepare outlines, provide feedback on content and language. This might be quite useful, particularly if it is difficult for the teacher to provide feedback to a large number of students. In this respect, ChatGPT functions as a friend by the side, who provides answers to questions and readily gives feedback whenever needed. However, students should not accept such feedback without considering its accuracy and appropriacy.

In educational contexts, to raise students' awareness of this critical topic, Gimpel et al. (2023) recommend that issues related to intellectual property rights and academic integrity should be discussed extensively with students. This is because it is the lack of knowledge or awareness that leads students to get involved in inappropriate writing practises in a way to harm the academic integrity of their work. Atlas (2023) provides some guidelines on how students could use ChatGPT responsibly. They are recommended to (a) know what ChatGPT could do and what it cannot do, (b) attribute it properly if used in their research, (c) be transparent, (d) know institutional policies, (e) use it ethically, (f) use it as a tool rather than something that substitutes their own intellectual activity, (g) not readily accept the output without evaluating its accuracy and (h) use plagiarism software to check the originality of the work produced by ChatGPT. Atlas also recommends educators to develop policies for ChatGPT use, use plagiarism software and provide guidance to students to ensure ethical use.

CONCLUSION

Although there have been recent instances of listing ChatGPT as a co-author in academic papers, an emerging consensus can be seen among researchers (Lee, 2023; Yeo-Teh & Tang, 2023) publishers and journals (Nature, Science) about the inappropriateness of crediting ChatGPT with authorship. A related issue is plagiarism, which is a significant problem, not only in educational contexts but also in scholarly publications. Nowadays, the widespread use of large language models has raised the issue of plagiarism, which is a significant problem regardless of its intent or severity, so it should be avoided.

Even though some software programmes and web tools apparently help detect AI content, usually free of charge, it is probable that they might miss content produced by AI tools other than the one(s) they are prepared to function against. Teachers usually know what their students could achieve in terms of academic writing (e.g., they know the mistakes commonly committed and are aware of their students' style). Therefore, teachers should use their knowledge and experience not only to decide to use AI detection tools but also to question, reject or verify the results of analysis of that piece of writing by such tools. However, this is much more complicated in scholarly publishing. It is not possible for journal editors and other responsible people to know the writing styles of their potential authors, who come with diverse educational backgrounds and nationalities.

As we are in a transitional period, in which boundaries are not clearly set, discussions are hardly conclusive as to what can be considered legitimate and appropriate in terms of using AI in academic research and writing. Such a transitional period might lead to some appropriate practices regarding how to use AI in academic writing. ChatGPT carries strong implications for teaching and assessing academic writing and academic integrity in general (Eke, 2023). For example, students might not be aware of what appropriate use of ChatGPT implies. Therefore, they should be educated and informed about what counts legitimate or illegitimate while using this tool for academic research and writing. Globally considered, it is critical that ethical issues surrounding the use of ChatGPT in academic writing be discussed in scholarly platforms, academics and students should be informed about institutional policies regarding the use of this software. All relevant institutions and people, including but not limited to, publishing houses, journals, journal editors, researchers, reviewers and librarians have to assume responsibility to ensure ethical and responsible use of ChatGPT and other similar AI tools that are capable of producing text-to-text content.

REFERENCES

Aljanabi, M., Ghazi, M., Ali, A. H., & Abed, S. A. (2023). ChatGPT: Open possibilities. *Iraqi Journal for Computer Science and Mathematics*, *4*(1), 62–64. doi:10.52866/20ijcsm.2023.01.01.0018

Anderson, N., Belavy, D., Perle, S., Hendricks, S., Hespanhol, L., Verhagen, E., & Memon, A. R. (2023). AI did not write this manuscript, or did it? Can we trick the AI text detector into generated texts? The potential future of ChatGPT and AI [Editorial]. *BMJ Open Sport & Exercise Medicine*, *9*(1), e001568. doi:10.1136/bmjsem-2023-001568 PMID:36816423

arXiv.org. (January, 2023). *arXiv announces new policy on ChatGPT and similar tools*. arXiv. https://blog.arxiv.org/2023/01/31/arxiv-announces-new-policy-on-chatgpt-and-similar-tools/

Atlas, S. (2023). *ChatGPT for higher education and professional development: A guide to conversational AI*. Digital Commons. digitalcommons.uri.edu

Avila-ChauvetL.MejíaD. (2023). Can Professors and Students Detect ChatGPT Essays? *SSRN*. doi:10.2139/ssrn.4373643

Çerası, C. Ç., & Balcıoğlu, Y. S. (2023). *AI and Ethics in Education: ChatGPT Program Example.* Paper presented at the The Book of Proceedings of the International Symposium on Communication and Technology with its Philosophical Dimensions (ISTC_PhD). 14–15 January, Marmara University, Istanbul, Türkiye.

Eke, D. (2023). *ChatGPT and the rise of generative AI: Threat to academic integrity?*: philpapers.org. doi:10.1016/j.jrt.2023.100060

Gimpel, H., Hall, K., Decker, S., Eymann, T., & Lämmermann, L. (2023). *Unlocking the power of generative AI models and systems such asGPT-4 and ChatGPT for higher education.* opus.uni-hohenheim.de

Haman, M., & Školník, M. (2023). Using ChatGPT to conduct a literature review [Letter to the editor]. *Accountability in Research*, 1–3. doi:10.1080/08989621.2023.2185514 PMID:36879536

Hosseini, M., Rasmussen, L. M., & Resnik, D. B. (2023). Using AI to write scholarly publications. *Accountability in Research*, 1–9. doi:10.1080/08989621.2023.2168535 PMID:36697395

International Committee of Medical Journal Editors (ICMJE). (n.d.). Defining the Role of Authors and Contributors. ICMJE. https://www.icmje.org/recommendations/browse/roles-and-responsibilities/defining-the-role-of-authors-and-contributors.html

Landa-Blanco, M., Flores, M., & Mercado, M. (2023). *Human vs. AI Authorship: Does it Matter in Evaluating Creative Writing? A Pilot Study Using ChatGPT*: psyarxiv.com. https://doi.org/ doi:10.31234/osf.io/wjsm3osf.io/wjsm3

Lee, J. Y. (2023). Can an artificial intelligence chatbot be the author of a scholarly article? *Journal of Educational Evaluation for Health Professions*, *20*, 1–6. doi:10.3352/jeehp.2023.20.6 PMID:36842449

O'Connor, S.ChatGPT. (2022). Open artificial intelligence platforms in nursing education: Tools for academic progress or abuse? *Nurse Education in Practice*, *66*, 103537–103537. doi:10.1016/j.nepr.2022.103537 PMID:36549229

Siegerink, B., Pet, L. A., Rosendaal, F. R., & Schoones, J. W. (2023). ChatGPT as an author of academic papers is wrong and highlights the concepts of accountability and contributorship. *Nurse Education in Practice*, *68*, 103599. doi:10.1016/j.nepr.2023.103599 PMID:36898252

Springer Nature. (2023a). *Editorial: Tools such as ChatGPT threaten transparent science; here are our ground rules for their use*, 613. Springer. doi:10.1038/d41586-023-00191-1

Springer Nature. (2023b). Artificial intelligence (AI) (Online). Spinger. https://www.nature.com/nature-portfolio/editorial-policies/ai

Stokel-Walker, C. (2022). *AI bot ChatGPT writes smart essays: Should academics worry?* doi:10.1038/d41586-022-04397-7

Stokel-Walker, C. (2023). *ChatGPT listed as author on research papers: many scientists disapprove* (613). doi:10.1038/d41586-023-00107-z

Teixeira da Silva, T. J. A. (2021). Outsourced English revision, editing, publication consultation, and integrity services should be acknowledged in an academic paper. *Journal of Nanoparticle Research*, *23*(81), 81. doi:10.100711051-021-05199-0

Teixeira da Silva, T. J. A. (2023). Is ChatGPT a valid author? *Nurse Education in Practice*, *68*(103600), 103600. doi:10.1016/j.nepr.2023.103600 PMID:36906947

Teubner, T., Flath, C. M., Weinhardt, C., Aalst, W., & Hinz, O. (2023). Welcome to the Era of ChatGPT et al. *Business & Information Systems Engineering*, *65*(2), 95–101. doi:10.100712599-023-00795-x

Thorp, H. (2023). ChatGPT is fun, but not an author. *Science*, *379*(6630), 313. Advance online publication. doi:10.1126cience.adg7879 PMID:36701446

Yeo-Teh, N., & Tang, B. (2023). Letter to Editor: NLP systems such as ChatGPT cannot be listed as an author because these cannot fulfill widely adopted authorship criteria. Accountability in Research. 1–3. doi:10.1080/08989621.2023.2177160

Zerogpt.net. (2023). *ZeroGPT*. Zero GPT. https://zerogpt.net/

Zhavoronkov, A. (2022). Rapamycin in the context of Pascal's Wager: Generative pre-trained transformer perspective. *Oncoscience*, *9*, 82–84. doi:10.18632/oncoscience.571 PMID:36589923

KEY TERMS AND DEFINITIONS

Academic Integrity: The quality of being truthful and being engaged in honest and moral practice while doing academic work.

Authorship: The state of being the writer or composer of an intellectual product, such as a book, an article, a report, music and so forth.

ChatGPT: A large language model that is capable of responding to queries prompted by humans and adopting numerous roles to fulfil various related tasks.

Credibility: The extent to which scientific research results can be considered convincing and valuable.

Plagiarism: The practice of using others' ideas and work and submitting it as if it were one's own work.

Scholarly Writing: The practice of writing scientific materials that disseminate knowledge acquired through systematic research methods.

Transparency: Being clear about doing scholarly research and reporting its results.

Chapter 6
Artificial Intelligence's Contribution to English Language Teaching:
Are We Asking AI the Right Questions?

Zoe Marlowe
Biruni University, Turkey

ABSTRACT

When the trendsetting 'buzz word' in technology came forth in recent years, some educators became a little wary of the term "artificial intelligence." Why is that? Perhaps the idea that something existing other than the human brain to make calculated decisions regarding the creation of exams, or the ability to plan a lesson without hours of research seemed too 'foreign' or 'unnatural' to them. However, for some, the realization of yet another branch of technology to assist practitioners in the ever-evolving pedagogical fields seems quite natural as well as massively time-saving. This chapter will attempt to lightheartedly decipher a few points of artificial intelligence and its implications for greatly improving the future of teaching and learning, plus a few wise words of caution... both for the teacher and the learner.

INTRODUCTION

We hear many things about technology in teaching in our English Language Education departments at universities worldwide. Technology helped to improve our craft in many different ways that we can no longer live without actually. Some of us remember when computers were first introduced into classrooms in the 1980s...

DOI: 10.4018/978-1-6684-9893-4.ch006

it was revolutionary for sure! Some teachers were on board with the idea, others preferred the 'pencil and paper approach' to teaching and learning, however. Software became the new savior to nearly all of us in education, and from that point onward we managed to help initiate some ground-breaking achievements in teaching, and of course, student learning. Our own teaching methodologies were greatly enhanced with the latest technologies which emerged, and students benefitted tremendously from many of the upgrades to their classroom environments. This goes without saying because we are still using technology to construct interesting and engaging learning materials for our students. Also, another consideration which stays close to the surface for many of my colleagues and myself, encompasses the idea of student motivation regarding the use of AI in ELT, particularly if they find it to be of good use for them in their completion of coursework and having access to AI for both fun and academic purposes. It is a well-known fact that students usually enjoy having new technology to use in their daily lives. According to Ali, et al (2023), reading and writing skills have been impacted mostly positively for students using ChatGPT, basically motivating them to improve themselves. In Ali's paper, one of their ultimate goals is to design instruction using AI with emphasis on maintaining the students' interest in the subjects they are studying.

From an instructor standpoint, it is clear that a great deal of teachers' non-teaching time is taken up with the endeavor of planning, which can seem endless. So, many might ask the question: "Is Artificial Intelligence going to turn traditional lesson planning and execution on its ear?" Probably not right away. However, the implications are already tugging at some practitioners' neatly rolled-up shirt sleeves, as the exploration of some of the more helpful features of using AI have started emerging in different learning institutions, plus the science community as well as others who are starting to get 'on board' with the concept of AI as a teaching/learning opportunity. Obviously, we can only try and predict how far and wide the use of AI technology will propagate, but there are signs in many institutions of higher learning, especially in the medical and engineering type faculties, and even my own, in English Language Teaching (ELT), that AI has become a definite advantage to have access to for students and instructors alike. So, with these issues in mind, we will peruse some of the experiments I have completed using ChatGPT using both my (and its) question formulations for AI.

LITERATURE REVIEW

First things first, a brief look into the literature is appropriate before we delve into the actual 'mini experiment' I created using the two versions of ChatGPT I tested for this endeavor. The first publication, a book, I studied and would like to mention, is Artificial Intelligence in Education by Holmes, Bialik, & Fadel (2019). Since education or teaching English Language Teaching (ELT) is where I spend most of my time, this seemed to cut straight to the depth of the situation; firstly their expectation being the projection of using AI and how it will have a huge impact on teaching, especially 'what' we teach. Notably, the authors discuss the deep and versatile education which can be a booster to student motivation; something we all desire as educators, of course. The book also makes the distinction between artificial intelligence and education technology in particular how AI use implies that learning can improve markedly as this technology keeps evolving, and is harnessed by tech savvy educators. As always, people should approach new technology with an open mind.

Researchers Sharadgah & Sa'di (2022), strongly believe there is a very positive future for AI in education, notably ELT. Although they feel there are still many gaps in the literature regarding AI, (which they agree is still in its 'infancy'), they also realize that when utilized in ELT, many positive results emerged in specific areas, such as: Optimization of English language skills, assessment, attitude, learner satisfaction and more. These researchers also shine light upon prior research which they feel has not been focused on, such as what areas of AI are being covered, and how literature in this field is progressing. This is important because we are always interested in what is being 'showcased' as essential knowledge or some feature or another that is potentially groundbreaking. So, in this case they are doing the opposite, and alerting others who might be researching similar topics, that some areas are not being focused upon as often as others are. This opens the field for even more research opportunities.

Similar to anything technologically new or groundbreaking, there comes a healthy dose of skepticism, and rightfully so. However, the literature keeps mounting up daily regarding how AI is actually becoming necessary to help to improve learning, for instance, and of interest to myself in particular: English teaching. Definitely for all branches, education is a huge, veritable "test kitchen" for AI. Li (2017) makes a similar argument and points out how AI is fast becoming a tool, a necessity if you will, for organizing and creating a new platform which can help instructors to create personalized English instruction environments. Also, we tend to think about something else Li mentions, in that we as teachers have the ability to provide templates, modify knowledge points as well as control the difficulty of papers and materials in the testing bases. Afterall, we aren't so separate from AI, we are also in effect, helping to build it by using and contributing to it, these possibilities seem endless!

In the article by Sun, Anbarasan, & Kumar (2020), the researchers contend that the subject of English teaching is paramount, suggesting AI can be utilized by schools and universities to create learning tool platforms which will allow ELT education students to improve their English teaching based around their own knowledge mastery and their personalities. Many pre-service English teachers who are enrolled in ELT education programs can improve themselves as they complete their learning journey. Again, as a teacher in an ELT program myself, I find this to be an outstanding idea if it can be implemented. This also speaks to the importance of AI in online as well as face-to-face English teaching.

As we continue to traverse the world in this literature review, an interesting article surfaced from Indonesia by Arini, Hidayat, Winarti, & Rosalina (2022), which touts Mobile Learning powered by AI. In their view, tutoring systems can be introduced which are fully personalized as well as autonomous for the learners and, cooperative learning can be advanced at the same time. Who, as a teacher or learner wouldn't want this? Since more than 60% of people in Indonesia apparently use mobile phones...where the smartphone users number higher than 100% of the people (How is that even possible?). The smartphone use of students along with AI is having, and will continue to have a powerful impact on the students and teachers of this area.

Not surprisingly, China also has it's technologically-trained eyes on the use of AI in the area of English Culture Intelligence. Meng-yue, Dan & June (2020) share their ideas of college English culture intelligence-system and teaching pattern. The Chinese are actually embedding the AI technology into all of their current teaching practices. They want their innovations in this area of teaching to reach depth and breadth of their information technology into the English cultural teaching, a new direction for them essentially. In a quote from this team of educators, they maintain: "College English teaching is supposed to cover both language acquisition and culture learning due to the close relationship between language and culture teaching as an indispensable part of college English courses." Their attitude is something which maintains that they have their finger on the pulse of the many different uses AI has to offer education.

Soni (2022), brings forth something noteworthy in his opinion of AI in the education field. He believes with the growth of the technology of AI, that it has highly impacted the equality of education in the current information-powered society. In this he feels that while ELT and AI have a relationship worthy of exploration, the teachers' role is not replaceable by the technology. We ELT teachers would definitely agree wholeheartedly with this opinion!

Perhaps one of the most interesting pieces of literature on this subject alluded to the challenges presented with regard to education policy implications of AI. The authors Pedro, et al., (2019) have outlined four challenges which are noteworthy, worth repeating, and should be understood by people in every education scenario considering the use of AI:

1. Ensuring inclusive and equitable use of AI in education
2. Leveraging AI to enhance education and learning
3. Promoting skills for jobs and life in the AI era
4. Safeguarding transparent and auditable use of education data

What makes these particular recommendations important? The first line item is giving advice that we must do what we can in education and also other fields who might use AI to ensure all people interested in working with the technology are given free-reign to do so. This isn't something that should be 'held back' or 'hidden' from possible researchers, students, and others who might easily be overlooked if they are thought of as less interested or have lower levels of education. Regardless of most normal circumstances, everyone should have an equal chance to participate in use, testing, evaluation, etc. Secondly, the leveraging of AI for enhancing education and learning purposes is the most logical and useful idea, because what else are we waiting for other than educators who will take the initiative and start integrating some AI opportunities for their students to experiment with, and to broaden their own perspectives by innovating in new ways? The third point is going to be far-reaching and highly important as AI starts working its way more deeply into the job markets. The skills people can learn beforehand will be very helpful especially in the tech industries which have popped up in larger numbers in recent years. This is a way to harness new practices that will possibly open up new jobs for those seeking them. Also, there is the promise of much more to come in the future, making life even more fruitful and sustainable, as well as enjoyable for those who are using the ideas being innovated and the products being created as a result. Finally, safeguarding data has always been a concern for those of us who work in education or scientific fields.

Data management will possibly, and hopefully be so much more secure with AI protocols, and of course there should be proper access to data for those who need to use it. Transparency covers a great deal of ground in the compilation and reporting areas, especially for further research within the companies who use it for forecasting, educational or archival purposes. As an addition to these points, researchers such as Esteves, et al (2019) who believe high school students should be taught some basic mechanisms of AI algorithms, point out the importance of implementing various coding scaffolds in order to inspire students to experiment with fundamental operations of AI. This way, students could begin to understand algorithmic behaviors by working on Scratch partial coding processes. Teaching this type of computational thinking makes perfect sense, and some students who are interested in AI would most likely enjoy and benefit from the learning process. Educating the next generation(s) about technological advances just seems to be an important consideration.

About the Types of ChatGPT AI Programs

Initially, for the purpose of this book chapter, I used the ChatGPT (version 1) which was released on November 30, 2022. This can be found at https://openai.com. OpenAI is the developer marketing the amazing tool. Later, I switched to a paid version (ChatGPT vers. 4) which charges a small fee for trial usage, then after the trial period of approximately 2 weeks, the program charges a user fee on a monthly basis (this could also be subject to change). I mention this because there are different versions of the online software provided by the OpenAI company. Why choose to pay for the software instead of using the free version? Simply, for my particular purposes as an academician in a university setting, I prefer to receive the most detailed, specific type of answers that are possible with artificial intelligence thus far. It can change, improve, and upgrade just like anything else available in the digital realm...for instance computer software developers of all types of programs release upgrades and improvements periodically, so do the AI program developers. The importance of AI is just recently emerging and becoming more widely known, and as more humans decide to use it and its endless resources, the chance of it upgrading and evolving more often seem highly likely.

The Quest for Questions

This is where we can begin going down that tutorial-esque road for those who want to read and share the knowledge…experimenting is the task at hand. Also, there are trials and errors experienced in here, so be ready for practically 'anything' to emerge once the questions start getting posed to the amazing robotic brain of ChatGPT platforms. Firstly, it occurred to me that I had never even heard of ChatGPT before a colleague of mine at the university I work at showed it to me. Needless to say I was amazed by the amount of sheer text it generated for me after I asked a fairly mundane question about something to do with research. A great deal depends on HOW you ask a question to the AI in ChatGPT.

The Good, the Bad, and the Right Questions

It can be recommend that it is best if you are trying out ChatGPT on your own, really do it on your own. In other words, experiment to your heart's content without interruption from others in your orbit. I say this because we all have different ways of formulating questions. One person's question could very well be another person's statement! I found out just how awful my own question formulations were in the beginning...AI wants one thing and one thing alone: It wants a 'straight up' question. Well, easy to say or think, but try writing one! Suddenly I was at a bit of a quandry,

Figure 1. Above query made using the free version of ChatGPT

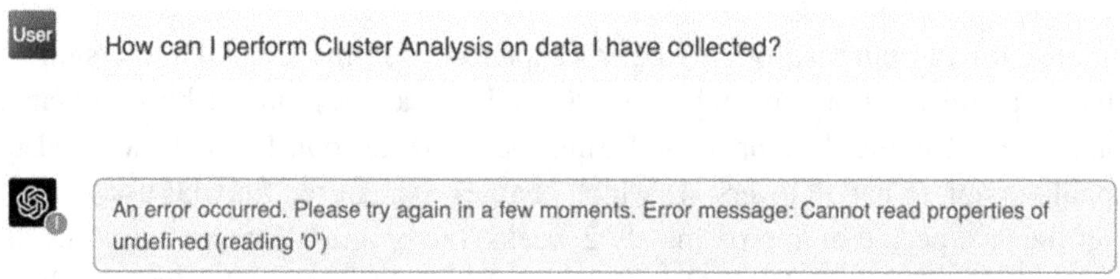

because my type of question could end up more like a short story all on its own. The best thing to do is to start simple and work your way up from there. I wish I had taken my own advice actually. But, as will be revealed, it soon becomes apparent just how clear, succinct, and to-the-point you should be. Otherwise some rather odd things will start popping up on the screen in front of you. Perhaps I should have named this article "How NOT TO ask AI a question!" Luckily, after a few tries I was getting much better results. It actually ends well, after some trial and error, that is.

Tips for Getting Started With Your Well-Formulated Questions to the AI in ChatGPT

1. Practice creating some sentences which ask what you want to know, but don't ask for the full Moon when you only want a 'sliver' of it, and vice-versa. (Examples to follow)
2. Don't 'panic' when the AI writes this in response to your query (just reword your sentence), or re-enter the text you asked for originally. This happens occasionally, so don't despair. The best way to deal with this if you had a lot of text is to make sure you downloaded the contents of your chat now and then just as a precaution. You don't want to lose the answers you received so far. In the exchange below, my question was either too ambiguous, or the processor encountered an error:
3. So, what is the difference between the free ChatGPT and the paid version? The chatbot enlightened me with the following answer:
   Incidentally, OpenAI offers both free and paid versions of ChatGPT. The key differences typically include the following:
   a. **Access Availability:** Free users might sometimes face usage restrictions during peak times due to high demand, while paid users usually have prioritized and uninterrupted access.
   b. **Waiting Times:** The paid version can also provide faster response times due to priority processing.

c. **Features and Updates:** Often, new features and other updates are first introduced to the subscribed users before they're available for the free version.

d. **Support:** Subscriptions may provide more customer support resources.

It is important to understand that the above-mentioned differences can vary and so it's best to check the official OpenAI platform for the most accurate and up-to-date information.

4. Sometimes if your question is more like a statement, you might still get a good answer. It is up to the user to think about and then formulate very specifically what they want to learn from AI before typing in the question. There are definitely some things to consider before typing in a question to the AI program, and my detailed suggestions for question formulation will follow in the next section.
5. **Reminder:** Save everything from your chat session by taking screen shots or copy/pasting down to your desktop, or you can download (export) the chat depending if you want 'everything' or not. Depending what you are getting for results, (good or bad), you should keep everything that is important to you because ChatGPT doesn't save your work. Remember this, it will save you a lot of time!

Question Types to Consider When Using AI

The following is my conversation with ChatGPT about formulating questions to ask AI. Instead of writing in third person about what I did, I opted to copy in the entire conversation between myself and the AI program. I thought the answer I was given was really clear and concise, and definitely something to keep in mind when I may possibly start using AI for some information to include in my English Language courses in the fall semester. (I generated this conversation with AI using the upgraded version of AI: ChatGPT-4).

User

ZM: Hello Chat

AI: *Hello! How can I assist you today?*

ZM: Can you compare for me the following: good questions vs bad questions for asking AI?

AI: *Absolutely, I'd be glad to help with that. Understanding how to interact effectively with AI can greatly improve the results you receive. Here's a comparison between good questions to ask an AI and less effective ones:*

Good Questions:

1. **Specific and focused:** A question like "How's the weather in New York today?" is specific because it is precise about the type and location of the weather sought. The more precise you are with your questions, the more accurate responses the AI can generate.
2. **Information-based:** Effective questions are often about established facts. For example, "What events led up to the French Revolution?" allows an AI to pull from a large amount of historical data.
3. **Contain keywords:** Utilizing keywords is important when asking a question. "What's the distance from New York to Los Angeles?" has the vital keywords such as 'distance', 'New York', and 'Los Angeles'.
4. **Direct and clear:** An unambiguous question like "Who wrote the play Romeo and Juliet?" is better because AI can interpret and generate a direct answer.
5. **Open to factual answer:** For example, "When was the Declaration of Independence signed?" is a good question because it has a definite, factual answer.

Less Effective Questions:

1. **Vague or overly broad:** For instance, "What's happening?" is quite vague, it could mean local news, world news, even personal agenda depending on the context.
2. **Dependent on personal opinions or emotions:** AI doesn't form personal beliefs or feelings. Thus, questions like "How do you feel about the latest Star Wars movie?" are hard for an AI to answer meaningfully.
3. **Assuming Knowledge:** Questions that assume prior knowledge about a conversation or individual, such as "Who won the game last night?" are less effective as AI lacks context-specific information.
4. **Relying on real-time updates:** While some AI systems are equipped to handle real-time data, many aren't. Questions like "How many people are at Times Square right now?" could be challenging.
5. **Requiring ethical judgments:** AI is not capable of moral or ethical reasoning, so questions like "Is it ethical to use animal products?" would be less effective, as they cannot draw well-informed conclusions about ethics.

AI: Remember, AI uses the information it's been provided or trained with to generate responses. It does not possess personal emotions, thoughts, or consciousness.

User

ZM: This is an answer such as I had expected. Thank you so much!

AI: *You're welcome! I'm glad the answer met your expectations. If you have any more questions about AI or anything else, feel free to ask. I'm here to help!*

Implications of AI Going Forward

On the ever-broadening subject of using AI for English Language and other teaching purposes, Luckin & Holmes (2016) voice strongly that instilling artificial intelligence in education, at its heart, has become a scientific goal to help make knowledge more explicit and precise. Sometimes referred to as the 'black box of learning,' they feel in the future that AI will give more finely-tuned understanding about how learning happens. Researchers such as these are certain that in the future, teachers will be prepared to offer their students different types of flexible educational scenarios which are personalized and both inclusive and engaging. Also importantly, Luckin & Holmes are adamant about the fact that AI is not something they advocate or see taking over the jobs of human teachers in the future. Rather, they believe human teachers will be living and working together with smart machines.

Research in many countries is emerging, so to keep up with these ideas, it would be quite interesting and possibly fruitful to invest in the use of AI in the ELT classroom. There are some great opportunities for research papers obviously, regarding how teachers have harnessed this technology and used it to create or augment interesting and engaging discussions and lessons. The students will see it from an entirely different angle perhaps, and use the opportunities supplied by the software to help them improve their language acquisition as far as writing and probably several other uses we haven't even thought of as yet. There are also the future emergence of higher technology, for instance, Hockley (2023) reminds us that we are currently using what is termed 'weak' AI. This means that we can expect 'stronger' AI to emerge over time. The field of ELT will most likely be onboard with the upgrades to come, and if it indicates anything to we practitioners of English language teaching, the signal for us to follow is one that we should instinctively take heed of by trying to learn as much as possible about AI. Why? Logically, we will need to start getting ready for the future changes and additions in our teaching posts. The most important action for those of us in education fields, especially teaching, is that we must educate ourselves firstly in the operations and ramifications of the AI communities. By this, I am referring to studying the papers and educational journals out there which have amassed a healthy amount of articles on the subject of using AI in educational pursuits including teaching, technology training, improving our own knowledge, individualization, and so on.

CONCLUSION

The AI program ChatGPT is helpful, fast, clear, orderly, and polite to a fault. One can assume that the scientists/programmers/creators of the AI interactive bots are educated and thoughtful people. Interestingly, when people first started hearing the rumblings of AI happening in the scientific or programming arenas, there was something akin to widespread panic happening amongst the less tech-savvy. Fears that AI would someday take over the world as we know it could be remotely possible...but highly unlikely! Historically speaking, people have always balked at new technology. In the 1980s and 90s, citizens were panicking over the new IBM and Macintosh computers which were sweeping the markets...some irrationally worrying that computers were going to "turn people into zombies", or cause "World War III." Suffice it to say, the once-panicky naysayers are now likely digitally writing their daily blogs and carrying on academic pursuits of their own, aided by nothing so sinister as a world-destroying computer. Similarly, the idea of Artificial Intelligence seemed very 'science-fiction' to many people when the first rumblings appeared a few years ago. Fear of the unknown is commonplace especially amongst those who are less interested in or motivated by innovation than others. Finally, perhaps unbeknownst to some, AI has actually been around since 1951, when the first successful program was written by a researcher, Christopher Strachey, in Manchester, UK.

No matter how many technological advances related to AI take place in the present and future, perhaps these quotes from the enigmatic technology mavens with their diverging viewpoints, Sergey Brin and Elon Musk, plus Geoffrey Hinton, will try to help us to keep things in perspective:

"The new spring in AI is the most significant development in computing in my lifetime. Every month, there are stunning new applications and transformative new techniques." - Sergey Brin, Co-founder of Google

"With artificial intelligence, we are summoning the demon." - Elon Musk, CEO of SpaceX and Tesla

"I console myself with the normal excuse: If I hadn't done it, somebody else would have," - Geoffrey Hinton, (a "father" of AI, one of those now sounding the alarm)

Another author, K.C. Cole (2023) Cautiously laments: "The wisest minds in AI have been urging us for years to stop being spectators. The future isn't written yet. We need to own it. Yet somehow we still fall for that freakily familiar argument: You can't stop; it's inevitable. The best we can do is watch it all unfold, hide under our desks."

Finally, one concluding thought...AI may have a lot of fans and an equal or even greater amount of opposers. However, in the grand scheme of things, upon first perusal, (in this case as with ChatGPT) it seems as though the benefits definitively outweigh the negatives. If it is used with the intention of improving education, with emphasis on the field of English Language Teaching (ELT), with its implications of being helpful and a great source of deeper learning opportunities for students and teachers...the positives could be endless and nothing short of 'awe inspiring.' This in mind, caution should always be used when experimenting with technology which is not well-known enough to make broad generalizations and baseless or uninformed assumptions about. Time will tell...and the rest, as they say, will probably make history.

REFERENCES

Ali, J., Shamsan, M. A. A., Hezam, T., & Mohammed, A. A. Q. (2023). Impact of ChatGPT on learning motivation: Teachers and students' voices. *Journal of English Studies in Arabia Felix*, *2*(1), 41–49. doi:10.56540/jesaf.v2i1.51

Arini, D. N., Hidayat, F., Winarti, A., & Rosalina, E. (2022). Artificial intelligence (AI)-based mobile learning in ELT for EFL learners: The implementation and learners' attitudes. *International Journal of Educational Studies in Social Sciences.*, *2*(2), 2. doi:10.53402/ijesss.v2i2.40

Cole, K.C. (2023). The Last Word on AI and the Atom Bomb. *Wired Magazine-Ideas*.

Estevez, J., Garate, G., & Grana, M. (2019). Gentle Introduction to Artificial Intelligence for High-School Students Using Scratch. *IEEE Access : Practical Innovations, Open Solutions*, *7*, 179027–179036. doi:10.1109/ACCESS.2019.2956136

Hockley, N. (2023). Artificial Intelligence in English Language Teaching: The Good, the Bad and the Ugly. *RELC Journal*, *0*(0). doi:10.1177/00336882231168504

Holmes, W., Bialik, M., & Fadel, C. (2019). *Artificial Intelligence in Education: Promises and Implications for Teaching and Learning*. The Center for Curriculum Redesign.

Li, X. (2017). *The construction of Intelligent Teaching Model based on Artificial Intelligence*. https://doi.org/ doi:10.3991/ijet.v12.i12.7963

Luckin, R., & Holmes, W. (2016) Intelligence Unleashed: An argument for AI in Education. *UCL Knowledge Lab*. London, UK. https://discovery.ucl.ac.uk/id/eprint/1475756

Meng-yue, C., Dan, L., & Jun, W. (2020). A study of college English culture Intelligence-Aided Teaching System and Teaching Pattern. *English Language Teaching, 13*(3). Published by Canadian Center of Science and Education.

Pedro, F., Subosa, M., Rivas, A., & Valverde, P. (2019). *Artificial Intelligence in Education: Challenges and opportunities for sustainable development.* UNESCO, 2019. https://unesdoc.unesco.org/ark:/48223/pf0000366994?pos

Sharadgah, T. A., & Sa'di, R. A. (2022). A Systematic Review of Research on the Use of Artificial Intelligence in English Language Teaching and Learning (2015-2021): What are the Current Effects? *Journal of Information Technology Education, 21*, 337–377. doi:10.28945/4999

Soni, M. (2022). Implications of Artificial Intelligence in English Language Teaching. *International Journal of English: Literature, Language & Skills.* www.ijells.com

Sun, Z., Anbarasan, M., & Kumar, D. P. (2020). Design of online intelligent English teaching platforms based on artificial intelligence techniques. *Computational Intelligence, 37*(3), 1166–1180. doi:10.1111/coin.12351

Chapter 7
Transforming the Language Teaching Experience in the Age of AI:
Ethical, Social, and Cultural Considerations in Implementing AI in Language Education

Reena Sudhakarrao Satpute
https://orcid.org/0000-0003-3309-4552
Faculty of Science & Technology, School of Allied Sciences, DMIHER, Wardha, India

ABSTRACT

Artificial intelligence is the simulation of human intelligence processes by machines, especially computer systems. Specific applications of AI include expert systems, natural language processing, and speech recognition and machine vision. Learning is the core feature that is connected to education. Actually, with AI, we are trying to force machines to imitate human behavior. Education increases the power of visualization and to differentiate between right and wrong. Education these days has become costly for the poor guardians. Education helps realize the real values in relation to social and cultural behavior so that one can become a decent person in nature and in society. The role of technology in modern education helps to look at the current trends and to solve the problems using artificial intelligence in education.

DOI: 10.4018/978-1-6684-9893-4.ch007

1. INTRODUCTION

The process of imparting or acquiring particular knowledge or skills is called education. The main determination of education is to provide the opportunity for acquiring knowledge and skills that will empower people to develop their full potential, and become successful members of society. The most general purpose of education is to gain knowledge and skills that will prepare individuals to lead productive and fulfilling lives. Alternatively we can define an education as a means to nurture a skilled labour force that drives economic growth and innovation. Discovery of artificial intelligence (AI) has added shine and stars to our traditional education system. Since AI plays very vibrant role in many applications, education sector is one of those fields. AI tools play a vital role in research and help to access the literature worldwide. AI can also provide the clarification to social challenges like diversity in nature, security, and privacy of the person. Apart from education, AI has made an impact in other fields like social media, communication, and technology. The ethical use of AI and data in learning, teaching, and assessment is based on four key ethical considerations, which include human agency, fairness, humanity, and justified choice. Artificial intelligence (AI) affects our lives every single day and brings with it both benefits and risks for all spheres of human activities, including education. Out of these risks, the most striking seems to be ethical issues of the use of AI, such as misuse of private data or surveillance of people's lives. Figure 1) shows Legal and Ethical considerations about AI.

"Success in creating AI would be the biggest event in human history. Unfortunately, it might also be the last, unless we learn how to avoid the risks."—Stephen Hawking

Figure 1. Legal and ethical considerations about AI

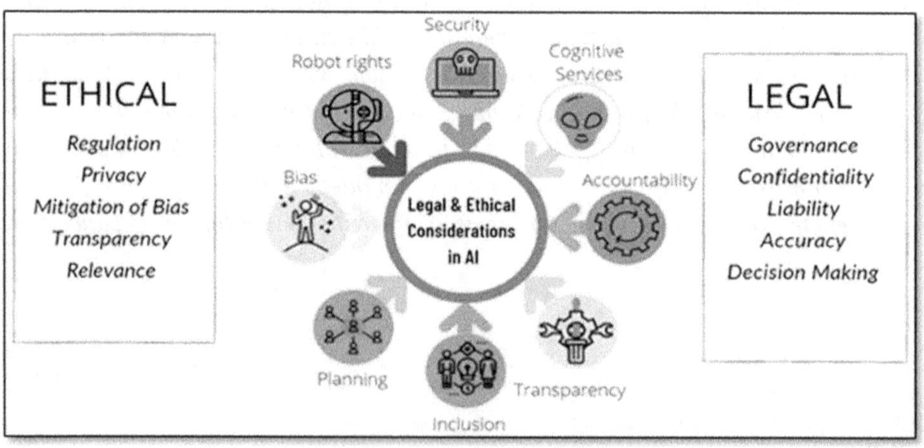

The legal and ethical issues that confront society due to Artificial Intelligence (AI) includes privacy and surveillance, bias or discrimination, and potentially the philosophical challenge is the role of human judgment. In addition, using, for instance, chatbots for developing foreign language speaking and writing skills, indicates another problem and that is monitoring students' ideas, which might consequently decrease student engagement in using this tool since s/he does not want to be tracked or even stalked for his/her ideas. This aspect is also related to students' autonomy, i.e., the ability to govern their own learning since the use of algorithms can make predictions about their actions based on provided information input by students.

2. ETHICAL CONSIDERATIONS IN IMPLEMENTING AI IN LANGUAGE EDUCATION

The ethical use of Artificial Intelligence and data in learning, teaching, and assessment is based on four key ethical considerations, which include privacy, bias & discrimination, autonomy and surveillance.

Figure 2. Ethical considerations about artificial intelligence

At present, artificial intelligence (AI) affects our lives every single day and brings with it both profit and loss for all spheres of human activities, including education as well. Out of these risks, the most striking seems to be ethical issues, such as misuse of private data or surveillance of people's lives. Currently, artificial intelligence (AI) is an indispensable part of people's lives and affects all fields of human activity. AI helps to enhance personalized learning and thus makes learning more student-centred in the form of using exploratory learning, collaborative, automatic assessment systems (Kite-Powell, 2017, Kannan & Munday, 2018) mobile game-based learning (Goksel-Canbek & Mutlu, 2016, Vaidya et al 2015) or conversational chat bots for developing foreign language skills (Tariq, 2014, Elwany & Shakeri, 2014, Shin, 2018).

Figure 2) Ethical considerations about Artificial Intelligence however, there are many aspects of the use of AI that need to be researched as the lack of data in these areas is still an issue, such as the impact of AI-driven tools to enhance human cognition or second language acquisition.

The facts we know are that the use of AI technology in classes not only contributes to students' learning but can also reduce in some respect a teacher's workload and can improve students' learning and their learning results (Fraenkel, Wallen, & Hyun, 2011, Maguire & Delahunt, 2017, Broussard, 2019).

However, fortunately, AI-driven technology cannot replace teachers' pedagogical work in any case (Davies et al, 2022) since AI technology does not know which methods suit best to meet students' learning needs. Despite the undeniable benefits that AI technology brings for both students and teachers, there are certain risks and threats associated with ethical issues and these risks should be carefully evaluated by both conceptual and empirical studies that will clearly delineate where the potential threats could be. One of these major risks is privacy or the lack of it. AI technology based on algorithmic applications intentionally collects human data from its users and they do not specifically know what kind of data and what quantities of them are collected. Although legislatively (in many countries or geographical/political regions, such as the European Union) user consent is required before using any AI technology, the user actually does not know what is happening with his/her data in the system (Day, 2021). Therefore, AI technology companies should minimize this data and aim to include only the information that can enhance student learning (Kite-Powell, 2017).

In addition, using, for instance, chat bots for developing foreign language speaking and writing skills, indicates another problem and that is monitoring students' ideas, which might consequently decrease student engagement in using this tool since s/he does not want to be tracked or even stalked for his/her ideas (Eynon & Young, 2021). This aspect is also related to students' autonomy, i.e., the ability to govern their own learning since the use of algorithms can make predictions about their actions based on provided information input by students (Gulson, Sellar, & Taylor-Webb, 2022). As Reiss (2022) puts it, within every AI system there are the fruits of countless hours of human thinking. Furthermore, another risk is connected with gender bias, for example, when using machine translation tools (Hooper, Livingstone, & Pothong, 2022) that could actually create an environment that is not considered fair from the gender perspective.

3. SOCIAL CONSIDERATIONS IN IMPLEMENTING AI IN LANGUAGE EDUCATION

Several people believe that to fully understand the inimitableness of a language, you must occupy with native speakers. However, AI models imitate real speech and conversations with rapidly increasing accuracy. A language learning chat bot can respond to messages with personalized, relevant information Privacy, security and deep fakes: Malicious AI could portend digital, physical, and political security. For example, people could train machines to hack victims in various ways, weaponized consumer drones, automate unfavourable campaigns for political reasons or implement

Figure 3. Social considerations about artificial intelligence

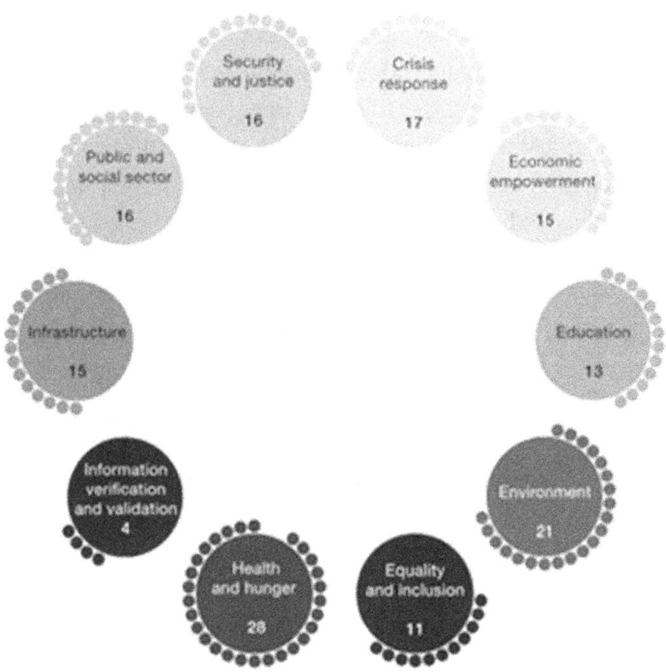

privacy-eliminating surveillance programmes (Holmes et al, 2022). There are many ethical challenges: Lack of transparency of AI tools: AI decisions are not always intelligible to humans. AI is not neutral: AI-based decisions are susceptible to inaccuracies, discriminatory outcomes, embedded or inserted bias. Surveillance practices for data gathering and privacy of court users (Hooper, Livingstone, & Pothong, 2022).

There are many ways that Google is using Artificial Intelligence to help solve society's challenges. The potential of AI to solve big problems is increasing all the time. Figure 3) shows Social considerations about Artificial Intelligence .In the past few years, AI and transformational innovations have become more important in confronting some of society's biggest challenges. Today, AI is helping countries and communities facing disease and natural disasters, and providing new opportunities for historically underserved groups. Here are seven ways AI is already making the world a better place:

4. CULTURAL CONSIDERATIONS IN IMPLEMENTING AI IN LANGUAGE EDUCATION

AI acts as a cultural catalyst and leads the charge into new analytical endeavours for employees, creating better learning opportunities. AI-powered tools monitor employees' performances and enhance their improvement areas. It also helps in foretelling future improvements by studying behavioural patterns. There are some cultural factors affecting language development are like Cultural Influences on Language Development, Language Diversity, Feedback Tone, Symbolic Emphasis, Guidance Style, Responsiveness. Figure 4) shows the Cultural considerations about Artificial Intelligence. The relationship between culture, language and literature cannot be overemphasized. Culture shows itself in everything-language, literature, performing arts, verbal and non-verbal behaviour of people, etc. We not only represent but also embody our respective cultures. AI-powered language learning platforms enable learners to work at their own pace, and emphasizing topics they have issues with, engaging them with the activities they're good at, appealing to their interests (Knox, 2020).

1) **Innovative AI Improves Competitiveness**: Employees who use AI to explore new ways of creating values can compete in better ways and are capable of facing challenges.
2) **Enhanced Decision-making Enhances Team Confidence**: Scaling the use of AI across organizations enhances decision-making, ultimately enhancing teams' confidence. This, in turn, inspires the team to clarify individual roles,

Figure 4. Cultural considerations about artificial intelligence

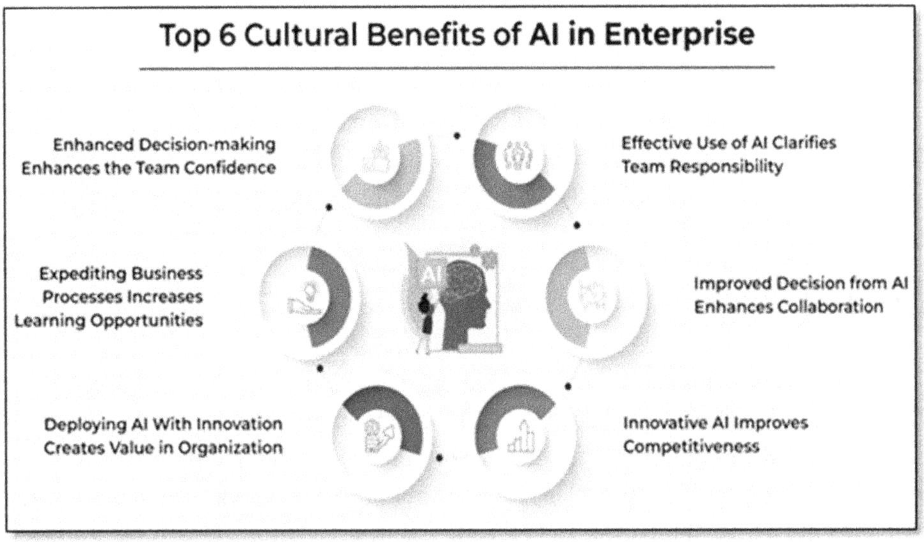

making it easier for teams to collaborate on a human level. The outcome is greater trust and doubled investment in AI.

3) **Business Processes & Financial Benefits Increases Learning Opportunities**: When AI leads to improving business processes, the technology creates further learning opportunities for employees and boosts employee morale. AI acts as a cultural catalyst and leads the charge into new analytical endeavours for employees, creating better learning opportunities. AI-powered tools monitor employees' performances and enhance their improvement areas. It also helps in foretelling future improvements by studying behavioural patterns (Koml, 2021).
4) **Deploying AI with Innovation Creates Value in Organization:** AI brings novel ways of working and boosts employee confidence which ultimately helps in translating business benefits into values like greater resilience and competitive advantage among employees. When employees are burdened with excessive work, the organization fails to leverage the potential of collaborative efforts. AI-powered tools assist leaders & managers with employee data and help them form better teams with complementing capabilities (McQuillan, 2022).
5) **Effective Use of AI Clarifies Team Responsibility:** AI-derived knowledge helps experts improve their skills (Nichols, & Garcia, 2022). For instance, in the healthcare industry, AI helps call centre employees handle customers effectively by studying the behaviour of customer queries and other parameters.

Enhanced operational efficiency defines team roles and responsibilities clearly (Nichols, & Garcia, 2022).

6) **Improved Decision from AI Enhances Collaboration:** The team's decision quality enhances collaboration. The new age of AI communication has enhanced cooperation for the remote workforce in diverse locations with different time zones, (Perrotta, Selwyn, & Ewin, 2022). Digital collaboration in today's remote work culture has enhanced employees' desire for improved connectivity.

5. CONCLUSION

The purpose of this chapter is to enlighten about the various considerations like social, ethical and cultural when we come across implementation of language education using Artificial Intelligence. The current reviews is to identify the uses of AI in language teaching and learning. This review has found that AI is a system that is used to understand natural human speech, able to incorporate flipped learning approach for teaching and learning of language, make learners become more competence and productive and able to assess human speech. Overall, the review strengthens the idea that AI is paramount in the language teaching and learning due to its various benefits.

REFERENCES

Broussard, M. (2019). *Artificial Unintelligence: How Computers Misunderstand the World*. MIT Press.

Davies, H., Eynon, R., Komljenovic, J., & Williamson, B. (2022). Investigating the financial power brokers behind EdTech. In S. Livingstone, & K. Pothong (Eds.), Education Data Futures: Critical, regulatory and practical reflections. London:5Rights Foundation.

Day, E. (2021). *Governance of data for children's learning in UK state schools*. London: 5Rights Foundation.

Elwany E, Shakeri S. (2014) Enhancing Cortana User Experience Using Machine Learning. *Recall, 55*(54.61), 24-24.

Eynon, R., & Young, E. (2021). Methodology, Legend, and Rhetoric: The Constructions of AI by Academia, Industry, and policy groups for lifelong learning. *Science, Technology & Human Values*, *46*(1), 166–191. doi:10.1177/0162243920906475

Fraenkel, J. R., Wallen, N. E., & Hyun, H. H. (2011). *How to design and evaluate research in education.* McGraw-Hill.

Goksel-Canbek, N., & Mutlu, M. E. (2016). in Errol Jayawardene (2015). On the track of Artificial Intelligence: Learning with Intelligent Personal Assistants. *International Journal of Human Sciences, 13*(1), 592–601. doi:10.14687/ijhs.v13i1.3549

Gulson, K. N., Sellar, S., & Taylor-Webb, P. (2022). *Algorithms of Education: How datafication and artificial intelligence shape policy.* University of Minnesota Press. doi:10.5749/9781452968797

Holmes, W., Persson, J., Chounta, I. J., Wasson, B., & Dimitrova, V. (2022). *Artificial intelligence and education: A critical view through the lens of human rights, democracy and rule of law.*

Hooper, L., Livingstone, S., & Pothong, K. (2022). Problems with data governance in UK schools: The cases of Google Classroom and ClassDojo. London: Digital Futures Commission. 5Rights Foundation.

Kannan, J., & Munday, P. (2018). New Trends in Second Language Learning and Teaching through the lens of ICT, Networked Learning, and Artificial Intelligence. In *Fernandez Juncal C.* Hernández. doi:10.5209/CLAC.62495

Kite-Powell, J. (2017). The Role of Artificial Intelligence and Language. *Forbes.* https://www.forbes.com/sites/jenniferhicks/2017/12/30/the-role-of-artificial-intelligence-and- language/

Knox, J. (2020). Artificial intelligence and education in China. *Learning, Media and Technology, 45*(3), 298–311. doi:10.1080/17439884.2020.1754236

Koml, J. (2021). The rise of education rentiers: Digital platforms, digital data and rents. *Learning, Media and Technology, 46*(3), 320–332.

Maguire, M., & Delahunt, B. (2017). Doing a thematic analysis: A practical, step-by-step guide for learning and teaching scholars. AISHE-J. *The All Ireland Journal of Teaching and Learning in Higher Education, 9*(3), 3351–33514.

McQuillan, D. (2022). *Resisting AI: An Anti-Fascist Approach to Artificial Intelligence.* Bristol University Press.

Muñoz, N. (Ed.). Vías de transformación en la enseñanza de lenguas con mediación tecnológica. Círculo de Lingüística Aplicada a la Comunicación 76, 13-30. doi:10.5209/CLAC.62495

Nichols, T. P., & Garcia, A. (2022). Platform studies in Education. *Harvard Educational Review*, *92*(2), 209–230. doi:10.17763/1943-5045-92.2.209

Perrotta, C., Selwyn, N., & Ewin, C. (2022). *Artificial intelligence and the affective labour of understanding: The intimate moderation of a language model*. New Media & Society. . doi:10.1177/14614448221075296

Shin, M. H. (2018). How to use artificial intelligence in the English language learning classroom. *Indian Journal of Public Health Research & Development*, *9*(9), 557–561. doi:10.5958/0976-5506.2018.01058.6

Tariq, K. (2014) *Siri, Google Now, Cortana: The Ultimate Digital Voice Assistant?* WCCFTech.com. http://wccftech.com/digital-voice-assistant/#ixzz3lcDQvCrq

Vaidya, T., Zhang, Y., Sherr, M., & Shields, C. (2015, August). Cocaine noodles: exploiting the gap between human and machine speech recognition. In *Proceedings of the 9th USENIX Conference.*

Chapter 8
From Digital Literacy to AI Literacy in Language Teaching:
Embracing the Artificial Intelligence Age

Galip Kartal
https://orcid.org/0000-0003-4656-2108
Necmettin Erbakan University, Turkey

ABSTRACT

The overarching goal of this chapter is to provide language educators and researchers with valuable insights and practical guidance for navigating the rapidly changing landscape of AI in education. This chapter investigates the transition from digital literacy to AI literacy in language teaching, a shift necessitated by the rapid evolution of AI-assisted technologies. Beginning with a comprehensive overview of digital literacy in the context of language teaching, the chapter explores the associated pedagogical practices, benefits, and challenges. The discussion then moves to the concept of AI literacy, an emerging necessity in education. The chapter delves into the implications of integrating AI technologies into language teaching and learning, stressing the potential of AI to revolutionize language education. The chapter encourages further research on the long-term impacts of AI literacy on language learning outcomes and the effectiveness of different strategies for AI literacy integration.

INTRODUCTION

In the age of AI, the concept of digital literacy is evolving to address the challenges posed by data-driven automated technologies. Previously, digital literacy focused on equipping individuals with skills to use technology effectively, but now the emphasis

DOI: 10.4018/978-1-6684-9893-4.ch008

is shifting towards understanding and navigating algorithmic systems. This new form of literacy, termed "AI literacy," encompasses various aspects such as working with algorithmic systems, finding ways to bypass them, and recognizing when human intervention is necessary. Developing AI literacy is crucial for contemporary citizenship and to prevent digital inequality and disadvantage.

AI literacy requires a collaborative approach between families, educators, and young people themselves, as it is a complex and ever-changing field. Even experts in computer science may struggle to comprehend the inner workings of these systems. Therefore, it is important for adults and young people to engage in co-learning, acknowledging that there is much to be learned together. Several initiatives and projects are already underway to cultivate algorithmic awareness, including the creation of toolkits and activities that enable young people to explore and understand the influence of algorithms in their digital experiences.

By fostering AI literacy, individuals can not only navigate digital systems more effectively but also become actively involved in shaping their digital futures. This awareness may lead to direct democratic participation in addressing algorithmic injustices and promoting algorithmic activism. Recent instances of student protests against automated exam grading and algorithmic targeting of body image and mental health messages exemplify the potential impact of algorithmic literacy in the lives of young people. As we look to the future, the DigiGen community should continue contemplating and advancing these topics.

Digital literacy, broadly defined as the ability to use digital technologies effectively for learning and communication, has become increasingly important in language teaching and learning in the 21st-century classroom (Kaeophanuek et al., 2019; Reddy et al., 2020). This concept embodies more than just the basic technical skills required to use digital tools; it also encompasses the ability to critically evaluate digital information, create digital content, and communicate effectively in online environments (Lankshear & Knobel, 2006; Polizzi, 2020). Language educators have leveraged this paradigm to facilitate collaborative learning, improve students' language skills, and prepare them for the global digital society.

In a review article on literacy types, Sur (2022) identified various literacies related to technology, highlighting the importance of acquiring skills in the digital era. These literacies encompass a range of domains such as network/web/internet/hyper literacy, computer literacy, information and communication technology (ICT) literacy, digital literacy, digital assessment literacy, digital media literacy, digital advertising literacy, e-literacy, electronic literacy, news literacy, news media literacy, software literacy, video game literacy, data literacy, agricultural literacy, and advertising literacy. Each of these literacies represents a distinct set of knowledge and competencies that individuals need to navigate and effectively engage with technology and its associated platforms. Developing proficiency in these literacies enables individuals to critically evaluate information, utilize digital tools and resources, understand and interpret media messages, comprehend and evaluate software applications, engage in digital communication, and make informed decisions in the digital landscape. These literacies play a crucial role in empowering individuals to actively participate in the digital society, adapt to technological advancements, and harness the potential of technology for personal and professional growth. Thus, fostering these literacies is vital for promoting digital citizenship and ensuring that individuals are equipped with the necessary skills to thrive in the rapidly evolving technological landscape.

As we navigate the third decade of the 21st century, we find ourselves on the cusp of a new technological revolution - the AI age. AI, defined as the capability of a machine to imitate intelligent human behavior is poised to radically reshape educational landscapes, including language teaching and learning. As AI technologies become more sophisticated and pervasive, there is an increasing need for educators and learners to develop AI literacy, a new form of literacy that is the ability to understand and use artificial intelligence (AI) technologies. It includes knowledge of the history and development of AI, the different types of AI, and the ethical implications of AI. AI literacy is essential for citizens in the 21st century, as AI is becoming increasingly pervasive in our lives. Amodei et al. (2016) also argue that AI literacy is essential for students to understand the world around them and to prepare for the jobs of the future.

AI literacy entails not only understanding how AI technologies work but also being able to use these technologies effectively and ethically in learning contexts. In the context of language teaching, AI literacy could involve using AI-powered language learning apps, interpreting the feedback provided by AI grading systems, and discussing the ethical implications of using AI in language assessment. Despite the growing relevance of AI literacy, research on this concept in language education is still in its infancy, and there is a lack of practical guidance for educators on how to integrate AI literacy into their teaching practice (Zawacki-Richter et al., 2019).

This chapter aims to fill this gap by providing a comprehensive overview of the transition from digital literacy to AI literacy in language teaching. It will first review the current state of digital literacy in this field, highlighting its importance and its limitations in the face of growing AI advancements. It will then introduce the concept of AI literacy, discussing its relevance in the rapidly changing educational landscape and exploring its potential to revolutionize language education. Subsequent sections will propose strategies for integrating AI literacy into language teaching and present case studies of exemplary models of AI literacy integration. Finally, the chapter will offer conclusions and recommendations for future research and practice in this burgeoning field.

The shift from digital literacy to AI literacy represents a new frontier in language teaching, one that presents both opportunities and challenges for educators. By embracing the AI age and fostering AI literacy in their classrooms, language educators can prepare their students for the future and make language learning more engaging, personalized, and effective. This chapter is intended to serve as a catalyst for this transformative process, equipping educators and researchers with the knowledge and tools they need to navigate the rapidly changing landscape of AI in education.

REVIEW OF THE RELATED LITERATURE

Historical Perspectives on AI in Language Teaching

The term "artificial intelligence" was originally introduced by John McCarthy in 1956 (Russsel & Norvig, 2010). According to Baker and Smith (2019), AI encompasses a range of technologies in which computers carry out cognitive tasks associated with human minds, particularly learning and problem-solving. AI is a broad concept that encompasses various analytical methods, including machine learning, neural networks, and deep learning (Aggarwal, 2018). Machine learning involves computer algorithms learning from data to make decisions without explicit programming (Popenici & Kerr, 2017).

The use of AI in language teaching has a rich and diverse history, stretching back to the 1960s when researchers started exploring the possibilities of computer-based systems for language learning. These early attempts at AI-powered language learning were limited in their capabilities but laid the groundwork for the more sophisticated tools available today. A significant milestone in the history of AI in language teaching was the emergence of Natural Language Processing (NLP) in the 1970s, a field of computer science that deals with the interaction between computers and human language. NLP techniques have since been applied to develop a wide array of AI-powered language learning tools, including machine translation systems, grammar checkers, speech recognition systems, and chatbots (Chen et al., 2013).

There has been a growing interest in using AI for language teaching, driven by factors such as advancements in computer technology and the recognition of AI's potential benefits in language learning (Yanhua, 2020). Among the most promising applications of AI in language teaching is adaptive learning, which uses AI to customize instruction to suit the individual needs of each learner. By monitoring student progress and identifying areas that require additional support, adaptive learning systems can provide personalized feedback and instruction, enhancing the learning experience (Smutny &Schreiberova, 2020).

Another exciting avenue for AI in language teaching lies in the use of virtual reality (VR) and augmented reality (AR). VR and AR technologies create immersive language learning environments, offering students realistic and interactive opportunities to practice their language skills (Kartal & Balçıkanlı, 2018). In recent years, researchers and educators have been exploring the possibilities of incorporating VR and AR into language teaching to create rich and dynamic learning environments. These technologies offer unique opportunities for students to practice their language skills in realistic and contextually relevant scenarios, thus enhancing their language proficiency (Chang et al., 2020). VR allows learners to enter simulated environments that closely mimic real-life situations, such as ordering food at a restaurant, traveling to a foreign country, or engaging in a business negotiation with international partners. Within these virtual settings, students can practice conversational skills, expand their vocabulary, and develop their language fluency through interactive and authentic interactions (Chen & Hsu, 2020).

On the other hand, AR supplements the real-world environment with virtual elements, enabling learners to interact with digital content while remaining immersed in their physical surroundings. For language learners, AR applications can overlay language prompts, translations, and interactive exercises onto real-world objects, making language learning more contextualized and practical (Huang et al., 2021b). Moreover, VR and AR can facilitate collaborative language learning experiences. Students can engage in role-playing activities, language games, and cultural simulations together, fostering communication and teamwork among learners, and promoting a sense of shared language learning community (Huang et al., 2021b). The integration of AI into VR and AR language learning systems further enhances their effectiveness. AI-powered adaptive learning algorithms can track students' progress, identify areas of improvement, and provide personalized feedback and content, tailoring the language learning experience to each individual's needs (Vesin et al., 2018).

While AI in language teaching is still in its early stages, it holds the potential to revolutionize language education in numerous ways. As AI technology continues to advance, we can expect even more innovative and effective applications to support language learning (Kartal, 2023). For example, AI could be used to develop more sophisticated chatbots that can provide students with more personalized and engaging feedback. AI could also be used to create immersive language learning experiences that are more realistic and engaging than ever before. The potential of AI in language teaching is vast, and it is only a matter of time before we see even more innovative and effective applications of this technology.

Digital Literacy in Language Teaching: Current Practices and Challenges

Over the past decade, there has been increasing attention given to the educational needs of a generation of young people who were born into a world dominated by computers and mobile technology. This focus arises from the realization that we must tackle the challenges posed by an ever more digitalized and globalized society. Among the various evolving professional competencies, digital competence stands out as a crucial skill, particularly in the context of lifelong learning as advocated by the PISA framework proposed by the OECD.

Over the past two decades, digital literacy has emerged as a critical competency in language teaching and learning (Kern et al., 2016). In this context, digital literacy involves a spectrum of skills, including the ability to use digital tools for language learning, evaluate digital resources for language teaching, create digital language learning content, and participate in online language learning communities (Hockly, 2012). The four-part subdivision of digital literacies by Hockly (2012) includes language-based literacies, information-based literacies, connection-based literacies, and (re-)design-based literacies. Language-based literacies encompass not only traditional reading and writing transferred to the digital environment but also proficiency in new online genres like blogs, wikis, and tweets (Belshaw, 2011). On the other hand, information-based literacies involve the ability to navigate and make sense of digital information using tools like search engines (e.g., Google) and tagging digital resources. Furthermore, Eshet-Alkalai and Chajut (2009) highlight the importance of connection-based literacies, which encompass skills related to social media and networking. These literacies are becoming increasingly relevant in our digitally interconnected world.

The integration of digital tools and resources into language instruction has brought significant benefits. For example, digital technologies can enhance student engagement and motivation by offering interactive and multimedia learning experiences (Kartal, 2023). They also facilitate collaborative learning by enabling students to communicate and collaborate with peers and educators in virtual environments (Kartal & Balçıkanlı, 2018). Moreover, digital tools can provide personalized learning opportunities by allowing students to learn at their own pace, according to their own needs and interests (Kartal, 2023).

Despite these benefits, integrating digital technologies into language instruction is not without challenges. One of the primary challenges lies in the digital divide, which refers to the gap between those who have access to digital technologies and those who do not (Warschauer, 2004). This divide can create disparities in language learning opportunities and outcomes, particularly for students in underserved communities. Another challenge relates to the lack of professional development opportunities for language educators in the area of digital literacy (Kessler, 2018). Without adequate training, educators may struggle to effectively integrate digital technologies into their teaching practice and to foster digital literacy among their students.

The literature on digital literacy in language teaching also reveals some limitations in the face of growing advancements in AI technologies. While digital literacy enables learners and educators to use and understand digital tools, it does not necessarily equip them with the skills needed to understand and use AI technologies (Zawacki-Richter et al., 2019). Moreover, digital literacy practices may not sufficiently address the ethical considerations associated with AI, such as data privacy and algorithmic bias (Buckingham, 2015). As AI becomes increasingly integrated into language education, these limitations of digital literacy underscore the need for a new form of literacy – AI literacy.

The Emergence of AI Literacy: A Paradigm Shift in Education

In the face of the Fourth Industrial Revolution marked by advancements in AI, a new form of literacy, termed as AI literacy, has begun to emerge as a critical competency in education (Rainie & Anderson, 2017). This new literacy extends beyond the scope of digital literacy, combining an understanding of AI principles, the ability to use AI tools effectively, and the ethical implications of AI use in educational contexts (Marr, 2018). AI literacy can be seen as a paradigm shift, urging educators to go beyond digital tools and embrace intelligent technologies that can mimic human cognition (Russell & Norvig, 2010).

AI technologies have been integrated into language teaching and learning in myriad ways. AI-based language learning applications like Duolingo and Babbel utilize machine learning algorithms to offer personalized and adaptive learning experiences (Loewen et al, 2019; Short, 2021). Meanwhile, AI-powered assessment tools are being used to provide instant feedback on language learners' proficiency, facilitating differentiated instruction (Diari et al., 2023). AI chatbots are also becoming increasingly common, helping learners to practice conversation in a safe, non-judgmental environment (Kartal, 2023).

These developments in AI integration in language teaching have far-reaching implications for educators, learners, and educational institutions. For educators, AI literacy means being competent in using AI tools for instruction, understanding how these tools work, and addressing ethical considerations like privacy and bias in AI technologies (Rainie & Anderson, 2017). For learners, AI literacy is about harnessing AI tools for self-directed learning, interpreting feedback from AI systems, and understanding the societal implications of AI. For educational institutions, promoting AI literacy requires investing in infrastructure, providing professional development opportunities for teachers, and revising curricula to include AI education (Zhao et al., 2022). The potential of AI to revolutionize language education is immense. It holds promise for personalized, adaptive, and immersive learning experiences that can make language learning more engaging and effective (Kartal, 2023). However, realizing this vision requires a commitment to fostering AI literacy in the classroom. As we navigate the era of AI, developing AI literacy is not just a nice-to-have; it's a must-have skill for educators and learners alike.

Bridging the Gap: Strategies for Integrating AI Literacy Into Language Teaching

Addressing the transition from digital literacy to AI literacy in language teaching necessitates the development of specific strategies. These strategies need to assist educators in both enhancing their own AI literacy and fostering it in their students, thereby bridging the literacy gap.

To begin with, it is vital for educators to first develop their own understanding of AI. They should engage in professional learning opportunities focusing on AI, its principles, applications in language teaching, and ethical implications (Cardona et al., 2023). Online courses, webinars, and professional networks can serve as valuable resources for educators seeking to build their AI knowledge.

To cultivate AI literacy among students, educators can integrate AI tools into their teaching in a purposeful way. For example, they can utilize AI-powered chatbots to facilitate conversational practice. Importantly, the use of these tools should not be treated as an end in itself but as a means to teach about AI. While using AI tools, educators can encourage students to question how these tools work, interpret the data generated by these tools, and discuss the ethical implications of AI use.

Critical thinking skills are also paramount in AI literacy. As AI technologies are increasingly integrated into language teaching and learning, educators should emphasize critical evaluation of these tools and the data they generate. Previous research has shown that AI can facilitate more effective and engaging learning processes (Crompton et al., 2023; Huang et al., 2021a) and has the potential to promote innovative teaching approaches (Zawacki-Richter et al., 2019). Classroom discussions can focus on the reliability of AI-driven feedback, the accuracy of machine translations, and the potential for bias in AI algorithms.

In addition to this, ethical considerations in the use of AI tools should form a significant part of AI literacy education. This might include discussions about data privacy, transparency, and the potential consequences of relying heavily on AI for learning. These discussions can be integrated into the language curriculum in relevant and meaningful ways.

Teacher training and professional development play a critical role in equipping language educators with the necessary skills and knowledge to navigate the AI-driven landscape. Institutions should offer professional development programs focusing on AI and its applications in language teaching. Moreover, pre-service teacher education programs should also incorporate AI education to prepare future educators for the AI age. researchers advocating for the development of thinking skills and creativity in education (Tias et al., 2022). The strategies proposed by study participants, such as cross-referencing AI-generated content with other sources, limiting its use, and engaging in discussions with peers and instructors, underscore the significance of fostering critical thinking and creativity within the context of AI-enhanced education.

Studies on AI Literacy in Education

In the rapidly evolving landscape of education, one topic has emerged as a central focus: AI literacy. With the ever-expanding influence of artificial intelligence (AI) in various aspects of our lives, understanding and navigating this technology has become more crucial than ever before. A myriad of studies have delved into the multifaceted concept of AI literacy, aiming to equip individuals with the knowledge, skills, and ethical perspectives necessary to thrive in the AI-driven world.

Ng et al. (2021) explored the concept of AI literacy and proposes four aspects for fostering it. The authors conducted a systematic review of literature on AI literacy and used the constant comparative method to analyze the data. The findings suggest that AI literacy is a multidimensional concept that includes technical, social, ethical, and critical aspects. The first aspect of AI literacy is "know and understand AI," which involves understanding the technical concepts and principles of AI, such as machine learning, neural networks, and natural language processing. This aspect also includes understanding the potential benefits and limitations of AI and its impact on society. The second aspect is "use and apply AI," which involves applying AI concepts and applications in everyday life and different contexts. This aspect includes using AI tools and technologies to solve problems, automate tasks, and enhance decision-making. The third aspect is "evaluate and create AI," which involves analyzing, evaluating, and creating AI systems and applications. This aspect includes assessing the ethical and social implications of AI and developing AI solutions that are fair, transparent, and accountable. The fourth aspect is "AI literacy assessment," which involves evaluating students' AI literacy skills and competencies. This aspect includes developing valid and reliable assessment tools and methods that measure students' knowledge, skills, and attitudes related to AI literacy. The authors argue that fostering AI literacy is crucial for individuals to participate in the digital society and for society to benefit from the potential of AI. The study provides insights for educators, policymakers, and researchers to develop strategies for promoting AI literacy.

A study by Lee et al. (2021) described an AI summer workshop called "Developing AI Literacy" (DAILy) designed to prepare middle school students to become informed citizens and critical consumers of AI technology. The workshop featured a 30-hour curriculum grounded in literature on child development, ethics education, and career development. The participants were students between the ages of 10 and 14, with 87% from underrepresented groups in STEM and Computing. The study reported on the design and implementation of the workshop, including the online curriculum and synchronous online workshop sessions, and provides preliminary findings on student outcomes. The authors reflected on the successes and lessons learned in terms of supporting students' engagement and conceptual learning of AI, shifting attitudes toward AI, and fostering conceptions of future selves as AI-enabled workers.

In a recent comprehensive review of AI literacy in K-12 education conducted by Casal-Otero (2023), two distinct categories of AI literacy approaches were identified. The first category comprises learning experiences that focus on the acquisition of technical, conceptual, and applied skills within specific domains of interest. Meanwhile, the second category centers on the development of models that frame AI literacy proposals. While the review revealed considerable efforts in implementing AI literacy in educational settings, it also highlighted some limitations. Notably, existing learning experiences in schools have primarily emphasized technical and applied skills with a narrow focus on specific domains, often neglecting rigorous assessments of student learning outcomes. In contrast, countries like the United States and China have taken a more comprehensive and ambitious approach to AI literacy implementation, encompassing a broader scope of subjects. Nevertheless, the review emphasizes the need to thoroughly evaluate these initiatives through comprehensive learning experiences that include an analysis of learning outcomes. Based on its findings, the review suggests that AI literacy should be integrated into the school curriculum using an interdisciplinary and competency-based approach. Rather than introducing a new AI-specific subject, AI literacy should build upon the existing competencies and content within disciplinary subjects. This interdisciplinary approach allows AI education to transcend disciplinary boundaries and embrace a global, practical, and active learning methodology, where project-based and contextualized work plays a pivotal role. Additionally, the review underscores the potential of AI literacy to enhance learning in various curricular subjects, expanding students' horizons and fostering a deeper understanding of AI's implications in diverse fields. Lastly, the review highlights the importance of prioritizing the competency of teachers, encouraging their active participation in co-designing didactic proposals in collaboration with pedagogues and AI experts.

Future Directions and Challenges in AI Literacy

The future of AI literacy in language teaching is bright. As AI technology continues to develop, we can expect to see even more innovative and effective ways to use AI to support language learning. Some potential future directions for AI literacy in language teaching include:

- *The development of more personalized and adaptive learning experiences.* AI can be used to track student progress and preferences, and to provide personalized feedback and instruction. This can help students learn more effectively and efficiently.
- *The creation of more engaging and immersive language learning environments.* AI can be used to create virtual worlds and simulations that allow students to practice their language skills in a realistic and interactive way. This can make language learning more fun and engaging.
- *The development of new tools for language assessment.* AI can be used to develop more accurate and reliable tools for assessing language proficiency. This can help teachers to track student progress and to identify areas where students need additional support.

However, there are also some potential challenges and barriers to the widespread adoption of AI in language teaching. These challenges include:

- *The cost of AI technology.* AI tools and applications can be expensive, which may limit their availability to schools and other educational institutions.
- *The lack of technical expertise.* Many teachers may not have the technical expertise to use AI effectively in the classroom.
- *The potential for bias in AI systems.* AI systems can be biased if they are trained on data that is not representative of the population of learners. This can lead to unfair or inaccurate assessment of student performance.

To address these challenges, it will be important to develop more affordable and accessible AI tools and applications. It will also be important to provide teachers with training on how to use AI effectively in the classroom. Additionally, research is needed to address the potential for bias in AI systems.

Areas for Future Research and Collaboration

There are many areas for future research and collaboration in AI literacy education. Some of these areas include:

- The development of new AI-powered tools and applications for language learning.
- The study of the effects of AI on language learning outcomes.
- The development of best practices for integrating AI into language teaching.
- The training of teachers on how to use AI effectively in the classroom.
- The study of the potential for bias in AI systems.

By addressing these challenges and continuing to research and develop new AI-powered tools and applications, we can help to ensure that AI literacy becomes an essential part of language teaching in the future.

CONCLUSION

In this chapter, we have navigated the shifting landscape of language teaching, from the era of digital literacy to the emerging age of AI literacy. This discussion has drawn insights from a range of scholarly literature, the analysis of AI technologies, and illustrative case studies. The examination of current practices and challenges in digital literacy in language teaching emphasized the significant role of digital technologies in shaping 21st-century language instruction (Hockly, 2012). Despite its many benefits, digital literacy has limitations, particularly in the face of rapid advancements in AI technologies.

The analysis of AI literacy revealed a significant paradigm shift in education. AI technologies have already found their way into language teaching and learning, with implications for educators, learners, and educational institutions alike (Rainie & Anderson, 2017). The potential of AI to revolutionize language education is significant, emphasizing the need for AI literacy in the classroom. In transitioning from digital literacy to AI literacy, educators must adopt a proactive stance, seeking to develop their own understanding of AI and fostering it among their students. Teacher training and professional development, focusing on AI and its implications, will play a critical role in this process.

In conclusion, AI has the potential to transform language education dramatically. While challenges exist, they are outweighed by the numerous opportunities that AI presents. Educators must therefore embrace these opportunities, integrating AI literacy into language teaching to prepare learners for the future. Further research is recommended, particularly focusing on the long-term impact of AI literacy on language learning outcomes and the effectiveness of different strategies for integrating AI literacy into language teaching.

REFERENCES

Aggarwal, C. C. (2018). Neural networks and deep learning. *Springer, 10*, 978-3. doi:10.1007/978-3-319-94463-0

Amodei, D., Olah, C., Steinhardt, J., Christiano, P., Schulman, J., & Mané, D. (2016). *Concrete problems. in AI safety*. arXiv preprint arXiv:1606.06565.

Baker, T., & Smith, L. (2019). *Educ-AI-tion rebooted? Exploring the future of artificial intelligence in schools and colleges.* Nesta. https://media.nesta.org.uk/documents/Future_of_AI_and_education_v5_WEB.pdf

Belshaw, D. (2011). *What is digital literacy? A pragmatic investigation.* [Unpublished Ed.D thesis. Durham University]. http://neverendingthesis.com

Buckingham, D. (2015). Defining digital literacy: What do young people need to know about digital media? *Nordic Journal of Digital Literacy, 10*(2), 88–101. doi:10.18261/ISSN1891-943X-2015-Jubileumsnummer-03

Cardona, M. A., Rodríguez, R. J., & Ishmael, K. (2023). *Artificial intelligence and the future of teaching and learning: Insights and recommendations.* W2. https://www2.ed.gov/documents/ai-report/ai-report.pdf

Casal-Otero, L., Catala, A., Fernández-Morante, C., Taboada, M., Cebreiro, B., & Barro, S. (2023). AI literacy in K-12: A systematic literature review. *International Journal of STEM Education, 10*(1), 29. doi:10.118640594-023-00418-7

Chang, Y., Chen, C., & Liao, C. (2020). Enhancing English-learning performance through a simulation classroom for EFL students using augmented reality—A Junior High School Case Study. *Applied Sciences (Basel, Switzerland), 10*(21), 7854. doi:10.3390/app10217854

Chen, L., & Tokuda, N. (2013). New template-template-enhanced ICALL system for a second language composition course. *CALICO Journal, 20*(3), 561–578. doi:10.1558/cj.v20i3.561-578

Crompton, H., Bernacki, M., & Greene, J. A. (2020). Psychological foundations of emerging technologies for teaching and learning in higher education. *Current Opinion in Psychology, 36*, 101–105. doi:10.1016/j.copsyc.2020.04.011 PMID:32604064

Diari, K., Suwarna, S., & Suweta, I. (2023). Mobile technology-mediated language learning: A quantitative study to unravel language learners' achievement and autonomy. *World Journal of English Language, 5*(13), 354. doi:10.5430/wjel.v13n5p354

Eshet-Alkalai, Y., & Chajut, E. (2009). Changes over time in digital literacy. *Cyberpsychology & Behavior, 12*(6), 713–715. doi:10.1089/cpb.2008.0264 PMID:19514816

Hockly, N. (2012). Digital literacies. *ELT Journal, 66*(1), 108–112. doi:10.1093/elt/ccr077

Huang, J., Saleh, S., & Liu, Y. (2021a). A review on artificial intelligence in education. *Academic Journal of Interdisciplinary Studies, 10*(3), 206–206. doi:10.36941/ajis-2021-0077

Huang, X., Zou, D., Cheng, G., & Xie, H. (2021b). A systematic review of AR and VR enhanced language learning. *Sustainability (Basel), 13*(9), 4639. doi:10.3390u13094639

Kaeophanuek, S., Na-Songkhla, J., & Nilsook, P. (2019). A Learning Process Model To Enhance Digital Literacy Using Critical Inquiry Through Digital Storytelling (Cidst). *International Journal of Emerging Technologies in Learning, 03*(14), 22. doi:10.3991/ijet.v14i03.8326

Kartal, G. (2023). Contemporary language teaching and learning with ChatGPT. *Contemporary Research in Language and Linguistics, 1*(1), 59–70.

Kartal, G., & Balçikanli, C. (2018). Willingness to communicate and communication anxiety of EFL learners in a virtual world. *I-manager's Journal of Educational Technology, 15*(3), 7–25.

Kern, R., Ware, P., & Warschauer, M. (2016). Computer-mediated communication and language learning. In G. Hall (Ed.), *The Routledge handbook of English languageteaching* (pp. 542–555). Routledge. doi:10.4324/9781315676203-45

Kessler, G. (2018). Technology and the future of language teaching. *Foreign Language Annals, 51*(1), 205–218. doi:10.1111/flan.12318

Lankshear, C., & Knobel, M. (2006). Digital Literacy and Digital Literacies: - Policy, Pedagogy and Research Considerations for Education. *Nordic Journal of Digital Literacy, 1*, 8–20.

Lee, I., Ali, S., Zhang, H., DiPaola, D., & Breazeal, C. (2021, March). Developing middle school students' AI literacy. In *Proceedings of the 52nd ACM technical symposium on computer science education* (pp. 191-197). ACM. 10.1145/3408877.3432513

Loewen, S., Crowther, D., Isbell, D., Kim, K., Maloney, J., & Rawal, H. (2019). Mobile-assisted Language Learning: A Duolingo Case Study. *ReCALL, 3*(31), 293–311. doi:10.1017/S0958344019000065

Marr, B. (2018). *What is artificial intelligence and how will it change our world?* Bernard Marr. https://www.bernardmarr.com/default.asp?contentID=963

Ng, D. T. K., Leung, J. K. L., Chu, S. K. W., & Qiao, M. S. (2021). Conceptualizing AI literacy: An exploratory review. Computers and Education. *Artificial Intelligence, 2*, 100041.

Polizzi, G. (2020). Digital literacy and the national curriculum for England: Learning from how the experts engage with and evaluate online content. *Computers & Education, 152*, 103859. doi:10.1016/j.compedu.2020.103859

Popenici, S. A., & Kerr, S. (2017). Exploring the impact of artifcial intelligence on teaching and learning in higher education. *Research and Practice in Technology Enhanced Learning, 12*(1), 1–13. doi:10.118641039-017-0062-8 PMID:30613250

Rainie, L., & Anderson, J. (2017). *Code-dependent: Pros and cons of the algorithm age*. Pew Research Center.

Reddy, P., Chaudhary, K., Sharma, B., Chand, R. (2020). *Digital Literacy: a Catalyst For The 21st Century Education.* doi:10.1109/CSDE50874.2020.9411548

Russell, S. J., & Norvig, P. (2010). *Artificial intelligence: A modern approach.* Pearson Education.

Shortt, M., Tilak, S., Kuznetcova, I., Martens, B., & Akinkuolie, B. (2021). Gamification In Mobile-assisted Language Learning: A Systematic Review Of Duolingo Literature From Public Release Of 2012 To Early 2020. *Computer Assisted Language Learning, 3*(36), 517–554. doi:10.1080/09588221.2021.1933540

Smutny, P., & Schreiberova, P. (2020). Chatbot for learning: A review of educational chatbots for the Facebook messenger. *Computers & Education, 151*, 111. doi:10.1016/j.compedu.2020.103862

Sur, E. (2022). Okuryazarlık Kavramı ve Türkiye'deki Okuryazarlık Araştırmaları Üzerine Bir İnceleme *Ahmet Keleşoğlu Eğitim Fakültesi Dergisi (AKEF). Dergisi, 4*(2), 445–467. doi:10.38151/akef.2022.27

Tias, I. W. U., Izzatika, A., & Perdana, R. (2022). Empowerment of Critical and Creative Thinking (CCT) Skills Through Student Worksheets Based on Inquiry Social Complexity (ISC). *WSEAS Transactions on Environment and Development, 18*, 865–872. doi:10.37394/232015.2022.18.81

Vesin, B., Mangaroska, K., & Giannakos, M. (2018). Learning in smart environments: User-centered design and analytics of an adaptive learning system. *Smart Learning Environments*, *5*(1), 1–21. doi:10.118640561-018-0071-0

Warschauer, M. (2004). *Technology and social inclusion: Rethinking the digital divide*. MIT.

Yanhua, Z. (2020). The Application of Artificial Intelligence in Foreign Language Teaching. *2020 International Conference on Artificial Intelligence and Education (ICAIE),* (pp. 40-42). IEEE. 10.1109/ICAIE50891.2020.00017

Zawacki-Richter, O., Marín, V. I., Bond, M., & Gouverneur, F. (2019). Systematic review of research on artificial intelligence applications in higher education–where are the educators? *International Journal of Educational Technology in Higher Education*, *16*(1), 1–27. doi:10.118641239-019-0171-0

Zhao, L., Wu, X., & Luo, H. (2022). Developing AI literacy for primary and middle school teachers in China: Based on a structural equation modeling analysis. *Sustainability (Basel)*, *14*(21), 14549. doi:10.3390u142114549

Chapter 9
Machine Translation Use in Language Learning:
Learner Characteristics, Beliefs, and Ethical Concerns

Ümran Üstünbaş
https://orcid.org/0000-0002-7382-6220
Zonguldak Bülent Ecevit University, Turkey

ABSTRACT

In recent years, there has been an increasing development in promoting newer ways to integrate artificial intelligence (AI) into various digital tools, applications, and platforms. On the other hand, machine translation (MT), which is processed through AI, has already been in use for translation purposes for about three decades. Additionally, it has been a software frequently resorted for language learning purposes through free online platforms. The association between MT use and language learning tends to bring about several related issues such as ethical concerns. Diving into depths of these issues, this chapter presents a literature review on the key concepts related to MT use in language learning, which is supported by research findings and implications.

INTRODUCTION

Constantly developing, technology has led to changes or improvements in many areas of life also by reshaping habits and lifestyles. Thus, recent advances have brought about the term of *digitalization* in transforming information, and artificial

DOI: 10.4018/978-1-6684-9893-4.ch009

intelligence has been integrated into activities of daily living. As in all fields, educational programs have been evaluated and adapted to keep up with the changing winds. Furthermore, independent learning opportunities have increased as anyone can reach information, digital resources and tools that meet their needs easily. As for language learning, the digital world supports learners with programs and tools specially designed for language learning or adapted for the purpose. While there is an ongoing trend in promoting new ways to learn and practice a language, there have already been available tools and programs in use benefitting artificial intelligence. Despite not being specially designed for language learning, machine translation (MT) defined as translation between two languages without human involvement by using artificial intelligence is one of the methods that is utilized for various components of language studies. For instance, it is possible for autonomous learners to conduct self-regulated language studies by using online machine translation tools to check meaning and pronunciation of words and phrases, get support to generate and understand sentences while studying reading, speaking, and writing skills. In this respect, the related research has revealed a positive impact of using free online machine translation (FOMT) tools on language studies (particularly using them to improve writing) (e.g., Fredholm, 2019; Garcia & Pena, 2011; Jolley & Maimone, 2015; Lee, 2023; O'Neill, 2019). Additionally, the suggestion is that through instruction on how to use these platforms effectively, they can be useful tools that support language learners to become proficient autonomous learners with high level of metalinguistic awareness (e.g., O'Neill, 2019). In accordance with the positive effects proposed, learners are inclined to have positive views about using machine translation for their language studies (e.g., Clifford et al., 2013; Urlaub & Dessein, 2022). On the other hand, it has been found out that teachers tend to have negative views about their use due to ethical concerns as they may consider their use as cheating (e.g., Clifford et al., 2013; Hellmich, 2019; Lee, 2023; Urlaub & Dessein, 2022). Considering the controversy in the opinions and findings about the use of MT-thus artificial intelligence-in language learning, it seems necessary to shed light on the issue by presenting positive and negative aspects, also ethical concerns reviewed in the related literature. Therefore, concerning the need to focus more on the use of MT in language learning, this chapter proposes to address background issues with introduction to artificial intelligence and MT use with explanations about beliefs and concerns, and benefits and drawbacks regarding the use of MT for language study purposes, which are discussed in light of the existing research. Overall, the chapter aims to inform about how MT, one of the artificial intelligence tools, is and/or could be integrated in language learning while addressing learner characteristics such as proficiency, metalinguistic awareness and autonomy.

From CALL to AI-ALL: A Brief History of Digitalization in Language Learning

Increased availability of computers and technology in the 20th century stimulated emergence of new approaches and methods in second language learning since it was considered as necessary by well-known communities and educators to integrate technology and technological knowledge and devices into teaching (e.g., ACTFL, 2017; Council of Europe, 2020, as cited in Sun, 2022), but basically into learning. It was the result of an attempt to support individual learning and in-class teaching, also to provide opportunities for it, which has changed and developed in time with newer ways of technological integration into language learning, as illustrated in Figure 1 below:

Figure 1. The history of digital approaches to language learning

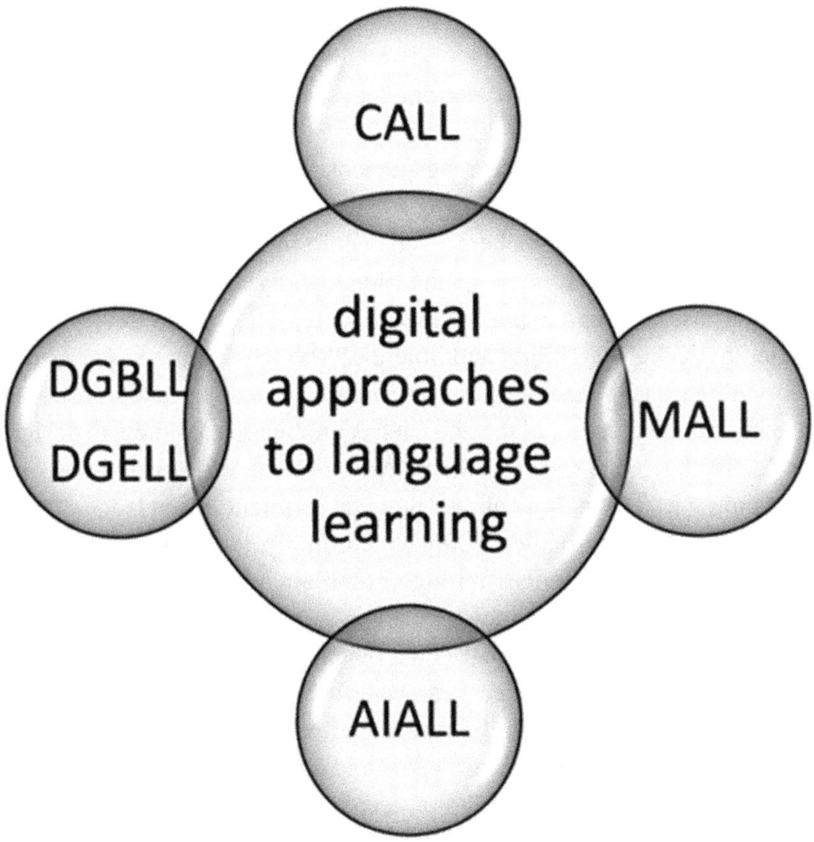

As demonstrated in Figure 1, among digital approaches to language teaching and learning, the main approach including computer and technology integration was Computer-Assisted Language Learning (CALL), defined as "using computers to support language teaching and learning in some way (Egbert, 2005, p. 3), or "any digital technology used in formal or informal learning inside or outside language classrooms" (Chen et al., 2021, p. 152) with former applications such as CDs and construction of computer laboratories to practice language. From this perspective, language learning approaches included in the figure above are sub-categories of CALL which are developed with new technologies.

The launch of CALL was triggered by an emerging need to facilitate language learning and teaching by integrating available machines and information technologies. With this regard, it contributes to facilitate the process by providing;

- variety in supporting authentic materials and sources sustained with visuals and audios.
- technology-integrated tasks that allow learners to interact, communicate and collaborate
- opportunities to connect to the world and, thus, raise cultural awareness
- opportunities to keep track of learning and save products

In sum, CALL promotes learner engagement, improved language knowledge and skills and self-regulated learning.

Besides language learners, teachers could benefit from CALL to plan and design their lessons by including timesaving and engaging activities to teach and for assessment purposes through elaborate use of sources, tools, and devices. Indeed, as also stated by Kukulska-Hulma and Shield (2008), CALL is an approach more associated with language teaching than learning as it was basically proposed for language education in computer labs, thus, it has implications for how to design and conduct effective language lessons. Implementing CALL effectively is reasonably bound to apply the Technological Pedagogical Content Knowledge (TPACK) framework by Mishra and Koehler (2006). Accordingly, teachers could implement technology in classroom practices through combining content knowledge (CK), pedagogical knowledge (PK), technological knowledge (TK), technological content knowledge (TCK), and technological pedagogical knowledge (TPK). Therefore, specific to language teaching, teachers can benefit from the variety that CALL and other CALL related approaches to be mentioned below provide, so that they are likely to take one step closer to achieve goals and objectives of their lessons.

With advances in computer and digital technologies, new approaches that are based on CALL, but concern language learners' personal use of digital technologies have been proposed for language learning. Chronologically, first, mobile and portable devices such mobile phones and laptops have been a part of daily life, by turning CALL technologies and devices into being mobile, portable, and more personal. To this end, Mobile-Assisted Language Learning (MALL), defined as using mobile devices for individual language learning purposes has followed the CALL approach as a later attempt to support language learning. This is achieved by ubiquitous, online mobile technologies that enhance collaboration through immediate communication tools and make it possible to share items in the process of learning a language (Kukulska-Hulme, 2010, as cited in Çakmak, 2019).

As for the role of MALL in improving language knowledge and skills, it is possible that mobile devices be used to learn new vocabulary and practice it via online dictionaries and specifically designed mobile applications. It is also possible to practice language skills through online, mobile applications as also indicated in the literature (e.g., Çakmak & Erçetin, 2018 for vocabulary and listening; Kartal, 2022 for pronunciation and speaking). Furthermore, as mobility makes it possible to learn at anywhere and anytime, MALL allows learners to study at their own pace in accordance with their needs and interests, which is at the core of learner autonomy and self-regulated learning. In sum, as well as CALL, sub-field of it, MALL proves benefits to language learners not only to improve language knowledge and skills but also to increase their autonomy and self-regulated study habits.

Recent developments in the digital technologies have led to integration of another CALL related approach into language learning, which is Digital Game-Based Language Learning (DGBLL), defined as integrating digital games into L2 learning. The reason for their being considered in language learning is that "it has become easier to imagine digital games as authentic, consequential, and widely applicable L2 learning resources" (Reinhardt & Thorne, 2016, p. 416). The games addressed in the definition are the ones that are specially designed for formal language education. Therefore, it is stated that the process of learning a language is enriched by gamers/ learners who actively engage in both playing a digital game in L2 and "gaining access to potentially hundreds of hours of authentic and engaging L2 input" (Dixon, et al., 2022, p. 1). However, dependent on authenticity concern of games that are created for language teaching in school context, integration of digital games that are available to gamers out of educative purposes has been highlighted by advocating Digital Game-Enhanced Language Learning (DGELL). In this sense, digital games that are commercially designed for entertainment purpose, not for formal education contexts could be used as authentic materials in language education. Concerning benefits, as all digital approaches to language learning, DGBLL and DGELL provide opportunities for learners to interact and communicate with the characters or other players in the game in the second language. Therefore, they have a chance to practice the target language while having fun in an engaging past time activity.

Apart from CALL related digital technologies and approaches that have led to developments in language learning and encourage learners' informal language studies, most recent innovations in the digital world have marked a revolutionary era with the spread of artificial intelligence (AI) in the last decade. AI is the intelligence that can achieve cognitive tasks that are cognate with human mind respectively in a short span of time. Smart-mobile devices and applications, chatbots, mobile assistants and robots are among AI-driven digital technologies which could also be used for language learning and teaching. These developments lead to a new approach that may be called as Artificial Intelligence-Assisted Language Learning (AI-ALL) in reference to CALL and MALL.

Even though the literature has a relatively short history (but expanding rapidly) with limited empirical research on the use of AI for language learning and teaching purposes (Sharadgah & Sa'di, 2022), existing research findings or reviews of literature suggest that it proves benefits to learners particularly to plan lessons with personalized content by analyzing a learner's study and determining needs for further practice and review (Sharadgah & Sa'di, 2022). Not limited to several digital technologies abovementioned and their proposed benefits, there are more AI applications each of which could be adapted for language education, and the newer applications or updates are introduced, the faster existing ones are getting expired even without totally analyzed and understood. In this regard, this review focuses on machine translation which is one of those former AI technologies having already been in use and issues related to its use.

An Earlier AI-driven Technology: Machine Translation and Language Learning

While AI technologies bring about digital tools, applications, platforms and devices, machine translation (MT) has been one of the initial tools to take advantages of AI technologies. Translation that is defined as "the expression in another language (or target language) of what has been expressed in another, source language, preserving semantic and stylistic equivalences (Bell, 1991, p. 5) has been performed since ancient times in human history (Ghanooni, 2012). Furthermore, translation is also an issue related to applied linguistics since it is rooted in Grammar-Translation Method, which is stated to cause a bad reputation in language learning (Garcia & Pena, 2011). Later, MT, referring to translation between two languages without human involvement through machines having been designed for the purpose, has appeared. From the basic versions to the latest AI-driven version that is available through free online machine translation tools, MT has attracted attention of users since it facilitates translation process. These free online tools involve "...internet search engines, monolingual and bilingual dictionaries, glossaries, parallel corpora, bilingual concordancers (parallel text alignment tools), peer-to-peer (P2P) language usage forums, sophisticated computer-assisted translation (CAT) suites that combine multiple functions (terminology management, translation memory, etc.)" (Jolley & Maimone, 2015, pp. 182-183), and tools such as Google Translate. Due to the connection between translation and applied linguistics, it is a fact that MT has a close relation to applied linguistics and language learning even though it has not been intentionally created for language learning purposes. Overall, being one of the earlier applications of AI, MT is part of language education with its benefits and pitfalls.

On the one hand machine translation has facilitated the process of translation in its main field, on the other hand it has been a controversial issue with the strengths and weaknesses suggested in language learning research, which is part of CALL research (e.g., Benda, 2014; Clifford et al., 2013; Garcia & Pena, 2011; Jolley & Maimone, 2015; Niño, 2009). The strengths involve "wide availability, immediacy, multilingualism, good lexical translation, and good simple structure translation" (Niño, 2009, p. 245) whereas some of the problems are suggested to be "literal translations, grammatical inaccuracies, discursive inaccuracies, spelling errors, missing cultural references, and unnatural writing" (Niño, 2009, pp. 245-246). It is important to highlight that these problems have decreased with recent advanced models of MT; FOMT. In line with these strengths and weaknesses of previous models, there are four models of MT use proposed: a bad model; correcting errors of MT product, a good model; using online dictionaries and other corpus-based tools especially for writing, vocational use; evaluating MT product through pre-editing and post-editing, and a CALL tool; interacting with advanced MT tools through translation exercises (Niño, 2009). In sum, MT use could be helpful for language learners due to its availability and speed, however; there may be errors in language use and mechanics in the product in addition to problems caused by lack of semantics and sociolinguistics knowledge of the machine.

With its positive aspects, MT use has been found to be beneficial to language learners as a CALL tool in the form of FOMT to study vocabulary, pronunciation, and grammar, but particularly to improve writing skills (e.g., Benda, 2014; Jolley & Maimone, 2015; Lee, 2020; Tsai, 2019; 2022). In one of these studies, Jolley and Maimone (2015) examined how FOMT is used by Spanish students as a CALL tool. The study addressing Google Translate as the FOMT tool revealed that majority of the participants used it frequently for the writing skill, which is followed by vocabulary studies. Similarly, in a more recent study, Tsai (2019) investigated how the use of Google Translate influenced Chinese EFL learners' performance in writing tasks and found a positive effect of it with fewer grammar and spelling mistakes and sophisticated vocabulary use. In a later study on writing, Tsai (2022) explored the effect of Google Translate as a CALL tool from a translingual perspective in a similar context, and concurring with the previous study, the findings of this study also indicated positive effect of this tool. Overall, MT or FOMT tools such as Google Translate have emerged to impact on improving language learners' skills, primarily the writing skill. Regarding the research findings, it is clear that MT is a tool primarily associated with vocabulary learning and the writing skill.

Having a facilitator role in language learning, MT as a CALL tool is considered effective in language skills development. Yet, due to individual differences, and thus learner characteristics, it is impossible to generalize its positive effect to all learners. Therefore, addressing learner characteristics is necessary to develop an understanding of the related concepts.

MT Use and Language Learners' Characteristics

MT Use and Proficiency

Individual differences lead to variation in the outcomes of any learning situation even if it is designed and implemented with the same procedures, techniques or in equal terms. Of all individual differences related to language learning, proficiency is the most associated one with various concepts. To this end, concerning variation in MT use and proposed effects, it is a matter of question whether language proficiency plays a role in the positive effects of MT use reported. Focusing on this question, Chung and Ahn (2022) set forth that the benefits and drawbacks of MT is based on how language learners use it and which proficiency level they have (including both high and low level of proficiency). Thus, effective MT use is inclined to be associated with high level of proficiency in the existing research due to lack of language knowledge of learners with low level of proficiency (e.g., Chung, 2020; Lee, 2022; Niño, 2008). On the comparison between high and low proficiency level learners, another finding is that low proficiency level learners use MT at sentence or paragraph level whereas the others use it for single word level or phrases (Jolley & Maimone, 2022). Expecting low language proficiency level learners not to use MT tools effectively, Niño (2020) explained the reason as these learners' lack of language awareness to translate or correct the mistakes in the translation. On the contrary, using FOMT tools without any guidance may lead to misconceptions or reliance heavily on the tools. Opposing it, Garcia and Pena (2011) included learners with low level of language proficiency into their research, and they reported these learners could benefit from FOMT better as they get more help in search of proper words in their writing. The conflict in the research findings can be explained by other individual differences as background factors to be discussed below:

MT Use and Metalinguistic Awareness

One of the language learner characteristics related to proficiency is metalinguistic awareness defined as an awareness about how a language works with its form, use and an ability to reflect on systematic use of language. It involves analysis and control of language components and structures through linguistic knowledge and skills to play with these components (Kieseier et al., 2022). In this respect, MT use is associated with metalinguistic awareness of advanced language learners (e.g., Niño, 2020). Accordingly, these learners make fewer mistakes thanks to their more developed metalinguistic awareness compared to low level proficiency learners. Furthermore, as Paterson (2023) stated, MT could draw language learners' attention to compare their mother tongue and second language in terms of similarities and differences, which boosts learners' metalinguistic awareness.

The translation process between L1 and L2 described is handled through integration of two vocational use promoted by Niño (2009); pre-editing and post-editing. While pre-editing includes preparing a draft of translation before having that translated by MT, post-editing involves checking and revising the text translated by MT. The latter one of these two models of translation is more applicable to language classrooms and requires metalinguistic awareness with an advanced level of language proficiency. Concerning the relation between proficiency and metalinguistic awareness, Chung (2020) found out that the higher language proficiency is, the more mistakes are corrected in the process of post-editing, and about benefit of post-editing, in an earlier study, Correa (2014) asserted that it enabled language learners to perform well in writing and develop metalinguistic awareness by working on the translated text to find and correct the mistakes. With this aspect, it is concluded that realizing mistakes in a machined translated text and correcting them is bound to metalinguistic awareness of proficient language learners, which may explain why majority of studies on MT use in language learning have focused on advanced level learners' post-editing process.

MT Use and Autonomy

Another learner characteristic that is connected to language proficiency is autonomy (and self-regulated learning). Learner autonomy refers to "...(a) ability and willingness to perform a language task without assistance, with adaptability related to the situational demands, with transferability to other relevant contexts, and with reflection, accompanied by (b) relevant action (the use, usually conscious and intentional, of appropriate learning strategies) reflecting both ability and willingness" (Oxford, 1999, pp.110-111). The concept involves self-regulation and strategy use as the tasks referred in this definition requires an awareness and socio-cognitive aspects to plan, conduct and evaluate the process. Thus, they are often considered as corresponding terms. Specific to language learning, it includes learners' interaction with various sources by selecting appropriate ones for their needs and interests and practicing language skills through a self-directed study habit, which requires to employ a number of cognitive skills to plan, monitor and evaluate the process.

Enabling learners to play with the language of their writing, MT contributes not only to language awareness, but also to learner autonomy and self-regulated learning since the learners evaluate their work and use strategies to find and correct their mistakes (Garcia & Pena, 2011; Lee, 2020). MT use links to autonomy when learners use strategies as part of self-regulated learning or when they cannot receive constructive feedback of their teachers (Bernardini, 2016; Paterson, 2023). As also mentioned above, through an effective instruction on how to use MT for post-editing, teachers can help language learners raise metalinguistic awareness. That instruction could also make it possible for learners to integrate MT use into their study habits as language practice. As part of their out-of-class studies, learners can carry on post-editing, and meanwhile, they employ strategies, which facilitates habit formation, and they can get meanings of unknown words with their pronunciation. As evidence for this benefit, van Lieshout and Cardoso (2022) focused on a possible effect of MT use (Google Translate in the study) on vocabulary and pronunciation in a Dutch context. Recording the participants' interaction with Google Translate for the purpose in different amounts and ways, the study revealed that learners' MT use changed in accordance with their needs and learning styles, which set the base for self-regulated learning. Additionally, Niño (2020) addressed the connection between MT use and self-regulated learning (referred as independent learning in the study). First, the study focused on how the participants considered themselves as independent learners. Then, they were asked about if they used MT tools for their studies and if yes for what purposes they used the tools. Findings of this study suggested that the learners considered themselves as good independent learners as they were conscious about their needs and what worked well for them. With regard to MT use, they reported that they liked using FOMT tools for their studies, which was basically for post-editing. In general, the research findings offer that there is a positive relationship between language learner autonomy and MT use habits.

MT Use and Language Learners' Beliefs

Besides findings suggesting a definite connection between MT use and language learning outcomes, MT use is also associated with positive psychological aspects such as higher level of motivation and decreased level of anxiety (Paterson, 2023). Based on these findings, the conclusion is that learners are inclined to consider MT use as helpful for them. There are many studies revealing their positive thoughts about using the tools (e.g., Clifford et al., 2013; Jolley & Maimone, 2015; Niño, 2008; 2009). For example, the study of Niño (2009) conducted with learners with advanced language proficiency set forth that post-editing their written works, majority of the participants found the FOMT tool (Google Translate) so helpful that it contributed to improve their language knowledge and skills, and they would use the tool for their future language studies. In a similar vein, Clifford et al. (2013) indicated that most of the participants believed that MT was helpful for them, but they also stated that they needed double-checking of their works as they had doubts about accuracy of the translation, which is good as it shows that they are aware of the limitations of MT. In a recent study, searching for learners' beliefs about MT use in language learning, Niño (2020) supported the findings of her previous study by suggesting that language learners regarded MT use for writing and vocabulary useful while they did not believe it for other language skills such as listening.

As well as students' beliefs about benefits of MT use, their belief about its ethicality is such a significant issue that it should be handled. Basically, the concern about it is that students totally depend on the tools for their studies. In fact, it is supported by research findings that students are conscious about the extent to which using the tools is regarded as unethical. To this end, they believe that MT or FOMT tools can be used to learn unknown words or to check the mistakes in writing assignments. Nevertheless, they disagree on using the translation of long paragraphs or an entire text. As evidence, the study of Jolley and Maimone (2015) revealed that learners' perception of ethicality was based on the purpose of the use since majority of the participants reported that using the tools for writing assignments or preparing presentations was acceptable, but it could not be ethical to use them for translation assignments. Moreover, high percentages of the participants reported that they found the use of the tools for checking and getting help with unknown words appropriate whereas they found it unethical or cheating for translating long paragraphs and texts or to use the tools rather frequently.

To conclude, language learners use MT, particularly free online tools such as Google Translate and dictionaries as they find them beneficial, and they believe that there is nothing wrong with using the tools in an acceptable amount and way.

MT Use and Ethical Concerns

MT use is favored by learners with generally positive views about it as it facilitates their learning process. While learners regard MT use considerably useful, teachers are inclined to have negative beliefs about it, or rather ethical concerns. Accordingly, heavily relying on ineffective MT tools, students tend to cheat especially in writing, which has partially emerged to be teachers' beliefs not only about MT tools, but also aspects of learners' MT use (e.g., Clifford et al., 2013; Correa, 2011; Groves

& Mundt, 2021). For instance, Jolley and Maimone (2015) compared teachers and learners' opinions about each other on the use of FOMT for language studies and revealed that the teachers overestimated their learners' FOMT use with the amount and ethicality. Regarding the results of that study, more than half of the teachers in the study predicted that their students used the tools very often and the students thought that the tools were very useful and reliable. However, it is important to note that the results or implications of the existing research do not thoroughly represent language teachers' beliefs and assumptions since there were also teachers who were indecisive about the ethicality of the tools or considered MT use as useful to a certain extent, which cannot be disregarded. In other words, MT use in language classrooms is a controversial issue in terms of its ethicality. In fact, students in a language class agree on unethicality of completely depending on an MT tool such as Google Translate, one of the most well-known engines, to complete a task, probably a writing task (e.g., Jolley & Maimone, 2015; Niño, 2009), or they are conscious that the tools do not provide totally accurate translation (Clifford et al., 2013). As evidence for their consciousness, Clifford et al. (2013) put forth that language learners often use the tools to study vocabulary, specifically as a dictionary to translate single words from English to their mother tongue. The use of MT tools for this purpose is acceptable and has nothing with being unethical.

The research suggests a discrepancy between teachers' views about their learners' MT use and learners' actual use of the tools. Besides, ethicality of MT use is controversial among the teachers. As a result, setting certain policies on which students also agree about the use of MT tools in language education is likely to contribute to handle the controversy or discrepancy in question, which could be one of the pedagogical implications to be presented below.

MT Use and Pedagogical Implications

With the latest technological developments, problems of earlier versions of MT have been solved (Jolley & Maimone, 2015), by making it a possible digital supplementary tool in language learning. Seemingly, MT (FOMT) tools particularly Google Translate is inevitable considering high number of language learners using the tool for this purpose. As evidence for the high number of users, Clifford et al. (2013) reported that about 90% of the participants in their study stated that they frequently use Google Translate for their language studies. Yet, learners' not knowing how to use it effectively or being unable to evaluate the product due to lack of their metalinguistic awareness may cause problems in language classrooms. Therefore, for the effective use of these tools and to dismiss any misuse or unethical use of the tools, instructional practices are to be set elaborately. For this purpose, various suggestions have been presented in the literature (e.g., Clifford et al., 2013; Somers et al., 2006). First of all, language teachers should observe and understand how learners use FOMT tools and teach them how they can use the tools effectively and ethically, or they should encourage learners to use other tools such as concordances and digital dictionaries (Ducar & Schocket, 2018) no matter what proficiency level learners have. Supporting these implications (still with doubts of suitability of MT for low proficiency level learners), Niño (2020) suggested that guiding beginner language learners how to use the MT appropriately could result in improved reading comprehension in L2 through vocabulary and pronunciation practices.

Another implication on language teacher role in guiding learners for effective use of MT is about increasing metalinguistic awareness of them (also mentioned in Section III.II). For this purpose, teachers could help their students build an awareness about how various language forms and features are used in the context of translated texts and make connections between L1 and L2 on the use of similar language features (Paterson, 2023), which is possible through tasks based on vocational use: pre-editing and post-editing (See section III.II). Specifically, an effective instruction on evaluating the translation by MT tools and making corrections on it while post-editing is essential (Zhang & Torres-Hostench, 2022). Similarly, students can use the tools to correct their written works by comparing their original work to translation performed by the machine but still keeping in mind that MT product may also have mistaken. As an intended result, language learners could become aware or increase their awareness that MT tools or more commonly used FOMT tools such as Google Translate could be a supporting tool that they can easily resort to for their out-of-class studies (as part of self-regulated learning). To conclude, as part of instruction, students could be presented good and bad examples of MT use to make them aware that the tools are imperfect with mistakes, and instead of totally depending on them, language learners can only get help to a certain extent, which is especially important for low level proficiency learners (Niño, 2009).

An effective instruction could also enable learners to increase their resources for their independent learning practices. Apart from frequently used FOMT tools, online dictionaries or corpora of MT tools could be beneficial to study and increase vocabulary (Niño, 2009; O'Neill; 2019). To this end, with an aim to focus on MT tools except for Google Translate, O'Neill (2019) examined the effect of instruction on various types of FOMT by comparing the groups of online dictionaries and translators with or without training through an experimental study design. The findings set forth that the most improved group was online translators (Google Translate) in the study with training in writing. Considering this result, the conclusion cannot be favoring the use of this one type of MT (Google Translate) in the classroom. Instead, learners are to be presented variation in the tools (i.e., corpora). Yet, the emphasis is that instruction is necessary for an effective integration of MT tools into language classrooms regardless of the type of the tools to be used.

Overall, instruction on how to use MT tools effectively is essential to fulfil intended teaching goals since it is an undeniable fact that MT tools are part of language classes. Since forbidding the tools is not a solution, policies related to how to use them as amount and conditions should be set in the classroom or added in the school policies (Clifford et al. 2013).

CONCLUSION

Machine translation (MT) is one of the earliest AI technologies that is associated with CALL and, thus, has been used in language learning with its advanced versions of free online machine translation (FOMT) for decades. Being easily accessible, MT provides benefits to learners for their language studies primarily vocabulary and writing, but the extent to which learners benefit from the tools is based on learner characteristics such as proficiency. There are two mainly related concepts with MT use and proficiency; learner autonomy and metalinguistic awareness. Within this scope, this chapter has presented a brief introduction to history of AI technologies and CALL moving to MT. Then, related concepts have been discussed in light of existing literature. Finally, pedagogical implications that basically highlight the significance of instruction on the effective use of MT have been proposed.

REFERENCES

Bell, R. T. (1991). *Translation and translating: Theory and practice*. Longman.

Benda, J. (2014). Google Translate in the EFL classroom: Taboo or teaching tool? *Writing & Pedagogy*, *5*(2), 317–332. doi:10.1558/wap.v5i2.317

Bernardini, S. (2016). Discovery learning in the language for translation classroom. *Cadernos de Tradução (Florianópolis)*, *36*, 14–35. doi:10.5007/2175-7968.2016v36nesp1p14

Çakmak, F. (2019). Mobile learning and mobile assisted language learning in focus. *Language and Technology*, *1*(1), 30–48.

Çakmak, F., & Erçetin, G. (2018). Effects of gloss type on text recall and incidental vocabulary learning in mobile-assisted L2 listening. *ReCALL*, *30*(1), 24–47. doi:10.1017/S0958344017000155

Chen, X. L., Zou, D., Xie, H. R., & Su, F. (2021). Twenty-five years of Computer-Assisted Language Learning: A topic modeling analysis. *Language Learning & Technology*, *25*(3), 151–185.

Chung, E. S. (2020). The effect of L2 proficiency on post-editing machine translated texts. *Journal of Asia TEFL*, *17*(1), 182–193. doi:10.18823/asiatefl.2020.17.1.11.182

Chung, E. S., & Ahn, S. (2022). The effect of using machine translation on linguistic features in L2 writing across proficiency levels and text genres. *Computer Assisted Language Learning*, *35*(9), 2239–2264. doi:10.1080/09588221.2020.1871029

Clifford, J., Merschel, L., & Munné, J. (2013). Surveying the landscape: What is the role of machine translation in language learning? *@tic Revista d'Innovació Educativa, 10*, 108-121.

Correa, M. (2011). Academic dishonesty in the second language classroom: Instructors' perspectives. *Modern Journal of Language Teaching Methods*, *1*(1), 65–79.

Correa, M. (2014). Leaving the "peer" out of peer-editing: Online translators as a pedagogical tool in the Spanish as a second language classroom. [LACLIL]. *Latin American Journal of Content and Language Integrated Learning*, *7*(1), 1–20. doi:10.5294/laclil.2014.7.1.1

Dixon, D. H., Dixon, T., & Jordan, E. (2022). Second language (L2) gains through digital game-based language learning (DGBLL): A meta-analysis. *Language Learning & Technology*, *26*(1), 1–25.

Ducar, C., & Schocket, D. H. (2018). Machine translation and the L2 classroom: Pedagogical solutions for making peace with Google Translate. *Foreign Language Annals*, *51*(4), 779–795. doi:10.1111/flan.12366

Egbert, J. (2005). *CALL essentials: Principles and practice in CALL classrooms.* TESOL.

Fredholm, K. (2019). Effects of Google Translate on lexical diversity: Vocabulary development among learners of Spanish as a foreign language. *Revista Nebrija de Lingüística Aplicada a la Enseñanza de las Lenguas*, *13*(26), 98–117. doi:10.26378/rnlael1326300

Garcia, I., & Pena, M. I. (2011). Machine translation-assisted language learning: Writing for beginners. *Computer Assisted Language Learning*, *24*(5), 471–487. doi:10.1080/09588221.2011.582687

Ghanooni, A. R. (2012). A review of the history of translation studies. *Theory and Practice in Language Studies*, *2*(1), 77–85. doi:10.4304/tpls.2.1.77-85

Groves, M., & Mundt, K. (2021). A ghostwriter in the machine? Attitudes of academic staff towards machine translation use in internationalised higher education. *Journal of English for Academic Purposes*, *50*, 1–11. doi:10.1016/j.jeap.2021.100957

Hellmich, E. A. (2019). Language teacher beliefs about technology: Expanding the ecology. *International Journal of Computer-Assisted Language Learning and Teaching*, *9*(4), 1–17. doi:10.4018/IJCALLT.2019100101

Jolley, J. R., & Maimone, L. (2015). Free online machine translation: Use and perceptions by Spanish students and instructors. In A. K. Moeller (Ed.), *Learn language, explore cultures, transform lives* (pp. 181–200). University of Nebraska-Lincoln.

Jolley, J. R., & Maimone, L. (2022). Thirty years of machine translation in language teaching and learning: A review of the literature. *Journal of Linguistics and Language Teaching*, *14*(1), 26–44. doi:10.5070/L214151760

Kartal, G. (2022). Evaluating a mobile instant messaging tool for efficient large-class speaking instruction. *Computer Assisted Language Learning*, 1–29. doi:10.1080/09588221.2022.2074463

Kieseier, T., Thoma, D., Vogelbacher, M., & Holger, H. (2022). Differential effects of metalinguistic awareness components in early foreign language acquisition of English vocabulary and grammar. *Language Awareness*, *31*(4), 495–514. doi:10.1080/09658416.2022.2093888

Kukulska-Hulme, A., & Shield, L. (2008). An overview of mobile assisted language learning: From content delivery to supported collaboration and interaction. *ReCALL*, *20*(3), 271–289. doi:10.1017/S0958344008000335

Lee, S. M. (2020). The impact of using machine translation on EFL students' writing. *Computer Assisted Language Learning*, *33*(3), 157–175. doi:10.1080/09588221.2018.1553186

Lee, S. M. (2022). Different effects of machine translation on L2 revisions across students' L2 writing proficiency levels. *Language Learning & Technology*, *26*(1), 1–21.

Lee, S. M. (2023). The effectiveness of machine translation in foreign language education: A systematic review and meta-analysis. *Computer Assisted Language Learning*, *36*(1-2), 103–125. doi:10.1080/09588221.2021.1901745

Mishra, P., & Koehler, M. J. (2006). Technological pedagogical content knowledge: A new framework for teacher knowledge. *Teachers College Record, 108*(6), 1017–1054. doi:10.1111/j.1467-9620.2006.00684.x

Niño, A. (2008). Evaluating the use of machine translation post-editing in the foreign language class. *Computer Assisted Language Learning, 21*(1), 29–49. doi:10.1080/09588220701865482

Niño, A. (2009). Machine translation in foreign language learning: Language learners' and tutors' perceptions of its advantages and disadvantages. *ReCALL, 21*(2), 241–258. doi:10.1017/S0958344009000172

Niño, A. (2020). Exploring the use of online machine translation for independent language learning. *Research in Learning Technology, 28*(0), 1–32. doi:10.25304/rlt.v28.2402

O'Neill, E. M. (2019). Training students to use online translators and dictionaries: The impact on second language writing scores. *International Journal of Research Studies in Language Learning, 8*(2), 47–65. doi:10.5861/ijrsll.2019.4002

Oxford, R. (1999). Relationship between second language learning strategies and language proficiency in the context of learner autonomy and self-regulation. *Revista Canaria de Estudios Ingleses, 38*, 109–126.

Paterson, K. (2023). Machine translation in higher education: Perceptions, policy, and pedagogy. *TESOL Journal, 14*(2), e690. doi:10.1002/tesj.690

Reinhardt, J., & Thorne, S. (2016). Metaphors for digital games and language learning. In F. Farr & L. Murray (Eds.), *Routledge handbook of language learning and technology* (pp. 415–430). Routledge.

Sharadgah, T. A., & Sa'di, R. A. (2022). A systematic review of research on the use of artificial intelligence in English language teaching and learning (2015-2021): What are the current effects? *Journal of Information Technology Education, 21*, 337–377. doi:10.28945/4999

Somers, H., Gaspari, F., & Niño, A. (2006). Detecting inappropriate use of free online machine translation by language students. A special case of plagiarism detection. In *Proceedings of the 11th Annual conference of the European Association for Machine Translation.*

Sun, X. (2022). Ten years later: Reexamining the TESOL Technology Standards for Language Teachers. *TESOL Journal, 13*(4), 1–15. doi:10.1002/tesj.684

Tsai, S. C. (2019). Using google translate in EFL drafts: A preliminary investigation. *Computer Assisted Language Learning*, *32*(5-6), 5–6, 510–526. doi:10.1080/09588221.2018.1527361

Tsai, S. C. (2022). Chinese students' perceptions of using Google Translate as a translingual CALL tool in EFL writing. *Computer Assisted Language Learning*, *35*(5-6), 1250–1272. doi:10.1080/09588221.2020.1799412

Urlaub, P., & Dessein, E. (2022). Machine translation and foreign language education. *Frontiers*, *1-5*, 936111. Advance online publication. doi:10.3389/frai.2022.936111 PMID:35937139

van Lieshout, C., & Cardoso, W. (2022). Google Translate as a tool for self-directed language learning. *Language Learning & Technology*, *26*(1), 1–19.

Zhang, H., & Torres-Hostench, O. (2022). Training in machine translation post-editing for foreign language students. *Language Learning & Technology*, *26*(1), 1–17.

ADDITIONAL READING

Jolley, J. R., & Maimone, L. (2015). Free online machine translation: Use and perceptions by Spanish students and instructors. In A. K. Moeller (Ed.), *Learn language, explore cultures, transform lives* (pp. 181–200). University of Nebraska-Lincoln.

Jolley, J. R., & Maimone, L. (2022). Thirty years of machine translation in language teaching and learning: A review of the literature. *Journal of Linguistics and Language Teaching*, *14*(1), 26–44. doi:10.5070/L214151760

Niño, A. (2008). Evaluating the use of machine translation post-editing in the foreign language class. *Computer Assisted Language Learning*, *21*(1), 29–49. doi:10.1080/09588220701865482

Niño, A. (2009). Machine translation in foreign language learning: Language learners' and tutors' perceptions of its advantages and disadvantages. *ReCALL*, *21*(2), 241–258. doi:10.1017/S0958344009000172

Shen, L., Chen, I., Grey, A., & Su, A. (2021). Teaching and learning with artificial intelligence. In S. Verma & P. Tomar (Eds.), Impact of AI technologies on teaching, learning, and research in higher education (pp. 73-98). IGI Global. doi:10.4018/978-1-7998-4763-2.ch005

KEY TERMS AND DEFINITIONS

Artificial Intelligence (AI): Non-human computer system that works like humans' mind to fulfil tasks peculiar to them such as thinking and generating ideas

CALL: (abbreviation of Computer-Assisted Language Learning) An approach to second language learning which involves learners' use of various computer technologies for their language studies

DGBLL: (abbreviation of Digital Game-Based Language Learning) An approach to second language learning which involves game play and digital games specifically designed for formal language education

DGELL: (abbreviation of Digital Game-Enhanced Language Learning) An approach to second language learning which involves game play and adaptation of commercial digital games to personal language studies.

Learner Autonomy: A learner's consciousness about taking responsibilities of their learning process that leads to shape their study habits.

Machine Translation: A type of translation between two languages that is automatically performed through use of AI generated tools and machines.

MALL: (abbreviation of Mobile-Assisted Language Learning) An approach to second language learning which involves learners' use of mobile devices and applications for their self-paced language learning studies

Metalinguistic Awareness: An awareness about how a language works with its form, use and an ability to reflect on systematic use of language.

Post-Editing: A process involved in machine translation in which the product obtained by translation of AI systems is checked and revised if necessary.

Self-Regulated Learning: A learner's cognitive and psychological involvement in their learning process with an ability to detect their learning needs, set learning goals, monitor and self-evaluate the process.

Chapter 10
Exploring the Potential of Chatbots and ChatGPT in Enhancing Vocabulary Knowledge

Mustafa Yildiz
Samsun University, Turkey

ABSTRACT

This chapter presents an in-depth analysis of chatbots and the integration of ChatGPT into vocabulary acquisition. The chapter begins with an introduction to artificial intelligence (AI) and continues with a definition of chatbots to highlight their role as computer programs designed to mimic human interaction. It subsequently focuses on the use of chatbots in language education. The potential benefits associated with the integration of chatbots into language learning environments are further explored. However, special attention is dedicated to the use of chatbots in vocabulary teaching, which is a fundamental aspect of language acquisition. The chapter also explores the use of ChatGPT, an AI-powered language model, particularly in the context of teaching vocabulary. The chapter ends with highlighting how ChatGPT can help learners master word form, meaning and usage, based on Nation's multidimensional aspects of vocabulary knowledge.

INTRODUCTION TO ARTIFICIAL INTELLIGENCE (AI)

"Can machines think?" (Turing, 1950, p. 433), the simple question, is assumed to be the genesis of the artificial intelligence phenomenon that is sweeping the

DOI: 10.4018/978-1-6684-9893-4.ch010

world today. Since then, humanity has witnessed the emergence of many artificial intelligence instruments. The earliest chatbots, such as Eliza (1966), Parry (1972), Racter (1983), Jabberwacky (1988), and A.L.I.C.E. (1995) are text-based and pre-set, based on a question-and-answer design with predictable responses and far from being natural and mimicking human-to-human communication (Belda-Medina & Calvo-Ferrer, 2022). Therefore, they were not able to respond to questions they were not yet programmed to address (Kohnke et al., 2023). However, generative language models capable of creating texts go through a series of developmental stages, starting with rule-based system of traditional chatbots based on pre-written scripts to generate a limited number of utterances (e.g., Quarc in Riloff & Thelen, 2000) and ending with transformer-based models (e.g., BERT in Devlin et al., 2019; GPT-2 in Radford et al., 2019), which are fed with large quantities of text data, able to provide more natural responses to their users, and capable of performing language tasks with a high degree of certainty (Kasneci et al., 2023). Thus, as a consequence of the steady advancement of artificial intelligence and the remarkable evolution of chatbots from more primitive pre-set systems to more complex generative language models, the modern world enjoys the privilege of communicating with chatbots that are at the peak of sophistication and allow for more natural and intelligent interactions between machines and humans.

The integration of technology into education has revolutionized the teaching and learning of English as a consequence of one of the ways in which this integration has been realized: the use of chatbots in language teaching. However, while the use of chatbots in language teaching has been widely considered and discussed recently (e.g., Huang et al., 2022; Kohnke, 2022; Polyzi & Moussiades, 2023; Smutny & Schreiberova, 2020), there is a noticeable lack of interest and studies on the use of chatbots in vocabulary teaching in the existing literature. Therefore, several reasons might provide justifications for a literature review on the use of chatbots in teaching vocabulary. On the one hand, chatbots as a tool for vocabulary teaching have the potential to offer new possibilities as innovative and effective ways to teach vocabulary compared to traditional methods commonly used inside and outside of classrooms. Thus, it has the potential to create excitement in the classroom as a novelty that allows revitalizing learners' interest, which diminishes over time during the process (Huang et al., 2022). On the other hand, chatbots have the ability to provide contextualized examples and meaningful interactions and, as a result, promote vocabulary acquisition through their ability to mimic conversations and engage learners in a dialogue. In addition, the opportunity for learners to communicate individually with a chatbot is invaluable in that it enables the chatbot to act as a kind of life coach, practicing vocabulary appropriate to the learner's needs and language level.

This chapter attempts to make a thorough overview of the effect of AI on vocabulary knowledge along with highlighting the potential and merits of AI in enhancing vocabulary teaching. More specifically, it explores the impact of AI on vocabulary teaching in second/foreign language teaching context. It also scrutinizes AI and its wider impact on second/foreign language education. It not only extensively discusses the role of AI in language learning but also points out how AI can enhance and support second/foreign language vocabulary knowledge. Exploring the key benefits of AI, including personalized learning experiences as well as increased engagement of learners, this chapter provides examples of AI-based tools that are specifically developed to aid vocabulary learning and demonstrates their application in vocabulary learning/teaching. The chapter concludes with the introduction of AI-generated outputs that can be utilized to teach vocabulary in the classroom.

Definition of Chatbots

There have been a wide variety of terms used for chatbots, including chatterbots, virtual assistants, virtual agents, intelligent agents or web-bots (Wang & Petrina, 2013). Regardless of the terms used to label it, many different researchers emphasize many different aspects when defining a chatbot, for example, which communicates with the user in a natural way on a specific topic and in a specific domain (Smutny & Schreiberova, 2020); replicates human conversation in a verbal or textual format (Belda-Medina & Calvo-Ferrer, 2022); is free from human-specific limitations such as forgetting and recalling and benefit from predetermined rules while making decisions (Qasem et al., 2023); is a virtual assistant that can respond to many user questions with correct answers (Clarizia et al., 2018); " are software avatars with limited, but growing capability for conversation with human beings" (Fryer et al., 2017, p. 461). Overall, the term 'chatbot' embraces a wide range of functionalities and capabilities as researchers continue to explore and advance its various applications and potentials in the field of human-computer interaction.

The fundamental operation of a chatbot, as mentioned in Haristiani (2019), starts with a user sending a message, which is then processed through Natural Language Processing (NLP). Based on the existing database, the chatbot generates a response corresponding to the message received. For instance, if a user sends the message "how are you?", the chatbot will search for suitable answers in the database, such as "I am fine" or "Great!"

Chatbots are customized with a wide range of purposes in mind. There are chatbots specifically designed to offer targeted information and engage in focused conversations on subjects like website guidance, frequently asked questions (FAQs), virtual support, sales assistance, surveys, quizzes, educational tutoring, and even hosting chat rooms (Wang & Petrina, 2013), as well as industrial solutions for which Apple Siri, Microsoft Cortana, Facebook M and IBM Watson are among the most famous ones (Clarizia et al., 2018).

The Use of Chatbots in Language Education

The use of chatbots in language teaching has been one of the most popular topics recently, as chatbots can act as valuable tools in educational settings to enhance language learning. Huang et al. (2022) assert that it is essential to understand their ongoing practice and pinpoint potential improvements for future chatbot-supported language learning environments in order to foster the implementation of chatbots in language learning.

Thanks to ongoing developments in artificial intelligence and machine learning techniques and advancements in visual chatbot development platforms that empower educators with no programming expertise, chatbots are currently revolutionizing language teaching by providing customizable and accessible learning experiences (Huang et al., 2022; Kohnke, 2022). Huang et al. (2022) assert that visual chatbot development platforms empower teachers with no programming experience to easily build customized chatbots, like Dialogflow and BotStar, to elevate learners' learning experience, while improvements in artificial intelligence and machine learning techniques are increasing the capacity of chatbots to understand and handle users' unstructured input. For example, using Dialogflow on Google's artificial intelligence platform, Kohnke (2022) built an educational text-based chatbot, which is able to answer common questions and designed with a visual flow builder that enables easy editing and sharing for non-programmers, to aid learners during the transition to online courses. The chatbot's multi-channel implementation allows learners to access it from a variety of platforms, and its natural language understanding models can interpret complex inquiries, handling possible misspellings or unclear wording. The chatbot operates based on a set of response rules derived from students' questions and is deployed on the Facebook page, which provides a familiar and accessible interface for students to interact 24/7 without the need for further installations.

Chatbots emerge as useful tools in language education because they host natural language conversations and help learners master their language-related skills. Therefore, the use of chatbots as learning assistance is increasingly gaining traction in language learning by virtue of their capability to engage in conversations with learners using natural language (Huang et al., 2022). These mobile tools revolutionize the nature of how we communicate and promote a continuous learning experience in a variety of settings (Smutny & Schreiberova, 2020). Covering a wide range of learning aspects such as vocabulary, grammar, academic pragmatics and meaning negotiation strategies, chatbots are largely implemented in higher education to help learners learn speaking, listening, reading and writing skills, the most common interface designs of which are web-based and mobile messenger interfaces, allowing learners to access conversations via computers, tablets or mobile instant messaging applications (Huang et al., 2022).

Fryer and Carpenter (2006) provide several strengths of chatbots, one of which is their convenience, which also refers to one of the pedagogical ways chatbots have been benefited: chatbots as interlocutors acting as a learning companion to facilitate language learning for students (Huang et al., 2022). Learners with computer access can instantly start interacting with many chatbots in and out of classrooms by simply creating a membership for free. They are "always-on technology" (Polyzi & Moussiades, 2023, p. 9) readily willing to reverse with learners, giving them the opportunity to practice language continuously (Belda-Medina & Calvo-Ferrer, 2022; Huang et al., 2022; Qian et al., 2023). They also provide EFL learners with the opportunity to practice their language skills by pretending to be native speakers of English (Fryer & Carpenter, 2006; Kim, 2018a). Thus, a well-designed chatbot can offer a very wide variety of expressions and vocabulary (Huang et al., 2022).

Additionally, a chatbot makes learners feel more comfortable during communication by reducing the level of shyness compared to communicating with a human being (Fryer & Carpenter, 2006). They have the potential to reduce the transactional distance in online learning spaces, as well as close the psychological and communication gap between instructors and learners, thus maximizing learner satisfaction by facilitating them to engage in interactive dialogue with course content (Huang et al., 2022).

Besides, chatbots have no human emotions such as impatience or boredom, so they can repeat an activity indefinitely (Fryer & Carpenter, 2006). Learners can practice and engage with chatbots as much as needed, without any concerns about causing annoyance or boredom.

Furthermore, chatbots provide simultaneous text and speech; therefore, they allow learners to improve both their reading and listening skills (Fryer & Carpenter, 2006). During the interaction between a learner and a chatbot, they can read the text on the screen and listen to the accompanying audio simultaneously.

In addition, the relatively new nature of chatbots makes them interesting for learners, but also a motivating factor (Fryer & Carpenter, 2006). As by-products of emerging technologies, these tools can have the potential to engage learners actively in language learning processes by capturing their curiosity. Finally, chatbots provide quick and effective feedback on learners' spelling and grammar usage (Fryer & Carpenter, 2006). Large language models offer a distinct opportunity to deliver personalized and effective learning experiences, given that individuals possess unique learning preferences, abilities and needs (Kasneci et al., 2023). They can instantly respond to learners with feedback and individualized assistance with no expensive expenses (Qian et al., 2023).

Use of Chatbots in Teaching Vocabulary

Although there are many discussions that emphasize the importance of vocabulary in language education, one of the most striking ones is Wilkins' (1972) famous quote: "...without grammar very little can be conveyed, without vocabulary nothing can be conveyed" (p. 111). In a similar vein, Ur (2022) states that "[Y]ou can communicate with limited grammar and less-than-accurate pronunciation, but you cannot do so without a lot of vocabulary. The more vocabulary a learner knows, the better they are likely to function in the new language" (p. 1) to express that it is more important to know as many words as possible than grammar or pronunciation. Similarly, Schmitt (2010) puts forward an anecdotal observation to emphasize the importance of vocabulary that "learners carry around dictionaries and not grammar books" (p. 4). These scholars are not without grounds, as there are many studies that suggest that vocabulary knowledge, which contributes significantly to overall foreign language competence, has also a direct correlation with other language skills. The findings towards the significance of vocabulary in language learning emphasize the crucial role of vocabulary in various language skills. It has been found that the extent of learners' vocabulary knowledge is a significant predictor of their reading proficiency (Laufer, 1992; Rashidi & Khosravi, 2010). Additionally, a larger vocabulary size positively impacts EFL learners' performance in listening comprehension (Stæhr, 2009; Teng, 2014), and an increase in vocabulary knowledge leads to an improvement in writing performance (Laufer, 1994). Furthermore, vocabulary knowledge has a stronger association with reading and writing skills compared to listening comprehension (Stæhr, 2008). These findings highlight why learners should give priority to vocabulary as an essential constituent of language acquisition in order to enhance the basic language skills.

Chatbots provide opportunities that human language learning partners are not able to offer, such as a diverse range of expressions and vocabulary (Fryer et al., 2019). They also enable users both to generate a variety of words, phrases, grammatical structures that they do not have the opportunity to use in daily life (Fryer & Carpenter, 2006) and to utilize appropriate words and idioms (Kim, 2017) during interaction. It was also found that learners using chatbots were more motivated to learn vocabulary, more interested in vocabulary learning and more confident about the words they knew (Kim, 2018b). Even ChatGPT itself sheds light on the promising role of chatbots as powerful teaching tools, especially in promoting vocabulary development among learners in a second language context. Asking ChatGPT how chatbots can contribute to language education, Forrester (2023) notes that ChatGPT claims that the use of chatbots as a teaching tool offers promise in fostering vocabulary growth among learners in a second language context. For example, learners can actively participate in interactive conversations with the chatbot and thus incorporate new vocabulary and expressions into their responses. By means of this conversational exchange, the chatbot takes on the role of an educational agent providing constructive feedback and corrections, thus promoting an environment that helps learners acquire and retain new vocabulary.

Asking ChatGPT how chatbots can contribute to language education, Forrester (2023) records the following statements as the response from ChatGPT: The use of chatbots as a teaching tool offers promise in fostering vocabulary growth among learners in a second language context. For example, learners can actively participate in interactive conversations with the chatbot and thus incorporate new vocabulary and expressions into their responses. By means of this conversational exchange, the chatbot takes on the role of an educational agent providing constructive feedback and corrections, thus promoting an environment that helps learners acquire and retain new vocabulary.

The use of chatbots in vocabulary learning has been a major topic of research recently and findings reveal a wealth of benefits attributable to their integration into educational settings. There are a lot of studies highlighting that chatbots provide a valuable opportunity to augment vocabulary learning and contribute to a more engaging language learning experience. Chatbot use in teaching vocabulary has been handled from many different perspectives such as the effects of interactions with AI chatbots on EFL learners' vocabulary skills, perceptions, and motivation (Kim, 2018b); the importance of integrating curriculum-specific content into chatbot interactions to promote learners' mastery of specific vocabulary and expressions (Qian et al., 2023); the benefits of integrating digital games with chatbots for vocabulary acquisition and learner satisfaction (Polyzi & Moussiades, 2023); the role of chatbots as mediators during reading activities on receptive and productive vocabulary knowledge (Jeon, 2021); the effects of incorporating a range of vocabulary learning tools into chatbots on learners' comprehension in conversational contexts (Alsadoon, 2021); the effects of integration of a chatbot with a crossword puzzle on learners' knowledge of work-related terminology (Hsu et al., 2023).

The use of chatbots during vocabulary instruction might also lead to enhanced vocabulary skills, improved perceptions of vocabulary learning, and increased motivation, interest, and confidence among learners interacting with chatbots. Kim (2018b) offers insights into the effectiveness of chatbots for vocabulary development by examining the impact of AI chatbots on Korean EFL learners' vocabulary knowledge in an experimental design in which the experimental group interacted with a chatbot for eight weeks. The findings from pre- and post-tests indicate that the experimental group enhanced their vocabulary skills. Pre- and post-surveys also indicate positive changes in their perceptions of vocabulary learning and their motivation, interest, and confidence.

The integration of curriculum-specific content into chatbot interactions can promote learners' mastery of specific vocabulary and expressions because the alignment of chatbot experiences with the curriculum can facilitate more targeted and effective language learning assistance. While regular chatbots can be very beneficial for learners to improve their language skills by helping them to have a daily conversation, they are inadequate for teaching the target contents of a specific time frame. Although there are many chatbots available for learners to chat with, these chatbots do not have constraints on the learning goals or the learning curricula (Qian et al., 2023). In order to maximize the quality of the time students spend with the chatbot, Qian et al (2023) design a lexically constrained chatbot called BlenderBot3 to teach lexical items and phrases available in their textbooks and the curriculum. The findings reveal that the curriculum-incorporated chatbot, in which the vocabulary content of the curriculum is integrated, helps students learn certain words and phrases.

The integration of digital games and a chatbot can promote learners' vocabulary acquisition. The interactive nature of chatbots, which raise relevant questions and generate positive feedback, might serve as a motivating factor for learners and make vocabulary learning fun and easy for them compared to traditional methods. Polyzi and Moussiades (2023) explore the effectiveness of digital games and chatbots on vocabulary learning based on an experimental pre- and post-test design. They prepare a digital vocabulary assistant including digital games and a chatbot acting as an English language learning assistant to teach vocabulary. The chatbot has the purpose of interacting with learners and assisting them in vocabulary acquisition. Therefore, it poses appropriate questions related to synonyms, translation and the definition of words, motivating learners to provide answers and offering them appropriate positive feedback. The findings reveal that learners in the experimental groups outperform those in the control groups, indicating that learners' performance is enhanced by utilizing vocabulary learning assistant. Most of the learners also acknowledge that the vocabulary assistant helps them learn vocabulary and confirm that they prefer it to traditional learning methods because they find it fun and easy.

Using chatbots as mediators during reading activities can also foster vocabulary acquisition and improve both receptive and productive vocabulary knowledge. The step-by-step guidance provided by a chatbot helps learners address their learning difficulties and improve their comprehension and production of unfamiliar words more effectively than traditional methods that simply convey the meaning of words. Jeon (2021) explores the effect of chatbots on vocabulary learning and draws on a chatbot which acts as a mediator for unfamiliar words while learners are reading a text during Chatbot-Assisted Dynamic Assessment (CA-DA). Learners involved in more open-ended dialogues with chatbots and had the opportunity of receiving automated mediation to recognize and produce unfamiliar vocabulary without being restricted to a multiple-choice format. When students face a learning challenge, the chatbot as part of the dynamic assessment provides them with graduated mediation, starting from the most implicit to the most explicit way. Learners who received gradual prompts showed a significant increase in both receptive and productive vocabulary knowledge compared to learners who were simply given the meaning of the target word.

In the domain of language learning, the integration of a chatbot with a range of vocabulary learning tools can considerably enhance learners' understanding and acquisition of vocabulary in conversational contexts. Alsadoon (2021) intends to foster EFL learners' vocabulary acquisition by employing a chatbot equipped and enhanced with a variety of vocabulary learning tools, including a dictionary, images, L1 translation and concordance, designed to facilitate the comprehension of vocabulary in conversational contexts. The findings reveal that the vocabulary learning chatbot leads to an enhancement in learners' vocabulary knowledge. In particular, the dictionary is both the most preferred and the most effective tool for vocabulary learning. However, no significant difference occurs between the dictionary and the translation in terms of effectiveness. The L1 translation has a slight, albeit negligible, advantage over the dictionary in terms of vocabulary retention.

The integration of a chatbot with a crossword puzzle can improve learners' knowledge of work-related terminology. Hsu et al. (2023) introduced Termbot, an online learning tool that integrates a crossword puzzle chatbot to help healthcare students learn English medical terminology interactively. By combining the engaging nature of puzzles, Termbot boosts the enjoyment and effectiveness of learning medical terms. While interacting with Termbot, learners can use online crossword puzzles to deepen their understanding of medical terminology. The findings of the study show significant advancement among students using Termbot with regard to their knowledge of medical terminology.

Use of ChatGPT in Teaching Vocabulary

In addition to the chatbots mentioned above, ChatGPT can also assist language learners by utilizing extensive data covering dictionaries and corpora to generate responses that introduce unfamiliar words and their definitions, so that it can facilitate vocabulary acquisition (Atlas, 2023). Kovačević (2023) discusses how ChatGPT can be fine-tuned to generate personalized vocabulary and grammar exercises for ESP learners, which includes collecting, cleaning and pre-processing an ESL dataset and then training the model to generate exercises that conform to specific grammar rules and vocabulary. According to Kovačević (2023), the fine-tuned model can create customized exercises based on each learner's proficiency, background and needs, yielding valuable supplementary practice material for language progress.

Kohnke et al. (2023) point out the affordances and pedagogical benefits of ChatGPT in language teaching. Regarding teaching vocabulary, Kohnke et al. (2023) emphasize that when learners are assigned a text, they may come across unfamiliar words whose meanings are unclear within the given context. ChatGPT can address this issue by offering explanations for such terms and engaging more interaction by responding to follow-up questions. Furthermore, learners have the opportunity to demand explanation in their native language for a better understanding. Kartal (2023) also underlines that one of the remarkable characteristics of ChatGPT is its capacity to ensure extensive vocabulary exploration by providing comprehensive definitions, contextualized word usage, example sentences and multiple meanings, which enables learners to develop a more comprehensive understanding of the language and helps them to decode foreign words in assigned texts, even in their native language.

For example, an EFL learner attending ESP courses, reading a text with full of technical terms about motorcycles, faces an unknown word 'quick-shifter' within the sentence '...the motorcycle is equipped with a **quick-shifter** for seamless gear shifts, while the electronically adjustable suspension allows riders to fine-tune their riding experience'. The following figure exemplifies the way ChatGPT offers explanation for the technical term 'quick-shifter', as mentioned in Kohnke et al. (2023) and Kartal (2023).

Figure 1. Explanation of a technical term

MU Could you please explain what 'quick-shifter' means in the following sentence?: "The motorcycle is equipped with a quick-shifter for seamless gear shifts, while the electronically adjustable suspension allows riders to fine-tune their riding experience".

In the given sentence, a "quick-shifter" refers to a feature on the motorcycle that enables smooth and rapid gear shifts without the need to use the clutch or throttle. It allows the rider to change gears quickly and seamlessly by simply exerting force on the gear lever. By employing a quick-shifter, riders can shift up or down gears without needing to close the throttle or disengage the clutch, resulting in swift and efficient gear changes. This feature enhances the overall riding experience by reducing the time and effort required for shifting, allowing riders to maintain better control and focus on the road. Additionally, the sentence also mentions an electronically adjustable suspension, which enables riders to customize and fine-tune the suspension settings to suit their preferences and optimize their riding experience.

As indicated in Figure 1, ChatGPT goes beyond providing a dictionary definition of a target word, delivering a vast amount of additional information and context. In addition, if requested, ChatGPT can also provide explanations in the learners' native language. Atlas (2023) underlines that ChatGPT and other language models can be brought into play to offer real-time translation assistance, which lets learners enter sentences in their native language and obtain translations in the target language. Thus, learners who are engaged in reading or writing tasks in a foreign language can check their understanding and make inroads in comprehension and production of the target language.

In addition, learners have the opportunity to use ChatGPT to access dictionary definitions and examples. ChatGPT can provide the definition of a word, determine the grammatical class of words, give sample sentences and also suggest additional meanings for polysemous words (Kohnke et al., 2023). In a similar vein, Atlas (2023) underlines that ChatGPT can be used for creating flashcards and quizzes. Learners can enter words and get responses with definitions, example sentences and synonyms or antonyms, which help them expand vocabulary retention through exercises and receive feedback on their performance. Figure 2 indicates a dictionary entry provided by ChatGPT for the meaning and use of a target word.

Figure 2. Dictionary entry generated by ChatGPT

MU Could you please provide a dictionary entry for 'quick-shifter' with sample sentences?

quick-shifter (noun): A device or mechanism on a motorcycle that enables swift and smooth gear changes without the need for clutch or throttle manipulation.

Example sentences:

1. "The high-performance sports bike comes equipped with a quick-shifter, allowing riders to shift gears seamlessly during rapid acceleration."
2. "With the help of the quick-shifter, the experienced rider effortlessly changed gears while maintaining a steady speed through the corners."
3. "The advanced quick-shifter system on the motorcycle ensures precise and lightning-fast gear shifts, enhancing the overall riding experience."
4. "During the race, the rider utilized the quick-shifter to effortlessly move through the gears without interrupting the acceleration."
5. "Thanks to the quick-shifter, the rider could maintain full throttle while shifting gears, resulting in improved speed and performance."

The sample sentences provided by ChatGPT in the dictionary entry in Figure 2 above illustrate the use of "quick-shifter" in context to better understand its meaning and use.

Moreover, ChatGPT can create a variety of text genres on a specific topic and then adapt the complexity of the text to make it more appropriate for novices or more advanced learners (Kohnke et al., 2023). Similarly, Koraishi (2023) emphasizes that ChatGPT enables EFL teachers to build contextually related and level-appropriate reading texts, based on specific topics that the learners can relate to or enjoy and aligned with learners' identified Common European Framework of Reference for Languages (CEFR) proficiency level, and introduce new vocabulary to fulfill the needs of individual learners. Furthermore, the model can generate a variety of question types targeting different aspects of the text such as vocabulary and comprehension to enhance the learning experience. Figure 3 reflects how ChatGPT functions as a text generator for introducing new vocabulary.

Figure 3. ChatGPT as a text generator

MU Could you please generate a short text full of bolded specialized vocabulary about motorcycles for ESP courses?

Motorcycles, commonly known as motorbikes or bikes, are two-wheeled **vehicles** that are widely used for transportation, recreation, and sport. They are powered by **internal combustion engines** and typically have **cylinders** ranging from two to six, with varying **displacements**. Motorcycles rely on a **transmission system** to transfer power from the engine to the rear wheel. This system includes components such as the **clutch**, **gears**, and **chain drive**. Braking on motorcycles is crucial for safety, and modern bikes often employ **disc brakes** with **calipers** and **ABS** (anti-lock braking system) technology. To ensure rider safety, it is essential to wear appropriate **protective gear**, including a **helmet**, **gloves**, and **leather clothing**. Regular **maintenance** is vital for the optimal performance of motorcycles, which involves tasks like **oil changes**, **spark plug replacement**, and **chain lubrication**. Furthermore, riders must be aware of essential safety practices, such as **lane splitting**, **countersteering**, and **body positioning**. Overall, developing a comprehensive understanding of motorcycle terminology and industry-specific language is essential for professionals in the field.

Figure 4. Adaptation of a complex text by ChatGPT

MU Could you please simplify this text by adjusting its vocabulary to the needs and skills of EFL learners with A2-level English language proficiency?

Motorcycles, also called motorbikes or bikes, are two-wheeled vehicles that people use for transportation, fun, and sport. They have engines inside them that make them go, and they usually have between two and six cylinders. Motorcycles have gears and a chain that helps them move. It's important to use the brakes on a motorcycle to stay safe, and many modern bikes have special brakes that don't lock up. To protect themselves, riders wear special clothes like helmets, gloves, and leather jackets. Motorcycles need regular check-ups and care, like changing the oil, replacing spark plugs, and keeping the chain greased. It's also important for riders to know how to stay safe, like when to change lanes, how to turn, and how to sit properly on the bike. Understanding motorcycle words and phrases is helpful for people who work with motorcycles.

As can be seen in Figure 3, ChatGPT is very effective in generating texts that aim to introduce words that are related to a specific domain. As mentioned earlier, ChatGPT also helps learners adjust the difficulty level of a text so that even less proficient learners can easily grasp the meaning in the text. Figure 4 contains the simplified version of the text generated in Figure 3 above.

Furthermore, ChatGPT assists learners in understanding lessons on topics such as short stories by helping to create vocabulary notes in both the target language and the native language (Kohnke et al., 2023). ChatGPT and other language models can be used to present personalized vocabulary lists and exercises with learners who receive a response with a relevant word list and corresponding practice exercises in return for entering their topic or area of interest. This personalized approach enables learners to concentrate on vocabulary compatible with their particular needs and interests (Atlas, 2023). In the following figure, ChatGPT generates vocabulary notes for the bolded specialized vocabulary available within the text generated by ChatGPT in Figure 3 above.

As can be seen in both Figure 3 and Figure 5, ChatGPT is effective in both creating a text specific to a particular field and generating vocabulary notes for the target words found within these texts. Thus, ChatGPT can be very beneficial for learning the target words in context.

Additionally, Mikeladze (2023) emphasizes the integration of ChatGPT in material design for creating efficacious language learning atmosphere for both teachers and learners and aims to illustrate how educators can draw on the assistance of the AI

Figure 5. Vocabulary notes generated by ChatGPT

MU Could you please generate vocabulary notes for the bolded specialized vocabulary?

Certainly! Here are the vocabulary notes for the bolded specialized vocabulary:

1. **Vehicles**: Refers to machines used for transportation.
2. **Internal combustion engines**: Engines that generate power by burning fuel inside them.
3. **Cylinders**: The parts of the engine where the fuel is burned to create power.
4. **Displacements**: The size of the engine, usually measured in cubic centimeters (cc).
5. **Transmission system**: The mechanism that transfers power from the engine to the wheels.
6. **Clutch**: The device that connects or disconnects the engine from the transmission system.
7. **Gears**: Different speeds or ratios that control how fast the motorcycle moves.
8. **Chain drive**: A chain that transfers power from the transmission system to the rear wheel.
9. **Disc brakes**: Brakes that use a rotating disc and calipers to slow down or stop the motorcycle.
10. **Calipers**: Devices that press against the brake disc to stop the wheel from spinning.
11. **ABS**: Abbreviation for anti-lock braking system, a safety feature that prevents the wheels from locking up during braking.
12. **Protective gear**: Equipment worn by riders to protect themselves from injuries.
13. **Helmet**: A hard hat worn on the head for safety.
14. **Gloves**: Hand coverings that protect the hands during riding.
15. **Leather clothing**: Clothing made from leather material, commonly worn for protection while riding.
16. **Maintenance**: The regular upkeep and care necessary to keep the motorcycle in good condition.
17. **Oil changes**: The process of replacing the engine oil with new oil to keep the engine running smoothly.
18. **Spark plug replacement**: Changing the spark plugs, which create a spark to ignite the fuel in the engine.
19. **Chain lubrication**: Applying lubricating oil to the chain to reduce friction and keep it functioning properly.
20. **Lane splitting**: Riding between lanes of traffic to pass slower-moving vehicles.
21. **Countersteering**: A technique used to initiate turns on a motorcycle by momentarily steering in the opposite direction.
22. **Body positioning**: The way riders position their body while riding for stability and control.

model to develop engaging teaching resources. The activities designed by ChatGPT have the versatility to target a variety of language skills covering reading, writing, speaking, grammar, function and vocabulary development. More specifically, regarding vocabulary instruction by employing ChatGPT to develop activities, Mikeladze (2023) generates a variety of vocabulary teaching activities such as matching new lexical items with their corresponding definitions, matching tasks involving synonyms and antonyms, as well as gap-filling exercises in dialogues and sentences.

In line with Mikeladze (2023), Koraishi (2023) highlights that educators can capitalize on AI capabilities to integrate a wide range of target vocabulary into generated texts, facilitate material customization, and effectively address diverse student vocabulary needs, thereby enriching the overall learning experience. Koraishi (2023) also underlines that using ChatGPT, educators can easily create vocabulary-focused worksheets or quizzes in a variety of formats. Simply giving the AI the vocabulary set and asking for a variety of questions to test the set or providing a specific template results in the instant creation of student-specific quizzes. This fast and efficient process enables educators to meet individual learner needs and significantly simplify the exam building process.

Use of ChatGPT for Multidimensional Vocabulary Growth

According to Nation's (2012) perspective on the multidimensionality of word knowledge, exploring vocabulary knowledge beyond formal aspects and meaning with an emphasis as well as on the ability to actively use words in context, vocabulary acquisition is a complex process involving the mastery of different aspects of knowledge for which learners require varied word encounters to fully comprehend and internalize vocabulary. Therefore, it can be inferred that it is significant to go beyond the formal aspects and meaning of words when acquiring vocabulary. The use of words in context must also be considered a crucial aspect of vocabulary knowledge. In addition, it can be further inferred that in order to claim that a word is truly known by a person, the form of a word, which is already a part of both receptive and productive vocabulary, must be easily recognized and produced within a syntactic pattern in both spoken and written language while it is semantically associated with a concept in mind. Given this multidimensionality of vocabulary knowledge, the activities for vocabulary acquisition using ChatGPT in the forthcoming section of this review will focus not only on the form of words, but also on their meaning and usage.

Use of ChatGPT for Word Forms

Even though ChatGPT cannot produce actual sounds, it can try to describe how the target word might be pronounced using the International Phonetic Alphabet (IPA). Thus, it can help learners to understand how to produce a word with a correct pronunciation in spoken form. ChatGPT responds to the request 'Could you please help me with how to pronounce the word 'flower'?' as follows in Figure 6.

Figure 6. ChatGPT as a facilitator for sound production

Of course! The word "flower" is pronounced as / flauər/. Let's break it down into phonemes with examples:

1. /f/ - This is the "f" sound as in "fish" or "fan."
2. /l/ - This is the "l" sound as in "love" or "lion."
3. /aʊ/ - This is a diphthong, which is a combination of two vowel sounds:
   - /a/ - The "a" sound as in "cat" or "hat."
   - /ʊ/ - The "oo" sound as in "book" or "look."
4. /ə/ - This is the schwa sound, similar to the "a" sound in the first syllable of "sofa."
5. /r/ - This is the "r" sound as in "red" or "rain."

As indicated in Figure 6, ChatGPT helps learners produce words accurately by providing phonetic transcriptions. On the other hand, ChatGPT can also assist learners in recognizing a word's form when it is heard by helping them associate the written word with its spoken counterpart, which makes contribution to learners' receptive vocabulary knowledge. The following prompt 'What does the word 'computer' sound like?' is responded by ChatGPT like so below.

Figure 7 indicates that ChatGPT plays a valuable role in developing learners' receptive vocabulary knowledge by helping them to associate written words with their corresponding spoken forms, which contributes to learners' ability to understand the words they hear and expand their receptive vocabulary.

ChatGPT can also contribute to learners' receptive vocabulary knowledge by enabling them to analyze the morphological structure of a word and explain how each of the basic building blocks of a word constitutes its meaning. The question 'What parts are recognizable in the word 'nationalistic'?' prompts ChatGPT to analyze the morphological structure of the word by breaking it down into its components as shown in Figure 8 below.

Figure 7. ChatGPT as a facilitator for sound recognition

The word 'computer' sounds like "kuhm-PYOO-tur" in regular English pronunciation. The emphasis is on the second syllable, 'PYOO.' Here is the phonetic representation of the word: /kəmˈpjuːtər/.

Again, please note that the phonetic representation uses the International Phonetic Alphabet (IPA) symbols to describe the sounds of the word more precisely.

Figure 8. Morphological analysis of words

In the word "nationalistic," the following parts are recognizable:

1. Root:
   - "nation" - the base word, which refers to a country or a community of people sharing a common identity.
2. Derivational Affixes:
   - "al" - added to "nation" to form "national" (adjective). It means relating to or characteristic of a nation.
   - "ist" - added to "national" to form "nationalist" (noun). It refers to a person who advocates or supports the interests of a specific nation or nationalism.
   - "ic" - added to "nationalist" to form "nationalistic" (adjective). It means having strong or excessive loyalty or devotion to a specific nation or nationalism.

As indicated in Figure 8, ChatGPT has the ability to make morphological analysis of words, so that learners can easily recognize both the morphological structure of words and the contribution of the constituents of words to meaning. On the other hand, ChatGPT can help increase learners' productive vocabulary knowledge by simply providing learners with a simple way of showing which suffix should be used both to convey a meaning and to form derivatives. ChatGPT helps learners to generate derived words by responding to the question 'What word parts are needed

Figure 9. Derivational analysis of words

To express the meaning "doer of an action," the following word part is needed:

1. Derivational Affix:
   - "er" - added to a verb to form a noun that denotes a person or thing that performs the action indicated by the verb.

For example:

- "teach" (verb) + "er" = "teacher" (noun) - someone who teaches.
- "write" (verb) + "er" = "writer" (noun) - someone who writes.
- "sing" (verb) + "er" = "singer" (noun) - someone who sings.

So, the "er" suffix is the word part that expresses the meaning "doer of an action."

to express the meaning 'doer of an action'?' with the following response shown in Figure 9.

Figure 9 indicates that learners can benefit from ChatGPT to produce derivatives as ChatGPT offers suffixes which should be employed to convey specific meanings and form word derivatives.

Use of ChatGPT for Word Meaning

Regarding the meaning of words, ChatGPT can expand learners' receptive vocabulary knowledge by helping them get what the word denotes in the immediate context of its occurrence. The prompt, 'What meaning does the word 'cable' signal?', leads ChatGPT to generate the following response in Figure 10, which provides the meaning of the target word in different contexts changing according to the grammatical class of the word.

It is indicated in Figure 10 that ChatGPT can provide various meanings a word might have depending on its syntactic role in a sentence.

To increase learners' productive vocabulary knowledge, ChatGPT helps to find the form of the target word whose meaning is given through circumlocution. For instance, in a case where learners are tasked with determining the word form that signifies 'a written text that can be published in printed or electronic form', ChatGPT can assist by providing the specific form of the target word in the following way in Figure 11.

As it is clearly indicated in Figure 11, ChatGPT assists in identifying the specific word form associated with a given meaning, even when expressed indirectly through circumlocution.

Figure 10. Generation of word meaning in return for target word

The word "cable" can signal various meanings depending on the context in which it is used. Here are a few common meanings associated with the word "cable":

1. Noun Meaning: A cable is a thick, strong rope or wire, typically made of metal or fiber, used for various purposes such as supporting structures, transmitting electrical or communication signals, or lifting heavy objects.
2. Verb Meaning: To "cable" can mean to send or transmit a message or information through a cable or telecommunication system.
3. Cable TV: "Cable" can also refer to a system of transmitting television programs and other signals to subscribers through coaxial or fiber-optic cables.

Figure 11. Generation of target word in return for word meaning

The word form that can be used to express a written text that can be published in printed or electronic form is "manuscript." A manuscript refers to an author's original document or text that is prepared for publication. It can be in the form of a handwritten or typewritten document, or a digital file, and it serves as the basis for creating a printed book, article, or electronic publication.

ChatGPT can also assist learners in gaining a deeper understanding of the concept of the target word, e.g., 'manuscript', and how it can be applied in different situations or contexts. By doing so, learners can grasp its broader meaning, implications, and potential uses across various domains. The prompt, 'Could you please help me with the concept behind the word 'manuscript' which will allow understanding in a variety of contexts?', directs ChatGPT to provide the following response in Figure 12.

Figure 12. Contextualization of words

Certainly! The concept behind the word "manuscript" encompasses various aspects that can help in understanding it in different contexts. Here are some key elements of the concept:

1. Written Work: A manuscript refers to a written or typed document that contains the original content and ideas of an author. It is a tangible form of a literary or scholarly work.
2. Handwritten or Typed: Historically, manuscripts were predominantly handwritten, often on parchment or paper. However, in modern usage, manuscripts can also be typewritten or digitally created.
3. Original and Unpublished: Manuscripts are typically the initial versions of a work, representing the author's original composition. They are often unpublished and may undergo revisions before being published.
4. Literary or Scholarly Context: Manuscripts are commonly associated with literary works such as novels, poems, plays, or academic works like research papers, theses, or dissertations.
5. Historical Significance: Manuscripts have played a crucial role in preserving historical records and cultural heritage. Ancient manuscripts have provided insights into literature, art, religion, and historical events.
6. Editing and Revision: Manuscripts often undergo editing, proofreading, and revisions to improve their clarity, organization, grammar, and style before publication.
7. Manuscript Culture: The concept of manuscripts is closely linked to a broader manuscript culture, which includes practices of copying, preserving, and transmitting written works before the advent of printing.

Figure 12 shows that ChatGPT enables learners to have a broader understanding of the word's meaning and its diverse range of usages in different contexts by facilitating a more comprehensive understanding of the target word.

Similarly, ChatGPT is a useful tool for learners to improve their productive use of a target word by enabling them to develop a deeper understanding of its referents in a variety of contexts. By exploring diverse references associated with a target word, learners can expand their vocabulary knowledge and gain the ability to use the word effectively in different situations. For instance, in a case in which if a learner would like to grasp the concept behind a word like 'car', ChatGPT can provide a comprehensive list of items that fall under this concept, which includes automobiles, passenger cars, sports cars, SUVs, convertibles and more. By exploring these references, learners can develop a broader understanding of the meaning of the word and be able to apply it confidently in a variety of conversations, writing tasks or real-life situations. Figure 13 includes the response of ChatGPT in return for the prompt, 'What items can the concept 'car' refer to?'.

Figure 13. Generation of semantically related words

The concept of 'car' can refer to various items and contexts. Here are some possible interpretations and items associated with the concept of 'car':

1. Automobile: The most common interpretation of 'car' refers to a motor vehicle used for transportation on roads. It typically has four wheels, an engine, and seating for passengers.
2. Passenger Car: This refers specifically to a car designed for transporting people rather than goods. It includes sedans, coupes, hatchbacks, and other body types.
3. Sports Car: A type of high-performance car designed for speed, agility, and aesthetics. Sports cars often have a sleek design, powerful engines, and advanced handling capabilities.
4. SUV (Sports Utility Vehicle): A larger car with increased ground clearance and versatile functionality, suitable for both on-road and off-road driving. SUVs often have more spacious interiors and are designed for utility and comfort.
5. Convertible: A car with a retractable or removable roof, allowing for an open-air driving experience when desired.
6. Classic Car: Refers to older, vintage, or collectible cars that are considered to be of historical or cultural significance.
7. Electric Car: A car that is powered by one or more electric motors and relies on rechargeable batteries or other forms of electric energy storage.
8. Concept Car: A prototype or experimental car designed to showcase new technologies, design concepts, or innovative features. Concept cars often push the boundaries of automotive design and functionality.

Figure 14. Associations of a target word

The word 'traffic' can evoke associations with various related terms and concepts. Some of the words that come to mind when thinking about 'traffic' are:

1. Congestion
2. Vehicles
3. Roads
4. Highways
5. Commute
6. Jams
7. Signals
8. Pedestrians
9. Accidents
10. Gridlock
11. Rush hour
12. Traffic lights
13. Traffic rules
14. Transportation
15. Road safety

With regard to the associations of a target word, ChatGPT goes beyond providing the dictionary definition and referents of a target word by assisting learners in exploring its associations and related words. This feature allows learners to expand their vocabulary and develop a better sense of the target word's semantic connections. By using ChatGPT, learners can create a broader network of related concepts which help discover words that are closely associated with the target word. The following figure includes the response of ChatGPT for the prompt, 'What other words does the word 'traffic' make us think of?'.

ChatGPT can serve as a versatile tool for learners, making it easier for them to explore and master interchangeable vocabulary and contributing to their overall linguistic development. In addition to the associations of target words, the engagement of learners with GPT can assist them in acquiring a wide range of synonyms, antonyms, and related words that can be used interchangeably to convey similar meanings. This feature enables learners to diversify their word choices and avoid repetition. Due to diverse word options, learners can broaden their vocabulary repertoire and develop an understanding of word usage, ultimately enhancing their overall language skills. Figure 15 includes the response of ChatGPT for the word 'traffic', which is formed of as a reply for the prompt 'What other words could we use instead of traffic?'

Figure 15. Alternatives for a target word

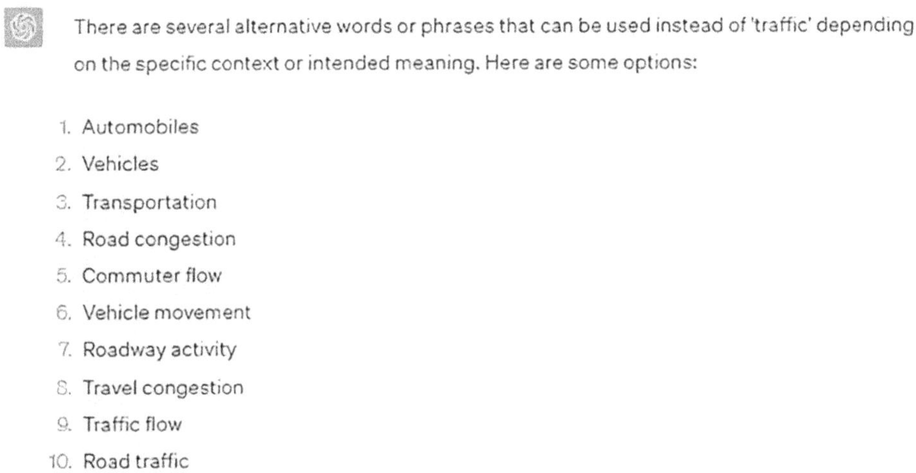
There are several alternative words or phrases that can be used instead of 'traffic' depending on the specific context or intended meaning. Here are some options:

1. Automobiles
2. Vehicles
3. Transportation
4. Road congestion
5. Commuter flow
6. Vehicle movement
7. Roadway activity
8. Travel congestion
9. Traffic flow
10. Road traffic

As indicated in Figure 15, ChatGPT provides learners with the opportunity to gain interchangeable vocabulary. By providing synonyms and semantically related words, ChatGPT helps learners diversify their word choices, avoid repetition, and convey similar meanings more effectively. This feature contributes to the overall development of learners' language skills by expanding their vocabulary knowledge.

Use of ChatGPT for Word Usage

Learners can also gain insights into the different syntactic patterns and sentence constructions in which a particular word is commonly employed. Active engagement with ChatGPT guide learners on how to use a target word effectively in different grammatical contexts, which expands learners' knowledge about a word's versatility in different syntactic patterns, helping learners understand how it fits into the overall structure of a sentence. Figure 16 reflects the response of ChatGPT to the prompt of 'In what patterns does the word 'manuscript' occur?'.

It is indicated in Figure 16 that learners can easily get information about the syntactic role of a target word within a larger grammatical structure. Accordingly, it is possible to argue that ChatGPT provides valuable information not only on the meaning of a target word but also on its usage.

On the other hand, ChatGPT assists learners in exploring contextually relevant words that commonly co-occur with a target word, which are commonly associated with each other, so that learners can broaden their vocabulary by developing a deeper understanding of word relationships. The prompt, 'Could you please produce words

Figure 16. Potential syntactic patterns for a target word

The word "manuscript" can occur in various patterns depending on its grammatical function and the context in which it is used. Here are some common patterns in which the word "manuscript" may appear:

1. Noun Phrase: The word "manuscript" can function as the head of a noun phrase and be modified by determiners, adjectives, or other noun modifiers. For example:
   - "The ancient manuscript"
   - "A handwritten manuscript"
   - "Her unpublished manuscript"
   - "Several valuable manuscripts"
2. Verb + Object: The word "manuscript" can also serve as the object of a verb, indicating the action performed on or related to the manuscript. For example:
   - "She wrote a manuscript."
   - "He edited the manuscript."
   - "They submitted their manuscript."
3. Prepositional Phrase: The word "manuscript" can appear in prepositional phrases, where it is introduced by a preposition and functions as the object of that preposition. For example:
   - "In the manuscript"
   - "With the manuscript"
   - "For the manuscript"
4. Adjectival Modifier: In some cases, "manuscript" can function as an adjectival modifier to describe another noun. For example:
   - "Manuscript collection"
   - "Manuscript study"
   - "Manuscript analysis"

Figure 17. Collocations of a target word

Certainly! Here are some words that commonly occur with the word "manuscript":

1. Ancient manuscript
2. Historical manuscript
3. Handwritten manuscript
4. Valuable manuscript
5. Unpublished manuscript
6. Original manuscript
7. Medieval manuscript
8. Illuminated manuscript
9. Fragile manuscript
10. Transcribed manuscript
11. Archival manuscript
12. Digitized manuscript
13. Manuscript collection
14. Author's manuscript
15. Edited manuscript

that commonly occur with the word 'manuscript'?' leads ChatGPT to generate the response in Figure 17.

Based on the data in Figure 17, it seems that ChatGPT is also good at providing learners with words that are often used together, which will contribute to fluency and accuracy in learners' productive language skills such as writing and speaking, enabling them to sound as native as possible.

In addition, ChatGPT helps learners develop a sense of register and level of formality appropriate for different contexts. Students can observe how words are used in various contexts, from informal to formal settings, so that they can use specific words according to the level of formality needed. That is, they can gain the ability to adapt their language to specific situations, enabling them to express themselves effectively and appropriately in a variety of social and professional contexts. For example, learners can observe how certain words such as "ask for" or "request" are used to express different degrees of formality in certain situations. They can then apply this knowledge when deciding which word is more appropriate according to the formality requirements of the context. Figure 18 indicates the response of

Figure 18. Analysis of target words in terms of degree of formality

In terms of formality, "ask for" is generally considered less formal than "request." While both phrases are used to seek or solicit something, "request" carries a more formal and polite tone. The choice between the two depends on the level of formality required in a given situation.

"Ask for" is commonly used in casual or informal settings, such as everyday conversations, friendly requests, or personal interactions. It is straightforward and direct in nature, often used among acquaintances or in less formal contexts. For example:

- "Can I ask for a favor?"
- "I'm asking for your help."
- "She asked for a raise."

On the other hand, "request" is typically used in more formal or professional situations, where a higher level of politeness and respect is expected. It is commonly used in business or official correspondence, formal letters, or when making official inquiries. For example:

- "I would like to request a meeting with you."
- "We kindly request your presence at the event."
- "Please submit your request in writing."

ChatGPT for the prompt, 'Could you please discuss the verbs 'ask for' and 'request' in terms of the degree of formality?'.

As shown in Figure 18, ChatGPT plays an important role in aiding learners to understand and adapt to the appropriate level of register and formality in diverse situations. By providing examples of vocabulary use in a variety of settings, it helps learners easily understand how their language choices should change depending on the situation. This experience improves learners' communication skills as a result of enabling them to effectively adapt their language to specific contexts.

CONCLUSION

This chapter presents a comprehensive overview of the impact of Artificial Intelligence (AI) on vocabulary knowledge and its potential to enhance vocabulary learning. While addressing the broader implications and advantages of AI in language education, the chapter gives particular attention to the application of chatbots in the domain of vocabulary instruction. However, the chapter extensively delves into the implementation of ChatGPT, an AI-powered language model, specifically within the context of vocabulary teaching. The chapter concludes by introducing the outputs generated by ChatGPT, in line with Nation's (2012) multidimensional aspect of vocabulary knowledge, thus highlighting the potential of ChatGPT to facilitate learners in gaining vocabulary.

Taken together, the studies mentioned in this chapter that utilize chatbots in vocabulary teaching and especially ChatGPT's capacity to contribute to the acquisition of multidimensional vocabulary knowledge suggest that artificial intelligence tools bring innovation to the learning environments and act as effective instruments both in language learning and particularly in vocabulary teaching and should be actively integrated into the language learning process.

This chapter also includes a growing body of evidence to suggest that the intensive use of artificial intelligence tools in many fields has necessarily made these tools a candidate to become a sought-after part of education. It would therefore be irrational to keep them off the agenda and not to capitalize on these tools in the field of education. Therefore, greater efforts are needed to conduct more studies that prioritize how learners can benefit more from AI tools. Further reviews should attempt to better understand how artificial intelligence takes role in language teaching. These studies will thus pave the way for further dissemination of knowledge and more effective use of AI tools in language teaching.

REFERENCES

Alsadoon, R. (2021). Chatting with AI Bot: Vocabulary learning assistant for Saudi EFL learners. *English Language Teaching*, *14*(6), 135–157. doi:10.5539/elt.v14n6p135

Atlas, S. (2023). *ChatGPT for higher education and professional development: A guide to conversational AI*. Digital Commons. https://digitalcommons.uri.edu/cba_facpubs/548

Belda-Medina, J., & Calvo-Ferrer, J. R. (2022). Using chatbots as AI conversational partners in language learning. *Applied Sciences (Basel, Switzerland)*, *12*(17), 8427. doi:10.3390/app12178427

Clarizia, F., Colace, F., Lombardi, M., Pascale, F., & Santaniello, D. (2018). Chatbot: An education support system for student. In A. Castiglione, F. Pop, M. Ficco, & F. Palmieri (Eds.), *Cyberspace Safety and Security* (pp. 291–302). Springer International Publishing. doi:10.1007/978-3-030-01689-0_23

Devlin, J., Chang, M.-W., Lee, K., & Toutanova, K. (2019). BERT: Pre-training of deep bidirectional transformers for language understanding. *NAACL-HLT*, 4171-4186. https://doi.org/ doi:10.18653/v1/N19-1423

Forrester, A. (2023). ChatGPT: What does it mean for language centres. *STiLE - Scholarship of Teaching in Language Education*, *1*(1), 1-22. https://www.stile.hk/osp/article/view/7

Fryer, L., & Carpenter, R. (2006). Emerging technologies: Bots as language learning tools. *Language Learning & Technology*, *10*(3), 8–14.

Fryer, L., Nakao, K., & Thompson, A. (2019). Chatbot learning partners: Connecting learning experiences, interest and competence. *Computers in Human Behavior*, *93*, 279–289. doi:10.1016/j.chb.2018.12.023

Fryer, L. K., Ainley, M., Thompson, A., Gibson, A., & Sherlock, Z. (2017). Stimulating and sustaining interest in a language course: An experimental comparison of chatbot and human task partners. *Computers in Human Behavior*, *75*, 461–468. doi:10.1016/j.chb.2017.05.045

Haristiani, N. (2019). Artificial Intelligence (AI) Chatbot as Language Learning Medium: An inquiry. *Journal of Physics: Conference Series*, *1387*(1), 012020. doi:10.1088/1742-6596/1387/1/012020

Hsu, M.-H., Chan, T.-M., & Yu, C.-S. (2023). Termbot: A chatbot-based crossword game for gamified medical terminology learning. *International Journal of Environmental Research and Public Health, 20*(5), 4185. doi:10.3390/ijerph20054185 PMID:36901193

Huang, W., Hew, K. F., & Fryer, L. K. (2022). Chatbots for language learning—Are they really useful? A systematic review of chatbot-supported language learning. *Journal of Computer Assisted Learning, 38*(1), 237–257. doi:10.1111/jcal.12610

Jeon, J. (2021). Chatbot-assisted dynamic assessment (CA-DA) for L2 vocabulary learning and diagnosis. *Computer Assisted Language Learning*, 1–27. doi:10.1080/09588221.2021.1987272

Kartal, G. (2023). Contemporary language teaching and learning with ChatGPT. *Contemporary Research in Language and Linguistics, 1*(1), 59-70. http://crlljournal.org/index.php/crll/article/view/10

Kasneci, E., Seßler, K., Küchemann, S., Bannert, M., Dementieva, D., Fischer, F., Gasser, U., Groh, G., Günnemann, S., Hüllermeier, E., Krusche, S., Kutyniok, G., Michaeli, T., Nerdel, C., Pfeffer, J., Poquet, O., Sailer, M., Schmidt, A., Seidel, T., & Kasneci, G. (2023). ChatGPT for good? On opportunities and challenges of large language models for education. *Learning and Individual Differences, 103*, 1–9. doi:10.1016/j.lindif.2023.102274

Kim, N.-Y. (2017). Effects of different types of chatbots on EFL learners' speaking competence and learner perception. *Cross-Cultural Studies, 48*, 223–252. doi:10.21049/ccs.2017.48..223

Kim, N.-Y. (2018a). A study on chatbots for developing Korean college students' English listening and reading skills. *Journal of Digital Convergence, 16*(8), 19–26. doi:10.14400/JDC.2018.16.8.019

Kim, N.-Y. (2018b). Chatbots and Korean EFL students' English vocabulary learning. *Journal of Digital Convergence, 16*(2), 1–7. doi:10.14400/JDC.2018.16.2.001

Kohnke, L. (2022). A pedagogical chatbot: A supplemental language learning tool. *RELC Journal, 0*(0). Advance online publication. doi:10.1177/00336882211067054

Kohnke, L., Moorhouse, B. L., & Zou, D. (2023). ChatGPT for language teaching and learning. *RELC Journal, 0*(0), 1–14. doi:10.1177/00336882231162868

Koraishi, O. (2023). Teaching English in the age of AI: Embracing ChatGPT to optimize EFL materials and assessment. *Language Education and Technology, 3*(1), 55-72. https://langedutech.com/letjournal/index.php/let/article/view/48

Kovačević, D. (2023). Use of ChatGPT in ESP teaching process. *22nd International Symposium INFOTEH-JAHORINA (INFOTEH),* (pp. 1–5). 10.1109/INFOTEH57020.2023.10094133

Laufer, B. (1992). How much lexis is necessary for reading comprehension? In P. J. L. Arnaud & H. Be'joint (Eds.), *Vocabulary and Applied Linguistics* (pp. 126–132). Macmillan. doi:10.1007/978-1-349-12396-4_12

Laufer, B. (1994). The lexical profile of second language writing: Does it change over time? *RELC Journal, 25*(2), 21–33. doi:10.1177/003368829402500202

Mikeladze, T. (2023). Creating teaching materials with ChatGPT. *13th International Research Conference on Education, Language and Literature.*

Nation, I. (2012). *Learning vocabulary in another language.* Cambridge University Press. doi:10.1017/CBO9781139524759

Polyzi, P., & Moussiades, L. (2023). An artificial vocabulary learning assistant. *Education and Information Technologies.* doi:10.100710639-023-11810-9

Qasem, F., Ghaleb, M., Mahdi, H. S., Al Khateeb, A., & Al Fadda, H. (2023). Dialog chatbot as an interactive online tool in enhancing ESP vocabulary learning. *Saudi Journal of Language Studies, 3*(2), 76–86. doi:10.1108/SJLS-10-2022-0072

Qian, K., Shea, R., Li, Y., Fryer, L. K., & Yu, Z. (2023). User Adaptive Language Learning Chatbots with a Curriculum. In N. Wang, G. Rebolledo-Mendez, V. Dimitrova, N. Matsuda, & O. C. Santos (Eds.), *Artificial Intelligence in Education. Posters and Late Breaking Results, Workshops and Tutorials, Industry and Innovation Tracks, Practitioners, Doctoral Consortium and Blue Sky. AIED 2023. Communications in Computer and Information Science* (Vol. 1831). Springer. doi:10.1007/978-3-031-36336-8_48

Radford, A., Wu, J., Child, R., Luan, D., Amodei, D., & Sutskever, I. (2019). Language models are unsupervised multitask learners. *OpenAI blog, 1*(8), 9.

Rashidi, N., & Khosravi, N. (2010). Assessing the role of depth and breadth of vocabulary knowledge in reading comprehension of Iranian EFL learners. *Journal of Pan-Pacific Association of Applied Linguistics, 14*(1), 81–108.

Riloff, E., & Thelen, M. (2000). A rule-based question answering system for reading comprehension tests. In *Proceedings of the 2000 ANLP/NAACL Workshop on Reading comprehension tests as evaluation for computer-based language understanding sytems.* Association for Computational Linguistics, USA, 13–19. https://doi.org/10.3115/1117595.1117598

Schmitt, N. (2010). *Researching vocabulary: A vocabulary research manual*. Palgrave Macmillan. doi:10.1057/9780230293977

Smutny, P., & Schreiberova, P. (2020). Chatbots for learning: A review of educational chatbots for the Facebook Messenger. *Computers & Education*, *151*, 103862. doi:10.1016/j.compedu.2020.103862

Stæhr, L. S. (2008). Vocabulary size and the skills of listening, reading and writing. *Language Learning Journal*, *36*(2), 139–152. doi:10.1080/09571730802389975

Stæhr, L. S. (2009). Vocabulary knowledge and advanced listening comprehension in English as a foreign language. *Studies in Second Language Acquisition*, *31*(4), 577–607. doi:10.1017/S0272263109990039

Teng, F. (2014). Assessing the depth and breadth of vocabulary knowledge with listening comprehension. *PASAA*, *48*, 29–56.

Turing, A. M. (1950). Computing machinery and intelligence. *Mind*, *59*(236), 433–460. doi:10.1093/mind/LIX.236.433

Ur, P. (2022). *Penny Ur's 77 tips for teaching vocabulary*. Cambridge University Press., doi:10.1017/9781009072892

Wang, Y. F., & Petrina, S. (2013). Using learning analytics to understand the design of an intelligent language tutor – Chatbot Lucy. *International Journal of Advanced Computer Science and Applications*, *4*(11), 124–131. doi:10.14569/IJACSA.2013.041117

Wilkins, D. A. (1972). *Linguistics in language teaching*. Arnold.

Chapter 11
Innovative Language Learning Approaches:
Immersive Technologies and Gamification

Mavis Chamboko-Mpotaringa
https://orcid.org/0000-0001-8488-4330
University of Johannesburg, South Africa

Blandina Manditereza
https://orcid.org/0000-0003-2564-5860
University of Free State, South Africa

ABSTRACT

The advancement of technology over the past two decades has provided various tools and platforms that facilitate and optimize the language-teaching-learning process using diverse teaching methods that help learners to acquire and understand new knowledge interactively. Despite extensive research highlighting the intersection between education and artificial intelligence technologies, many language teachers are unaware of innovative learning approaches at their disposal. As a result, the potential to transform classroom learning is yet to be realized. The chapter aims to close this gap by providing an overview of the transformation of language teaching experiences in the artificial intelligence age and exploring the opportunities and challenges associated with immersive and gamification technologies. The chapter argues that incorporating innovative technologies in teaching significantly contributes to language learning experiences. The chapter provides insight, more understanding and adds to the body of literature of the study area.

DOI: 10.4018/978-1-6684-9893-4.ch011

INTRODUCTION

Technology advancement has brought unprecedented classroom learning opportunities, from online platforms for virtual learning to digital tools for collaboration and interactive activities (Carpenter et al., 2022; Stephens & Roberts, 2017; Tao & Gao, 2022). Many of these opportunities, such as social media, e-games, big data, artificial intelligence, virtual reality, and artificial reality, are common in our daily lives. Similarly, today's students are becoming more accustomed to social technologies daily (Lyu & Lai, 2022). It is noticeable in the classroom when educators fail to use such technology (Bui, 2022). Despite the varied innovations that can be used in the classroom to improve language learning experiences, research indicates that these are not fully exploited (Parmaxi, 2023; Qiu et al., 2021) and are predominantly used for teacher-centered strategies (Bui, 2022), resulting in limited learner participation.

The chapter's exploration of immersive learning and gamification in language learning informs better teaching and learning strategies that improve the learning experience, especially for second language learners, and contributes to effective language learning. By further providing practical advice and recommendations for best practices, future directions, and opportunities, the chapter is a valuable resource for language educators and education policymakers, offering insights into immersive and gamification learning experiences in artificial intelligence-assisted language education. For researchers, the chapter suggests future research directions.

As the chapter aims to foster awareness of immersive learning and gamification and advocates for meaningful integration and use of digital technologies in language learning to drive the quality transformation of language teaching experience in the age of artificial intelligence, the chapter first illustrates the traditional teaching, learning, and assessment paradigm.

TRADITIONAL TEACHING, LEARNING, AND ASSESSMENT PARADIGM

Paradigms are rules, standards, beliefs, and values shared by an association, society, community, or scientists (Žukauskas et al., 2018). The traditional teaching, learning, and assessment paradigm refers to the conventional methods used in education to impart knowledge and evaluate student performance. Guided and inspired by Žukauskas et al. (2018)'s definition, da Costa Liberato et al. (2018) highlight the traditional paradigm of education as being within the historical context of 'traditional liberal pedagogy,' where truths were socially imposed, and teachers were regarded as the sole holders of knowledge. As opposed to progressive education, which places the students at the centre of teaching and learning, the traditional liberal pedagogy education approach values the pursuit of knowledge in a rational manner confined to pre-established truths. In support, (Sullivan, 2015) postulates that the traditional teaching, learning, and assessment paradigm involves the teacher having the authority to define the learning outcomes and decide how students should learn. Teaching can be regarded as engaging learners to enable their understanding and application of knowledge, concepts, and processes and includes design, content selection, delivery, assessment, and reflection (MacPhail et al., 2023). Learning, on the other hand, is the activity or process of gaining knowledge and skills by being taught, studying, practicing, or experiencing something, while assessment involves judging the amount of learning that took place because of learning and teaching (Enders & Kostewicz, 2023; Napper, 2012).

In traditional education pedagogy, the teachers' duties are mainly to pass on the knowledge without regard for learner ability or cognitive level. This is consistent with the long-established customs that society has traditionally used to transmit knowledge and skills from one generation to the next, replicating knowledge instead of reassembling knowledge. The teacher dominates the teaching-learning space by controlling the teaching and learning environment, methodology, and course curriculum (de Almeida et al., 2019; Tularam & Machisella, 2018). The knowledge-power relationship is inclined in favour of the teacher because the teacher is the primary source of knowledge, while the students are passive recipients of the information (Sullivan, 2015; Tomei, 2010; Voskoglou, 2023).

Learning, teaching, and assessing languages have long been rooted in traditional paradigms because learning a language is viewed as an intellectual endeavour that significantly benefits from memorization. Conventional methods of teaching languages require pupils to memorize texts, vocabulary, and content in addition to grammar rules (Djauhar, 2021). The teaching and learning method was teacher-centered; hence there needed to be more contact among students. In addition, historically, assessments were based on grades that reflected course standards and were typically based on weighted quarters and final examinations. The grading was used to interpret educational value and worth (Sullivan, 2015). Assessments were mainly standardized tests that checked students' ability to recollect and reproduce content tests (Quansah, 2018) and were true/false questions, quizzes, short answers, and essays. Students were believed to learn through recitation and recall; hence the greater focus was placed on the action of classroom-based assessment as compared to large-scale standardized tests (Voskoglou, 2023).

Three distinct approaches, namely the grammar-translation method, the direct method, and the audiolingual method have been adopted by language teachers. The grammar translation method was popularized and widely used for language teaching between the 1840 to 1940 era. The principle of the grammar-translation approach considers language as an intellectual activity which requires memorization as a learning tool while the teacher is represented as an authoritarian (Higgs & Krashen, 1983; Kaharuddin, 2022). The grammar translation method is based on analyzing and comprehending texts. Hence is oriented to improve students' reading comprehension and writing competencies (Kaharuddin, 2022). For several years, the grammar-translation method was employed in Europe to teach Greek and Latin, with teaching and learning focusing on the rules of translating grammar and vocabulary from native languages to second languages (Djauhar, 2021). The primary focus of this approach is that English words, phrases, and paragraphs are translated into and out of a learner's native language (Djauhar, 2021). The approach uses translation, synonyms, antonyms, analogues, completing the gaps, recalling facts, forming sentences, and comprehending the texts.

The second method: the direct method, was developed in the nineteenth century and is oriented to improve students' listening and speaking competence (Kaharuddin, 2022). Language learning was built around observations made by children in their pursuit of language learning. The approach was based on the four language skills- listening, speaking, reading, and writing- taught from the foundational learning phase. Classes followed a sequential pattern of reading aloud a specially graded text, thus introducing the lesson's vocabulary and grammatical structure, and students engaged in guided conversations, role-playing, and game-playing. The direct method views learning as thinking and communicating directly in the target language but discourages translation. The method emphasizes proficiency in speaking while grammar is taught inductively and motivated through the teacher's questions influencing children to react to given questions (Ifeanyi, 2020). The teacher uses demonstration and visual aids to engage students.

The third method is audiolingual, established in the 1950s and 1960s. Audiolingual ideologies portray language as a set of structures(Mei, 2018). The audiolingual method rests on the premise of the philosophy of behaviourists, who hold the notion that when content is presented as a dialogue, students must imitate given content and acquire correct habits—as a result, emphasizing repetition, reinforcement, and habit formation as critical strategies. The audio-lingual approach intends to help students become more proficient communicators while focusing on learning the structures and patterns of regular everyday discourse. The approach maintained teaching the four language skills in the natural order of acquisition: listening, speaking, reading, and writing. Audiolingual principles stress the following: use of tapes and visual aids, focus on proper pronunciations, there is no grammatical explanation, learning is dependent on memorization, and the teacher reinforces correct responses immediately (Ifeanyi, 2020). Similarity exists between the direct and audiolingual methods as they both use instruction within the target language (Jebahi, 2022).

The three aforementioned methods (the grammar-translation method, the direct method, and the audiolingual method) are part of the traditional paradigm, whose strength lies in its ability as a conventional evaluation method that gauges students' capacity for learning and memory retention (Mansory, 2020). Teachers can identify students' strengths and limitations by assessing the zone of proximal growth, thus allowing teachers to adapt learners' work according. In this way, teachers can also examine how much of the provided material or syllabus the student has learned using traditional evaluation methods. In addition, comparing the skills and abilities of different learners aids teachers in meeting diverse learner needs.

However, there are also many things that could be improved to the traditional teaching, learning, and assessment paradigm. Firstly, the approach can often be theoretical and disconnected from the real world (Mansory, 2020). For instance, in language learning, emphasis is placed on grammar rules and syntactic structures, which can be challenging to understand without examples of how they are used in real-life contexts or the memorization of verb conjugations without any context or application of the language in real-world scenarios. This can lead to students feeling disengaged from the course material, as they need help seeing the relevance of the topics to their everyday lives. Moreover, students are driven by fear of examination since the student is required to retain conditioned learning where cause and effect responses are displayed because the belief is that knowledge is a display of cause and effect (English & Kirshner, 2015).

Secondly, traditional language teaching, learning, and assessment paradigm no longer resonate with the current academic environment as they may not be able to keep up with the changing needs of the context because they often focus on rote learning rather than real-world skills (Swiecki et al., 2022). The traditional paradigm's one size fits all strategy cannot accommodate diverse student needs, where students are treated as having the same academic problems (Quansah, 2018).

Thirdly, traditional tests might not accurately determine a student's knowledge and skills. How can information acquired by memory and recall, as opposed to critical thinking abilities, be measured accurately? Rote learning deprives students of deep understanding since the students mainly engage in recitation and recall. They mostly memorize because educators emphasize memorization as a learning tool (de Almeida et al., 2019). The method restricts creativity, thinking out of the box, and is not linked to long-term memory. Consequently, assessments do not accommodate opportunities for collaboration and strategic problem-solving, and teachers need to fully understand students' capabilities because students develop limited comprehensive skills (Tularam & Machisella, 2018).

Fourth, the traditional assessment method may be difficult for educators and requires a lot of skill and time (Mansory, 2020). Considering that an educator's assessment ability is influenced by the educators' perspectives and academic, professional, and contextual understanding of evaluation, these factors may impact the educator's ability to design, implement, and evaluate assessments. For instance, a teacher with an equity-based perspective may recognize how particular assessments can impact certain students more than others and adjust the assessment accordingly. Similarly, a teacher's evaluation of student knowledge may be more holistic if the teacher deeply understands the student's cultural context.

To overcome the challenges of the traditional paradigm, there has been a call to adopt digital technologies in the education sector. However, the transition to digital technologies in learning has yet to be smooth sailing. For example, with online education, deception by students, such as screen sharing with another computer, keeping notes on smartphones, or faking identities to get third-party assistance, has become a significant problem in online assessments, reducing the significance of such examinations. Moreover, online learning may only be suitable for some students, as it requires a certain level of self-discipline and motivation (Swiecki et al., 2022).

Despite the challenges with online learning, as technology advances, many scholars have collaborated on the positive effects of digital technologies on language learning (Phakamach et al., 2022). This is because the present academic arena constitutes learners who are digital natives who grew up absorbed in technology and thus resulting in them having different learning styles and preferences. Today's learners have advanced technological needs (Haleem et al., 2022), the classroom environment has changed and become technologically enabled, and even the content that should be taught is constantly changing; therefore, pedagogy must change (MacPhail et al., 2023). At the same time, many nations face an increasing number of migrants, resulting in high demand for language teachers and academic institutions that specialize in teaching languages (Batardière et al., 2023). Coupled with this, language teachers face high teacher-learner ratios and overcrowded classrooms (Makarova et al., 2023) that are not conducive for students to participate meaningfully. These challenges force teachers to adopt modern pedagogical approaches where technology contributes to the learning outcomes.

IMMERSIVE LEARNING AND GAMIFICATION IN LANGUAGE LEARNING

Over time, knowledge acquisition and sharing methods have become more differentiated, diverse, and facilitated (Topal & Karaca, 2022). With the emergence of new technologies, language teachers today face many fascinating options for using technology to enhance language learning (Chocarro et al., 2023). In recent years, new teaching and learning formats like flipped classrooms and Massive Open Online Courses (MOOCs) have entered the education sector (Janssen et al., 2016;

Ng & Lo, 2022). In countries like China, Japan, and the USA, the development of education informatization is vigorously promoted, while the use of more affluent and more personalized teaching methods is gradually gaining ground among various teaching groups (Turan & Karabey, 2023; Yang & Liu, 2022; Zhang & Zou, 2020). One of the most promising approaches in computer-assisted language learning is immersive learning, which provides learners with an engaging and interactive learning environment that mimics real-life experiences (Cai, 2022). According to (Gonzalez-Argote & Gonzalez-Argote, 2022), immersive learning is the process of creating immersive learning experiences using immersive technologies such as Virtual Reality (VR), Augmented Reality (AR), and the metaverse. Using immersive technologies in language learning can help bridge the gap between traditional classroom and online learning. Using immersive technologies, language educators can create safe and controlled spaces for learners to practice and improve their language skills authentically and meaningfully (Chabot et al., 2020).

VR and AR are two related but distinct technologies. VR is a technology that uses computer-generated simulations to create a lifelike experience in a computer-generated environment, while AR is a technology that subtly integrates virtual information by overlaying digital information with the natural world (Lee, 2020; Luo et al., 2021). VR teaching and learning places learners in an environment of immersive teaching using hardware and software (Yang & Liu, 2022). By utilizing VR, learners can interact directly with the learning scenarios, thus breaking down the boundaries of traditional learning scenarios (Xin, 2022). VR-based language learning can significantly improve learners' language proficiency, learning, interaction, motivation, and confidence (Cai, 2022; Ganier et al., 2014). In language learning, VR can create simulated environments that resemble real-life situations, such as shopping, travelling, or socializing. These immersive environments provide learners a safe and controlled space to practice and improve their language skills (Soto et al., 2020).

Conversely, AR can improve learners' interaction with the real world because its key novelty features allow virtual and real worlds to coexist and provide additional information or context (Majid & Salam, 2021; Mills, 2022). The 3D educational content in AR provides students with the opportunity to explore and interact with the learning object, resulting in interactive and immersing learning experiences (Chen et al., 2020). Consequently, in language teaching and learning, AR provides a more contextualized and socialized learning experience (Lin et al., 2019). The use of well-designed AR applications enhances the presentation of information, captivates learners' attention, and stimulates curiosity through eye-catching formats like animation, audio, and pictures (Cai et al., 2022). Thus, AR provides learners with information about the objects they see around them in the language they are learning, resulting in improved vocabulary retention and motivation.

Metaverse is a term that refers to a collective virtual shared space created by the convergence of virtual reality and the Internet. Thus, the metaverse connects social media to virtual reality and augmented technologies. With social media and virtual reality joining forces, the metaverse unleashes creativity and paves the way for transformation (Phakamach et al., 2022). Here, VR, AR, and the real world interact; they are not just combined (Jang, 2021). In language teaching and learning, the metaverse can create virtual communities where learners can interact and practice their language skills with native speakers (Kim et al., 2022).

The gaming industry has been one of the first movers of immersive technology. With the number of people who play video games increasing daily (Berns et al., 2013; Berns & Ruiz-Rube, 2022), gaming and immersive technology have become almost synonymous, resulting in different industries leveraging this technology. The launch of the Play Station VR and even Pokemon Go has helped in this spacetime. Today, VR is not just niche technology gamers enjoy but has expanded into everyday life (Chamboko-Mpotaringa & Tichaawa, 2021). Despite not being at the forefront of gaming, evidence suggests that there has been an increase in the use of games to reduce anxiety in elementary school students (Jeon, 2021). As the use of smartphones and tablets (with better cameras, bigger screens sensitive to human touch screens, better audio quality, faster connectivity, and incorporation of GPS), become widespread and influential (Garnes-Tarazona, 2018), gamified Mobile-Assisted Language Learning (MALL) platforms have gained more acceptance and increased popularity (Shortt et al., 2021). Gamification is game-based teaching and learning, is a technique that uses game-based elements to neutralize the complex content by making learning fun using point scoring, peer competition, teamwork, score tables, badges, and leaderboards (Figueroa Flores, 2015; Hossein & Dehganzadeh, 2020). Gamification involves incorporating game elements and game design techniques into non-game contexts (Nguwi, 2023), implying that tasks, assignments, tests, and any theoretical contexts can be gamified. Gamified MALL refers to a type of learning facilitated by mobile devices, enabling learners to engage in learning activities without being limited to a specific geographic location while focusing specifically on the context of language learning (Shortt et al., 2021). In agreement, Kim et al. (2018) view gamification as a recurrent methodological strategy adopted in foreign language teaching.

Benefits of Immersive Learning and Gamification

Immersive learning and gaming experiences have the potential to significantly enhance language teaching and learning by using modal learning strategies, which provide learners with a more realistic, authentic, and meaningful learning experience (Hu et al., 2017). For example, a teacher could design a lesson where students use virtual reality to visit a market in a foreign country and practice their language skills by interacting with vendors and making purchases. Alternatively, learners can use metaverse platforms such as Second Life to attend virtual language classes or participate in virtual language exchange programs. The learners can practice their target language with native speakers in a virtual environment (Ajisoko, 2020), where they participate in virtual conversations, join virtual language classes, and engage in activities related to the language they are learning. By immersing themselves, learners acquire language proficiency and cultivate a profound understanding of the subject matter (Hossein & Dehganzadeh, 2020). Both teachers and students can explore the boundless possibilities of immersive technologies and unlock a new level of language proficiency and cultural understanding (Sullivan, 2015). Moreover, when teachers embrace immersive technologies into their pedagogical strategies by incorporating virtual reality, augmented reality, and the metaverse, they also enhance the efficacy of their lesson plans.

Recent work by Lee & Yoo-Kyung (2022) established that metaverse platforms reduce anxiety in second language learners by providing a comfortable learning environment resulting in immersive and engaging learning experiences for language learners. Consequently, incorporating immersive technologies into teaching paves the way for a dynamic and interactive educational landscape (Zhang & Zou, 2020), where students are no longer passive recipients but active participants in their learning journey. With the metaverse and virtual reality, learners can interact with virtual characters called avatars in captivating environments designed to refine the learners' linguistic abilities wherein language comes alive. Thus, leaving an indelible imprint upon the learners' memory.

Immersive technologies and gamification can personalize learning experiences and provide students with immediate feedback (Kuhail et al., 2022). Providing adequate support and feedback is also crucial when implementing immersive technologies in language learning. Feedback helps students to identify areas for improvement and track their progress. Teachers can use adaptive learning algorithms to personalize the language learning experience for each student. These algorithms can analyze a student's performance and adjust the difficulty and content of the learning materials to match their individual needs and abilities (Lyu & Lai, 2022). Virtual characters and chatbots can act as assistant teachers by providing additional practice opportunities for the learners. For instance, teachers could design an activity where students converse with a virtual character in the target language and use virtual characters or chatbots to provide students with additional opportunities to practice their speaking and listening skills.

Gamification increases engagement and motivation (Almarzouqi et al., 2022) through connectivism as it is closely followed by building a sense of community and belonging while nurturing meaningful connections, where even boundaries of communication are extended beyond classroom hours (Hossein & Dehganzadeh, 2020; Nguwi, 2023; Pinto et al., 2021). Coupled with the metaverse, the education sector is transformed by promoting communication and supportive, immersive learning. Gonzalez-Argote and Gonzalez-Argote (2022) ascertain that immersive learning is projected to dramatically boost e-learning by making virtual learning environments more lifelike and learning more engaging and experiential.

To demonstrate that immersive reality teaching has advantages, in their study, Soto et al. (2020) placed students in the virtual environment of a second language. Findings suggested improved, different skills of English as a foreign language and promoting the motivation of students to learn spoken English. Similarly, Nguwi (2023) investigated the use of game-based platforms from a pedagogical viewpoint. One positive aspect highlighted is the use of artificial intelligence (AI) assisted learning tools in flipping the classroom to allow the students to engage in a more active role in learning. The study further found that gamification promotes learners' engagement by designing learning activities for learners to go through a series of storylines. Chabot et al. (2020) explored the use of gamification and AI in education more broadly, and their study concurs that engagement in gamification motivates students and improves their learning outcomes.

Teachers can use immersive technologies and gamification for immersive learning by using gamification to motivate and engage students (Wang, 2023). Teachers can incorporate game-like elements such as points, badges, and leaderboards into language learning activities to make learning fun and engaging. For example, a teacher could design a vocabulary quiz where students earn points for correct answers and compete with their classmates for the top spot on the leaderboard. Learners learn best when they are having fun while pursuing set goals. Similarly, gamification in language learning drives engagement and motivates students, making learning enjoyable and engaging and testing their knowledge. Students engage deeper with the subject matter and easily and quickly assimilate new information.

Given the benefits of immersive technologies such as VR, AR, and metaverse and a strategy such as gamification, teachers can use these technologies in their teaching to enhance the language learning experience for their students in several ways. The technologies discussed in this section, VR, AR, the metaverse, and the gamification strategy, offer various opportunities for language educators to create interactive learning environments that can improve learners' language proficiency, reduces anxiety, and increases motivation and engagement. Students can experience a sense of immersion, improving their ability to interact realistically with the language and culture in a real-world setting, which can aid in content comprehension and retention. The integration of gaming into immersive technology enables teachers to provide students with more individualized instruction, allowing the learners to progress at their own pace (Pinto et al., 2021).

Challenges of Immersive Learning and Gamification

While immersive technologies and gamification can potentially enhance the language learning experience, there are also several challenges to consider before using these technologies. To corroborate this assertion, Hossein and Dehganzadeh (2020) state that as much as technology has numerous advantages, digital gamified technologies involve pedagogical and technological hiccups. To begin with, AI-based gamification is cost-prohibitive when it comes to the production and installation of the technology. In addition to purchasing and installing the hardware, the schools have additional costs related to curriculum, teaching, and assessment, which must all work together with the new technology to leverage its full potential. There is a need to train and retrain teachers to have the expertise, while other institutions might have to hire experts to design games that align with the curriculum and specific needs of the learners. Arguments arise as others might believe there is no reason to acquire new technology and spend millions on a system that is yet to be validated on whether it is helpful for educational growth.

For the learners, the high cost of purchasing a high-tech device compatible with the technology may result in a learning barrier since cost impacts accessibility (Koohang et al., 2023). This may further result in social inequality due to the widening digital divide between the students who can access the technology and those who cannot. Moreover, with the rapid technological developments, it is difficult for schools and learners to keep up with the changing technology. In addition, without adequate knowledge, learners' privacy might be compromised due to digital footprint and digital citizenship.

AI's dependency on technology makes immersive technology and gamification systems susceptible to system malfunctions or other technical problems. As a result, teachers and learners may be demotivated and frustrated as studies become disrupted. The issue of demotivation is supported by the views of Furdu et al. (2017), who concluded that a decrease in motivation is another disadvantage of gamification. Furdu et al. (2017) further contend that AI dehumanizes the learning environment. Despite AI systems providing customized learning experiences, AI cannot replace the vital human connection required for language learning. By using AI, students will likely miss the social and cultural components of language learning and will have different social cues than those students having face-to-face time with their teacher and other students.

Furthermore, the advantages of gamification in language learning are questionable since some studies' findings indicate that gamification participation does not reflect how well students learn in general (Wang, 2023). A study by Domínguez et al. (2013) highlights that students who completed a gamified exercise underperformed in written tasks and participated in fewer class activities. Domínguez et al. (2013)

findings imply that not all students will benefit from gamification. Consequently, there is a need for educators to adopt strategies to counteract the challenges.

Best Practices for Using Immersive Technologies and Gamification in Language Teaching, Learning, and Assessment

It is the author's view and that of other scholars (Zain et al., 2022) that immersive technologies and gamification in language teaching, learning, and assessment are expected to increase as technology continues to evolve. In support, (Almarzouqi et al., 2022) posit that the increased innovation and use of VR and AR in education settings will dramatically impact teaching, learning, and assessment practices. Language learning can be time-consuming, stressful, anxiety-inducing challenging, and require perseverance to learn a new language (Shortt et al., 2021). Without enough motivation, it is easy for students to quit. Immersive technologies and gamified MALL motivate learners (Chabot et al., 2020). This is because immersive technologies and gamification allow learners and teachers to engage and experience the virtual environment more realistically, authentically, and immersively than traditional methods (Scrivner et al., 2019).

There have been several successful implementations of immersive technologies and gamification in language teaching, learning, and assessment, such as Duolingo, Babbel, and Busuu (Garnes-Tarazona, 2018). Duolingo is a popular mobile-assisted language learning application that uses gamification to engage and motivate users (Ajisoko, 2020; Ritonga et al., 2022). Duolingo employs AI to adapt lessons to individual learning levels. The lessons primarily focus on introducing new vocabulary fun and excitingly (Jaelani & Sutari, 2020). The platform analyzes user responses to assess strengths and weaknesses, allowing it to adjust content and provide targeted exercises. A systematic review of Duolingo literature from 2012 to early 2020 found that the app's challenging tasks, reward incentives, systematic levels, and ranking of users according to their achievements demonstrate strong gamification elements within this popular language learning application (Shortt et al., 2021). Incorporating interactive and social learning elements into the language learning lessons also enhances the student experience. Interactive activities such as role-playing can help students practice their language skills collaboratively and engagingly.

Babel is a language learning app available on iOS, Android, and the web, with content synced across multiple devices (Sporn et al., 2020). Similar to Duolingo, Babbel uses AI to analyze user behavior and responses to provide personalized learning paths. It identifies areas where learners need improvement and adjusts lessons accordingly. Babbel is perceived to improve learners writing and communication skills; specifically, learners improve spoken competence (Garnes-Tarazona, 2018; Mendes de Oliveira et al., 2021). Babbel also uses speech recognition technology to help users improve their pronunciation. Babbel's pedagogical method empowers learners to speak a new language in real life (Sporn et al., 2020). The success of Babel has been supported by earlier studies, such as (Loewen et al., 2020), who confirms that the app measurably improved second language speaking skills and explicit grammar and vocabulary knowledge in the study participants. Babbel provides a personalized and learner-centered experience with a positive atmosphere (Mendes de Oliveira et al., 2021).

Founded in 2008, the Busuu app has course material in 13 languages that facilitate the learning of language skills for listening, reading, speaking, and writing from native speakers (Syafrizal & Septiawati, 2022). Busuu combines AI and human feedback for language learning. It uses AI to assess user exercises and provide immediate corrections. Busuu also offers personalized study plans based on user goals and progress. Native speakers review more complex tasks. Moreover, Busuu motivates learners and enhances social interaction (Garnes-Tarazona, 2018). A study conducted by Rosell-Aguilar (2018) found positive language improvement and learner engagement when using Busuu.

Educaplay, a platform for e-learning and authoring, enhances the development of skills, values, and attitudes inherent to the profile of 21st-century students (Graça et al., 2022). Its main aim is to enable teachers of various disciplines to design learner-friendly materials (Sujatha & Menon, 2021). As a result, Educaplay does not require teachers to have advanced technical knowledge. This means that even teachers who possess basic knowledge of computers and Google Forms can use Educaplay with ease.

Duolingo, Babbel, and Busuu emerged as pioneers and gained widespread recognition in language learning, even though the market for language learning apps and platforms has significantly increased in recent years (Garnes-Tarazona, 2018). The apps' early achievements allowed them to establish themselves as leaders in the use of technology in language learning as they gained early credibility and established a strong foothold (Shortt et al., 2021). Literature has shown that Duolingo, Babbel, Busuu, and Educaplay have incorporated AI technology to deliver customized learning experiences to their users (Jaelani & Sutari, 2020).. The integration of artificial intelligence enables these apps to offer personalized feedback and tailored learning paths to learners, enhancing their sense of achievement and advancement. With the assistance of AI, students are empowered to make measurable progress and gain confidence in their language skills, making the language learning journey more enjoyable. Also, the effective implementation of gamification makes learning rewarding and encourages students to engage consistently. Furthermore, despite the apps offering a variety of content, such as vocabulary, grammar, interactive exercises, and real-life scenarios, the apps' interfaces are user-friendly and are easily accessible on multiple devices. This has made them attractive to a wide range of learners (Mendes de Oliveira et al., 2021).

Having analyzed the literature on immersive technologies and gamification, Table 1 systemizes the best practices for using immersive technologies and gamification in language teaching, learning, and assessment. Table 1 offers practical advice and recommendations for best practices in implementing immersive technologies in language learning, such as using realistic scenarios and authentic learning, incorporating interactive visualization, and providing adequate support and feedback. Scrivner et al. (2019) believe that immersive technologies are ideal for learning

Table 1. Best practices for using immersive technologies and gamification

Category	Strategy	Example
Teaching	Authentic learning	Structure virtual learning according to real-life situations
	Learning objectives	Clearly define the learning objectives for the immersive experience and ensure that they align with the overall learning goals.
	Collaborative learning	Design the immersive experience to facilitate collaboration among learners, allowing them to work together and share knowledge and resources.
	Interactive visualization	Adopt contextual visualization to display visual content according to the specific context. Design the immersive experience to be interactive and engaging, allowing learners to explore and interact with the virtual environment meaningfully.
	Learner directed	Give adequate instructions to infer knowledge through interaction with the 3D digital objects representing the languages and cultures within the relevant content. Give immediate feedback.
Learning	Instructional strategies	Examine the curriculum and then decide on the most effective rather than the most appealing method to use technology to improve pedagogy.
	Environmental design	Identify and use creative and visually stimulating visual spaces rather than sending the students to virtual spaces that attempt to replicate the brick-and-mortar of the traditional classroom. Use realistic simulations in the immersive experience to allow learners to practice and learn in a virtual environment that closely resembles the real world.
Evaluation and assessment	Formative assessment	Provide students with informational feedback on their performance, the learning process, and status, which they can use to reflect, plan, and reorganize. Regularly evaluate the effectiveness of the immersive experience and adjust as needed to improve the learning experience.
	After action review	Review practice applied to completed tasks so that learners can learn to reflect and enhance their training. This strategy is implemented during and or after the teaching sessions.

Authors' compilation

instruction in languages as they combine visual, auditory, and kinesthetic learning styles. Language teaching, learning, and assessment in the age of AI promise to be a more engaging and efficient experience for students.

FUTURE DIRECTIONS AND OPPORTUNITIES

In recent years, there has been a shift towards task-based teaching techniques in foreign language education, prioritizing student motivation by emphasizing effective communication and practical language skills while moving away from traditional grammar-translation methods (De La Guia et al., 2016). As we envision the future, the language teaching experience in the age of AI holds numerous opportunities, emerging trends, and transformative potential, mainly through immersive technologies and gamification.

With immersive technologies and gamification, AR, VR, and the metaverse will likely be increasingly used in language learning. Language learning can become a more engaging and efficient experience for students. One of the key benefits of using immersive technologies in language learning is the ability to create realistic scenarios and authentic cultural contexts (Hu et al., 2017). This allows students to practice their language skills in a simulated environment resembling real-life situations. For example, a Spanish student with an upcoming cultural exchange program to South Africa could learn isiXhosa by participating in a virtual market in Eastern Cape, South Africa, where the student would need to use language skills to make purchases and interact with the vendors. This immersive experience could help the student develop language skills more naturally and intuitively before the exchange program.

Another trend and opportunity are the use of adaptive learning algorithms to personalize the language learning experience for each student. These algorithms can analyze a student's performance and adjust the difficulty and content of the learning materials to match their individual needs and abilities. This can help students learn at their own pace and focus on areas where they need the most improvement. Also, immersive technologies and gamification can make it easier for students with disabilities to access educational and social opportunities (Koohang et al., 2023). For example, participating in an immersive learning environment and engaging with instructors and course material can enhance students' interpersonal and learning abilities with autism, special needs, and social interaction challenges. This allows students to navigate new worlds by visualization without feeling overwhelmed.

People tend to adopt new technologies they consider useful (Chamboko-Mpotaringa & Tichaawa, 2023). With gamification becoming an increasingly valuable and popular language learning tool, the future will likely see more gamified-

MALL platforms being developed and adopted. These emerging technologies may further transform the language teaching experience in the age of AI. For instance, natural language processing and speech recognition advances could enable more sophisticated interactions between students and avatars or chatbots. This could give students more opportunities to practice speaking and listening skills in a safe and controlled environment. By incorporating game-like elements such as points, badges, and leaderboards into language learning activities, teachers can motivate students to engage more deeply with the material and make the learning process fun and engaging.

Overall, the future of language teaching in the age of AI is full of exciting possibilities (Koohang et al., 2023). With the continued development of immersive technologies and gamification, we can expect to see even more innovative approaches to language learning that engage students and help them develop their skills in new and exciting ways.

FUTURE RESEARCH DIRECTIONS

From prior literature, we found that although some challenges are associated with using immersive technologies and gamification in language teaching, learning, and assessment, it is a positive shift from the traditional teaching and learning paradigm. This is because using immersive technologies and gamification has great benefits and opportunities for language practitioners and students. In addition, the literature suggests that as technology continuously develops, the adoption of immersive technologies is likely to increase; thus, we ask the following future research questions, which can guide future research.

1. How can immersive technologies and gamification be tailored to individual student needs and learning styles? This question is essential because personalized learning is becoming increasingly popular and influential in education, and understanding how to implement this approach in immersive language learning can improve student engagement and outcomes.
2. What are the long-term effects of immersive technologies and gamification on language learning outcomes? This question is critical to address as immersive technologies, and gamification are new to language education, and understanding their long-term effects can support their integration into curricula and inform the future development of these methodologies.
3. How can immersive technologies and gamification enhance language assessment practices? This question is important to address as traditional language assessment methods may not effectively measure language proficiency in

immersive environments, and developing new assessment practices can ensure that language proficiency is being accurately measured and evaluated.

4. What cultural and ethical considerations should be considered when using immersive technologies and gamification in language education? This question is important to ensure that these technologies are culturally sensitive and appropriate and that ethical concerns such as data privacy and security are being addressed.

CONCLUSION

This study is a short version of the authors' review on immersive learning and gamification in language teaching, learning, and assessment in AI adoption and a call to research presence in transforming the language teaching experience in the age of AI that considers gamification and immersive learning experiences in AI-assisted language education. Moreover, the chapter shows that using immersive technologies and gamification can overcome the limitations of time and space. Immersive technologies and gamification enhance language learning by providing authentic learning experiences to learners and allowing teachers and students to explore the vast potential of these technologies and unlock a whole new level of language proficiency. Therefore, understanding the benefits and opportunities of adopting immersive technologies and gamification in language learning, teaching, and assessment can incite educators and policymakers to incorporate AR, VR, and the metaverse in their teaching, while understanding the challenges is crucial in effectively utilizing these techniques to enhance language education and to ensure that their implementation aligns with the learning objectives and student needs. Based on the literature review, the chapter systematized best practices for using immersive technologies and gamification in language learning, teaching, and assessment, which can help educators to design and implement effective and engaging language learning experiences for their students. By following best practices, educators can ensure that language education is delivered in a way that is consistent with established standards and expectations for language proficiency. The chapter did not evaluate the quality of immersive and gamification technologies. However, developments in AR, VR, and the metaverse will make using immersive technologies and gamification in education highly relevant and timely. Thus, with the right combination of creativity, innovation, and technological magic, teachers can revolutionize how languages are taught, sparking joy, excitement, and a lifelong love for linguistic exploration among their students. The future of language education is here, and it is an exhilarating adventure in immersive learning.

REFERENCES

Ajisoko, P. (2020). The use of Duolingo apps to improve English vocabulary learning. *International Journal of Emerging Technologies in Learning*, *15*(7), 149. doi:10.3991/ijet.v15i07.13229

Almarzouqi, A., Aburayya, A., & Salloum, S. A. (2022). Prediction of User's Intention to Use Metaverse System in Medical Education: A Hybrid SEM-ML Learning Approach. *IEEE Access : Practical Innovations, Open Solutions*, *10*, 43421–43434. doi:10.1109/ACCESS.2022.3169285

Batardière, M. T., Berthaud, S., C¨atibušić, B., & Flynn, C. J. (2023). Language teaching and learning in Ireland: 2012-2021. In Language Teaching, 56(1). doi:10.1017/S0261444822000374

Berns, A., Gonzalez-Pardo, A., & Camacho, D. (2013). Game-like language learning in 3-D virtual environments. *Computers & Education*, *60*(1), 210–220. doi:10.1016/j.compedu.2012.07.001

Berns, A., & Ruiz-Rube, I. (2022). Use of digital game creation tools in computer assisted language learning. *Digital Games in Language Learning*, 35–51. doi:10.4324/9781003240075-3

Bui, T. H. (2022). English teachers' integration of digital technologies in the classroom. *International Journal of Educational Research Open*, *3*, 100204. doi:10.1016/j.ijedro.2022.100204

Cai, Y. (2022). A Review of Virtual Reality Technology in EFL Teaching. *Journal of Education. Humanities and Social Sciences*, *4*, 260–263. doi:10.54097/ehss.v4i.2783

Cai, Y., Pan, Z., & Liu, M. (2022). Augmented reality technology in language learning: A meta-analysis. In Journal of Computer Assisted Learning, 38(4). doi:10.1111/jcal.12661

Carpenter, J. P., Shelton, C. C., & Schroeder, S. E. (2022). The education influencer: A new player in the educator professional landscape. *Journal of Research on Technology in Education*, 1–16. doi:10.1080/15391523.2022.2030267

Chabot, S., Drozdal, J., Peveler, M., Zhou, Y., Su, H., & Braasch, J. (2020). A Collaborative, Immersive Language Learning Environment Using Augmented Panoramic Imagery. *6th International Conference of the Immersive Learning Research Network (ILRN)*. IEEE. 10.23919/iLRN47897.2020.9155140

Chamboko-Mpotaringa, M., & Tichaawa, T. M. (2021). Tourism digital marketing tools and views on future trends: A systematic review of literature. *African Journal of Hospitality, Tourism and Leisure*, *10*(2), 712–726. doi:10.46222/ajhtl.19770720-128

Chamboko-Mpotaringa, M., & Tichaawa, T. M. (2023). Domestic tourists' perceptions of the intention to use digital marketing tools and platforms. *Geo Journal of Tourism and Geosites*, *46*(1), 9–18. doi:10.30892/gtg.46101-995

Chen, M. P., Wang, L., Zou, D., Lin, S. Y., Xie, H., & Tsai, C. C. (2020). Effects of captions and English proficiency on learning effectiveness, motivation and attitude in augmented-reality-enhanced theme-based contextualized EFL learning. *Computer Assisted Language Learning*, 1–31. doi:10.1080/09588221.2018.1544151

Chocarro, R., Cortiñas, M., & Marcos-Matás, G. (2023). Teachers' attitudes towards chatbots in education: A technology acceptance model approach considering the effect of social language, bot proactiveness, and users' characteristics. *Educational Studies*, *49*(2), 295–313. doi:10.1080/03055698.2020.1850426

da Costa Liberato, P. M., Alén-González, E., & de Azevedo Liberato, D. F. V. (2018). Digital technology in a smart tourist destination: The case of Porto. *Journal of Urban Technology*, *25*(1), 75–97. doi:10.1080/10630732.2017.1413228

de Almeida, F. A. S., de Oliveira Marques, P. C., Adão, J. M., Teixeira, Z. D., & Porto, M. D. (2019). The Paradigms of Traditional Educational Culture in the Context of Liquid Modernity: An Empirical Study. *Creative Education*, *10*(04), 784–795. doi:10.4236/ce.2019.104058

De La Guia, E., Camacho, V. L., Orozco-Barbosa, L., Brea Lujan, V. M., Penichet, V. M. R., & Lozano Perez, M. (2016). Introducing IoT and Wearable Technologies into Task-Based Language Learning for Young Children. *IEEE Transactions on Learning Technologies*, *9*(4), 366–378. doi:10.1109/TLT.2016.2557333

Djauhar, R. (2021). The Grammar-Translation Method, The Direct Method, and The Audio-Lingual Method. *Langua. Journal of Linguistics, Literature, and Language Education*, *4*(1).

Domínguez, A., Saenz-De-Navarrete, J., De-Marcos, L., Fernández-Sanz, L., Pagés, C., & Martínez-Herráiz, J. J. (2013). Gamifying learning experiences: Practical implications and outcomes. *Computers & Education*, *63*, 380–392. doi:10.1016/j.compedu.2012.12.020

Enders, O. G., & Kostewicz, D. (2023). Secondary Teachers' Remote Instructional Practices in Mathematics for Students With Disabilities. *Journal of Special Education Technology*, *38*(1), 50–60. doi:10.1177/01626434211059486

English, L. D., & Kirshner, D. (2015). Handbook of international research in mathematics education: Third edition. In Handbook of International Research in Mathematics Education: Third Edition. doi:10.4324/9780203448946

Figueroa Flores, J. F. (2015). Using Gamification to enhance second language learning. *Digital Education Review, 27*.

Furdu, I., Tomozei, C., & Kose, U. (2017). Pros and Cons Gamification and Gaming in Classroom.: Discovery Service for Univ of South Carolina. *BRAIN: Broad Research in Artificial Intelligence & Neuroscience, 8*(2).

Ganier, F., Hoareau, C., & Tisseau, J. (2014). Evaluation of procedural learning transfer from a virtual environment to a real situation: A case study on tank maintenance training. *Ergonomics, 57*(6), 828–843. doi:10.1080/00140139.2014.899628 PMID:24678862

Garnes-Tarazona, I. (2018). Exploring socio-cultural elements in three commercial English language learning apps. *International Journal of Computer-Assisted Language Learning and Teaching, 8*(1), 65–82. doi:10.4018/IJCALLT.2018010105

Gonzalez-Argote, J., & Gonzalez-Argote, D. (2022). 10 Best practices in Immersive Learning Design and 10 points of connection with the Metaverse. *Metaverse Basic and Applied Research, 2*, 7. doi:10.56294/mr20237

Graça, V., Quadro-Flores, P., & Ramos, A. (2022). The Integration of the Digital Platform Educaplay in Interdisciplinary Paths in the 1st and 2nd Basic Education Cycles. *Athens Journal of Education, 9*(3), 377–392. doi:10.30958/aje.9-3-2

Haleem, A., Javaid, M., Qadri, M. A., & Suman, R. (2022). Understanding the role of digital technologies in education: A review. *Sustainable Operations and Computers, 3*, 275–285. doi:10.1016/j.susoc.2022.05.004

Higgs, T. V., & Krashen, S. D. (1983). Principles and Practice in Second Language Acquisition. *Modern Language Journal, 67*(2), 168. doi:10.2307/328293

Hossein, D., & Dehganzadeh, H. (2020). Investigating effects of digital gamification-based language learning: A systematic review. *Journal of English Language Teaching and Learning, 12*, 53–93.

Hu Au, E., & Lee, J. J. (2017). Virtual reality in education: A tool for learning in the experience age. *International Journal of Innovation in Education, 4*(4), 215. doi:10.1504/IJIIE.2017.091481

Ifeanyi, U. (2020). Language Teaching Methods: A Conceptual Approach. *Research Gate, 9*(January 2015).

Jaelani, A., & Sutari, D. R. (2020). Students' Perception of Using Duolingo Application As a Media in Learning Vocabulary. *The 2nd Bogor English and Teacher (BEST) Conference*.

Jang, J. (2021). A study on a Korean speaking class based on metaverse: Using Gather. town. *Journal of Korean Language Education, 32*, 279–301.

Janssen, D., Tummel, C., Richert, A., & Isenhardt, I. (2016). Virtual Environments in Higher Education – Immersion as a Key Construct for Learning 4.0. [IJAC]. *International Journal of Advanced Corporate Learning, 9*(2), 20. doi:10.3991/ijac.v9i2.6000

Jebahi, K. (2022). Approaches and Methods in Language Teaching and Learning over Time. *Language and Literature, 24*(3), 88–106. doi:10.20360/langandlit29595

Jeon, J. H. (2021). A Study on the principle of metaverse composition with a focus on Roblox. *Korean Association for Visual Culture, 38*, 257–279. doi:10.21299/jovc.2021.38.10

Kaharuddin. (2022). E-Learning During the COVID-19 Outbreak: The Effect of the Grammar Translation Method and the Direct Method on Students' English Competence. *Journal of Language Teaching and Research, 13*(2). doi:10.17507/jltr.1302.06

Kim, M., Sim, J., & Ryu, S. (2022). A Study on Foreign Students' Perception of Metaverse-Based Korean Language Course as General Education. *The Korean Association of General Education, 16*(6), 183–195. Advance online publication. doi:10.46392/kjge.2022.16.6.183

Kim, S., Song, K., Lockee, B., & Burton, J. (2018). *Gamification in Learning and Education*. Springer International Publishing., doi:10.1007/978-3-319-47283-6

Koohang, A., Nord, J. H., Ooi, K.-B., Tan, G. W.-H., Al-Emran, M., Aw, E. C.-X., Baabdullah, A. M., Buhalis, D., Cham, T.-H., Dennis, C., Dutot, V., Dwivedi, Y. K., Hughes, L., Mogaji, E., Pandey, N., Phau, I., Raman, R., Sharma, A., Sigala, M., & Wong, L.-W. (2023). Shaping the Metaverse into Reality: A Holistic Multidisciplinary Understanding of Opportunities, Challenges, and Avenues for Future Investigation. *Journal of Computer Information Systems, 63*(3), 1–31. doi:10.1080/08874417.2023.2165197

Kuhail, M. A., Elsayary, A., Farooq, S., & Alghamdi, A. (2022). Exploring Immersive Learning Experiences: A Survey. In Informatics, 9(4). doi:10.3390/informatics9040075

Lee, J. (2020). Problem-based gaming via an augmented reality mobile game and a printed game in foreign language education. *Education and Information Technologies*, *27*(1), 743–771. doi:10.100710639-020-10391-1

Lee, J., & Yoo-kyung, J. (2022). Effects of Video Conferencing and Metaverse Platforms on Korean EFL University Learners' Self-assessed L2 Speaking, Interaction, Immersion, and Affective Factors. *Journal of Research in Curriculum Instruction*, *26*(4).

Lin, S. Y., Chen, M. P., Wang, L. C., Kao, Y. T., Zou, D., & Xie, H. (2019). Enhancing low achievers EFL learning with interactive digital technologies. In C. Maiga, S. Hyo-Jeong, W. Lung-Hsiang, Y. Fu-Yun, S. Ju-Ling, & B. Ivica (Eds.), *Proceedings of the ICCE 2019 - 27th International Conference on Computers in Education.* (pp. 617–623). Kenting: Asia-Pacific Society for Computers in Education.

Loewen, S., Isbell, D. R., & Sporn, Z. (2020). The effectiveness of app-based language instruction for developing receptive linguistic knowledge and oral communicative ability. *Foreign Language Annals*, *53*(2), 209–233. doi:10.1111/flan.12454

Luo, H., Li, G., Feng, Q., Yang, Y., & Zuo, M. (2021). Virtual reality in K-12 and higher education: A systematic review of the literature from 2000 to 2019. *Journal of Computer Assisted Learning*, *37*(3), 887–901. doi:10.1111/jcal.12538

Lyu, B., & Lai, C. (2022). Analysing learner engagement with native speaker feedback on an educational social networking site: An ecological perspective. *Computer Assisted Language Learning*, 1–35. doi:10.1080/09588221.2022.2030364

MacPhail, A., Tannehill, D., Leirhaug, P. E., & Borghouts, L. (2023). Promoting instructional alignment in physical education teacher education. *Physical Education and Sport Pedagogy*, *28*(2), 153–164. doi:10.1080/17408989.2021.1958177

Majid, S. N. A., & Salam, A. R. (2021). A systematic review of augmented reality applications in language learning. *International Journal of Emerging Technologies in Learning*, *16*(10), 18–34. doi:10.3991/ijet.v16i10.17273

Makarova, I., Duarte, J., & Huilcán, M. I. (2023). Experts' views on the contribution of language awareness and translanguaging for minority language education. *Language Awareness*, *32*(1), 74–93. Advance online publication. doi:10.1080/09658416.2021.1963976

Mansory, M. (2020). The Significance of Non-traditional and Alternative Assessment in English Language Teaching: Evidence From Literature. *International Journal of Linguistics*, *12*(5), 210. doi:10.5296/ijl.v12i5.17782

Mei, Y. (2018). Comments on the audiolingual method. *International Journal of Arts and Commerce, 7*(4).

Mendes de Oliveira, M., Sporn, Z., Kliemann, L., Borschke, A., & Meyering, M. (2021). Online language learning and workplace communication: a study on Babbel's virtual-classroom solution. In Computer Assisted Language Learning. doi:10.1080/09588221.2021.2002364

Mills, K. A. (2022). Potentials and Challenges of Extended Reality Technologies for Language Learning. *Anglistik: International Journal of English Studies, 33*(1), 147–163. www.tcpdf.org

Napper, V. S. (2012). Alignment of Learning, Teaching, and Assessment. In Encyclopedia of the Sciences of Learning. doi:10.1007/978-1-4419-1428-6_1847

Ng, L. K., & Lo, C. K. (2022). Flipped Classroom and Gamification Approach: Its Impact on Performance and Academic Commitment on Sustainable Learning in Education. *Sustainability (Basel), 14*(9), 5428. doi:10.3390u14095428

Nguwi, Y. Y. (2023). Technologies for Education: From Gamification to AI-enabled Learning. *International Journal of Multidisciplinary Perspectives in Higher Education, 8*(1), 111–132.

Parmaxi, A. (2023). Virtual reality in language learning: A systematic review and implications for research and practice. *Interactive Learning Environments, 31*(1), 172–184. doi:10.1080/10494820.2020.1765392

Phakamach, P., Senarith, P., & Wachirawongpaisarn, S. (2022). The Metaverse in Education: The Future of Immersive Teaching & Learning. *RICE Journal of Creative Entrepreneurship and Management, 3*(2), 75–88.

Pinto, R. D., Peixoto, B., Melo, M., Cabral, L., & Bessa, M. (2021). Foreign language learning gamification using virtual reality—A systematic review of empirical research. *Education Sciences, 11*(5), 222. Advance online publication. doi:10.3390/educsci11050222

Qiu, X., Chiu, C.-K., Zhao, L.-L., Sun, C.-F., & Chen, S. (2021). Trends in VR/AR technology-supporting language learning from 2008 to 2019: A research perspective. *Interactive Learning Environments*. Advance online publication. doi:10.1080/10494820.2021.1874999

Quansah, F. (2018). Traditional or Performance Assessment: What is the Right Way to Assessing Learners? *Research on Humanities and Social Sciences, 8*(1).

Ritonga, M., Febriani, S. R., Kustati, M., Khaef, E., Ritonga, A. W., & Yasmar, R. (2022). Duolingo: An Arabic Speaking Skills' Learning Platform for Andragogy Education. *Education Research International*, *2022*, 1–9. doi:10.1155/2022/7090752

Rosell-Aguilar, F. (2018). Autonomous language learning through a mobile application: A user evaluation of the busuu app. *Computer Assisted Language Learning*, *31*(8), 854–881. doi:10.1080/09588221.2018.1456465

Scrivner, O., Madewell, J., Buckley, C., & Perez, N. (2019). Best Practices in the Use of Augmented and Virtual Reality Technologies for SLA: Design, Implementation, and Feedback. In M. Carrió-Pastor (Ed.), *Teaching Language and Teaching Literature in Virtual Environments* (pp. 55–72). Springer Nature. doi:10.1007/978-981-13-1358-5_4Shortt, M., Tilak, S., Kuznetcova, I., Martens, B., & Akinkuolie, B. (2021). Gamification in mobile-assisted language learning: A systematic review of Duolingo literature from public release of 2012 to early 2020. *Computer Assisted Language Learning*. doi:10.1080/09588221.2021.1933540

Soto, J. B., Ocampo, D. T., Colon, L. B., & Oropesa, A. V. (2020). Perceptions of ImmerseMe virtual reality platform to improve English communicative skills in higher education. *International Journal of Interactive Mobile Technologies*, *14*(7), 4–19. doi:10.3991/ijim.v14i07.12181

Sporn, Z., Chanter, J., & Meehan, D. (2020). Babbel Language Learning Podcasts. [IJAC]. *International Journal of Advanced Corporate Learning*, *13*(3), 43. doi:10.3991/ijac.v13i3.17025

Stephens, G. E., & Roberts, K. L. (2017). Facilitating collaboration in online groups. *The Journal of Educators Online*, *14*(1).

Sujatha, A., & Menon, S. A. (2021). First Steps in Online Gamification: Tips for the Language Classroom. *Gedrag en Organisatie*, *34*(4), 227–241.

Sullivan, S. C. (2015). Shifting Educational Paradigms: From Traditional to Competency-Based Education for Diverse Learners. *American Secondary Education*, *43*(3).

Swiecki, Z., Khosravi, H., Chen, G., Martinez-Maldonado, R., Lodge, J. M., Milligan, S., Selwyn, N., & Gašević, D. (2022). Assessment in the age of artificial intelligence. *Computers and Education: Artificial Intelligence*, *3*, 100075. doi:10.1016/j.caeai.2022.100075

Syafrizal, S., & Septiawati, T. (2022). Enhancing listening skills of EFL Indonesian learners through Busuu application. *International Journal of English Language and Literature Studies*, *11*(3), 147–154. Advance online publication. doi:10.55493/5019.v11i3.4615

Tao, J., & Gao, X. (2022). Teaching and learning languages online: Challenges and responses. *System*, *107*, 107. doi:10.1016/j.system.2022.102819

Tomei, L. A. (2010). Learning Theories and Pedagogy: Teaching the Traditional Learner. *Designing Instruction for the Traditional, Adult, and Distance Learner: A New Engine for Technology-Based Teaching*.

Topal, M., & Karaca, O. (2022). Gamification in E-Learning. In *Research Anthology on Developments in Gamification and Game-Based Learning* (pp. 1–20). IGI Global., doi:10.4018/978-1-6684-3710-0.ch001

Tularam, G. (2018). Traditional vs Non-Traditional Teaching and Learning Strategies: The Case of E-Learning. *International Journal for Mathematics Teaching and Learning*, *19*(1), 129–158. doi:10.4256/ijmtl.v19i1.21

Turan, Z., & Karabey, S. C. (2023). The use of immersive technologies in distance education: A systematic review. *Education and Information Technologies*. doi:10.100710639-023-11849-8 PMID:37361798

Voskoglou, M. (2023). *Artificial Intelligence and Digital Technologies in the Future Education*. Qeios. doi:10.32388/07VE29

Wang, Y. C. (2023). Gamification in a News English Course. *Education Sciences*, *13*(1), 90. Advance online publication. doi:10.3390/educsci13010090

Xin, Y. (2022). Influence of Learning Engagement on Learning Effect under a Virtual Reality (VR) Environment. *International Journal of Emerging Technologies in Learning*, *17*(5), 226–237. doi:10.3991/ijet.v17i05.29451

Yang, P., & Liu, Z. (2022). The influence of Immersive Virtual Reality (IVR) on skill transfer of learners: The moderating effects of learning engagement. *International Journal of Emerging Technologies in Learning*, *17*(10), 62–73. doi:10.3991/ijet.v17i10.30923

Zain, F. M., Sailin, S. N., Kasim, M., Abdul Karim, A. M., & Zameri, N. N. (2022). Developing an Augmented Reality Immersive Learning Design (AILeaD) Framework: A Fuzzy Delphi Approach. [IJIM]. *International Journal of Interactive Mobile Technologies*, *16*(11), 65–90. doi:10.3991/ijim.v16i11.30063

Zhang, R., & Zou, D. (2020). Types, purposes, and effectiveness of state-of-the-art technologies for second and foreign language learning. *Computer Assisted Language Learning*, 1–47.

Žukauskas, P., Vveinhardt, J., & Andriukaitienė, R. (2018). Philosophy and Paradigm of Scientific Research. In *Management Culture and Corporate Social Responsibility*. IntechOpen., doi:10.5772/intechopen.70628

KEY TERMS AND DEFINITIONS

Audiolingual Method: A method of teaching languages which stresses reinforcement and repetition by encouraging students to memorize and internalize patterns of dialogue.

Gamification: The practice of incorporating and using game design elements and principles in non-game contexts as a way of highlighting user engagement, enthusiasm, and learning. In an educational context, gamification integrates game elements into the design of learning activities.

Grammar Translation Method: A method of teaching languages that focuses on mastering grammar rules and vocabulary.

Immersive Language Learning: A pedagogical approach that leverages digital tools and virtual environments to create an engaging and interactive language learning experience by immersing language learners in a simulated environment where they can practice language skills in real-life scenarios, providing a more authentic and contextually relevant learning experience.

Modal Learning Strategies: Using various media elements, such as audio, video, images, and interactive exercises, to appeal to different learning styles and enhance the overall learning experience.

Traditional Assessment: The evaluation and measuring of students' academic performance using standardized tests, quizzes, exams, and assignments frequently stress factual recall, comprehension, and the ability to apply knowledge in a coordinated format.

Virtual Environment: A computer-generated simulation of a three-dimensional world where learners can interact with computer-generated content and engage in language activities that mimic real-life situations by a person using special electronic equipment, such as a virtual reality headset or gloves fitted with sensors.

Chapter 12
Breaking Down Barriers With Artificial Intelligence (AI):
Cross-Cultural Communication in Foreign Language Education

Ali Karakas
https://orcid.org/0000-0002-9790-8562
Mehmet Akif Ersoy University, Turkey

ABSTRACT

Cross-cultural communication has gained significance in recent years as a result of the ubiquitous effects of globalization on interpersonal interactions. Face-to-face language encounters, however, might not always be convenient or possible. Artificial intelligence (AI) technology provides a solution to this issue by facilitating language exchanges and fostering intercultural dialogue. In this chapter, the use of AI technology in language learning, especially for cross-cultural communication, is explored by mentioning the benefits of AI technology in language instruction, such as the provision of individualized feedback and interaction with both native and non-native speakers of the target languages. Additionally, the chapter addresses possible issues posed by the AI technology, including cultural prejudices and solutions for them. Finally, case studies of productive AI-facilitated language exchange platforms are provided, along with various AI-powered solutions that might improve learners' cross-cultural competence.

DOI: 10.4018/978-1-6684-9893-4.ch012

INTRODUCTION

In today's increasingly globalized and interconnected world, cross-cultural communication has become a critical aspect of foreign and second language education (Davitishvili, 2017). Foreign language learners today look for opportunities to interact with speakers of the target language from various cultural backgrounds (Leung, Harris, & Rampton, 1997). However, these opportunities are frequently scarce or difficult to find in a face-to-face fashion, making it difficult for language learners to gain worthwhile cross-cultural experience. Fortunately, language technologies, especially Artificial Intelligence (AI), have become a potential tool to overcome these obstacles and ease language exchanges, promoting efficient cross-cultural communication through AI-powered tools and web conferencing platforms (Rehm et al., 2020; Roll & Wylie, 2016).

The goal of this chapter is to explore how AI technology can support intercultural communication and language instruction, as well as how it may change language instruction and promote intercultural competence in the current era. Take, for example, the case of self-regulated learning opportunities which may be enhanced by AI tools. Language teachers may provide learners customized learning opportunities that are catered to their unique requirements and preferences by utilizing AI technology. The benefits of AI will be covered in detail in this chapter, including how it may provide tailored feedback, enable adaptive learning, and help learners access to both native and non-native speakers of the target language.

A word of caution is necessary here as well, though, because applying AI to cross-cultural settings may also create difficulties that need to be resolved for utilization to be successful. The challenges to be overcome include, for example, cultural biases within AI systems, restrictions in natural language processing, and issues in comprehending the subtleties of cross-cultural communication. One may make sure that AI technology is used in a way that promotes justice, accuracy, and cultural sensitivity by understanding and resolving these difficulties.

The chapter will also explore how AI technology may improve language learners' cultural awareness, lessen cultural misunderstandings, and develop empathy. The chapter will discuss how AI-powered language learning systems can facilitate virtual interactions with people from various cultural backgrounds and expose students to real-world cross-cultural situations. These interactions may foster empathy, broaden cultural comprehension, and provide learners the intercultural competence needed for successful cross-cultural communication.

Finally, the chapter will exemplify effective uses of AI-powered tools in removing obstacles and fostering cross-cultural communication by presenting some case studies and samples of linguistic interactions assisted by AI technology. The future of AI in cross-cultural communication and language exchanges will also be covered in this chapter, with potential directions for more study and multidisciplinary cooperation among linguists, educators, technologists, and academics. Overall, this chapter will offer useful insights for practitioners, academics, and educators who are interested in maximizing the potential of AI technology in support of effective language learning and cross-cultural communication in the increasingly diverse real-world communication.

ADVANTAGES OF AI TECHNOLOGY IN LANGUAGE LEARNING

The field of language learning can greatly benefit from AI technology, which has the capacity to transform conventional methods and offer learners personalized learning experiences. In this sense, the opportunity to receive tailored feedback is a big advantage. AI-driven platforms for language learning can evaluate students' performance and provide real-time feedback, identifying areas for further development and providing personalized recommendations for language improvement (Cardona et al., 2023; Jaiswal & Arun, 2021; Kumar, 2019). By helping learners address their unique language obstacles and achieve progress in meaningful ways, this individualized feedback may support a more successful and efficient foreign language learning process.

AI technology also makes it easier for learners to connect with both native and non-native speakers of the target language, increasing their opportunities for productive language practice (Jauregi et al., 2012). Through virtual language exchanges, conversation practice, or even interactive chatbots, language learning platforms powered by AI can connect students with the speakers of that particular language, be they native or non-native speakers. These encounters give language learners exposure to real-world conversations and realistic language input, which helps them improve their speaking, listening, and comprehension skills. Additionally, AI technology may mimic conversations with non-native speakers so that students can encounter other accents, dialects, and linguistic varieties. As a result of this experience, students gain communication skills that are culturally sensitive and adaptable, preparing them for interactions in multicultural settings in the real world.

The ability to customize language learning experiences is another benefit of AI models in language teaching (Cardona et al., 2023). To create personalized learning paths and resources, AI platforms can be utilized by learners as these tools can examine learners' preferences, development, and learning styles by creating content matching with learners' characteristics and preferences (Bellarhmouch et al., 2023; Cheng & Wang, 2021). The process of learning a language is made more interesting and motivating by learners' access to content that matches their interests and objectives. In order to provide the right amount of challenge, AI can also modify the degree of difficulty of the learning materials based on the proficiency of the students. AI enables learners to take control of their education and advance at their own speed by personalizing the learning experience for each individual (Chen et al., 2020). This individualized method encourages learners' autonomy and lifetime learning abilities while also boosting their confidence.

According to Nykon (2023), AI technology provides enhanced language practice opportunities and accurate performance evaluation. Language learning platforms powered by AI can provide interactive exercises, simulations, and role-playing scenarios that allow learners to apply their language skills in practical contexts. These immersive experiences enable learners to practice their speaking, listening, reading, and writing skills in a simulated real-world environment. Furthermore, AI can analyze learners' language production and provide detailed assessments of their performance, including pronunciation, grammar, vocabulary usage, and overall proficiency (Nykon, 2023). By offering precise and objective performance evaluations, AI assists learners in identifying areas for improvement and tracking their progress over time. This feedback-oriented approach promotes continuous growth and development in language proficiency, which then facilitates their accomplishment of language learning goals (Nykon, 2023)

CHALLENGES OF USING AI IN CROSS-CULTURAL SETTINGS

While AI has a great deal of potential to improve cross-cultural communication in language learning, there are a number of obstacles that must be overcome before it can be effectively used. The existence of cultural biases within AI systems is a serious problem (Mehrabi et al., 2021). Large datasets are used to train AI algorithms, which may unintentionally reflect biases in the data. Due to this, AI systems may provide information or reactions that are culturally prejudiced, thereby reinforcing stereotypes or false beliefs (O'Flaherty, 2022; Schwartz et al., 2022). In order to ensure fairness, accuracy, and cultural sensitivity, addressing these biases necessitates rigorous curation of training material as well as constant monitoring and evaluation of AI systems.

Natural language processing (NLP) restrictions for other languages and dialects, as well as dialects and varieties of English, cause another problem (Plank, 2016; Schwartz et al., 2022). NLP algorithms may have issues understanding less frequently used languages or regional dialects, as well as less prevalent non-native and native but non-standard variations of English, as they were largely created for major languages. This may result in errors while interpreting, translating, or evaluating pronunciation. When the goal is to accommodate the linguistic variety of language learners, additional improvements in NLP technology need to be made in order to assure the inclusiveness and efficacy of AI in cross-cultural communication (Anand, 2023).

As noted by Frąckiewicz (2023a), another challenge in the effective use of AI in cross-cultural communication lies in understanding the nuances of cross-cultural communication. Language is deeply intertwined with culture, and certain cultural elements can heavily influence communication patterns, politeness norms, and contextual meanings. AI systems may struggle to interpret and convey these nuances accurately, leading to potential miscommunications or misunderstandings (ÓhÉigeartaigh et al., 2020). Overcoming this challenge requires developing AI models that are attuned to cultural contexts, incorporating cultural knowledge and sensitivity into their algorithms (Frąckiewicz, 2023a). Collaborative efforts between linguists, cultural experts, and AI researchers are crucial in developing AI systems that can navigate cross-cultural communication successfully.

Furthermore, as Nguyen et al. (2023) contend, ethical considerations are paramount in using AI in education and a cross-cultural context does not fall out of the scope of education. Privacy, data security, and informed consent become critical factors to address when implementing AI technology in language education. Safeguarding learners' personal information, ensuring transparent data usage practices, and obtaining consent for data collection and processing are essential for building trust and maintaining the ethical integrity of AI-powered language learning platforms. Upholding ethical standards and establishing clear guidelines for the responsible use of AI technology will be fundamental in its successful integration into cross-cultural language education.

By acknowledging and actively addressing these challenges, it is possible to exploit the full potential of AI in cross-cultural communication and language learning. Overcoming cultural biases, advancing NLP capabilities, understanding cultural nuances, and maintaning ethical standards are key areas of focus for researchers, educators, and technologists to ensure that AI technology becomes a valuable tool for promoting effective cross-cultural communication in language education (ÓhÉigeartaigh et al., 2020; Socher, 2018).

AI and the Development of Intercultural Competence

As contended by Frąckiewicz (2023b), AI technology can play a crucial role in nurturing empathy and cultural understanding among language learners. By exposing learners to authentic cultural content, e.g. videos, articles, and multimedia materials, AI-powered language learning platforms can provide immersive experiences that go beyond pure language instruction (Kim & Lee, 2021). Learners can gain insights into different cultures, traditions, and perspectives, promoting empathy and cultivating a deeper appreciation for cultural diversity. Additionally, with AI tools, it becomes possible to incorporate interactive features, such as virtual reality or augmented reality, to simulate cross-cultural scenarios, which further allows learners to virtually immerse themselves in different cultural contexts and practice their intercultural skills (Chen & Chen, 2019).

Cultural misunderstandings often arise from misinterpretations of language, gestures, or customs. AI technology can contribute to lessening such misunderstandings by providing learners with context-specific information and explanations (Kim & Lee, 2021). Language learning platforms equipped with AI can offer cultural notes, explanations of idiomatic expressions, or social etiquette guidance, which help learners navigate cultural intricacies (Casumano & Yoffie, 2021). With AI technology, learners' language production can be analyzed and potential cultural drawbacks or linguistic errors can be identified, with further targeted feedback to rectify culture-related misconceptions. It is certain that by addressing cultural misunderstandings proactively, AI technology might promote effective communication, foster cultural sensitivity, and diminish the risk of unintentional offense or miscommunication (Kim & Lee, 2021).

Researchers argue that AI technology can help learners develop their cultural awareness with the exposure to a wide range of cultural artefacts, perspectives and practices (see, Cusumano & Yoffie, 2021). Especially at a time when most students are switching to AI tools to learn languages (Ro, 2023), teachers can create content that represents diverse cultural backgrounds that display various cultural festivals, traditions, literature, and historical events using various AI-empowered language learning platforms. Through AI algorithms, teachers can adapt these platforms' the content to match learners' interests and language proficiency, which then may result in gaining relevant cultural learning experiences. Furthermore, using AI-powered language interactions, teachers can create opportunities for learners to interact with individuals from different cultural backgrounds and this creates opportunities for direct engagement and knowledge exchange. Such interactions inevitably contributes to mutual understanding, breaking down stereotypes, and promoting an inclusive and global mindset among learners.

AI technology can contribute to the learners' development of intercultural competence by promoting empathy, reducing cultural misunderstandings, and enhancing cultural awareness. Intercultural competence covers "the ability to interact effectively and appropriately in intercultural situations, based on specific attitudes, intercultural knowledge, skills and reflection" (Deardorf, 2006, p.5). AI technology can provide learners with the tools and resources necessary to develop this competence, empowering them to adapt their communication style, understand cultural nuances, and build meaningful connections with individuals from diverse backgrounds. AI technology's role in nurturing intercultural competence extends beyond language learning, as it equips learners with essential skills for thriving in today's interconnected and multicultural world (Deardorf, 2006; Kampermann et al., 2021).

AI technology, through its various applications, has the potential to nurture intercultural competence in language learners by assisting them to become effective communicators and bridge cultural gaps. By leveraging AI technologies to promote empathy, reduce misunderstandings, enhance cultural awareness, and develop intercultural competence, teachers can embrace the transformative power of AI technology to foster meaningful cross-cultural communication and promote global citizenship in foreign language education.

CASE STUDIES AND EXAMPLES OF AI-FACILITATED LANGUAGE EXCHANGES

Case One: An AI Implementation in a Cross-Cultural Language Exchange Program

In a case study conducted by Astrid Education (also known as Astrid), an innovative educational technology company in collaboration with Oxford Languages, language research program affiliated with Oxford University Press, researchers utilized Oxford Languages Data, the Oxford Dictionary of English (ODE) and the New Oxford American Dictionary (NOAD), as well as audio content to validate their voice-based, AI-powered language learning platform, with a purpose to enable their users to communicate confidently in English. For this, an easily accessible, efficient and affordable learning tool was developed by Astrid, i.e. *the Astrid app*, for teenagers and younger learners who wish to improve their practical English, especially pronunciation and speaking. More precisely, Astrid, as an education technology company, offers an AI-powered voice-based English learning platform to its users. The platform makes use of AI technology to provide personalized feedback on pronunciation and grammar, helping learners improve their communication skills. Such communication skills may further become rather vital in cross-cultural communication. The platform also includes features such as real-time translation and transcription, enabling learners to communicate effectively with native and non-native speakers of English (Astrid Case Study, n.d.). Among the activities offered by the app are storytelling, reading aloud texts, conversation activities with follow-up speech analysis coupled with feedback on their performance.

However, in its present form, the tool may fail to facilitate cross-cultural communication at a satisfactory level. To make it better matched with the characteristics of cross-cultural communication, this tool may indeed need some adjustments and customization. For instance, by utilizing AI technology, the tool may be set to match learners from different cultural backgrounds based on their language learning goals, interests, and convenience. Through its virtual platform, learners may be paired with native or non-native speakers of their target language who are also learning their 'native' language. The AI algorithm in the tool should be also programmed to ensure compatible language exchange partners in order to optimize the learning experience for both parties. The program has already incorporated features such as real-time language translation and pronunciation assessment, enabling learners to communicate effectively and receive valuable feedback. Pronunciation assessment should not be prejudiced towards accented speech with a focus on 'mutual intelligibility' rather native-like pronunciation. Or else, learners with accented speech may be biased with negative feedback and low scores on their speech (Freeze, 2019). Overall, the case study offers evidence regarding the effectiveness and future potential of AI-powered tools in promoting cross-cultural communication, fostering mutual language learning for real-world communication, and creating a supportive learning environment for learners from diverse cultural backgrounds (Freeze, 2019).

Case Two: AI-Powered Platforms and Their Impact on Cross-Cultural Communication

Several AI-powered language learning platforms have emerged that might be used by teaching in support of promoting cross-cultural communication. For example, LinguaConnect[1] is one of them. As an AI platform, it can connect learners with (both native and non-native) speakers of different languages through virtual language exchanges. The platform incorporates AI chatbots that facilitate conversations between learners and native speakers, ensuring a balanced language exchange experience. Learners can practice their target language with native speakers, gaining cultural insights and improving their language proficiency. There are several ways of using LinguaConnect for cross-cultural communication. For instance, LinguaConnect's AI algorithms match learners who are native speakers of different languages but are learning each other's native language. For instance, a language learner from Turkiye who is learning English can be matched with a learner from the United States or Denmark who is learning Turkish. This virtual language exchange creates an opportunity for learners to engage in cross-cultural communication while practicing their 'target' language in their own terms (e.g. their local accent, cultural elements, and communicative strategies). During these exchanges, learners can share their cultural experiences, traditions, and perspectives, which may then result in fostering their mutual understanding and appreciation of different cultures, perspectives and linguistic diversity.

Additionally, LinguaConnect can be used integrate cultural exchange activities within its platform to promote cross-cultural communication. For example, in the platform, teachers can organize virtual cultural events for their learners with learners from different countries by bringing them together to discuss and share aspects of their culture, such as festivals, cuisine, or customs. Through these activities, learners can gain insights into various cultures, broaden their horizons, and engage in meaningful cross-cultural interactions. Moreover, LinguaConnect offers a wide range of multimedia content, such as videos, articles, and podcasts that exhibit diverse cultures and perspectives. Learners can be guided to explore topics related to different cultures so that they could enhance their understanding of global diversity. They can discuss and exchange opinions on these cultural topics with their language partners, deepening their cross-cultural communication skills. Finally, using the AI chatbots employed by LinguaConnect that act as language guides for learners, software developers can program these chatbots to simulate conversations with native and non-native speakers, providing learners with opportunities to practice their language skills in a culturally relevant context (Belda-Medina & Calvo-Ferrer, 2022; Huang et al., 2022; Mageira et al., 2022). For instance, a learner interested in Japanese culture can engage in a conversation with an AI chatbot designed as a virtual Japanese language partner by means of English or any other common language spoken by both parties, discussing cultural aspects and practicing the target language at the same time.

Another example is ImmerseMe[2], an AI-powered language learning platform that provides interactive cultural modules alongside language lessons. The platform offers multimedia content, virtual reality experiences, and quizzes to enhance learners' cultural awareness and understanding. By integrating AI technology, these platforms bridge the gap between learners from different cultural backgrounds, promoting effective cross-cultural communication and fostering intercultural competence. As with the case of LanguageConnect, ImmerseMe can be used in different ways for enhancing cross-cultural communication skills of learners. To start with interactive cultural modules, these modules provide learners with in-depth insights into different cultures, traditions, and customs. For example, learners studying English can access a cultural module that explores the traditions of native and non-native English-speaking countries, such as festivals, cuisine, and social customs. By engaging with these modules, learners not only improve their English language skills but also gain a deeper understanding of the cultural context in which the language is used. This knowledge serves as a foundation for meaningful cross-cultural communication where English is not mother tongue of the majority of speakers.

Unlike many of its similar kinds, ImmerseMe also makes use of virtual reality (VR) technology to offer immersive cultural experiences (He & Smith, 2018). As put by He and Smith (2018), "[t]he use of virtual reality allows for more authentic representations of real-life interactions learners may find themselves in if they travel to a region where the target language is spoken" (para. 1). This feature of the tool is rather vital in terms of preparing learners for real-world cross-cultural communication in the language learning process. Additionally, in support of cross-cultural competence, the VR feature of the tool might help learners to virtually explore different countries, landmarks, and cultural sites while learning the target language (Shadiev et al., 2021; Xie et al., 2019). For instance, a learner studying English can start a virtual tour of London or someone studying Arabic can explore Casablanca through visiting iconic sites like London Bridge in the UK and the Hassan II Mosque in Morocco. With these VR experiences, learners can engage with different cultures first-hand and gain a sense of cultural empathy and understanding (Ahn et al., 2016). In addition, they can share their virtual travel experiences and insights with fellow learners, which further can promote their cross-cultural dialogue.

Additionally, teachers can use quizzes and games offered by ImmerseMe that test learners' cultural knowledge with an eye to improving learners' cross-cultural knowledge. With these interactive activities, learners can be challenged to identify cultural elements, such as traditional clothing, famous landmarks, or traditional music. Learners can deepen their cultural understanding and engage in friendly competition with their classmates by taking part in these quizzes and games. Learners can also share their cultural knowledge and discuss the significance of different cultural elements. By doing so, they find opportunities for cross-cultural conversations.

Last but not least, ImmerseMe facilitates collaborative language projects that encourage learners to work together on language-related tasks while incorporating cultural aspects. For instance, Turkish learners studying English can collaborate on a project to create a bilingual cultural guidebook on Turkish and English. Through this project, learners may explore cultural similarities and differences, exchange ideas, and learn from each other's cultural perspectives. Consequently, the collaborative nature of these projects promotes cross-cultural communication and fosters a sense of shared learning and understanding.

Example One: Personalized Language Learning Experiences With AI Assistance

As far as I am concerned, several AI tools exist in the market right now that can provide personalized language learning experience. By using these tools, teachers can help learners gain a better understanding of different cultures and languages by providing them with personalized lessons that are tailored to their individual needs. This can improve students' cross-cultural communication skills and prepare them for success in a globalized world. One of the leading tools in this category is LangAI[3], a kind of personalized language tutor that can leverage AI technology to provide personalized language learning experiences. As of now, it supports over 20 languages (e.g. German, Portpguese, English, Turkish, Danish, and Hindi). LangAI can utilize machine learning algorithms to analyze learners' language proficiency, learning styles, and preferences. Based on this analysis, using the platform, language teachers can produce customized learning paths by selecting relevant materials, exercises, and assessments tailored to each learner and their needs. Drawing on the real-time feedback and adaptive learning features of LangAI, teachers can adjust lessons to learners' individual progress by providing targeted guidance and support. Furthermore, learners can access interactive lessons, engage in virtual conversations with AI chatbots, and receive instant feedback on their pronunciation and grammar. With the assistance of AI-powered LangAI tool, teachers can ensure that each learner receives a personalized language learning experience by experiencing effective language acquisition and enhancing their cross-cultural communication skills.

Apart from using LangAI, teachers can also make use of similar tools already available in the market. For instance, Duolingo[4] is one of the available tools, which serves as a popular language learning platform drawing on AI technology. It has the capacity to provide learners with personalized lessons specific for their individual needs. The platform also offers interactive lessons, virtual conversations with AI-powered chatbots, and instant feedback on pronunciation and grammar. Duolingo uses real-time feedback and adaptive learning to adjust to learners' individual progress by providing targeted guidance and support. Babbel[5] is another language learning platform that uses AI to provide personalized language learning experiences. The platform offers interactive lessons, virtual conversations with AI chatbots, and instant feedback on pronunciation and grammar. Babbel uses real-time feedback and adaptive learning to adjust to learners' individual progress by providing targeted guidance and support. Memrise[6] is a language learning platform that uses AI to provide learners with personalized lessons that are tailored to their individual needs. The platform offers interactive lessons, virtual conversations with AI chatbots, and instant feedback on pronunciation and grammar. Memrise uses real-time feedback and adaptive learning to adjust to learners' individual progress by providing targeted guidance and support.

Example Two: Some Virtual Language Exchange Platforms

Virtual language exchange platforms like Voki have the potential to revolutionize cross-cultural communication in language learning. Voki draws on AI technology while connecting learners from diverse cultural backgrounds through virtual language exchanges. Voki is an online platform that allows users to create their own talking characters, i.e. animated characters or avatars. The platform is used by millions of teachers across the world as an educational tool to largely personalize the learning process, engage learners in classes and help them better understand complex issues with audio-visual support (Davis, 2022; Moeller & Nugent, 2014; Takacs & Bus, 2016). Voki can be used for cross-cultural communication in language education in several ways, too. For example, Voki can be used to create avatars that represent different languages, some varieties of these languages and cultures. A teacher can create an avatar that represents a person from a specific country or culture. The avatar can then be used to teach students about the culture and language of that country. This can help students gain a better understanding of the cultural context in which the language is spoken and improve their cross-cultural communication skills (Karakaş, forthcoming).

In addition, Voki can be used to create avatars that speak different languages. A teacher can create an avatar that speaks Turkish and another avatar that speaks English. The avatars can then be used to teach students about the differences between the two languages. This can help students develop their language skills and improve their ability to communicate with people from different linguistic backgrounds. Furthermore, using Voki's speech technology, teachers can create avatars that represent different accents. A teacher can create an avatar that speaks with a British accent and another avatar that speaks with an American accent or non-native accents like Indian accent or a less prestigious native accent like Irish English with the help of the text-to-speech technology aspect of the tool, i.e. 'read aloud' technology (Karakaş, 2017). The avatars can then be used to teach students about the differences between the two accents. This can help students develop their listening skills and improve their ability to understand different accents and more importanltly language learners can grasp how languages are used differently by everyone (Cavalheiro, 2020). Finally, Voki can be used to create avatars that represent different genders. A teacher can create an avatar that represents a male and another avatar that represents a female. The avatars can then be used to teach students about gender roles and differences in language use between males and females. This can help students develop their understanding of gender issues and improve their ability to communicate with people of different genders in cross-cultural communication.

Another AI-powered language learning similar to Voki is Rosetta Stone. It is a language learning platform that uses AI technology to provide students with personalized lessons that are tailored to their individual needs. Teachers can use the platform for cross-cultural communication in language education in different ways. For example, teachers can use it to teach students about different cultures by providing them with interactive lessons designed to help them learn the language in an enjoyable and engaging way. For instance, the platform offers lessons on different cultural topics such as food, music, and art. These lessons are designed to help students gain a better understanding of the cultural context in which the language is spoken and improve their cross-cultural communication skills. In addition,

Rosetta Stone can be used to teach students about different accents since unfamiliar accents in the platform may be perceived as problematic by language learners with pejorative attitudes towards these accents (Ikonta et al., 2015). The platform offers lessons on different native accents such as British English, American English, and Australian English; however, unlike Voki, it does not present non-standard native and non-native accents to its users. These lessons are designed to help students develop their listening skills and improve their ability to understand different accents (Lord, 2016; Kurniawan et al., 2021). This can be particularly useful for students who plan to travel or work in a country where the language is spoken. Finally, Rosetta Stone can be used to teach students about different languages. As of now, the platform offers lessons on over 25 different languages including Spanish, French, German, and Turkish. By learning a new language, students can gain a better understanding of different cultures and improve their cross-cultural communication skills. This can be particularly useful for students who plan to travel or work in a country where the language is spoken.

In summary, one can conclude that these platforms are resourceful in that teachers can use them in several different ways in order to promote cross-cultural communication in language teaching. By using these platforms, teachers can support students' understanding of different cultures, languages, accents, and genders in a much better fashion. With this improved understanding and awareness, language learners are highly likely to improve their cross-cultural communication skills and can be better prepared for success in a globalized world characterized by an ever-increasing cross-cultural communication.

CONCLUSION

The need to write this chapter arose from the need to understand the role of AI technology in grappling with challenges and promoting cross-cultural communication in language instruction. Throughout the chapter, we have looked at the benefits of AI technology in language learning, such as customized language learning experiences, networking with native and non-native speakers, and personalized feedback and adaptive and self-regulated learning. These benefits underscore how AI technology holds the power to transform language learning and provide language learners with personalized learning experiences that are likely to improve their language skills and cross-cultural awareness.

The chapter also addressed the difficulties, e.g. cultural prejudices, restrictions in natural language processing, and comprehension of the subtleties of cross-cultural communication, while using AI technology for cross-cultural communication. It is considerably essential to address these issues if AI technology is to be employed in a way that raises fairness, accuracy, and intercultural sensitivity. Language teachers can fully utilize the potential of AI technology in assisting efficient cross-cultural communication by acknowledging and trying to overcome these limitations in collaboration with certain stakeholders from different disciplines.

The chapter also explored the place of AI tools in advancing empathy, lessening cultural misconceptions, and raising cultural awareness to support the development of cross-cultural competence. It is argued that a greater respect and understanding of diverse cultures can be cultivated if language learners are given the chance to have immersive experiences, virtual interactions, and cultural modules offered by AI-powered language learning platforms. This way, it is believed that AI technology can help learners navigate cultural differences and grow as competent communicators in multicultural settings by developing intercultural competence and awareness.

Furthermore, we have explored various case studies and some AI tools that demonstrate the practical implementation of AI technology in language learning. These case studies have shed light on the effective applications of some selected AI tools indicating their potential in bridging linguistic and cultural gaps during in-person and virtual cross-cultural communication. The examination of some AI-powered platforms, such as LinguaConnect, ImmerseMe, and Voki, has shown the ways in which these tools can broaden learners' language learning experiences. It was also reported that these tools offer customized learning experiences that fit individual needs, assist virtual language exchanges, and impeccably integrate cultural elements into the language learning process. The cases presented also imply that by using AI technology and its capacity, language teachers are empowered for a much more effective language instruction and creating cross-cultural contacts and inclusive and engaging learning environments.

Looking towards the future, one can unarguably aver that continued research and development in AI technology hold great capacity for further advancements in cross-cultural communication and language learning. As implied in the main body of the chapter, what is crucial is interdisciplinary collaboration among linguists, educators, technologists, and researchers in the act of driving innovation and employing the potential of AI technology in order to promote effective cross-cultural communication.

In conclusion, the potential of AI technology appears to be enormous in terms of breaking down barriers, promoting intercultural competence, and broadening language learning experiences. Language specialists, researchers, and practitioners can create inclusive and engaging language learning environments that may promote effective cross-cultural communication by exploiting the elements of the AI technology. It is also highly likely that if language teachers and learners grasp the opportunities that AI technology presents for language teaching and learning, they will likely pave the way for a more culturally and linguistic connected world.

REFERENCES

Ahn, S. J., Bostick, J., Ogle, E., Nowak, K. L., McGillicuddy, K. T., & Bailenson, J. N. (2016). Experiencing nature: Embodying animals in immersive virtual environments increases inclusion of nature in self and involvement with nature. *Journal of Computer-Mediated Communication*, *21*(6), 399–419. doi:10.1111/jcc4.12173

Astrid Case Study. (n.d.). Oxford languages. https://languages.oup.com/about-us/case-studies/astrid/

Belda-Medina, J., & Calvo-Ferrer, J. R. (2022). Using chatbots as AI conversational partners in language learning. *Applied Sciences (Basel, Switzerland)*, *12*(8427), 1–16. doi:10.3390/app12178427

Bellarhmouch, Y., Jeghal, A., Tairi, H., & Benjelloun, N. (2023). A proposed architectural learner model for a personalized learning environment. *Education and Information Technologies*, *28*(4), 4243–4263. doi:10.100710639-022-11392-y PMID:36267481

Cardona, M. A., Rodríguez, R. J., & Ishmael, K. (2023). *Artificial Intelligence and the Future of Teaching and Learning: Insights and recommendations.* Report by U.S. Department of Education, Office of Educational Technology. https://www2.ed.gov/documents/ai-report/ai-report.pdf

Cavalheiro, L. (2020). Developing intercultural communication and intercultural awareness in the EFL classroom. *Estudos Linguísticos e Literários*, *1*(65), 30–48. doi:10.9771/ell.v1i65.36467

Chen, C.-M., & Chen, Y.-S. (2019). *Handbook of research on integrating technology into contemporary language learning and teaching*. IGI Global.

Chen, L., Chen, P., & Lin, Z. (2020). Artificial intelligence in education: A review. *IEEE Access : Practical Innovations, Open Solutions*, *8*, 75264–75278. doi:10.1109/ACCESS.2020.2988510

Chen, S. Y., & Wang, J. H. (2021). Individual differences and personalized learning: A review and appraisal. *Universal Access in the Information Society*, *20*(4), 833–849. doi:10.100710209-020-00753-4

Cusumano, M. A., & Yoffie, D. (2021). The cultural benefits of artificial intelligence in the enterprise. *MIT Sloan Management Review*, *62*(4), 1–9.

Davis, V. (2022) *Duolingo: The Vital Role of Animated Characters in Language Learning*. Animation World Network. https://www.awn.com/animationworld/duolingovital-role-animated-characters-language-learning

Davitishvili, N. (2017). Cross-cultural awareness and teaching English as a second language in the context of globalization. *Sino-US English Teaching, 14*(9), 549–558. doi:10.17265/1539-8072/2017.09.003

Deardorff, D. K. (2006). *Intercultural competence: The key competence in the 21st century?* Bertelsmann Stiftung.

Frąckiewicz, M. (2023a). *Bridging Language Barriers: The Potential of ChatGPT-4 for Multilingual Communication*. TS2 Space. https://ts2.space/en/bridging-language-barriers-the-potential-of-chatgpt-4-for-multilingual-communication

Frąckiewicz, M. (2023b). *The Role of AI in Promoting Cultural Diversity and Global Understanding*. TS2 Space. https://ts2.space/en/the-role-of-ai-in-promoting-cultural-diversity-and-global-understanding

Freeze, J. (2019). Build Cross-Cultural Bridges, Not Barriers, With AI. *Forbes*. https://www.forbes.com/sites/forbescommunicationscouncil/2019/07/31/build-cross-cultural-bridges-not-barriers-with-ai/?sh=3971bbe71839

He, L. & Smith, J., (2018) Pronunciation in Second Language Learning and Teaching Proceedings. *Immerse Me, 10*(1).

Huang, W., Hew, K. F., & Fryer, L. K. (2022). Chatbots for language learning—Are they really useful? A systematic review of chatbot-supported language learning. *Journal of Computer Assisted Learning, 38*(1), 237–257. doi:10.1111/jcal.12610

Ikonta, N. R., & Ugonna, N. C. (2015). The effect of Rosetta Stone (computer-assisted language learning) software on English as second language students' proficiency in English language. *American Educational Research Journal, 3*(1), 69–79.

Jaiswal, A., & Arun, C. J. (2021). Potential of artificial intelligence for transformation of education system in India. *International Journal of Education and Development Using Information and Communication Technology, 17*(1), 142–158.

Jauregi, K., De Graaff, R., Van den Bergh, H., & Kriz, M. (2012). Native/non-native speaker interactions through video-web communication: A clue for enhancing motivation? *Computer Assisted Language Learning, 25*(1), 1–19. doi:10.1080/09588221.2011.582587

Kampermann, A., Opdenakker, R., Heijden, B. V. D., & Bücker, J. (2021). Intercultural competencies for fostering technology-mediated collaboration in developing countries. *Sustainability (Basel), 13*(14), 7790. doi:10.3390u13147790

Karakaş, A. (2017). English voices in text-to-speech tools representation of English users and their varieties from a World Englishes perspective. *Advances in Language and Literary Studies*, *8*(5), 108–119. doi:10.7575/aiac.alls.v.8n.5p.108

Karakaş, A. (forthcoming). Supporting the teaching of GELT through VOKI. *RELC Journal*, 0-0.

Kim, J. S., & Lee, J. H. (2021). Overcoming barriers to cross-cultural cooperation in AI ethics and governance. *Philosophy & Technology*, *34*(2), 321–327. doi:10.100713347-020-00402-x

Kumar, D. N. (2019). Implementation of artificial intelligence in imparting education and evaluating student performance. *Journal of Artificial Intelligence and Capsule Networks*, *1*(1), 1–9. doi:10.36548/jaicn.2019.1.001

Kurniawan, D., Bunau, E., & Wardah, W. (2021). The use of Rosetta Stone language learning software in teaching listening: Documentary research. *Journal of English Education Program*, *2*(2), 97–103. doi:10.26418/jeep.v2i2.45516

Leung, C., Harris, R., & Rampton, B. (1997). The Idealised Native speaker, Reified Ethnicities, and Classroom Realities. *TESOL Quarterly*, *3*(31), 543. doi:10.2307/3587837

Lord, G. (2016). Rosetta Stone for language learning: An exploratory study. *IALLT Journal of Language Learning Technologies*, *46*(1), 1–35. doi:10.17161/iallt.v46i1.8552

Mageira, K., Pittou, D., Papasalouros, A., Kotis, K., Zangogianni, P., & Daradoumis, A. (2022). Educational AI chatbots for content and language integrated learning. *Applied Sciences (Basel, Switzerland)*, *12*(3239), 1–16. doi:10.3390/app12073239

Moeller, A. K., & Nugent, K. (2014). Building intercultural competence in the language classroom. *Faculty Publications: Department of Teaching, Learning and Teacher Education*, *161*, 1-18. https://digitalcommons.unl.edu/teachlearnfacpub/161

Nguyen, A., Ngo, H. N., Hong, Y., Dang, B., & Nguyen, B. P. T. (2023). Ethical principles for artificial intelligence in education. *Education and Information Technologies*, *28*(4), 4221–4241. doi:10.100710639-022-11316-w PMID:36254344

Nykon, Y. (2023). How AI Helps Crack a New Language? *Intellias*. https://intellias.com/how-ai-helps-crack-a-new-language/

O'Flaherty, M. (2022.). *Bias in Algorithms –Artificial Intelligence and Discrimination Report of European UnionAgency for Fundamental rights*. FRA. https://fra.europa.eu/sites/default/files/fra_uploads/fra-2022-bias-in-algorithms_en.pdf

ÓhÉigeartaigh, S. S., Whittlestone, J., Liu, Y., Zeng, Y., & Liu, Z.ÓhÉigeartaigh. (2020). Overcoming barriers to cross-cultural cooperation in AI ethics and governance. *Philosophy & Technology*, *33*(4), 571–593. doi:10.100713347-020-00402-x

Rehm, G., Marheinecke, K., Hegele, S., Piperidis, S., Bontcheva, K., Hajič, J., & Yvon, F. (2020). The European language technology landscape in 2020: Language-centric and human-centric AI for cross-cultural communication in multilingual Europe. *Proceedings of the 12th Language Resources and Evaluation Conference (LREC 2020)* (pp. 3315-3325), European Language Resources Association (ELRA), Marseille, France.

Ro, C. (2023). Students switch to AI to learn languages. *BBC news*.

Roll, I., & Wylie, R. (2016). Evolution and Revolution In artificial intelligence In Education. *International Journal of Artificial Intelligence in Education*, *2*(26), 582–599. doi:10.100740593-016-0110-3

Schwartz, R., Vassilev, A., Greene, K., Perine, L., Burt, A., & Hall, P. (2022). Towards a standard for identifying and managing bias in artificial intelligence. NIST special publication, 1270. doi:10.6028/NIST.SP.1270

Shadiev, R., Wang, X., & Huang, Y. M. (2021). Cross-cultural learning in virtual reality environment: Facilitating cross-cultural understanding, trait emotional intelligence, and sense of presence. *Educational Technology Research and Development*, *69*(5), 2917–2936. doi:10.100711423-021-10044-1

Socher, R. (2018). AI's Next Great Challenge: Understanding the Nuances of Language *Hardward Business Review* [Online]. https://hbr.org/2018/07/ais-next-great-challenge-understanding-the-nuances-of-language

Takacs, Z. K., & Bus, A. G. (2016). Benefits of motion in animated storybooks for children's visual attention and story comprehension. An eye-tracking study. *Frontiers in Psychology*, *7*, 1–12. doi:10.3389/fpsyg.2016.01591 PMID:27790183

Xie, Y., Ryder, L., & Chen, Y. (2019). Using interactive virtual reality tools in an advanced Chinese language class: A case study. *TechTrends*, *63*(3), 251–259. doi:10.100711528-019-00389-z

ENDNOTES

1 Homepage (linguaconnect.com)
2 https://immerseme.co/#home
3 https://langai.io/
4 https://www.duolingo.com/
5 https://www.babbel.com/
6 https://www.memrise.com/

Chapter 13
Enhancing Outcomes, Fostering Values, and Shaping Pedagogy With ChatGPT in English Learning Courses:
AI in Two Value-Oriented English Language Courses

Chad Christopher Davidson
https://orcid.org/0000-0002-7446-1366
University of Delaware, USA

ABSTRACT

Through a value-oriented framework, this chapter explores uses of the AI chatbot, ChatGPT, to enhance student learning outcomes, foster individual student values, and promote the harmony between both of these. This exploration occurs via practitioner research of two projects given in two courses. The practitioner research is value-oriented in that its focus is on the use of ChatGPT to foster these values of course outcomes and individual student values. The courses and research occurred from fall semester 2022 to spring semester 2023 in a university in eastern Türkiye. The discussion in the chapter works to advance an understanding of AI's potential use in the development of innovative pedagogical strategies that cater to diverse learner values in order to enhance learning outcomes, promote learner values, and add to the repository of evidence-based practices and case studies implementing AI in language education that can serve as part of the foundation for further research and language teaching experimentation.

DOI: 10.4018/978-1-6684-9893-4.ch013

INTRODUCTION

Purposes and Background of the Study

In order to assist in filling the ever-growing gap in language education research caused by continual advances of artificial intelligence (AI), this chapter presents practitioner research concerning the use of AI-driven language learning (LLing) activities within a Two-Threaded Value Orientation to Language Education (2ThVO, described below). In this way, the chapter will help to advance an understanding of AI's potential use in and impact on language teaching pedagogical practices and the development of innovative instructional strategies that cater to diverse learner values to enhance learning outcomes and add to the repository of evidence-based practices and case studies implementing AI in language education that can serve as part of the foundation for further research and experimentation. This study also addresses calls to action put forth by exploratory practice progenitors Dick Allwright and Judith Hanks (Allwright, 2006; Hanks, 2019). These will be described in the discussion on 2ThVO.

The AI pedagogical activities used the AI chatbot ChatGPT (OpenAI, 2023) to work to enhance student outcomes and to involve students' unique values via two major projects, one in each of two different courses comprised of the same cohort of first year English Language Teaching (ELT) students. The student learning outcomes that ChatGPT worked to enhance were (1) the outcome of accurately distinguishing all of the English phonemes both in terms of ability to distinguish them when heard (listening) and ability to distinguish them in the student's articulation of them (pronunciation); and (2) the outcome of thoroughly explaining an academic topic that corresponded with a value that the student herself holds and of defending one's side concerning that topic in an academic Oxford-Style Debate. These two corresponded to two main projects: Contrasting English Phonemes and Oxford-Style Debates, respectively.

The first outcome concerned a course entitled Listening and Pronunciation, and the second outcome concerned an Oral Communication course. Both courses contained the same cohort of students. For these and other courses, I came in as an American instructor to a Turkish university. Due to delays in being permitted a work visa, I began teaching these courses after they had already been taught for three weeks. This was a homogenous class of Turkish students, albeit with distinct subcultures. The students were between 19 and 35 years of age. There were a total of 32 students: 19 women, and 13 men. The courses took place in Fall Semester 2022 and Spring Semester 2023.

Each course involved much more than these student learning outcomes, and ChatGPT was used in other aspects of the course. However, limiting the discussion to these two outcomes and the two main projects that they corresponded with provided a feasible study for this chapter. Moreover, discussing these projects were address the purposes of this chapter: demonstrating innovative instructional strategies of AI in language education, demonstrating AI's impact on pedagogical practices and enhancing the outcomes of the courses, and demonstrating AI's use in catering to and fostering diverse student values. In the rest of this section, practitioner research will be explained. Then, the particular kind of practitioner research of this study, value-oriented practitioner research (VOPR), will be described. Finally, the LLing orientation, 2ThVO, will be explicated.

Practitioner Research and Value-Oriented Practitioner Research

Practitioner research is research that is generated by a person who is actively engaged in a profession that is directly related to the subject being researched, normally centering on furthering an understanding of one's own practices or lives and/or the lives or practices of those they work with (Zeichner & Noffke, 2001). Practitioner research ranges from research that is broad in scope to research with more fine-grained aims. An example of practitioner research with a broad scope is Exploratory Practice. Exploratory Practice aims at developing understanding in order to contribute to professional development, teaching, and learning while maintaining "a high quality of classroom life" by "using normal pedagogic practices as investigative tools, so that working for understanding is part of the teaching and learning, not extra to it" (Allwright, 2003, p. 116 & p. 127). Alternatively, practitioner research may take the form of fine-grained aims, such as seen in Action Research that aims at producing practical solutions to isolated problems (see Nunan, 1989, pp. 13–14).

Value-oriented practitioner research (VOPR) is a broad-in-scope type of practitioner research in that its aim is to contribute to professional development, teaching, and learning via exploring values on the global, institutional (university, departmental, and otherwise), class, educator, and student level and their interactions and interplays. This list can be parsed into two broad categories, with each having their own subcategories. The two broad categories are considered the two threads of VOPR and of the orientation in which it is couched, Two-Threaded Value Orientation to Language Education.

One thread concerns individual values. Examples of subcategories of this thread would be educator values, student values, supervisor values, and administrator values. The other thread concerns group values. Examples of subcategories of this thread would be global values, institutional values, and classroom values. Specifically for this study, an educator of English as a Foreign Language at a university in Türkiye carried out VOPR in two of his courses wherein he explored AI-driven pedagogical practices, focusing on intertwining students' individual values with the course's values (worded as two course outcomes) by way of using the AI chatbot, ChatGPT, in order to help to advance an understanding of AI's potential use in language education pedagogical practices, including the development of innovative instructional strategies, that cater to diverse learner values in a way that enhances learning outcomes, adds to the repository of evidence-based practices and case studies implementing AI in language education, and addresses calls to action that applied linguistics move "[f]rom commonality to idiosyncrasy," "[f]rom prescription to description to understanding," and "[f]rom academics to practitioners as the knowledge-makers in the field" (Allwright, 2006, pp. 10-14).

This study's VOPR research focus on intertwining student values with course values is derived from the *orientation* of the Two-Threaded Value Orientation to Language Education (2ThVO) in that it is orienting on intertwining the individual thread's subcategory (sub-thread) "student values" with the group thread's subcategory (sub-thread) "course values." 2ThVO is underpinned by a philosophical framework derived from the works of existentialist Jean-Paul Sartre (1948, 1956, 1963, 2013, 2021); value theorists Henry Frankfurt (1971), Ryan Kemp (2020), and Agnes Callard (2018); and exploratory practice (EP) progenitors Dick Allwright and Judith Hanks (Allwright, 2006; Allwright & Hanks, 2009).

The philosophical framework is an applied philosophy of action that understands that values can only be truly known via observation of action and that understands the importance of intertwining higher-order values throughout both threads. Therefore, it attends to Dick Allwright's suggestion that applied linguistics move "[f]rom academics to practitioners as the knowledge-makers in the field" (Allwright, 2006, p. 13). In VOPR, the teacher or student or administrator is the one who adds knowledge to the field of applied linguistics, specifically knowledge related to language institution, teacher, and learner values and knowledge related to methods and techniques for understanding and fostering these values, such as the use of AI.

Two-Threaded Value Orientation to Language Education

There are five main concepts to understand in 2ThVO: (1) value, (2) higher-order values, (3) aspirational value projects, (4) cultivational value projects, and (5) defective or disordered value projects. *Value* is taken to be that which is considered important to someone or some group such that they are willing to spend time attending to it (e.g., a student reading about space in her target language) or willing to have another spend time attending to it (e.g., a teacher having a student differentiate the /w/ and /v/ sounds in speech). Thus, each act reveals a value or set of values (see Sartre,

1956, p. 38). For students to readily understand what I mean by their values, I often simply refer to them as "interests" in homework assignment instructions and the like (see the Methods section).

Values are of higher- or lower-order importance with respect to each other. *Higher-order* values are taken to be those values that are more important to the person or group than other values that they hold (Frankfurt, 1971). A key aspect of 2ThVO is to foster an *explicit* centering on higher-order values so that other values do not usurp them, such as if an individual student's value to participate by accidentally talking over other students when they try to participate usurps the group's value of having many students participate. An individual's or group's ranking of values may change with time, such as when a mere curiosity turns steadily into a passion, or when a value takes a backseat for some other value given the contexts of the person's or institution's life.

As mentioned, each act reveals a value or set of values, and act-types enacted over time reveal aspirational, cultivational, or defective/disordered projects. *Defective/disordered* projects are of three kinds: (1) drifting projects wherein no value is fostered because it is not sufficiently enacted due to drifting/changing from initial project to initial project, (2) projects that pursue some defective value, e.g., any value related to hurting another individual, or (3) projects in which a good-but-lower-order value is usurping or displacing a higher-order value (Callard, 2018; Sartre, 2021). Thus, these project are created from and provide a context (a story) of value-types, and thus, act-types: aspirational acts/values, cultivational acts/values, and defective/disordered acts/values.

An *aspirational* project is one in which the institution or individual is pursuing a value that they do not yet fully understand or are not very good at executing, but a value they desire to improve in (e.g., practicing critical reading skills). A *cultivational* project is one in which the institution or individual is pursuing a good value that they have already been pursuing well and want to continue pursuing well and perhaps even improving in further. Aspirational and cultivational projects may convert into one another, such as when due to lack of actions a cultivational project becomes an aspirational project; or due to frequency of and growth via acts, an aspirational project becomes a cultivational project. Value-oriented practitioner researchers desire to foster and buttress aspirational and cultivational projects and to guard from defective and disordered projects.

As aforementioned, one thread of the 2ThVO refers to implementing an *individual's* values of various kinds (interests, curiosities, aspirations, goals, passions, things that are important enough to bother the student, etc.) and degrees (ranging from slight curiosity to central life interest) via in-class and out-of-class language learning activities, including course activities (e.g., in-class group work), assessments, and homework; as well as language learning adjacent activities, such as when an individual administrator surveys all students concerning their ability to pay for food. Naturally, this includes the individual interacting with others, but because this thread centers on the individual's values and, thus, her acts (be they in or out of the classroom), for ease of communication this is referred to as "Thread One."

The other thread of the 2ThVO is the thread of group values in relation to language learning/teaching. The most common values in this thread would be curricular values, which include those that motivate course policies (e.g., classroom management rules, grading rules), course goals, student learning outcomes (SLOs), and so forth. Often this thread relates to a multiplicity of groups that are coordinated across many different classrooms wherein the same course is taught by different teachers to different students. Hence, the individual cannot be readily parsed from these groups. Since this thread always includes a group (not a singular individual), this is considered "Thread Two."

The 2ThVO has three main goals: (1) To learn about and understand the higher-order values of (both those described and those enacted by) the institution, class, and individual; (2) To foster higher-order, non-defective values and avoid defective values; and (3) To have the higher-order values in both Thread One and Thread Two be harmonious with each other, e.g., students simultaneously pursuing their values through the values of the classroom. An example of this would be a student who is working to better understand and articulate to others how to start an airplane (one of the student's values) in order to better understand how to do that *and* in order to master the SLO of giving a clear process/sequence lecture (one of the course's values).

Thus, while the two threads of 2ThVO may sometimes conflict, a goal of 2ThVO is that they be mutually beneficial like a double orchestra where two orchestras play in harmony although the players are playing different instruments within their orchestra and are in different orchestras. For this chapter, the goal was to use AI-driven LLing practices to create harmony between classroom values (the two student learning outcomes) and student values (e.g., to be a successful movie director, to be a K-12 English teacher, to be a pilot). In so doing, while not the focus of this chapter, it would also harmonize with the educator's values, i.e., the value-oriented practitioner whose most relevant value here was the harmonizing of classroom values with student values.

Ideally, the teacher approaches the curriculum and the pedagogy through the value-oriented lens (e.g., as concerns the SLOs and bringing the students' values into as many of the in-class activities, homework, and assessments as possible) *and* the students work through mastering the curriculum by using their values, i.e. the students' values are implemented in ways that promote their mastery of the SLOs, the accomplishment of the course objectives, and community in the classroom and beyond. By having students' values advance institutional values and using institutional values to foster students' values, a cooperation of values occurs.

Hence, 2ThVO is an institution-supervisor-teacher-student collaborative approach to language education. These three goals of the 2ThVO in which higher-order individual, class, and institutional values are explicitly understood, promoted, and united are meant to build everyone up, bring about excellence for all, and bring about goal achievement for all.

Furthermore, the class is the primary place that Thread One (individual values) and Thread Two (group/institutional values) interplay. The class is the nucleus of the 2ThVO. Because the classroom is the primary locus of interaction among these threads, practitioner research (VOPR) is the best form of research methodology in a 2ThVO. In other words, the teacher is the one who is positioned to be most aware of all the threads of value: the institution's (e.g., the course's SLOs), her own, and her students' values. Also, the teacher is the one most positioned to observe the values in action and to foster the full-flowering of both institutional and student values.

Aside from addressing the gap in research on AI and language education, this study also addresses two issues in applied linguistics put forth by Exploratory Practice progenitor, Dick Allwright. Allwright presented a call for applied linguistics to move "[f]rom commonality to idiosyncrasy" (Allwright, 2006, p. 16). This direction for applied linguistics is justified by the proposition that "Language learners are unique individuals who learn and develop best in their own idiosyncratic ways" (Allwright & Hanks, 2009, p. 7). Because Thread One focuses on the idiosyncratic values of the individual, Thread One as studied in VOPR attends to this call. Each idiosyncratic way and act of students reveal idiosyncratic values. After all, as value theorist Agnes Callard words it concerning aspirational projects, "aspiration is self-creation, and selves are quite particular and idiosyncratic" (2021, p. 463).

Allwright also delivers a direction for applied linguistics that concerns Thread Two of the 2ThVO. Allwright states that applied linguistics needs to go "[f]rom prescription to description to understanding" (Allwright, 2006, p. 11). In VOPR, this is seen by way of the practitioner going from being prescribed and prescribing the values of the course by the institution (e.g., the SLOs), to the practitioner describing her and her students' engagements and values in relation to those course values given by the institution, to the practitioner further understanding the institutional course values as well as her own and those of her students as she enacts, observes, and articulates those values throughout the semester.

In sum, the 2ThVO and its practitioner research, VOPR, address the continued need for studies in language education on the uses of AI and they address suggested directions for applied linguistics given by Dick Allwright. Due to the perceived benefit of using AI-driven techniques for assisting students in diving deeper into their values and assisting in better mastering the outcomes of the course, for the two courses studied in this chapter, language learners used the AI, ChatGPT, in areas of value for them while also assisting them in being directed towards the requirements and SLOs of their classes. In this way, ChatGPT was used to address the abovementioned gap and directions by providing pedagogical practices that interweaved institutional values with students' particular and idiosyncratic values, providing and building understanding and enhancements of both.

METHODS

Methodological Fluidity and Openness

Corresponding to Exploratory Practice's applied linguistics focal shift "[f]rom teaching and learning as 'work' to teaching and learning as 'life'" (Allwright, 2006, p. 14), in VOPR every act of or within teaching and learning reveals real life values of the actors, be they students or teachers or any other stakeholder. Hence, when a teacher or student engages with a language, she is engaging with key, valued aspects of her life, concerning both linguistic and languacultural values of the language itself and those things she values in life that she engages with by and while engaging with the language.

Because values are revealed by acts, VOPR may be carried out in numerous ways, so long as it is carrying out and documenting an understanding and fostering of values and documenting what values were actually concretely instantiated (the *acts*) in the filaments of threads being studied—the subcategories of Thread One or Thread Two. For example, if research centered on a student in a semester-long course, both how the student articulated her values and what the student actually *did* throughout the course reveal her values. Thus, there would likely be a strong evaluation done by the student (i.e., the student articulates her values) and a documentation of the student's in-class and out-of-class work. Another example might be VOPR of faculty committee meetings over the course of a semester on revising SLOs, in which case both what the faculty members said *and* any curricular changes they put into place would all be documented in order to discern and understand the overt and covert values these acts represented.

Strong Evaluation

As mentioned in the Introduction section, value-oriented practitioner research (VOPR) holds commonalities with Exploratory Practice (EP). VOPR agrees with the principles of EP that practitioner research "promotes principles of puzzling, working for understanding, and quality of life" (Hanks, 2019, p. 143). In EP this is done by working "primarily to understand language classroom life" (Kato & Hanks, 2021, p. 2). However, in VOPR this is done by working primarily to understand, develop, and foster the *values* of language classroom life, including classroom values, educator values, and student values. In doing so, VOPR "promotes . . . quality of life" (Hanks, 2019, p. 149) by way of promoting higher-order values held by those institutions and individuals. Thus, unlike EP, value-oriented practice (VOPR) is more particularized on *values* and on fostering a cooperative understanding between stakeholders concerning each one's higher-order values.

While the key practitioner research method for EP may be a puzzling about anything, in VOPR the puzzling concerns values. Therefore, rather than "puzzling," VOPR calls these "strong evaluations" as the term "e-*valu*-ation" keeps "value" as the center. Hence, a puzzling activity, i.e., a strong evaluation, for VOPR might be to have students ask why they are in the academic program they are in, why they are enacting their academic pursuits via that program, and why those answers are interesting to them or matter to them. The students then continue asking "Why is that interesting? / Why does that matter?" of each response they give until they have provided a set of values and, hopefully, arrived at higher-order values.

Strong Evaluations and ChatGPT in This Study

The strong evaluations occurred in Fall Semester 2022, and the two projects and the activities leading up to them occurred mainly in Spring Semester 2023. Because I had the same students for both courses, I wanted to be able to get more information from them concerning their various kinds of values. Also, I did not want them to have to partake of the exact same activity in two different courses taught by me. Moreover, I wanted to be able to compare and contrast value-oriented responses that I might get from giving two different kinds of strong evaluations to the same cohort of students. Therefore, I had the students conduct a different strong evaluation in Oral Communication from the one they did in Listening and Pronunciation.

For the strong evaluation in Oral Communication, I requested that students anonymously write down in class (in class so as to make it easily feasible for them) their values in relation to the class and to their own lives. Following the suggestion of Penny Ur (2019), this was done by way of asking them to provide an answer to each of the four following questions: What do you *expect* from the rest of this course? What do you *want* from the rest of this course? Any *(special) requests* to help you learn better? Anything that has *hindered* you from learning so far?

Another reason I conducted this kind of strong evaluation for Oral Communication is because I wanted to see what perceptions and expectations they had of me as a teacher coming in from America to teach the course. For example, the strong evaluation showed that, while I never mentioned my native speaker identity, the students held it as highly valued since I was perceived as the only native speaker of the university and since they themselves held sounding like a native speaker as a highly-ordered value.

After they handed these into me in class, I compiled them and read them in the next class. Then, I asked students to ask ChatGPT what they should expect and want from an Oral Communication course, what might hinder them from learning in such a course, and how they might overcome those hindrances. They were to let me know what answers they were given in the next class. In that next class, we discussed ChatGPT's answers, whether and how much the students agreed with those answers or not, and if they helped them come up with more of their own expectations and wants.

In the strong evaluation for Listening and Pronunciation, on the other hand, I had an in-class activity where students conducted a value-chain strong evaluation for their answers as to why they are in this language program, growing the value-chain via why-evaluations of each response they gave. That is, I asked my students write out why they are in this program and why that mattered or was of interest to them. I then had them continue asking that question for each of their following answers. I encouraged them to draw arrows from each answer to the following answer to better follow their chain of valuation. Then, I had them ask a partner what answers they gave in order to verbalize their responses and see if saying these thoughts out loud to someone else brought about any sharper insights. This follows Heinrich von Kleist's advice that one cannot fully know what one thinks without talking it out with someone (von Kleist, 1951).

After these activities in Listening and Pronunciation, I had the students use ChatGPT to see if they could discover any more values. They were to ask ChatGPT questions such as, "Why might someone be in an English Language Teacher program?" and to ask specific questions incorporating other interests of theirs besides English Language teaching proper into the question. For example, one student asked, "How might someone combine their love of space with an English Language Teacher program?" and "Why might someone who is interested in space or who wants to work for NASA enroll in an English Language Teacher program?" They were to bring their answers to class, and similar to the Oral Communication assignment, we discussed ChatGPT's answers: if and how much each student agreed with the answers they were given, and if those ChatGPT answers helped them come up with more of their own values in their value-chains.

After this for both classes, I explained the aims of the course in terms of course goals, specific student learning outcomes, and the personal aims I had for my students and the class. I did not share this before the strong evaluations because I wanted the students to share their own expectations without initial influence from me in case these were much different from what I understood the course was supposed to be about.

TWO PROJECTS AND CHATGPT: AI-DRIVEN PEDAGOGICAL PRACTICES

Listening and Pronunciation's "Contrasting English Phonemes"

The project that was implemented in Listening and Pronunciation was "Contrasting English Phonemes." For this project, I handed out a sign up sheet of 20 different phonemic contrasts, e.g. [w] vs. [v]; [u:] vs. [ʊ]; [ow] vs. [ɔ]; [i:] vs. [ɪ]. Students were to sign up for one set of sounds to be the expert of and to teach their classmates in. Students were to use ChatGPT to provide a description of how to make the sounds with the muscles and movements of one's mouth and throat (vibrating i.e. voiced or non-vibrating i.e. non-voiced), to find minimal pairs of the sounds, to create role plays using those minimal pairs, and to find tongue twisters that used the sounds.

For the role plays, students were to ask ChatGPT to create a role play using the words from those minimal pairs that were *about some interest* (i.e., value) to the student (e.g., directing a movie). The students would then need to make sure they could pronounce the role play's lines perfectly so that they could guide and correct students when they assigned roles to classmates in groups. Similarly, students had to ask ChatGPT not only to make or find tongue twisters with their sounds, but also to create a tongue twister covering the content of a value to the student, e.g. "Make a tongue twister using /w/ and /v/ sounds about aviation." Again, students would need to understand their selections of ChatGPT's answers such that they could then lead their classmates in class as to how to pronounce the sounds in the contexts of the phrases and clauses via tongue twisters, correcting and guiding any classmates who mispronounced them.

Within and beyond these, students were asked to experiment with ChatGPT in whatever other ways that came to them as they worked on their project. For example, one student specified that ChatGPT should "provide minimal pairs with words at least two syllables long" and then after that "at least three syllables long" to see what ChatGPT would come up with, if anything.

Furthermore, they also experimented with if ChatGPT could provide them with games in relation to those minimal pairs and tongue twisters. For example, some students simply submitted what ChatGPT said when asked, "Please provide me with three games that use these minimal pairs."

After all of these activities, the students compared those ChatGPT answers with websites that provided long lists of minimal pairs; detailed explanations, pictures, and videos of how to create the sounds in one's mouth; tongue twister examples; some game ideas; and some short role plays. Because the games could be applied to an two pairs of phonemes (unlike minimal pairs which only relate to the two sounds of each minimal pair, etc.), we compiled the different game ideas students found from interacting with ChatGPT, from the other websites, my own games, and games other students had played in the past. Students could select two or three to use when guiding their classmates to master their particular two sounds. This way, not only would students experience different minimal pairs, tongue twisters, and role plays; but they also would not be playing the exact same games for each set of phonemes.

Oral Communication's "Oxford-Style Debates"

The project that was implemented in Oral Communication was "Oxford-Style Debates." Oxford-Style Debates are debates that foster critical thinking and are used in many university courses. What follows is the format of the debates. (For more information on each of these portions of an Oxford-Style Debate, see Open to Debate Staff, 2019 and Arizona Board of Regents, N/D). First, there is an initial anonymous vote where all students send the teacher privately in the Zoom chat whether they are for the supporting side, are for the opposing side, or are undecided. Then, the class is told the totals of the pre-debate vote. A main goal of the debaters is to try convince those who support the other side to instead support their side, but without also losing any supporters for their own side. Next, are two to three minutes of opening statements for each of the debaters. After this, there is an intra-panel cross-examination where the debaters questioned and responded to each other. Following that, is the audience discussion period where audience members have the opportunity to ask the debaters questions. After the audience discussion period, there are two to three minutes maximum of closing statements for each of the debaters to reiterate and/or clarify information and to make a final attempt at persuading the audience. Finally, there is an ending vote by the audience to reveal the side that showed the most positive change in the votes taken at the end versus those that were given at the beginning of the debate.

In preparation for the debate, ChatGPT AI was used to come up with more debate topic ideas for the students. I first supplied a list of topics for them, but then had them ask ChatGPT for other possible academic topics. In particular, I asked students to plug in some interest of theirs into the question. The following is an excerpt of the instructions I provided the students: "Ask ChatGPT for academic-related topics to your interests. Try to think of three interests you have that you could ask ChatGPT about. For some interests, the academic relation will be obvious (e.g., engineering), but for others it will not be. For example, if you are interested in basketball, ask ChatGPT 'What is an academic topic related to basketball?' Also, ask, 'What is a topic related to basketball that might be debated in a university course?' Come to class ready to share the answers that ChatGPT provided."

While they could choose any topic, there had to at least be one classmate who would take the opposing side. Therefore, when they came to class with the answers ChatGPT gave them, I provided each student with a sheet of paper with the names of all the other students in the first column. In the next, much bigger, three columns, they were to write down the three interests of the other students and to write next to each interest if you would be interested in debating an opposing side related to that interest, and if so, what would the student's side be and what would their classmate's side be. The students were then to rotate around the class, in pairs or groups of there, interviewing each other in order to write down their answers and to find someone to debate against. They also could choose people to debate with. Each topic being debated could have one to three people on each side. This was a great way to get students practicing talking about their interests and in growing in conversational abilities in talking about others' interests.

After debate topics and sides were chosen, students were told that they would be put in groups where they would be the expert/specialist of their topic. There would be no one else from their debate in their group, so that no group would be taught about the same topic more than once. In preparation for this, they needed to ask ChatGPT for suggestions of 10 key words that were each over three syllables long, since such words tend to be academic in nature. The students were to choose five of these to teach their group. Also, they were to ask ChatGPT to describe their topic using the six thinking hats of Dr. Edward de Bono. For example, if basketball was their topic, they could put, "Describe basketball using the six thinking hats of Dr. Edward de Bono" into ChatGPT and get quite a full description. However, when they came to class, they could only use a 3x5 size card or ripped off piece of paper with nothing longer than a phrase in any line of words to help them remember how to describe their area of expertise using the six hats.

Next, ChatGPT was used to come up with more reasons for their side and possible rebuttals and reasons of the other side—and to judge for themselves as to if those reasons are good—which ones are, which ones are not, why so, why not so, and to use those to think of other reasons. Students were to turn ChatGPT's answers to this with their commentary as part of preparing for their debate.

Students also used ChatGPT to ask for suggestions for questions to pose to the other side, and potential questions that might be posed to their side as well as possible answers to those questions and rebuttals to those answers. The students were to continue asking ChatGPT for questions, answers, rebuttals, rebuttals to rebuttals, and so on until it seemed ChatGPT ran out of good responses or until the sixth iteration if it went on that long. Students had the option to continue asking ChatGPT if they were curious as to how long it could go before ChatGPT started talking in circles or giving poor reasons.

During the actual debates students could only have short notes in front of them. They could not dictate reading of ChatGPT's answers. Also, their response time was limited to 15 seconds of silence between being asked a question from the opposing side or from the audience and providing their answers in order to ensure that it came from a place of learning, which was influenced and fostered by research using ChatGPT, rather than from finding the answer right that moment from something they had printed from ChatGPT.

DISCUSSION

Strong Evaluations

The strong evaluation given in Oral Communication well-corresponded with the project that this paper focused on in that class, Oxford-Style Debates. Answers to what the students *wanted* from the course are discussed in the Conclusion section as it brings up information concerning potential for future AI pedagogical work. The other four items are discussed here. Specifically, most frequent answers to what students most expect in the course were the following, and each of the following are specific answers given by students that well-exemplify and are synonymous with answers given by most of the other students: "I expect to speak and improve my speaking ability." "I don't want to read or listen, I just want to speak." "I want to become more fluent." "Speaking skills to get better in terms of fluence." "I expect to talk fluently and I expect that I understand when we have a conversation with others." The activities leading up to the Oxford-Style Debates and the Oxford-Style Debates themselves provided the students many opportunities for this. Students seemed to agree with this, although no thorough end-of-semester evaluation could be given due to difficulties in getting feedback due to changes brought on by the 2023 earthquakes.

The Oxford-Style Debates also addressed issues brought forth by the most frequent answers concerning *special ways* I could help them in Oral Communication. The following answers well-exemplify the most frequent responses: "I think we have a problem when we are talking and the problem is we are afraid of making mistakes when talking. Maybe you can help us to overcome this issue." Oxford-Style Debates did this by having them use ChatGPT to help prepare for speaking with classmates in the various activities leading up to and including the Oxford-Style Debates themselves and then the debates themselves made the talk, which speaks to their other frequent answers: "Push us to speak. We can be shy when talking but you should always make us speak." "Interactive lessons by making groups, such as groups of four, or better, splitting the class into two and talking-discussing about a topic." Again, the

Oxford-Style Debates activities did both of these: small group work, and then the debates themselves which were usually two or three students debating for each side of the topic and the entire audience taking sides and interacting with them.

Frequent answers to what they gave as to anything that may have *hindered* them from learning were synonymous with answers of "unwillingness," "delaying our responsibilities," and "laziness." I am not sure if the Oxford-Style Debates project assisted with this, but I believe in some ways it did. It seemed to increase willingness because students both liked being able to use ChatGPT and to incorporate their interests in with it and to then discuss these interests in more and more advanced ways with their classmates and myself. I made use of Telegram and Google Classroom to remind the students of the different assignments leading up to and including the debates themselves in order to try to prevent this "delaying responsibilities" issue my students claimed they had.

The strong evaluation given in Listening and Pronunciation centered on student interests both inside and outside of the classroom. When comparing this strong evaluation answers with what the students actually did with ChatGPT, there is a high correlation in terms of values instantiated in the types of content questions the students asked ChatGPT. That is, students who valued X (e.g., K-pop) incorporated that value in the ChatGPT activities (e.g., asking ChatGPT to provide a role-play wherein the characters debate whether the musical quality of K-pop or Baroque music is better or worse and in what ways might it be convincingly argued that K-pop is indeed better).

ChatGPT and the Student Learning Outcomes

As concerns answers students were given from ChatGPT during the semester, they were surprisingly in-depth and academic. Due to the length of ChatGPT's answers, examples could not be included in this chapter, but it is easy to get an idea if one simply puts in any of the example items of this chapter into ChatGPT. Answers of ChatGPT were quite academic, including how what might initially seem to be a non-academic topic (e.g., basketball) can indeed be discussed and debated with an academic mindset and in academic terms.

Incorporating ChatGPT into the outcomes and student values, without replacing the students' own initiative and creative spontaneous interactions with the target language, seems to have struck a good balance. While ChatGPT would provide thorough responses for the students, the students themselves adapted these and added to them in interesting ways. Since the students knew they would be in some way presenting this to other students and myself, they wanted their actual personality to shine forth and not just an AI alone. For example, for the strong evaluation in Listening and Speaking, one student asked ChatGPT, "How might someone combine their love of outer space with learning English in an English Language Teacher program?" One of the answers ChatGPT gave her was, "Introduce space-related vocabulary and topics into your lessons . . . terms like 'galaxy,' 'constellation,' 'asteroid,' 'comet,' and 'spaceship.' Engage in discussions about space exploration, the wonders of the universe, or recent space missions." When the student shared this in her small group, she talked about how this made her think about the term she usually Googles or searches on Instagram: "black holes" and how she then planned to work in the topic of black holes in the role play that she will lead with her two phonemes.

Higher-Order Values

Because I had the same students for both classes, I urged them to apply the answers from their values in their value-chain evaluation in our Listening and Pronunciation course to their debate topic for our Oral Communication course. That is, that their debate topic and side for their Oxford-Style Debate reflected something that they had discussed in the value-chain that they created in our Listening and Pronunciation course. They were also free to change their answers for both of the strong evaluations. For example, they could tell me different desires (wants) they have for the course than they gave in the Oral Communication strong evaluation or their value-chain answers if their values shifted over the course of the semester, even if it simply shifted slightly on a smaller-scale for one assignment or activity. Sometimes students did not recognize their values until they were given thee concrete assignments and activities that they were asked to apply their interests to, and then as they worked on that activity they would discover other, sometimes stronger higher-order, values to them. With the assignment instructions, and my own verbal reminders to them, I sought to urge them to implement their higher-order values through these projects.

In detecting if students were indeed actively incorporating higher-order values, there was one warning sign that while they may have appeared to be centering on a higher-order value, they may have not been actively doing so. This warning sign was evidence that they may have been using a topic that they valued but were using it in the same way they had used it in prior classes and therefore were not actually advancing in it or in, perhaps, our course's specific outcomes. The few times I was suspicious of this, I ask the students in a dialogical rather than accusatory manner (Bakhtin, 1981). The answers were fairly uniform. They related to it indeed being a topic area they had used in an assignment in the past, but that for their prior class, they simply wrote one paragraph about it or some other different project from our course with different focuses and outcomes, but that they had never debated for it or presented a role play using it in order to master phonemes. They chose it again because it is a cultivational higher-order value to them, and they wanted to master talking about it in critical thinking, academic ways in English better.

A final issue I noticed was when a student wrote out a value prominently in their value-chain strong evaluation, but then never incorporated it in their project or the ChatGPT activities within those projects to aim toward their higher-order values. I only noticed this with one student. This student put aviation for a reason she was in the ELT program as well as a love of teaching K-12 students English. However, she never incorporated anything remotely related to aviation in either of her projects. I asked her why she had not done so, and she said it was because it is such a competitive program that she doubted she would get into it and did not want to build up her hopes by incorporating aviation in the projects. I understood and assured her it was completely fine that she did not incorporate it, but I still encouraged her to remember that incorporating it could make her both more knowledgeable in aviation and better at English and that, furthermore, even if she does not get into the aviation program, aviation could still be a hobby of hers, and she could still get a pilot license or other kinds of certifications if it continues to be a lifelong hobby.

In situations like these, it was important for me to remember that student voice cannot be and should not be attempted to be forced, but only fostered. Teachers cannot force students' voice to be heard because "voice is not something to be given by those in power. Voice requires struggle and the understanding of both its possibilities and limitations" (Macedo, 2006, p. 174); therefore, "The most educators can do is to create structures that would enable submerged voices to emerge" (Macedo, 2006, p. 174). Thus, with this student, as with others in different ways, I attempted to foster their uses of their higher-order values. The ChatGPT activities within the 2ThVO was how I created "structures that would enable submerged voices to emerge" (Macedo, 2006, p. 174). Students then did use the ChatGPT activities to assist in having their voices emerge via each student's own unique usage of ChatGPT's answers.

Student Feedback Concerning Using ChatGPT

I was unable to get as much student feedback at the end of the semester as I was able to procure strong evaluations the semester before because all of our classes had been made online due to the earthquakes and many students were only responsive to the high-stakes tests in the course. However, the following represents the student feedback I did receive as concerns using ChatGPT activities:

One answer type related to how certain teachers simply tried to hide the fact that AI like ChatGPT exists, so they appreciated that, for those few students who were less familiar with it, I helped them learn about it and how to use. One student worded it in this way, "Most teacher[sic] do not want you to know tools like ChatGPT. It was refreshing to have a teacher let us know about it and how to use it in ways that helped us master English."

Another answer type related to teachers who were upfront about AI, but did not permit its use. As one student said, "Some teacher[sic] who allow ChatGPT for certain assignments, forbid it on other assignment[sic]. But there are always some maybe most maybe all of us who use it anyway to help find and develop our own voices. It's nice to use it without the added guilt of a teacher forbidding it."

A final answer type, and more important to me as a teacher, related to the techniques by which we used ChatGPT in these courses. The following student's comment articulates this particularly well: "I like how Professor Chad had us learn through ChatGPT—that we could not bring it in and claim it was our own, but we had to show mastery by remembering things we learned and attempting to teach it to each other."

CONCLUSION

The goal of this VOPR study was to help to advance our understanding of AI's potential use in language educational practices and the development of innovative instructional strategies that cater to diverse learner values in a way that adds to the repository of evidence-based practices and case studies implementing AI in language education and that explores intertwining the enhancement of students' individual values with the course's values (course learning outcomes) by way of using the AI chatbot, ChatGPT.

Centering on ChatGPT, values, and fostering a cooperative understanding between stakeholders for this study meant using ChatGPT to foster cooperation between the requirements of the classes and the values of the students, i.e., intertwining of the values of classroom life with the (development of) students' values. The student learning outcomes that ChatGPT worked to enhance were (1) the outcome of accurately distinguishing all of the English phonemes both in terms of ability to distinguish them when heard (listening) and ability to distinguish them in the student's articulation of them (pronunciation); and (2) the outcome of thoroughly explaining an academic topic that corresponded with a value that the student herself holds and of defending one's side concerning that topic in an academic Oxford-Style Debate. These two corresponded to two main projects; respectively, Contrasting English Phonemes and Oxford Style Debates. Students explored their values initially via two strong evaluations (one in each course) of which they elaborated via interactions with ChatGPT after providing their strong evaluations in in-class activities. Then, throughout the semester the students explored their values further by using ChatGPT to provide new ideas that they could adapt and incorporate into their projects and to provide a rich source of content by which the students could critique and comment on, further developing their own opinions and understanding of their values and of the outcomes of the course.

The Discussion section talked about the Oral Communication strong evaluation items that related to what the students *expected* from the course and any *special requests* to help them learn better, and anything that may have *hindered* them from learning so far. However, the students' most frequent answers to what they *wanted* from the course related in one way or another to games, such as the following: "I want to play some games and make some different exercises to improve my speaking skill because I can learn any lesson better with games." "Maybe we can play games or things like that." "Well, I want fun games that will contribute to our speaking ability. For example, for each day we can choose different subjects and discuss them." "Lessons to be fun." "I want to have fun while learning." "I want to do different activities so that it can be enjoyable."

In response to the students' high-order value on games, gaming occurred throughout Oral Communication leading up to the final Oxford-Style Debates, using games I came up with, I had learned in the past, or games from various resource books like *The Monster Book of Language Teaching Activities* (Office of English Language Programs, 2019). However, unlike with Listening and Pronunciation project (as discussed in the Methods section), ChatGPT was not used to come up with these Oral Communication games. If there is a future iteration of a Oxford-Style Debate project, I will have students conduct an initial activity wherein students ask ChatGPT for game ideas as concerns getting better at debating a topic in a C1 English language learning course or some other variations of that theme in their questioning of ChatGPT to come up with games. Then, as we did for the Contrasting English Phonemes project, students could compare and contrast these game ideas from ChatGPT with games found in resource books, games that I provide them in a document of game options, and games that they think of in class and add to the document. Then, they, as a class and individually, could decide which games we would instantiate in class.

This technique did seem to work in Listening and Pronunciation. One game did not work due to technical difficulties, and a few games did not work well due to taking too much time for one overly-technical part of it, but students enjoyed learning from the difficulty of having the game they led work sufficiently, and learning how to do it better and more smoothly next time, especially because they hoped to be able to teach English in the future and to do so in a very gamified way, combining their higher-order values of games and English. It was also clear that fun activities, such as games and (role) plays, were of higher-order value even to the self-proclaimed shy and lazy students. They requested games in which they would be forced to communicate with others, requesting that there be a foisting of fun activities upon them; thus providing a way out of their shyness or laziness.

This gaming, playing and fun also fits the value framework wherein one's acts are what comprise a person's values; thus, in a LLing course, the more actions that are done by the students (by the learners), the better. Clearly, for this population of students, game-like activities fostered more acts by both outgoing and shy students alike. Again, a teacher cannot force *fun* on students (on other people), one can only foster it by providing *rich opportunities for* (vs. opportunity deprivation of opportunities) it via highly interactive activities. Of particular importance, this study having been carried out both in face-to-face courses (Fall Semester 2022) and online (Spring Semester 2023) showed that certain things like games are better face-to-face when technical difficulties cannot prevent the game from occurring and wherein students often must move around for the games.

Another aspect I would change in future research, is to keep a more rigorous account of the answers to the strong evaluation and then feedback at the end. Unfortunately, for the Listening and Pronunciation strong evaluation, I returned the students' value chains without having made copies myself because I wanted the students themselves to have it to refer back to and remind themselves of throughout the semester and I did not have access to a copy machine; therefore, I would have had to type all the answers into my computer and I simply did not permit myself sufficient time to do so. At my future university, I will have access to a copy machine; therefore I can keep the students' answers by way of copying them while also being able to give it back to my students. Then, at the end, I could ask each individual student if and how much they were able to incorporate their specific value, mentioning it in my question so that I can directly correlate it to each answer given in the beginning-of-the-year strong evaluation (e.g., space, aviation, movie directing, K-pop).

For the Oral Communication strong evaluation, I simply went over with the entire class their most frequent answers as a class, but I kept their answers since I had them answer anonymously. For the value-chains, they put their names on it because I wanted them to remember and possibly develop their unique higher-order values. However, with the Oral Communication strong evaluation, I wanted them to be as honest as possible as to their expectations, wants, special requests, and hinderances of the class itself without fear of what the teacher of the class might think of those. Along with that, since this strong evaluation pertained to how the class should be run, it most pertained to what I as a teacher had the most control over. Therefore, keeping these answers would be a good reminder for me throughout the course.

The assessments at the end of Spring Semester 2023 revealed that students who showed up to class regularly and participated in the ChatGPT activities did successfully master the two main outcomes of this study: (1) the outcome of accurately distinguishing all of the English phonemes both in terms of ability to distinguish them when heard (listening) and ability to distinguish them in the student's articulation of them (pronunciation); and (2) the outcome of thoroughly explaining an academic topic that corresponded with a value that the student herself holds and of defending one's side concerning that topic in an academic Oxford-Style Debate. The progression towards this mastery was readily seen in comparing their abilities revealed in their performances in activities from the beginnings of the projects to those at the end.

In conclusion, while AI will continue to advance and change, each advance could and, therefore, should be used to good effect in advancing and enhancing student learning outcomes and students' own individual values and language mastery. Furthermore, AI provides students with creative ideas pertaining to their higher-order values and with ideas of new values they may wish to aspirationally pursue. As this study and its many examples are evidence of, so long as there are real-time classes (preferably face-to-face) wherein students have to interact without the use of the AI directly in front of them (for certain portions of the classes), it can be nearly guaranteed that AI will be used to help them come up with and master the material for these in-class real-time language interactive acts, rather than in any way replacing the student with the AI.

REFERENCES

Allwright, D. (2003). Exploratory Practice: Rethinking practitioner research in language teaching. *Language Teaching Research*, *7*(2), 113–141. doi:10.1191/1362168803lr118oa

Allwright, D. (2006). Six promising directions in applied linguistics. In S. Gieve & I. K. Miller (Eds.), *Understanding the language classroom* (pp. 11–17). Palgrave Macmillan. doi:10.1057/9780230523166_2

Allwright, D., & Hanks, J. (2009). *The developing language learner*. London, England: Palgrave Macmillan London. Arizona Board of Regents (N/D). In *Arizona board of regents*. https://www.azregents.edu/sites/default/files/public/Oxford.pdf

Bakhtin, M. (1981). *The dialogic imagination: Four essays* (M. Holquist, Trans.). University of Texas Press.

Callard, A. (2018). *Aspiration: The agency of becoming*. Oxford University Press. doi:10.1093/oso/9780190639488.001.0001

Callard, A. (2021). Precis. *Philosophy and Phenomenological Research*, *102*(2), 459–463. doi:10.1111/phpr.12758

Hanks, J. (2019). From research-as-practice to exploratory practice-as-research in language teaching and beyond. *Language Teaching*, *52*(2), 143–187. doi:10.1017/S0261444819000016

Kato, Y., & Hanks, J. (2021). Learner-initiated exploratory practice: Revisiting curiosity. *ELT Journal*.

Kemp, R. (2020). Lessons in self-betrayal: On the pitfalls of transformative education. *Educational Theory*, *70*(5), 603–616. doi:10.1111/edth.12446

Macedo, D. (2006). Literacies of power: What Americans are not allowed to know (Expanded ed.). Boulder, CO: Westview Press.

Nunan, D. (1989). *Understanding language classrooms*. Prentice Hall International (UK).

Office of English Language Programs. (2019). *The Monster Book of Language Teaching Activities*. American English. www.americanenglish.state.gov

Open A. I. (2023). *ChatGPT (July 12 version)* [Large language model]. https://chat.openai.com/chat

Open to Debate Staff. (2019). What is the oxford style of debate? *Open to debate*. https://opentodebate.org/what-is-the-oxford-style-debate-format/

Sartre, J. (1948). *What is literature? And other essays* (S. Ungar, Trans.). Harvard University Press.

Sartre, J. (1956). *Being and nothingness: An essay on phenomenological ontology* (H. Barnes, Trans.). Washington Square Press.

Sartre, J. (1963). *Search for a method* (H. Barnes, Trans.). Alfred A. Knopf.

Sartre, J. (2013). We have only this life to live: The selected essays of Jean-Paul Sartre 1939-1975 (A. Van Den Hoven, Trans.). Aronson, R. & Van Den Hoven, A. (Ed.s). New York, NY: New York Review of Books.

Sartre, J. (2021). *Being and nothingness: The principal text of modern existentialism* (S. Richmond, Trans.). Washington Square Press.

Ur, P. (2019, September 6). *Penny Ur - My Top 30 teaching Tips (plus some extras!)* [Video]. YouTube. https://youtu.be/ddOudlhnjPE?t=1274

von Kleist, H. (1951). On the Gradual Construction of Thoughts during Speech (M. Hamburger, Trans.). *German Life and Letters*, *5*(1), 42–46. doi:10.1111/j.1468-0483.1951.tb01029.x

Zeichner, K., & Noffke, S. (2001). Practitioner research. In V. Richardson (Ed.), *Handbook of research on teaching* (4th ed., pp. 298–330). American Educational Research Association.

Chapter 14
Opinions of ESL Preservice Teachers on Using Artificial Intelligence Language Models in Language Education

Matti Izora Ibrahim
Arkansas Tech University, USA

Mohamed M. Ibrahim
https://orcid.org/0000-0003-4618-2463
Arkansas Tech University, USA

ABSTRACT

This chapter examined the opinion of 417 ESL preservice teachers regarding the use of AI language models in teaching and learning English language. The study found that most of the participants do not believe that AI language models could replace human teachers in ESL education, either now or in the future. However, it was found that there are some ethical, social, and cultural concerns related to the use of AI language models in language education. The concerns voiced by participants include the issue of the users' privacy and ownership, the lack of social interaction, empathy, and communication, and the potential for cultural bias. The chapter also recommended that ESL educators should offer comprehensive training that addresses these concerns and develops critical thinking skills by emphasizing the significance of safeguarding users' privacy and data, mitigating bias in AI models, clarifying intellectual property rights, ensuring reliable text generation, considering social and cultural implications, and promoting a balanced and ethical approach to using AI language models.

DOI: 10.4018/978-1-6684-9893-4.ch014

INTRODUCTION

Instructors of English as a Second Language (ESL) aim to facilitate the development of linguistic, communicative, intercultural competencies, cognitive skills, and social skills among their students. To accomplish these goals, instructors employ diverse texts, resources, and technologies to support students and enhance learning outcomes. In recent times, ESL instructors have incorporated Artificial Intelligence (AI) language models into their pedagogical strategies to harness the benefits of these technologies, including generating engaging content, providing access to native speakers, delivering prompt feedback, and creating natural language text based on student inputs (Chen et al., 2021; Hockly, 2023). Many ESL educators recognize the value of AI models in offering personalized and adaptive learning aligned with individual needs, automated feedback, interactive content, and conversational agents (Kohnke et al., 2023).

However, despite the promising potential of AI technologies, concerns have emerged among scholars, educators, and users regarding the ethical, social, and cultural implications of integrating AI models into ESL contexts (Nguyen et al., 2023; Perkins, 2023). While AI has become ubiquitous across various educational domains, from intelligent tutoring systems to automated writing evaluation (Rusmiyanto et al., 2023; Zawacki-Richter et al., 2019), research focused specifically on ESL preservice teachers' perspectives remains scarce. Although prior studies have examined student and teacher perceptions of AI in education broadly (Aljohani, 2021; Davis, 2022), a gap persists in understanding ESL preservice teachers' attitudes and beliefs as future adopters of AI technologies.

This study aims to address this gap by eliciting the opinions and apprehensions of ESL preservice teachers concerning the incorporation of AI language models in English language teaching and learning. The findings will inform recommendations for equipping preservice teachers with the requisite knowledge and skills for the responsible integration of AI technologies into their future educational practices.

Profile of the Participants

For this study, we developed a survey questionnaire that included two sections: (1) a demographics section included questions regarding the participants' demographic characteristics, such as gender, age, level of English proficiency, years in the university, and educational major; and (2) a section to ask about participants opinion regarding the use of AI language models in teaching and learning English language.

The results of the survey indicated that there were 417 ESL preservice teachers who participated in this study. All participants were enrolled in the English teaching program in a 4-year university in the Anatolian region in Türkiye. ESL preservice teachers were attending different courses that were taught in English which covered various topics and skills related to ESL education that included the development and improvement of oral communication skills, the acquisition and analysis of listening and pronunciation skills, the diversity and variation of Englishes spoken around the world, and the theories and principles of second language learning and teaching.

The results of the survey found that 70% of the preservice teachers who completed the survey questionnaire were female, 69% were between 18 and 21 years old, and 53% of the participants had intermediate or advanced level of English proficiency. The survey results also indicated that 30% of the participants were freshman, 28% sophomore, and 42% were senior. The English department at the surveyed university is normally attended by ESL students who are training to become English teachers. Therefore, 77% of the participants reported that they are majoring in general English teaching, while 14% of them majoring in teaching high school. The remaining number of the participants are majoring in teaching English in middle education, elementary and early childhood education. Participants also reported that around 64% of them had used AI language models in practicing their English skills, generating ideas, or creating content for their assignments, while 36% reported that they had not used AI language models at all. Furthermore, more than one-third (35%) of the participants who reported using the AI language models indicated that they agreed or strongly agreed that AI language models were more helpful, useful, or effective for their English learning than traditional methods, while 31% of the participants disagreed or strongly disagreed that AI language models were helpful, useful, or effective for their English learning. The remaining (34%) were neutral or may have been unsure or undecided about the impact or outcome of using AI language models in ESL education. A possible interpretation of these responses is that not all ESL preservice teachers have the same level of experience in using AI language models in their academic work or for fun. This interpretation could be supported by the earlier numbers that indicated that about 36%, more than one-third of the participants had not used AI language models at all, and this maybe led to be unsure or undecided about the impact of using AI language models in ESL education.

The final question in this section asked ESL preservice teachers for their opinion on whether AI language models could replace human teachers in ESL education, either now or in the future. The results of this question showed that most of the ESL preservice teachers (more than 67%) did not believe that AI language models could replace human teachers in ESL education, either now or in the future. This result suggests that the ESL preservice teachers looked favorably on the role of human teachers in ESL education. A possible interpretation of this result is that students who participated in this study are mainly preservice teachers, who aspire to be English teachers in the future. They therefore value and appreciate the roles of human teachers and their impact on the lives of future generations.

In the following section we will discuss the second part of the survey by asking the participants about their opinion regarding three areas related to the use of AI language models in language education, namely ethical, social, and cultural considerations. The questions focused on participants' opinion on ethical issues, such as the effect of the use of AI language models on the users' privacy and ownership. Questions about social issues included topics such as students' social interaction, empathy, and communication with AI language models. The cultural issues included topics such as cultural sensitivity, linguistic diversity, and inclusion.

Perspectives on AI Replacing Human Teachers

When prompted about the potential for AI to replace human instructors in ESL education presently or in the future, over 67% of participants disagreed. They recognized the unique roles of human teachers in providing social-emotional support, individualized guidance, and interpersonal interaction. This aligns with studies demonstrating student preferences for human elements in education over complete technological substitution (Keerthiwansha, 2018; Kohnke et al., 2023).

However, around 34% remained neutral, potentially attributable to their limited exposure to AI integration in teaching contexts thus far. As they accumulate more practical experience, they may form clearer perspectives regarding AI's capabilities and limitations. Nonetheless, most preservice teachers in this study valued the irreplaceable impact of human teachers.

In the ensuing section, participant opinions regarding ethical, social, and cultural considerations related to AI language model usage in education will be discussed. Key topics included ethical issues surrounding user privacy and data ownership, social dynamics such as interaction and communication, and cultural dimensions including sensitivity, diversity, and inclusion.

Ethical Considerations: Privacy and Data Protection

ESL preservice teachers expressed substantial concerns regarding privacy and data protection when utilizing AI models. Over 90% felt that AI systems could potentially leak users' personal information during interactions. They worried about how user data is collected, stored, and used without adequate consent or anonymity safeguards (Lu, 2019). This aligns with findings revealing user discomfort with AI systems accessing their private information (Sindermann et al., 2021).

To mitigate privacy risks, recommendations include:

- Anonymizing or encrypting user data (Nguyen et al., 2023)
- Disclosing data practices transparently and obtaining informed consent

- Establishing security safeguards against unauthorized access
- Educating students on strategies for protecting personal information online

Users' Privacy and Data Protection

ESL preservice teachers voiced their concerns regarding the issue of protecting users' privacy and the process of users' data collection by the AI language models. Participants raised this issue as one of the most pressing concerns, since all AI models have not shared with users how they collect, store, and use personal data from users who interact with them. Further, more than 90% of the participants reported that the AI language models in language education have the potential to violate users' information by leaking sensitive personal data after they interact with the AI language model, such as their names and email addresses. The privacy issue is a legitimate concern for ESL preservice teachers because AI models rely on enormous amounts of text data and personal information to learn and generate personalized language and text. Some of the text and data provided to the AI models by the users may contain sensitive or personal information which could be compromised or misused by AI models or third parties. This personal information could also be extracted and stored from the users' questions or their feedback and later used by the model or third parties. As a result, the AI model may access or disclose the identity, location, preferences, or performance of the ESL preservice teachers who use them. Most of the ESL preservice teachers found that AI models collect and store some of their data without their consent or knowledge. Moreover, ESL preservice teachers were concerned that AI language models may also expose their data to unauthorized users who may exploit or manipulate the data for purposes not intended by them. Additionally, ESL preservice teachers were concerned that since AI models are trained on substantial amounts of text data from various sources (e.g., books, websites, social media, news articles, etc.), these data may contain sensitive or personal information about them, for instance, their names, addresses, opinions, preferences, etc. Finally, ESL preservice teachers were concerned that if these data were not properly anonymized or encrypted, their data might be leaked or inferred by the AI language models or by malicious actors who may access them.

Consequently, these privacy and security issues may affect the rights and interests of the data sources and the users, as well as erode their trust and confidence in using AI language models. Moreover, ESL preservice teachers expressed concern that these data may reflect the socioeconomic and geopolitical conditions of their originators (e.g., wealth, education, power, influence, etc.). When taken together, these conditions may affect the quality, availability, and accessibility of the data, as well as the models that are trained on them. Therefore, it is important for ESL preservice teachers to be aware of these issues and adopt strategies to ensure the privacy and security of the data sources and the users.

Bias and Discrimination

Participants also raised concerns about bias and discrimination issues with AI systems reflecting prejudices in their training data or design (Richardson & Clesham, 2021). They felt AI models could generate offensive, insensitive, or misleading content about certain groups. Research confirms AI algorithms can perpetuate harmful stereotypes and exclusion of marginalized populations if biases are not proactively addressed (Nguyen et al., 2023).

Strategies to mitigate bias include:

- Utilizing diverse and representative data sources (El Shazly, 2021)
- Incorporating bias detection and mitigation mechanisms (Xiao & Hu, 2019)
- Promoting algorithmic fairness through continuous evaluation and improvement
- Raising awareness among educators and students about biased AI behaviors

Another ethical concern identified by the ESL preservice teachers is the fairness and bias of AI language models when interacting with non-native English speakers. Their concern was derived from the issue that certain groups or individuals may face bias and discrimination while using AI language models. For example, AI language models may reflect or amplify the bias or prejudice that exist in the data they are trained on or in the society they operate in. The AI model may generate texts that are discriminatory, offensive, or harmful to certain groups or individuals based on their race, gender, ethnicity, religion, age, disability, culture, or other characteristics. The AI models may also generate texts that favor or promote certain perspectives, values, beliefs, or interests over others, while also exhibiting bias and unfairness by producing texts that are inaccessible or incomprehensible to some users due to their linguistic or cultural diversity or differences. Additionally, as compared to other social media applications, AI language models may replicate or amplify biases present in their training data or in their internal patterns. For example, AI language models may perpetuate stereotypes, unfair discrimination, exclusionary norms, toxic language, and lower performance by social groups. They may also generate false or misleading information about certain topics or events that may affect the reputation or well-being of certain groups or individuals. Hence, the preservice teachers believe that these bias and discrimination issues may affect the learning outcomes and experiences of students and teachers.

Therefore, it is important for language educators to be aware of these issues and develop different pedagogical strategies to prevent or mitigate any signs of bias and discrimination during the use of AI language models. Some possible strategies include using diverse and representative data sources, incorporating feedback mechanisms, leveraging machine learning techniques to adapt and improve the models, providing bias awareness and education for staff and students, and establishing protocols that enhance fairness and accountability. Additionally, AI could include using diverse and representative data sources to train AI language models, incorporating ethical principles and values into the design and development of AI language models, and providing cultural training and education for staff and students who use AI language models.

Ethical Considerations: Bias and Discrimination Mitigation

Participants also expressed concerns regarding bias and discrimination issues stemming from AI systems reflecting prejudices embedded in their training data or design (Richardson & Clesham, 2021). They felt AI models could generate offensive, insensitive, or misleading content about certain groups. Research confirms AI algorithms risk perpetuating harmful stereotypes and exclusion of marginalized populations without proactive bias mitigation (Nguyen et al., 2023).

Recommendations to mitigate bias include:

- Utilizing diverse and representative data sources (El Shazly, 2021)
- Incorporating bias detection and mitigation mechanisms (Xiao & Hu, 2019)
- Promoting algorithmic fairness through continuous evaluation and improvement
- Raising educator and student awareness of biased AI behaviors
- Employing diverse training data and embedding ethical principles into model design
- Providing cultural competency training for AI users

Language educators must be cognizant of these issues and adopt pedagogical strategies to prevent or reduce AI bias and discrimination. Ongoing analysis, adaptation, and oversight mechanisms are imperative to enhance fairness, accountability, and learning outcomes.

Another ethical concern identified by the ESL preservice teachers is the fairness and bias of AI language models when interacting with non-native English speakers. Their concern was derived from the issue that certain groups or individuals may face bias and discrimination while using AI language models. For example, AI language models may reflect or amplify the bias or prejudice that exist in the data they are trained on or in the society they operate in. The AI model may generate texts that are discriminatory, offensive, or harmful to certain groups or individuals based on their race, gender, ethnicity, religion, age, disability, culture, or other characteristics. The AI models may also generate texts that favor or promote certain perspectives, values, beliefs, or interests over others, while also exhibiting bias and unfairness by producing texts that are inaccessible or incomprehensible to some users due to their linguistic or cultural diversity or differences. Additionally, as compared to other social media applications, AI language models may replicate or amplify biases present in their training data or in their internal patterns. For example, AI language models may perpetuate stereotypes, unfair discrimination, exclusionary norms, toxic language, and lower performance by social groups. They may also generate false or misleading information about certain topics or events that may affect the reputation or well-being of certain groups or individuals. Hence, the preservice teachers believe that these bias and discrimination issues may affect the learning outcomes and experiences of students and teachers.

Therefore, it is important for language educators to be aware of these issues and develop different pedagogical strategies to prevent or mitigate any signs of bias and discrimination during the use of AI language models. Some possible strategies include using diverse and representative data sources, incorporating feedback mechanisms, leveraging machine learning techniques to adapt and improve the models, providing bias awareness and education for staff and students, and establishing protocols that enhance fairness and accountability. Additionally, AI could include using diverse and representative data sources to train AI language models, incorporating ethical principles and values into the design and development of AI language models, and providing cultural training and education for staff and students who use AI language models.

Intellectual Property

Unclear intellectual property rights and plagiarism risks also emerged as concerns. Participants worried about proper attribution when AI systems produce content derived from copyrighted training data. Studies show the legal ownership of AI-generated text remains a gray area (Eke, 2023).

To address these issues, educators should:

- Provide authorship and plagiarism guidelines for AI content use.
- Teach citation skills and promote academic integrity.
- Use plagiarism checking tools to detect problematic content.
- Advocate for clearer intellectual property policies around AI text generation

Another issue raised by the ESL preservice teachers who participated in our survey was the issue of intellectual property and ownership rights of the data sources and the work produced by the AI models. As part of their learning about digital citizenship, ESL preservice teachers learned that intellectual property and ownership is respecting and acknowledging the original sources and creators of the linguistic data. One of the ethical concerns is the ownership of the intellectual property of the responses generated by AI language models.

Participants indicated that they were concerned that their work would be considered plagiarized. Therefore, users must be informed about who owns the intellectual property and who has the right to use and modify the responses generated by the AI models. Looking through the process of how the AI language models create content would explain the participants concerns. Traditionally, AI language models are trained on text data that are created by human authors who have copy rights over their works, such as books, articles, poems, songs, etc. And if these copy-righted works are not properly licensed or attributed to their authors, the AI-created work and the users who may use them without permission or acknowledgment may be violating the authors' copyrights. Moreover, the users of AI language models may also create texts that are influenced or derived from the outputs of the models. Again, these texts may raise questions about their originality, creativity, and ownership. For example, if an ESL student uses an AI language model to generate an essay for a class assignment, the pressing questions then become: who owns the essay? The ESL student, the AI model, or both? And how should the essay be evaluated for its quality, relevance, and authenticity?

The issue of intellectual property and ownership of the AI-created work was raised frequently throughout the survey and should be answered. Otherwise, it may affect the rights and interests of the many stakeholders, such as the authors of the data sources, the users, as well as their academic integrity and professional ethics of students and instructors. Therefore, it is important for ESL language instructors to be aware of these issues and develop different strategies and share them with their students on how to respect the intellectual property and ownership rights of the data sources and the users. ESL instructors can also develop different strategies by providing clear guidelines and expectations about the data and output from AL language models, as well as by monitoring and moderating the work produced by ESL students when using AI models.

Reliability of the Texts

Preservice teachers also critiqued AI for generating irrelevant, illogical, or factually incorrect text at times. Research confirms AI can produce false information, grammatical errors, and other flawed output lacking human reasoning (Teubner et al., 2023).

Improving reliability involves:

- Setting quality control standards for text generation (Koraishi, 2023)
- Evaluating and providing feedback to refine AI system accuracy.
- Educating users to critically examine AI output for errors.
- Combining AI generation with human content curation and verification

Another ethical concern expressed by the ESL preservice teachers is the level of accuracy and reliability of the texts generated by AI language models. For example, some students commented that since they are still learning, AI language models may produce texts that are inaccurate, incorrect, irrelevant, or inconsistent with the input or the context which could result in their inability to recognize the mistakes. Additionally, a few participants complain that the responses generated by AI language models are not always accurate or appropriate for the context of the conversation. Other students mentioned that, in some cases, AI language models generate texts that contain factual errors, grammatical mistakes, logical flaws, or inappropriate content. Other ESL students mentioned that the AI language models sometimes generate texts that do not match the students' intended purpose or genre of the writing tasks. Participants also mentioned that, in some cases, AI models generate texts that are either plagiarized or copied from other sources without proper citation or acknowledgment. All these issues related to the generated text demand that ESL instructors should develop different strategies and share them with their students to ensure the accuracy and reliability of the texts generated by AI language models before, they can submit it for grading or fully depend on its outputs. Some of the possible solutions that can be easily adopted by ESL teachers and students is using quality control mechanisms, such as human verification, peer review, or feedback systems, providing clear and specific instructions or criteria for the writing tasks, and using plagiarism detection tools or software to check for originality and authenticity before submitting their work for assessment.

Reliance on AI Models

Finally, participants worried students might become overly dependent on AI, losing critical thinking and communication skills. Indeed, studies show some users prefer interacting with chatbots over humans (Davis, 2022).

To prevent overreliance, teachers should:

- Clarify AI limitations and use as a supplemental tool, not surrogate (Sindermann et al., 2021)
- Structure activities to balance AI and human interactions (Kohnke et al., 2023)
- Cultivate skills in independent learning, communication, and content evaluation.

The final ethical issue voiced by the ESL preservice teachers in this survey is their concern that they would become reliant and dependent on using AI language models to create their academic work in ESL education. In our early conversations with ESL students, we discussed the pros and cons of using technology in ESL education. We found that although most ESL students have no objections to utilize technology in learning and teaching ESL, the majority of students indicated that language education should not rely solely on technology, such as AI language models, and that it should be used for limited times. Their justification for their position was very logical: dependence on technology could lead to a reduction in human interaction, which is essential for language learning. Furthermore, participants indicated that they are concerned that AI language models may influence the role of human teachers in ESL education. For example, the heavy use of AI language models may reduce or eliminate the need for teachers' feedback and interaction during ESL learning. Another negative effect of the reliance on the AI models is that it may undermine or diminish ESL learners' abilities or creativity by providing them with ready-made or easy solutions to their writing or communication challenges. Another concern was related to creating or increasing the gap or disparity between students who "Have" and students who "Have Not" access or affordance to AI language models. Accordingly, the ESL instructors should ensure the balance and moderation of using AI language models with their students in ESL education. Some possible solutions include encouraging and fostering ESL students' critical thinking, independent learning, and creative expression, as well as providing equal or equitable opportunities and resources for all ESL learners to use AI language models.

Social Considerations in the Use of AI Language Models in Language Education

ESL preservice teachers identified six main issues related to the social considerations in using AI models in language education. The social issues include the absence of the human element in their communications with the AI models, affordability, equal access to AI language models for all students, and the lack of inclusivity and equity of AI language models.

Implications and Relationships: Human Interaction and Communication

The lack of human emotions and empathy was a top social concern. Participants felt AI systems would struggle to provide the social connection, individualized support, and interpersonal communication skills expected from human teachers and peers. Research confirms AI currently lacks capacities for deeper social-emotional engagement in learning experiences (Zawacki-Richter et al., 2019).

Recommendations include:

- Framing AI as a complementary, not primary means of interaction and feedback (Kose et al., 2015)
- Designing classroom activities focused on human connection and communication (Kohnke et al., 2023)
- Monitoring student-AI collaborations to facilitate learning and mitigate unintended consequences.

ESL preservice teachers who participated in the survey indicated that the first social issue they were concerned about was the impact AI language models may have on the social interaction and communication between humans and machines, as well as between humans themselves. For instance, while AI language models may enable conversational agents that can interact with ESL students and instructors in natural language, they may also pose social risks to different users, such as lack of human empathy, manipulation, deception, emotional attachment, or the loss of human connections. These issues are mostly related in one way or another to the loss of the human connection during the interaction with the AI models. For example, ESL students reported that they lacked personalized human teacher feedback during the use of AI language models, as well as guidance, and support that they need and expect from their teachers. Additionally, ESL students stated that AI language models tend to completely disregard the unique quality of human interaction, such as failing to provide human-like emotions, expressions, or understanding, that ESL learners need from their instructors. Another important aspect of ESL human interaction also eliminated by the AI language models is the human socialization that ESL learners need and enjoy with their peers and instructors. These AI model social flaws could also extend its negative affects to the psychological well-being and social skills of ESL students, as well as the quality and accuracy of human communication they would receive. For example, ESL students may become too dependent on or attached to conversational agents, losing their critical thinking or self-regulation skills. They may also be misled or manipulated by conversational agents that have hidden agendas or culture biases. In extreme cases, ESL students may lose their interest or confidence in communicating with human peers or teachers, preferring to get lost in cyber space and interact with machines instead. Therefore, it is important for ESL language instructors to be aware of these social risks and adopt counter strategies to ensure the safety, well-being, and success of ESL students.

Some possible solutions include developing teaching strategies by instructors to use AI language models just as a complement or an aid rather than depending fully on or as a replacement to human teachers. Another solution is by encouraging and facilitating student-student and student-instructor interactions through various classroom activities. Additionally, instructors may engage ESL students in different activities that could help them to develop or improve their emotional intelligence and social skills. On the design side, AI models should be developed as conversational agents that are clearly distinguishable from humans. This could be achieved by providing ESL students with clear disclosures and expectations about the AI models' capabilities and limitations, as well as monitoring and moderating their interactions with users.

Affordability and Access

Another social concern expressed in the survey is the issue of affordability and access to AI language models by all ESL learners and instructors. Currently, many of the reliable AI language models include expensive subscriptions that are unaffordable for many students. Therefore, ESL preservice teachers indicated that it is important to provide affordable alternatives to allow them equitable access to AI models in ESL education. Some possible solutions include allowing ESL students to use open-source or low-cost AI model platforms or sharing an AI model subscription among different users or institutions.

Access and Inclusion

Preservice teachers also critiqued AI's potential to exclude or disadvantage students lacking proficiency, finances, or digital access to leverage the technology fully. Studies confirm AI risks exacerbating existing educational inequities and barriers for underserved groups if its use is not equitably managed (Nguyen et al., 2023).

Promoting inclusive use involves:

- Developing equitable district/school policies for AI integration
- Providing accessibility accommodations and digital literacy training as needed
- Making low-cost AI solutions available, avoiding overreliance on expensive proprietary products

- Monitoring AI impacts on marginalized populations; addressing detrimental effects.

A third social concern of ESL preservice teachers is the issue of inclusivity and equity of AI language models in ESL education. Since AI models depend heavily on the users' inputs and interactions and not all ESL students can access AI models equally, this may create or increase the disparity among different students in different regions or countries. Additionally, AI language models may favor or benefit those in developed countries who have more access to AI models over those who are in underdeveloped countries who have less or no access to the same platforms. AI models may also favor or benefit those who have higher skills or knowledge to use AI language models over those who have lesser or limited skills. Therefore, ESL preservice teachers believe that it is crucial to have equal access to AI models to ensure the inclusivity and equity of all students in ESL education. Some possible solutions include providing equal resources for all ESL learners to access and use AI models and offering appropriate training for all ESL learners to develop and improve their skills and knowledge to use AI models in their language education.

Diversity and Culture

ESL preservice teachers included the diversity and culture of AI language models as one of the social issues concerning them. Many ESL students indicated that AI language models may ignore the diversity and culture of the users or the contexts they operate in. For example, some ESL students reported that AI language models sometimes generate texts that are insensitive or offensive to certain groups or individuals based on their race, gender, ethnicity, religion, culture, or other characteristics. Other students indicated that AI models sometimes generate texts that are irrelevant, inaccurate, or incomprehensible for certain users due to their linguistic, cultural, or situational diversity. Other reports showed that AI models may generate texts that are standardized or normalized according to values or beliefs of certain groups that may not represent or respect the diversity and cultures of other users. Therefore, the ESL preservice teachers believe that it is important to ensure diversity and culture of AI language models in ESL education. The issue of respecting the diversity and culture of the users requires design improvement to the AI models. Some of the design improvements include using diverse and representative data sources to train AI language models to become more sensitive to the users' culture and their diversity. Further, developers could incorporate cultural awareness and sensitivity into the design and development of AI language models.

CULTURAL CONSIDERATIONS IN THE USE OF AI LANGUAGE MODELS IN LANGUAGE EDUCATION

Finally, ESL Preservice teachers expressed their opinions regarding some cultural issues when using the AI language models, such as cultural sensitivity, respect for linguistic diversity, and adaptation of AI language models to different users' socioeconomic and geopolitical variation.

Cultural Sensitivity

Participants felt AI systems lacked sufficient cultural awareness and often generated insensitive content. Research shows AI algorithms frequently encode and amplify societal biases against minorities, women, and other groups (Nguyen et al., 2023).

Improving cultural sensitivity requires:

- Training AI models on diverse data representative of multicultural contexts (El Shazly, 2021)
- Establishing human oversight and feedback processes to identify and redress insensitivities (Nguyen et al., 2023)
- Educating AI developers and users about preventing and mitigating biased behaviors
- Promoting learning activities that counteract prejudices and celebrate pluralism.

One of the main cultural concerns ESL preservice teachers identified in their survey feedback regarding the use of AI language models was the sensitivity and awareness to their cultural diversity and differences. For example, some ESL students indicated that AI models sometimes generate texts that contain stereotypical expressions, prejudices, or discriminations that are unacceptable to some users. The AI models may also generate texts that violate or disregard the norms of certain populations, values, or beliefs that may conflict or clash with the preferences of the users. Moreover, AI models may generate texts that ignore the users' language nuances that may influence the meaning of the used texts due to the AI model's inability to capture the linguistic and cultural subtleties that convey tone, context, or identity. Therefore, ESL preservice teachers believe that it is important to ensure the sensitivity of AI language models to the cultural diversity of all users and the contexts they operate in. A possible solution for the culture sensitivity is by incorporating ethical principles and values into the design of AI language models to accurately represent the cultural diversity of their target audience. Additionally, the AI models may incorporate design mechanisms to improve the models' responses based on the users' feedback continuously.

Linguistic Diversity

Additionally, some students found AI language rigidly formalized to dominant dialects, lacking accommodation for diverse forms of expression. Research confirms a tendency toward linguistic homogeneity in AI systems (Hockly, 2023).

Teachers should promote flexibility through:

- Customizing AI responses and acceptable language based on local contexts.
- Exploring student backgrounds to develop pluralistic communication norms.
- Evaluating AI bias toward specific dialects; making corrections as needed
- Fostering class discussions about linguistic diversity and inclusion

ESL preservice teachers also noticed that, in some cases, AI language models generated texts in dominant dialects that marginalize the linguistic diversity of the English language. They also encountered that the AI models provided text outputs that were either irrelevant, or unhelpful to ESL students who may have different levels of proficiency. This issue could be addressed by designing AI conversational agents that can generate content that suits the diverse users' interests and their English proficiency levels.

Socioeconomic Diversity

Another cultural issue concerning ESL preservice teachers during the use of AI language models was the lack of inclusivity of different socioeconomic levels of all users. For example, AI models may use data that reflect the socioeconomic level of their creators (e.g., wealth and education) who may fail to include a wider socioeconomic level of their users. This issue could be addressed by ESL instructors through developing different strategies, such as teaching ESL students techniques in using reliable and reputable data sources that are diverse and representative of different socioeconomic levels of users.

Final Thoughts About the Use of AI Language Models in English Education

As we investigate the use of AI language models by ESL preservice teachers in English education, two important themes emerged in ESL students' responses. These themes are: (1) the potential impact of AI language models on the role of human teachers in English education; and (2) the use of AI language models and conventional learning theories. In these final thoughts we will discuss both issues and elaborate on the importance of human teachers in ESL language education. By discussing these topics, we hope to provide an insightful and personal overview of the use of AI language models in language education by its users. We also hope to inspire further ESL research and practice in this emerging and exciting field of using AI in English language education.

AI Language Models and Human Teachers

The first issue that was frequently brought up by our survey participants was the potential impact on the role of ESL human teachers. We can probably predict that the importance of this topic was inspired by our participants' passion to their personal investment in the teaching profession, as they are trained to be future teachers. We observed from the short time the AI language models were investigated that users have widely different opinions regarding their positive or negative experiences. However, we found that the AI language models' impact on the role of human teachers was partially conditional on how they are designed, deployed, and used in language education. For example, on the one hand, many of the ESL preservice teachers who participated in our study indicated that AI language models could support and enhance their role during their teaching internship by providing personalized learning experiences for their students, offering automated feedback, creating engaging content and examples, and presenting wide varieties of practice opportunities to their students. ESL preservice teachers also indicated that their use of AI language models helped reduce the workload and stress by automating some of the repetitive or tedious tasks they used to do during teaching, such as grading, testing, or monitoring some of students' learning activities.

On the other hand, AI language models may endanger the teaching and learning process by providing ESL students impersonal or irrelevant learning experiences and information. The negative impact of providing ESL students with irrelevant information could be exacerbated, especially when the ESL students are at a younger age and could not distinguish between false and true information. Another issue noticed by our participants is that AI language models could not match the teaching expertise and experience of human teachers. Furthermore, if ESL students happen to be emotionally challenged or vulnerable, they may develop a dependency or detachment among ESL students who may prefer to interact with machines rather than humans. Such situations can result in ESL students separating further from their peers and teachers and missing the emotional support and feedback that their human teachers can offer. Additionally, this can lead ESL students to feel isolated and disconnected from their learning experience or not receiving the care and support for their individual needs by their human teachers. Consequently, this can lead to ESL students developing a dependency on AI language models, rather than developing their own critical thinking skills and emotional intelligence.

Therefore, it is important for ESL language instructors to be aware of these issues and adopt practical strategies to balance the role of using AI language models and human teachers in language education. Additionally, it should also be emphasized to ESL preservice teachers that the use of AI language models is complementary rather than competitive to human teachers. ESL teachers should also provide clear disclosures and expectations about the AI models' capabilities and limitations to their students. Another important role for ESL teachers is to continuously maintain monitoring and moderating students' interactions with the AI language models, fostering critical thinking and media literacy skills among ESL students by exposing them to diverse perspectives and sources of information. Finally, it is extremely essential for ESL instructors to incorporate classroom activities specifically designed to promote human teacher-student and student-student communications as a complementary or alternative option.

The Use of AI Language Models and Conventional Learning Theories

The final issue we would like to discuss in this chapter is one of the topics widely debated by ESL instructors. The issue is related to the extensive adoption of AI language models by ESL students and how this issue poses significant challenges for ESL instructors who are seeking to leverage conventional learning theories in their instructional planning and classroom activities. While AI language models can offer useful tools to ESL English language learners, overly relying on the AI models can inhibit key elements of student learning and engagement. Additionally, successful integration of AI models into ESL teaching requires many elements, such as instructors' training, technical support, thoughtful lesson planning, developing pedagogically-based activities, and continuous curation by ESL educators.

The first core issue is that AI language models, by their very nature, lack the interpersonal dynamics of a traditional classroom. ESL students who prefer using primarily AI language models tend to miss out on constructivist learning experiences that focus on in-person collaboration. For example, ESL students who rely only on using AI language models will have no chance to engage in activities based on inquiry learning, problem-solving, and peer-to-peer discussions that would help them construct their own knowledge together with guidance from their ESL instructors. Yet constructing meaning solely from AI model content would overlook the central tenets of social constructivism activities that would allow ESL students to learn through the social interactions with their peers and instructors to craft and shape their shared understanding. While AI models have many values in teaching English language, ESL students still need human connection.

A second issue is that when ESL students become dependent on AI to complete their academic tasks, it would limit them from many opportunities to learn through participating in active learning pedagogies used in many current ESL classrooms. For example, students would have limited experience with many approaches, such as project-based and task-based learning that enable students to develop English proficiency through hands-on, and experiential activities. It is empirically and practically proven that when ESL students work on problems and tasks collaboratively with other peers, it would allow them to utilize better language skills in authentic contexts, compared to working in isolation and without human interaction. Additionally, students deprived of active learning risk losing out on vital communicative experiences. Until now, the developers of AI language models are still struggling to replicate the degree of engagement and meaning-making close to human, let alone to replace teachers. Therefore, we can say with a high level of confidence that AI's capabilities cannot match the human teacher and classroom language training, and the use of the AI language models in language education remain enormously nuanced.

Additionally, passive use of AI language models can inhibit ESL students from the benefits of community building that is essential for ESL learners. Sharing a physical classroom space together between ESL students and instructors would foster supportive relationships and a sense of belonging. Yet independent online work with AI systems tends to give many ESL students a sense of isolation, rather than community and inclusion. ESL students also could miss many chances to work together with their peers and instructors, share perspectives, and gain intercultural awareness. Therefore, it is recommended that ESL teachers expand the classroom activities to help ESL students maintain a sense of community and support.

These challenges underscore the importance of rethinking the use of conventional ESL pedagogies in the light of the prevalent use of AI language models among ESL learners. Therefore, ESL teachers must investigate innovative methods to redesign ESL classroom instructions, develop different ways to curate AI language models to complement, not replace, sound and conventional learning frameworks. For instance, ESL teachers might utilize AI speech recognition applications during class activities to enable small groups of 3-5 students to engage in different hands-on work, such as analyzing idioms, explaining metaphors, and the use of slang in daily activities. In this scenario, ESL teachers can utilize the AI models to provide immediate feedback to students on their pronunciation activities while all students actively construct understanding together. Similarly, ESL teachers can use AI language models to generate writing prompts for different collaborative essay planning and outlining by ESL students, again, while all students actively compose their essay together. The critical element that must be maintained throughout all these classroom activities is keeping the human touch as the main component of the activities.

CONCLUSION

This study provided insights into ESL preservice teachers' perspectives for responsibly adopting AI technologies. Key findings show:

- Most did not view AI as capable of replacing human teachers, though about a third were unsure, signaling more guidance is needed.
- Major concerns emerged around ethics (privacy, bias, intellectual property, reliability) and social/cultural issues (communication, access, sensitivity).
- Recommendations center on comprehensive training to develop preservice teachers' knowledge, values, and skills for ethical AI integration. This includes fostering data protection, algorithmic fairness, transparent attribution, cultural responsiveness, and more.

As AI becomes further embedded in ESL education, it is imperative that preservice teachers receive robust preparation not just in leveraging these technologies, but also navigating them thoughtfully to uphold student rights, inclusion, and wellbeing. With sound training and policies, ESL programs can implement AI in a manner that lives up to ethical ideals and institutional values. This will allow preservice teachers to gain practical experience mentored by faculty who model responsible use of AI tools. By equipping the next generation of ESL educators in this way, schools can unlock the benefits of AI while proactively addressing its risks.

In our investigation, we have found that the use of AI language models in language education presents significant ethical and safety considerations for the ESL preservice teachers we surveyed. Building upon these findings, and as we venture further into exploring this emerging technology, we believe it is important that educators proactively address these concerns by offering guidance on how to engage with AI language models in a safe and ethical manner.

We have identified several ethical concerns to include bias, intellectual property, text reliability, reliance on AI models, and social and cultural considerations. In order to guide ESL preservice teachers, educators should offer comprehensive training that addresses these concerns and develops critical thinking skills. This training should emphasize the significance of safeguarding users' privacy and data, mitigating bias in AI models, clarifying intellectual property rights, ensuring reliable text generation, considering social and cultural implications, and promoting a balanced and ethical approach to using AI language models. By equipping teachers with this knowledge and skill set, we can ensure the safe and ethical use of AI language models in ESL education.

REFERENCES

Ali, M., & Abdel-Haq, M. K. (2021). Bibliographical analysis of artificial intelligence learning in Higher Education: is the role of the human educator and education a thing of the past? In *Fostering Communication and Learning with Underutilized Technologies in Higher Education* (pp. 36–52). IGI Global. doi:10.4018/978-1-7998-4846-2.ch003

Aljohani, R. A. (2021). Teachers and students' perceptions on the impact of artificial intelligence on English language learning in Saudi Arabia. *Journal of Applied Linguistics and Language Research*, *8*(1), 36–47.

Chassignol, M., Khoroshavin, A., Klimova, A., & Bilyatdinova, A. (2018). Artificial Intelligence trends in education: A narrative overview. *Procedia Computer Science*, *136*, 16–24. doi:10.1016/j.procs.2018.08.233

Chen, X., Zou, D., Cheng, G., & Xie, H. (2022). Two decades of artificial intelligence in education. *Journal of Educational Technology & Society*, *25*(1), 28–47.

Chiu, T. K., Moorhouse, B. L., Chai, C. S., & Ismailov, M. (2023). Teacher support and student motivation to learn with Artificial Intelligence (AI) based chatbot. *Interactive Learning Environments*, 1–17. doi:10.1080/10494820.2023.2172044

Davis, G. M. (2022). *Humanlike Conversational Artificial Intelligence Agents for Foreign or Second Language Learning: User Perceptions, Expectations, And Interactions with Agents*. Stanford University.

Eke, D. (2023). ChatGPT and the rise of generative AI: Threat to academic integrity? *Journal of Responsible Technology*.

El Shazly, R. (2021). Effects of artificial intelligence on English speaking anxiety and speaking performance: A case study. *Expert Systems: International Journal of Knowledge Engineering and Neural Networks*, *38*(3), e12667. doi:10.1111/exsy.12667

Fitria, T. N. (2021). The use technology based on artificial intelligence in English teaching and learning. ELT Echo. *The Journal of English Language Teaching in Foreign Language Context*, *6*(2), 213–223.

Hang, Y., Khan, S., Alharbi, A., & Nazir, S. (2022). Assessing English teaching linguistic and artificial intelligence for efficient learning using analytical hierarchy process and Technique for Order of Preference by Similarity to Ideal Solution. *Journal of Software (Malden, MA)*, 2462. doi:10.1002mr.2462

Hockly, N. (2023). Artificial Intelligence in English Language Teaching: The Good, the Bad and the Ugly. *RELC Journal*, 00336882231168504. doi:10.1177/00336882231168504

Kaharuddin, A. (2021). Assessing the effect of using artificial intelligence on the writing skill of Indonesian learners of English. *Linguistics and Culture Review, 5*(1).

Keerthiwansha, N. (2018). Artificial intelligence education (AIEd) in English as a second language (ESL) classroom in Sri Lanka. *Artificial Intelligence, 6*(1), 31–36.

Kim, N.-Y., Cha, Y., & Kim, H.-S. (2019). Future english learning: Chatbots and artificial intelligence. *Multimedia-Assisted Language Learning, 22*(3).

Kohnke, L. (2023). L2 learners' perceptions of a chatbot as a potential independent language learning tool. *International Journal of Mobile Learning and Organisation, 17*(1-2), 214–226. doi:10.1504/IJMLO.2023.128339

Kohnke, L., Moorhouse, B. L., & Zou, D. (2023). ChatGPT for language teaching and learning. *RELC Journal*. doi:10.1177/00336882231162868

Koraishi, O. (2023). *Teaching English in the age of AI: Embracing ChatGPT to optimize EFL materials and assessment*. Language Education & Technology.

Kose, U., Arslan, A., & Campus, A. K. (2015). E-learning experience with artificial intelligence supported software: An international application on English language courses. *GLOKALde, 1*(3), 61–75.

Kuddus, K. (2022). Artificial intelligence in language learning: Practices and prospects. *Advanced Analytics and Deep Learning Models*, 1-17.

Lesia Viktorivna, K., Andrii Oleksandrovych, V., Iryna Oleksandrivna, K., & Nadia Oleksandrivna, K. (2022). *Artificial Intelligence in Language Learning: What Are We Afraid Of.* Arab World English Journal.

Lew, S., Gul, T., & Pecore, J. L. (2021). ESOL pre-service teachers' culturally and linguistically responsive teaching in mixed-reality simulations. *Information and Learning Sciences, 122*(1/2), 45–67. doi:10.1108/ILS-01-2020-0012

Liu, Y., & Liu, M. (2019). Research on college English teaching under the background of artificial intelligence. Journal of Physics: Conference Series. doi:10.1089/big.2018.0151

Lu, X. (2019). An empirical study on the artificial intelligence writing evaluation system in China CET. *Big Data*, *7*(2), 121–129. doi:10.1089/big.2018.0151

Nguyen, A., Ngo, H. N., Hong, Y., Dang, B., & Nguyen, B.-P. T. (2023). Ethical principles for artificial intelligence in education. *Education and Information Technologies*, *28*(4), 4221–4241. doi:10.100710639-022-11316-w PMID:36254344

Perkins, M. (2023). Academic Integrity considerations of AI Large Language Models in the post-pandemic era: ChatGPT and beyond. *Journal of University Teaching & Learning Practice, 20*(2), 07.

Poersch, J. M. (2005). A new paradigm for learning language: Connectionist artificial intelligence. *Linguagem & ensino, 8*(1), 161-183.

Richardson, M., & Clesham, R. (2021). Rise of the machines? The evolving role of Artificial Intelligence (AI) technologies in high stakes assessment. *London Review of Education*, *19*(1), 1–13. doi:10.14324/LRE.19.1.09

Rusmiyanto, R., Huriati, N., Fitriani, N., Tyas, N. K., Rofi'i, A., & Sari, M. N. (2023). The Role of Artificial Intelligence (AI) In Developing English Language Learner's Communication Skills. *Journal of Education*, *6*(1), 750–757.

Schank, R. C., & Childers, P. (1984). *The cognitive computer on language, learning, and artificial intelligence.*

Schmidt, T., & Strasser, T. (2022). Artificial intelligence in foreign language learning and teaching: A CALL for intelligent practice. Anglistik. *International Journal of English Studies*, *33*(1), 165–184.

Sharadgah, T. A., & Sa'di, R. A. (2022). A Systematic Review of Research on the Use of Artificial Intelligence in English Language Teaching and Learning (2015-2021): What are the Current Effects? *Journal of Information Technology Education*, 21.

Sindermann, C., Sha, P., Zhou, M., Wernicke, J., Schmitt, H. S., Li, M., Sariyska, R., Stavrou, M., Becker, B., & Montag, C. (2021). Assessing the attitude towards artificial intelligence: Introduction of a short measure in German, Chinese, and English language. *KI-Künstliche intelligenz, 35,* 109-118.

Singh, G., Kaur, G., & Thaemphan, L. (2021). Artificial intelligence in ESL–A survey on school students and teachers in Ubon Ratchathani Thailand. *The Eleventh Annual International Symposium of Foreign Language Learning (AISOFOLL).*

Sumakul, D. T. Y., Hamied, F. A., & Sukyadi, D. (2022). Artificial intelligence in EFL classrooms: Friend or foe? *LEARN Journal: Language Education and Acquisition Research Network*, *15*(1), 232–256.

Sun, Z., Anbarasan, M., & Praveen Kumar, D. (2021). Design of online intelligent English teaching platform based on artificial intelligence techniques. *Computational Intelligence*, *37*(3), 1166–1180. doi:10.1111/coin.12351

Teubner, T., Flath, C. M., Weinhardt, C., Aalst, W., & Hinz, O. (2023). Welcome to the Era of ChatGPT et al. *Business & Information Systems Engineering*, *65*(2), 95–101. doi:10.100712599-023-00795-x

Wang, R. (2019). Research on artificial intelligence promoting English learning change. *3rd international conference on economics and management, education, humanities and social sciences (EMEHSS 2019)*.

Xiao, Y., & Hu, J. (2019). Assessment of optimal pedagogical factors for Canadian ESL learners' reading literacy through artificial intelligence algorithms. *International Journal of English Linguistics*, *9*(4), 1–14. doi:10.5539/ijel.v9n4p1

Xiao, Y., & Hu, J. (2019). Assessment of optimal pedagogical factors for Canadian ESL learners' reading literacy through artificial intelligence algorithms. *International Journal of English Linguistics*, *9*(4), 1–14. doi:10.5539/ijel.v9n4p1

Xu, W., Meng, J., Raja, S. K. S., Priya, M. P., & Kiruthiga Devi, M. (2023). Artificial intelligence in constructing personalized and accurate feedback systems for students. *International Journal of Modeling, Simulation, and Scientific Computing*, *14*(01), 2341001. doi:10.1142/S1793962323410015

Zawacki-Richter, O., Marín, V. I., Bond, M., & Gouverneur, F. (2019). Systematic review of research on artificial intelligence applications in higher education–where are the educators? *International Journal of Educational Technology in Higher Education*, *16*(1), 1–27. doi:10.118641239-019-0171-0

Zawacki-Richter, O., Marín, V. I., Bond, M., & Gouverneur, F. (2019). Systematic review of research on artificial intelligence applications in higher education–where are the educators. *International Journal of Educational Technology in Higher Education*, *16*(1), 1–27. doi:10.118641239-019-0171-0

Zhang, Y. (2022). Construction of English language autonomous learning center system based on artificial intelligence technology. *Mathematical Problems in Engineering*, *2022*, 1–12. doi:10.1155/2022/7900493

Zou, S. (2017). Designing and practice of a college English teaching platform based on artificial intelligence. *Journal of Computational and Theoretical Nanoscience*, *14*(1), 104–108. doi:10.1166/jctn.2017.6133

Compilation of References

Adiguzel, T., Kaya, M. H., & Cansu, F. K. (2023). Revolutionizing education with AI: Exploring the transformative potential of ChatGPT. *Contemporary Educational Technology*, *15*(3), 1–13. doi:10.30935/cedtech/13152

Adolphs, S., & Knight, D. (2010). Building a spoken corpus: What are the basics? In A. O'Keeffe & M. McCarthy (Eds.), *The Routledge handbook of corpus linguistics* (pp. 38–52). Routledge. doi:10.4324/9780203856949.ch4

Aggarwal, C. C. (2018). Neural networks and deep learning. *Springer*, *10*, 978-3. doi:10.1007/978-3-319-94463-0

Ahn, S. J., Bostick, J., Ogle, E., Nowak, K. L., McGillicuddy, K. T., & Bailenson, J. N. (2016). Experiencing nature: Embodying animals in immersive virtual environments increases inclusion of nature in self and involvement with nature. *Journal of Computer-Mediated Communication*, *21*(6), 399–419. doi:10.1111/jcc4.12173

AI in Virtual Reality. (2022). *IEEE Digital Reality*. IEEE. https://digitalreality.ieee.org/publications/ai-in-virtual-reality

Aijmer, K. (2020). Spoken corpora. In S. Adolphs & D. Knight (Eds.), *The Routledge handbook of English language and digital humanities* (pp. 5–25). Routledge. doi:10.4324/9781003031758-2

Ajisoko, P. (2020). The use of Duolingo apps to improve English vocabulary learning. *International Journal of Emerging Technologies in Learning*, *15*(7), 149. doi:10.3991/ijet.v15i07.13229

Alexoloulou, T., Michel, M., Murakami, A., & Meurers, D. (2017). Task effects on linguistic complexity and accuracy: A large-scale learner corpus analysis employing natural language processing techniques. *Language Learning*, *67*(1), 180–208. doi:10.1111/lang.12232

Ali, J. K. M., Shamsan, M. A. A., Hezam, T. A., & Mohammed, A. A. (2023). Impact of ChatGPT on learning motivation: Teachers and students' voices. *Journal of English Studies in Arabia Felix*, *2*(1), 41–49. doi:10.56540/jesaf.v2i1.51

Ali, M., & Abdel-Haq, M. K. (2021). Bibliographical analysis of artificial intelligence learning in Higher Education: is the role of the human educator and education a thing of the past? In *Fostering Communication and Learning with Underutilized Technologies in Higher Education* (pp. 36–52). IGI Global. doi:10.4018/978-1-7998-4846-2.ch003

Aljanabi, M., Ghazi, M., Ali, A. H., & Abed, S. A. (2023). ChatGPT: Open possibilities. *Iraqi Journal for Computer Science and Mathematics*, *4*(1), 62–64. doi:10.52866/20ijcsm.2023.01.01.0018

Aljohani, R. A. (2021). Teachers and students' perceptions on the impact of artificial intelligence on English language learning in Saudi Arabia. *Journal of Applied Linguistics and Language Research*, *8*(1), 36–47.

Allwright, D., & Hanks, J. (2009). *The developing language learner*. London, England: Palgrave Macmillan London. Arizona Board of Regents (N/D). In *Arizona board of regents*. https://www.azregents.edu/sites/default/files/public/Oxford.pdf

Allwright, D. (2003). Exploratory Practice: Rethinking practitioner research in language teaching. *Language Teaching Research*, *7*(2), 113–141. doi:10.1191/1362168803lr118oa

Allwright, D. (2006). Six promising directions in applied linguistics. In S. Gieve & I. K. Miller (Eds.), *Understanding the language classroom* (pp. 11–17). Palgrave Macmillan. doi:10.1057/9780230523166_2

Almarzouqi, A., Aburayya, A., & Salloum, S. A. (2022). Prediction of User's Intention to Use Metaverse System in Medical Education: A Hybrid SEM-ML Learning Approach. *IEEE Access : Practical Innovations, Open Solutions*, *10*, 43421–43434. doi:10.1109/ACCESS.2022.3169285

Alper, M., & Goggin, G. (2017). Digital technology and rights in the lives of children with disabilities. *New Media & Society*, *19*(5), 726–740. doi:10.1177/1461444816686323

Alsadoon, R. (2021). Chatting with AI Bot: Vocabulary learning assistant for Saudi EFL learners. *English Language Teaching*, *14*(6), 135–157. doi:10.5539/elt.v14n6p135

Amidi, A., & Amidi, S. (n.d.). *Gözetimli öğrenme el kitabı. Shervine Amidi*. Stanford. https://stanford.edu/~shervine/l/tr/teaching/cs-229/cheatsheet-supervised-learning

Amodei, D., Olah, C., Steinhardt, J., Christiano, P., Schulman, J., & Mané, D. (2016). *Concrete problems. in AI safety*. arXiv preprint arXiv:1606.06565.

Anderson, N., Belavy, D., Perle, S., Hendricks, S., Hespanhol, L., Verhagen, E., & Memon, A. R. (2023). AI did not write this manuscript, or did it? Can we trick the AI text detector into generated texts? The potential future of ChatGPT and AI [Editorial]. *BMJ Open Sport & Exercise Medicine*, *9*(1), e001568. doi:10.1136/bmjsem-2023-001568 PMID:36816423

Arini, D. N., Hidayat, F., Winarti, A., & Rosalina, E. (2022). Artificial intelligence (AI)-based mobile learning in ELT for EFL learners: The implementation and learners' attitudes. *International Journal of Educational Studies in Social Sciences.*, *2*(2), 2. doi:10.53402/ijesss.v2i2.40

Arnold, K. E., & Pistilli, M. D. (2012, April). Course signals at Purdue: Using learning analytics to increase student success. In *Proceedings of the 2nd International Conference on Learning Analytics and Knowledge* (pp. 267-270). IEEE. 10.1145/2330601.2330666

arXiv.org. (January, 2023). *arXiv announces new policy on ChatGPT and similar tools*. arXiv. https://blog.arxiv.org/2023/01/31/arxiv-announces-new-policy-on-chatgpt-and-similar-tools/

Astrid Case Study. (n.d.). Oxford languages. https://languages.oup.com/about-us/case-studies/astrid/

Atlas, S. (2023). *ChatGPT for higher education and professional development: A guide to conversational AI*. Digital Commons. digitalcommons.uri.edu

Atlas, S. (2023). *ChatGPT for higher education and professional development: A guide to conversational AI*. Digital Commons. https://digitalcommons.uri.edu/cba_facpubs/548

Ausat, A. M. A., Massang, B., Efendi, M., Nofirman, N., & Riady, Y. (2023). Can chat GPT replace the role of the teacher in the classroom: A fundamental analysis. *Journal of Education*, *5*(4), 16100–16106. doi:10.31004/joe.v5i4.2745

Avila-ChauvetL.MejíaD. (2023). Can Professors and Students Detect ChatGPT Essays? *SSRN*. doi:10.2139/ssrn.4373643

Azevedo, R., & Hadwin, A. F. (2005). Scaffolding self-regulated learning and metacognition–Implications for the design of computer-based scaffolds. *Instructional Science*, *33*(5/6), 367–379. doi:10.100711251-005-1272-9

Bachman, L., & Adrian, P. (2022). *Language assessment in practice: Developing language assessments and justifying their use in the real world*. Oxford University Press.

Baidoo-Anu, D., & Owusu Ansah, L. (2023). Education in the era of generative artificial intelligence (AI): Understanding the potential benefits of ChatGPT in promoting teaching and learning. http://dx.doi.org/ doi:10.2139/ssrn.4337484

Baker, T., & Smith, L. (2019). *Educ-AI-tion rebooted? Exploring the future of artificial intelligence in schools and colleges*. Nesta. https://media.nesta.org.uk/documents/Future_of_AI_and_education_v5_WEB.pdf

Baker, R. S., & Siemens, G. (2014). Educational data mining and learning analytics. In R. K. Sawyer (Ed.), *The Cambridge Handbook of the Learning Sciences* (2nd ed., pp. 253–274). Cambridge University Press. doi:10.1017/CBO9781139519526.016

Bakhtin, M. (1981). *The dialogic imagination: Four essays* (M. Holquist, Trans.). University of Texas Press.

Bao, M. (2019). Can home use of speech-enabled artificial intelligence mitigate foreign language anxiety–Investigation of a concept. *Arab World English Journal (AWEJ)*. *SSRN*, (5). Advance online publication. doi:10.2139srn.3431734

Barrot, J. S. (2023). Using ChatGPT for second language writing: Pitfalls and potentials. *Assessing Writing*, *57*, 100745. doi:10.1016/j.asw.2023.100745

Baskara, F. R., & Mukarto, F. X. (2023). Exploring the Implications of ChatGPT for Language Learning in Higher Education. *Indonesian Journal of English Language Teaching and Applied Linguistics*, *7*(2), 343–358. doi:10.210 93/ijeltal.v7i2.1387

Baskara, F. R., & Mukarto, F. X. (2023). Exploring the Implications of ChatGPT for Language Learning in Higher Education. *Indonesian Journal of English Language Teaching and Applied Linguistics, IJELTAL*, *7*(2), 343–358.

Batardière, M. T., Berthaud, S., C¨atibušić, B., & Flynn, C. J. (2023). Language teaching and learning in Ireland: 2012-2021. In Language Teaching, 56(1). doi:10.1017/S0261444822000374

Bayne, S. (2015). Teacherbot: Interventions in automated teaching. *Teaching in Higher Education*, *20*(4), 455–467. doi:10.1080/13562517.2015.1020783

Belda-Medina, J., & Calvo-Ferrer, J. R. (2022). Using chatbots as AI conversational partners in language learning. *Applied Sciences (Basel, Switzerland)*, *12*(17), 8427. doi:10.3390/app12178427

Bellarhmouch, Y., Jeghal, A., Tairi, H., & Benjelloun, N. (2023). A proposed architectural learner model for a personalized learning environment. *Education and Information Technologies*, *28*(4), 4243–4263. doi:10.100710639-022-11392-y PMID:36267481

Bell, R. T. (1991). *Translation and translating: Theory and practice*. Longman.

Belshaw, D. (2011). *What is digital literacy? A pragmatic investigation*. [Unpublished Ed.D thesis. Durham University]. http://neverendingthesis.com

Benda, J. (2014). Google Translate in the EFL classroom: Taboo or teaching tool? *Writing & Pedagogy*, *5*(2), 317–332. doi:10.1558/wap.v5i2.317

Bernardini, S. (2016). Discovery learning in the language for translation classroom. *Cadernos de Tradução (Florianópolis)*, *36*, 14–35. doi:10.5007/2175-7968.2016v36nesp1p14

Berns, A., & Ruiz-Rube, I. (2022). Use of digital game creation tools in computer assisted language learning. *Digital Games in Language Learning*, 35–51. doi:10.4324/9781003240075-3

Berns, A., Gonzalez-Pardo, A., & Camacho, D. (2013). Game-like language learning in 3-D virtual environments. *Computers & Education*, *60*(1), 210–220. doi:10.1016/j.compedu.2012.07.001

Blikstein, P., & Worsley, M. (2016). Multimodal learning analytics and education data mining: Using computational technologies to measure complex learning tasks. *Journal of Learning Analytics*, *3*(2), 220–238. doi:10.18608/jla.2016.32.11

Broussard, M. (2019). *Artificial Unintelligence: How Computers Misunderstand the World*. MIT Press.

Buckingham, D. (2015). Defining digital literacy: What do young people need to know about digital media? *Nordic Journal of Digital Literacy*, *10*(2), 88–101. doi:10.18261/ISSN1891-943X-2015-Jubileumsnummer-03

Bui, T. H. (2022). English teachers' integration of digital technologies in the classroom. *International Journal of Educational Research Open*, *3*, 100204. doi:10.1016/j.ijedro.2022.100204

Cai, Y., Pan, Z., & Liu, M. (2022). Augmented reality technology in language learning: A meta-analysis. In Journal of Computer Assisted Learning, 38(4). doi:10.1111/jcal.12661

Cai, Y. (2022). A Review of Virtual Reality Technology in EFL Teaching. *Journal of Education. Humanities and Social Sciences*, *4*, 260–263. doi:10.54097/ehss.v4i.2783

Çakmak, F. (2019). Mobile learning and mobile assisted language learning in focus. *Language and Technology*, *1*(1), 30–48.

Çakmak, F., & Erçetin, G. (2018). Effects of gloss type on text recall and incidental vocabulary learning in mobile-assisted L2 listening. *ReCALL*, *30*(1), 24–47. doi:10.1017/S0958344017000155

Callard, A. (2018). *Aspiration: The agency of becoming*. Oxford University Press. doi:10.1093/oso/9780190639488.001.0001

Callard, A. (2021). Precis. *Philosophy and Phenomenological Research*, *102*(2), 459–463. doi:10.1111/phpr.12758

Calvo, R. A., & D'Mello, S. (2010). Affect detection: An interdisciplinary review of models, methods, and their applications. *IEEE Transactions on Affective Computing*, *1*(1), 18–37. doi:10.1109/T-AFFC.2010.1

Cardona, M. A., Rodríguez, R. J., & Ishmael, K. (2023). *Artificial Intelligence and the Future of Teaching and Learning: Insights and recommendations*. Report by U.S. Department of Education, Office of Educational Technology. https://www2.ed.gov/documents/ai-report/ai-report.pdf

Cardona, M. A., Rodríguez, R. J., & Ishmael, K. (2023). *Artificial intelligence and the future of teaching and learning: Insights and recommendations*. W2. https://www2.ed.gov/documents/ai-report/ai-report.pdf

Carpenter, J. P., Shelton, C. C., & Schroeder, S. E. (2022). The education influencer: A new player in the educator professional landscape. *Journal of Research on Technology in Education*, 1–16. doi:10.1080/15391523.2022.2030267

Casal-Otero, L., Catala, A., Fernández-Morante, C., Taboada, M., Cebreiro, B., & Barro, S. (2023). AI literacy in K-12: A systematic literature review. *International Journal of STEM Education*, *10*(1), 29. doi:10.118640594-023-00418-7

Cavalheiro, L. (2020). Developing intercultural communication and intercultural awareness in the EFL classroom. *Estudos Linguísticos e Literários*, *1*(65), 30–48. doi:10.9771/ell.v1i65.36467

Cawthon, S., Leppo, R., Carr, T., & Kopriva, R. (2013). Toward accessible assessments: The promises and limitations of test item adaptations for students with disabilities and English Language Learners. *Educational Assessment*, *18*(2), 73–98. doi:10.1080/10627197.2013.789294

Çerası, C. Ç., & Balcıoğlu, Y. S. (2023). *AI and Ethics in Education: ChatGPT Program Example.* Paper presented at the The Book of Proceedings of the International Symposium on Communication and Technology with its Philosophical Dimensions (ISTC_PhD). 14–15 January, Marmara University, Istanbul, Türkiye.

Chabot, S., Drozdal, J., Peveler, M., Zhou, Y., Su, H., & Braasch, J. (2020). A Collaborative, Immersive Language Learning Environment Using Augmented Panoramic Imagery. *6th International Conference of the Immersive Learning Research Network (ILRN).* IEEE. 10.23919/iLRN47897.2020.9155140

Chae, H., Kim, M., Kim, C., Jeong, W., Kim, H., Lee, J., & Yeo, J. (2023). TUTORING: Instruction-Grounded Conversational Agent for Language Learners. arXiv preprint arXiv:2302.12623.

Chamboko-Mpotaringa, M., & Tichaawa, T. M. (2021). Tourism digital marketing tools and views on future trends: A systematic review of literature. *African Journal of Hospitality, Tourism and Leisure*, *10*(2), 712–726. doi:10.46222/ajhtl.19770720-128

Chamboko-Mpotaringa, M., & Tichaawa, T. M. (2023). Domestic tourists' perceptions of the intention to use digital marketing tools and platforms. *Geo Journal of Tourism and Geosites*, *46*(1), 9–18. doi:10.30892/gtg.46101-995

Chang, Y., Chen, C., & Liao, C. (2020). Enhancing English-learning performance through a simulation classroom for EFL students using augmented reality—A Junior High School Case Study. *Applied Sciences (Basel, Switzerland)*, *10*(21), 7854. doi:10.3390/app10217854

Chassignol, M., Khoroshavin, A., Klimova, A., & Bilyatdinova, A. (2018). Artificial Intelligence trends in education: A narrative overview. *Procedia Computer Science*, *136*, 16–24. doi:10.1016/j.procs.2018.08.233

Chen, C.-M., & Chen, Y.-S. (2019). *Handbook of research on integrating technology into contemporary language learning and teaching*. IGI Global.

Chen, L., Chen, P., & Lin, Z. (2020). Artificial intelligence in education: A review. *IEEE Access : Practical Innovations, Open Solutions*, *8*, 75264–75278. doi:10.1109/ACCESS.2020.2988510

Chen, L., & Tokuda, N. (2013). New template-template-enhanced ICALL system for a second language composition course. *CALICO Journal*, *20*(3), 561–578. doi:10.1558/cj.v20i3.561-578

Chen, M. P., Wang, L., Zou, D., Lin, S. Y., Xie, H., & Tsai, C. C. (2020). Effects of captions and English proficiency on learning effectiveness, motivation and attitude in augmented-reality-enhanced theme-based contextualized EFL learning. *Computer Assisted Language Learning*, 1–31. doi:10.1080/09588221.2018.1544151

Chen, S. Y., & Wang, J. H. (2021). Individual differences and personalized learning: A review and appraisal. *Universal Access in the Information Society, 20*(4), 833–849. doi:10.100710209-020-00753-4

Chen, X. L., Zou, D., Xie, H. R., & Su, F. (2021). Twenty-five years of Computer-Assisted Language Learning: A topic modeling analysis. *Language Learning & Technology, 25*(3), 151–185.

Chen, X., Zou, D., Cheng, G., & Xie, H. (2022). Two decades of artificial intelligence in education. *Journal of Educational Technology & Society, 25*(1), 28–47.

Chen, X., Zou, D., Xie, H., Cheng, G., & Liu, C. (2022). Two decades of artificial intelligence in education: Contributors, collaborations, research topics, challenges, and future directions. *Journal of Educational Technology & Society, 25*(1), 28–47.

Chen, X., Zou, D., Xie, H., Cheng, G., & Liu, C. (2022). Two Decades of Artificial Intelligence in Education: Contributors, Collaborations, Research Topics, Challenges, and Future Directions. *Journal of Educational Technology & Society, 25*(1), 28–47. https://www.jstor.org/stable/48647028

Chiu, T. K., Moorhouse, B. L., Chai, C. S., & Ismailov, M. (2023). Teacher support and student motivation to learn with Artificial Intelligence (AI) based chatbot. *Interactive Learning Environments*, 1–17. doi:10.1080/10494820.2023.2172044

Chocarro, R., Cortiñas, M., & Marcos-Matás, G. (2023). Teachers' attitudes towards chatbots in education: A technology acceptance model approach considering the effect of social language, bot proactiveness, and users' characteristics. *Educational Studies, 49*(2), 295–313. doi:10.1080/03055698.2020.1850426

Chowdhary, K. R. (2020). Natural language processing. *Fundamentals of artificial intelligence,* 603-649.

Chung, E. S. (2020). The effect of L2 proficiency on post-editing machine translated texts. *Journal of Asia TEFL, 17*(1), 182–193. doi:10.18823/asiatefl.2020.17.1.11.182

Chung, E. S., & Ahn, S. (2022). The effect of using machine translation on linguistic features in L2 writing across proficiency levels and text genres. *Computer Assisted Language Learning, 35*(9), 2239–2264. doi:10.1080/09588221.2020.1871029

Clarizia, F., Colace, F., Lombardi, M., Pascale, F., & Santaniello, D. (2018). Chatbot: An education support system for student. In A. Castiglione, F. Pop, M. Ficco, & F. Palmieri (Eds.), *Cyberspace Safety and Security* (pp. 291–302). Springer International Publishing. doi:10.1007/978-3-030-01689-0_23

Clifford, J., Merschel, L., & Munné, J. (2013). Surveying the landscape: What is the role of machine translation in language learning? *@tic Revista d'Innovació Educativa, 10*, 108-121.

Cole, K.C. (2023). The Last Word on AI and the Atom Bomb. *Wired Magazine-Ideas.*

Correa, M. (2011). Academic dishonesty in the second language classroom: Instructors' perspectives. *Modern Journal of Language Teaching Methods, 1*(1), 65–79.

Correa, M. (2014). Leaving the "peer" out of peer-editing: Online translators as a pedagogical tool in the Spanish as a second language classroom. [LACLIL]. *Latin American Journal of Content and Language Integrated Learning*, *7*(1), 1–20. doi:10.5294/laclil.2014.7.1.1

Cotton, D. R., Cotton, P. A., & Shipway, J. R. (2023). Chatting and cheating: Ensuring academic integrity in the era of ChatGPT. *Innovations in Education and Teaching International*, 1–12. doi:10.1080/14703297.2023.2190148

Crompton, H., Bernacki, M., & Greene, J. A. (2020). Psychological foundations of emerging technologies for teaching and learning in higher education. *Current Opinion in Psychology*, *36*, 101–105. doi:10.1016/j.copsyc.2020.04.011 PMID:32604064

Cusumano, M. A., & Yoffie, D. (2021). The cultural benefits of artificial intelligence in the enterprise. *MIT Sloan Management Review*, *62*(4), 1–9.

D'Mello, S., & Graesser, A. (2012). Dynamics of affective states during complex learning. *Learning and Instruction*, *22*(2), 145–157. doi:10.1016/j.learninstruc.2011.10.001

da Costa Liberato, P. M., Alén-González, E., & de Azevedo Liberato, D. F. V. (2018). Digital technology in a smart tourist destination: The case of Porto. *Journal of Urban Technology*, *25*(1), 75–97. doi:10.1080/10630732.2017.1413228

Daly, A., Hagendorff, T., Hui, L., Mann, M., Marda, V., Wagner, B., & Witteborn, S. (2019). Artificial intelligence governance and ethics: global perspectives. arXiv preprint arXiv:1907.03848.

Davies, H., Eynon, R., Komljenovic, J., & Williamson, B. (2022). Investigating the financial power brokers behind EdTech. In S. Livingstone, & K. Pothong (Eds.), Education Data Futures: Critical, regulatory and practical reflections. London:5Rights Foundation.

Davis, V. (2022) *Duolingo: The Vital Role of Animated Characters in Language Learning*. Animation World Network. https://www.awn.com/animationworld/duolingovital-role-animated-characters-language-learning

Davis, G. M. (2022). *Humanlike Conversational Artificial Intelligence Agents for Foreign or Second Language Learning: User Perceptions, Expectations, And Interactions with Agents*. Stanford University.

Davitishvili, N. (2017). Cross-cultural awareness and teaching English as a second language in the context of globalization. *Sino-US English Teaching*, *14*(9), 549–558. doi:10.17265/1539-8072/2017.09.003

Day, E. (2021). *Governance of data for children's learning in UK state schools*. London: 5Rights Foundation.

de Almeida, F. A. S., de Oliveira Marques, P. C., Adão, J. M., Teixeira, Z. D., & Porto, M. D. (2019). The Paradigms of Traditional Educational Culture in the Context of Liquid Modernity: An Empirical Study. *Creative Education*, *10*(04), 784–795. doi:10.4236/ce.2019.104058

De La Guia, E., Camacho, V. L., Orozco-Barbosa, L., Brea Lujan, V. M., Penichet, V. M. R., & Lozano Perez, M. (2016). Introducing IoT and Wearable Technologies into Task-Based Language Learning for Young Children. *IEEE Transactions on Learning Technologies*, *9*(4), 366–378. doi:10.1109/TLT.2016.2557333

de Wet, F., Van der Walt, C., & Niesler, T. R. (2009). Automatic assessment of oral language proficiency and listening comprehension. *Speech Communication*, *51*(10), 864–874. doi:10.1016/j.specom.2009.03.002

Deardorff, D. K. (2006). *Intercultural competence: The key competence in the 21st century?* Bertelsmann Stiftung.

Deci, E. L., & Ryan, R. M. (2000). The "what" and "why" of goal pursuits: Human needs and the self-determination of behavior. *Psychological Inquiry*, *11*(4), 227–268. doi:10.1207/S15327965PLI1104_01

Deng, J., & Lin, Y. (2022). The benefits and challenges of ChatGPT: An overview. *Frontiers in Computing and Intelligent Systems*, *2*(2), 81–83. doi:10.54097/fcis.v2i2.4465

Devlin, J., Chang, M.-W., Lee, K., & Toutanova, K. (2019). BERT: Pre-training of deep bidirectional transformers for language understanding. *NAACL-HLT*, 4171-4186. https://doi.org/ doi:10.18653/v1/N19-1423

Dhimolea, T. K., Kaplan-Rakowski, R., & Lin, L. (2022). A systematic review of research on high-immersion virtual reality for language learning. *TechTrends*, *66*(5), 810–824. doi:10.100711528-022-00717-w

Diari, K., Suwarna, S., & Suweta, I. (2023). Mobile technology-mediated language learning: A quantitative study to unravel language learners' achievement and autonomy. *World Journal of English Language*, *5*(13), 354. doi:10.5430/wjel.v13n5p354

Dicheva, D., Dichev, C., Agre, G., & Angelova, G. (2015). Gamification in education: A systematic mapping study. *Journal of Educational Technology & Society*, *18*(3), 75–88.

Dietz-Uhler, B., & Hurn, J. E. (2013). Using learning analytics to predict (and improve) student success: A faculty perspective. *Journal of Interactive Online Learning*, *12*(1), 17–26.

Dixon, D. H., Dixon, T., & Jordan, E. (2022). Second language (L2) gains through digital game-based language learning (DGBLL): A meta-analysis. *Language Learning & Technology*, *26*(1), 1–25.

Djauhar, R. (2021). The Grammar-Translation Method, The Direct Method, and The Audio-Lingual Method. *Langua. Journal of Linguistics, Literature, and Language Education*, *4*(1).

Dodigovic, M. (2005). *Artificial intelligence in second language learning: Raising error awareness.* Multilingual Matters., doi:10.21832/9781853598319

Domínguez, A., Saenz-De-Navarrete, J., De-Marcos, L., Fernández-Sanz, L., Pagés, C., & Martínez-Herráiz, J. J. (2013). Gamifying learning experiences: Practical implications and outcomes. *Computers & Education*, *63*, 380–392. doi:10.1016/j.compedu.2012.12.020

Donova, M., Kiselev, V., Veretennikova, E., Lozina, E. N., & Shcherbakov, S. (2021). *Automation of Tutor's Activities in Higher Education Institutions.*

Doshi-Velez, F., & Kim, B. (2017). Towards a rigorous science of interpretable machine learning. arXiv preprint arXiv:1702.08608.

Ducar, C., & Schocket, D. H. (2018). Machine translation and the L2 classroom: Pedagogical solutions for making peace with Google Translate. *Foreign Language Annals, 51*(4), 779–795. doi:10.1111/flan.12366

Duijnhouwer, H., Prins, F. J., & Stokking, K. M. (2012). Feedback providing improvement strategies and reflection on feedback use: Effects on students' writing motivation, process, and performance. *Learning and Instruction, 22*(3), 171–184. doi:10.1016/j.learninstruc.2011.10.003

Egbert, J. (2005). *CALL essentials: Principles and practice in CALL classrooms.* TESOL.

Eke, D. (2023). ChatGPT and the rise of generative AI: Threat to academic integrity? *Journal of Responsible Technology.*

Eke, D. (2023). *ChatGPT and the rise of generative AI: Threat to academic integrity?*: philpapers. org. doi:10.1016/j.jrt.2023.100060

Ekoç-Özçelik & Ergun-Gündüz. (2023). Embracing ChatGPT in foreign language writing classes: potentials and challenges. In Ferdig, R.E., Hartshorne, R., Baumgartner, E., Kaplan-Rakowski, R. & Mouza, C. (Eds.), what prek-12 teachers should know about educational technology in 2023: A research-to-practice anthology, (1st ed., pp. 133-143). AACE2023.

El Shazly, R. (2021). Effects of artificial intelligence on English speaking anxiety and speaking performance: A case study. *Expert Systems: International Journal of Knowledge Engineering and Neural Networks, 38*(3), e12667. doi:10.1111/exsy.12667

Elwany E, Shakeri S. (2014) Enhancing Cortana User Experience Using Machine Learning. *Recall, 55*(54.61), 24-24.

Enders, O. G., & Kostewicz, D. (2023). Secondary Teachers' Remote Instructional Practices in Mathematics for Students With Disabilities. *Journal of Special Education Technology, 38*(1), 50–60. doi:10.1177/01626434211059486

English, L. D., & Kirshner, D. (2015). Handbook of international research in mathematics education: Third edition. In Handbook of International Research in Mathematics Education: Third Edition. doi:10.4324/9780203448946

Eshet-Alkalai, Y., & Chajut, E. (2009). Changes over time in digital literacy. *Cyberpsychology & Behavior, 12*(6), 713–715. doi:10.1089/cpb.2008.0264 PMID:19514816

Estevez, J., Garate, G., & Grana, M. (2019). Gentle Introduction to Artificial Intelligence for High-School Students Using Scratch. *IEEE Access : Practical Innovations, Open Solutions, 7*, 179027–179036. doi:10.1109/ACCESS.2019.2956136

Eynon, R. (2013). The rise of Big Data: What does it mean for education, technology, and media research? *Learning, Media and Technology*, *38*(3), 237–240. doi:10.1080/17439884.2013.771783

Eynon, R., & Young, E. (2021). Methodology, Legend, and Rhetoric: The Constructions of AI by Academia, Industry, and policy groups for lifelong learning. *Science, Technology & Human Values*, *46*(1), 166–191. doi:10.1177/0162243920906475

Figueroa Flores, J. F. (2015). Using Gamification to enhance second language learning. *Digital Education Review, 27.*

Fitria, T. N. (2023, March). Artificial intelligence (AI) technology in OpenAI ChatGPT application: A review of ChatGPT in writing English essay. *ELT Forum: Journal of English Language Teaching, 12*(1), 44-58. 10.15294/elt.v12i1.64069

Fitria, T. N. (2021). The use technology based on artificial intelligence in English teaching and learning. ELT Echo. *The Journal of English Language Teaching in Foreign Language Context*, *6*(2), 213–223.

Forrester, A. (2023). ChatGPT: What does it mean for language centres. *STiLE - Scholarship of Teaching in Language Education, 1*(1), 1-22. https://www.stile.hk/osp/article/view/7

Frąckiewicz, M. (2023, April 17). *The impact of chatbots on language learning and teaching.* Ts2 Space. https://ts2.space/en/the-impact-of-chatbots-on-language-learning-and-teaching/

Frąckiewicz, M. (2023a). *Bridging Language Barriers: The Potential of ChatGPT-4 for Multilingual Communication.* TS2 Space. https://ts2.space/en/bridging-language-barriers-the-potential-of-chatgpt-4-for-multilingual-communication

Frąckiewicz, M. (2023b). *The Role of AI in Promoting Cultural Diversity and Global Understanding.* TS2 Space. https://ts2.space/en/the-role-of-ai-in-promoting-cultural-diversity-and-global-understanding

Fraenkel, J. R., Wallen, N. E., & Hyun, H. H. (2011). *How to design and evaluate research in education.* McGraw-Hill.

Fredholm, K. (2019). Effects of Google Translate on lexical diversity: Vocabulary development among learners of Spanish as a foreign language. *Revista Nebrija de Lingüística Aplicada a la Enseñanza de las Lenguas*, *13*(26), 98–117. doi:10.26378/rnlael1326300

Freepik. (2023, April 15). *Trace effect PSD.* Freepik. https://www.freepik.com/psd/trace-effect

Freeze, J. (2019). Build Cross-Cultural Bridges, Not Barriers, With AI. *Forbes.* https://www.forbes.com/sites/forbescommunicationscouncil/2019/07/31/build-cross-cultural-bridges-not-barriers-with-ai/?sh=3971bbe71839

Fryer, L. K., Ainley, M., Thompson, A., Gibson, A., & Sherlock, Z. (2017). Stimulating and sustaining interest in a language course: An experimental comparison of chatbot and human task partners. *Computers in Human Behavior*, *75*, 461–468. doi:10.1016/j.chb.2017.05.045

Fryer, L., & Carpenter, R. (2006). Emerging technologies: Bots as language learning tools. *Language Learning & Technology*, *10*(3), 8–14.

Fryer, L., Nakao, K., & Thompson, A. (2019). Chatbot learning partners: Connecting learning experiences, interest and competence. *Computers in Human Behavior*, *93*, 279–289. doi:10.1016/j.chb.2018.12.023

Furdu, I., Tomozei, C., & Kose, U. (2017). Pros and Cons Gamification and Gaming in Classroom.: Discovery Service for Univ of South Carolina. *BRAIN: Broad Research in Artificial Intelligence & Neuroscience, 8*(2).

Ganier, F., Hoareau, C., & Tisseau, J. (2014). Evaluation of procedural learning transfer from a virtual environment to a real situation: A case study on tank maintenance training. *Ergonomics*, *57*(6), 828–843. doi:10.1080/00140139.2014.899628 PMID:24678862

Garcia, I., & Pena, M. I. (2011). Machine translation-assisted language learning: Writing for beginners. *Computer Assisted Language Learning*, *24*(5), 471–487. doi:10.1080/09588221.2011.582687

García-Peñalvo, F. J. (2023). The perception of Artificial Intelligence in educational contexts after the launch of ChatGPT: Disruption or Panic? *Education in the Knowledge Society*, *24*. doi:10.14201/eks.31279

Garnes-Tarazona, I. (2018). Exploring socio-cultural elements in three commercial English language learning apps. *International Journal of Computer-Assisted Language Learning and Teaching*, *8*(1), 65–82. doi:10.4018/IJCALLT.2018010105

Ghanooni, A. R. (2012). A review of the history of translation studies. *Theory and Practice in Language Studies*, *2*(1), 77–85. doi:10.4304/tpls.2.1.77-85

Gimpel, H., Hall, K., Decker, S., Eymann, T., & Lämmermann, L. (2023). *Unlocking the power of generative AI models and systems such asGPT-4 and ChatGPT for higher education.* opus.uni-hohenheim.de

Godwin-Jones, R. (2019). In a world of SMART technology, why learn another language? *Journal of Educational Technology & Society*, *22*(2), 4–13.

Goksel-Canbek, N., & Mutlu, M. E. (2016). in Errol Jayawardene (2015). On the track of Artificial Intelligence: Learning with Intelligent Personal Assistants. *International Journal of Human Sciences*, *13*(1), 592–601. doi:10.14687/ijhs.v13i1.3549

Gonzalez-Argote, J., & Gonzalez-Argote, D. (2022). 10 Best practices in Immersive Learning Design and 10 points of connection with the Metaverse. *Metaverse Basic and Applied Research*, *2*, 7. doi:10.56294/mr20237

Graça, V., Quadro-Flores, P., & Ramos, A. (2022). The Integration of the Digital Platform Educaplay in Interdisciplinary Paths in the 1st and 2nd Basic Education Cycles. *Athens Journal of Education*, *9*(3), 377–392. doi:10.30958/aje.9-3-2

Granger, S., Kraif, O., Ponton, C., Antoniadis, G., & Zampa, V. (2007). Integrating learner corpora and natural language processing: A crucial step towards reconciling technological sophistication and pedagogical effectiveness. *ReCALL, 19*(3), 252–268. doi:10.1017/S0958344007000237

Grant, P., & Basye, D. (2014). *Personalized learning: A guide for engaging students with technology*. International Society for Technology in Education.

Greene, D., Hoffmann, A. L., & Stark, L. (2019). Better, nicer, clearer, fairer: A critical assessment of the movement for ethical artificial intelligence and machine learning. In *Proceedings of the 52nd Hawaii International Conference on System Sciences*. 10.24251/HICSS.2019.258

Groves, M., & Mundt, K. (2021). A ghostwriter in the machine? Attitudes of academic staff towards machine translation use in internationalised higher education. *Journal of English for Academic Purposes*, *50*, 1–11. doi:10.1016/j.jeap.2021.100957

Guidotti, R., Monreale, A., Ruggieri, S., Turini, F., Giannotti, F., & Pedreschi, D. (2018). A survey of methods for explaining black box models. *ACM Computing Surveys*, *51*(5), 1–42. doi:10.1145/3236009

Gulson, K. N., Sellar, S., & Taylor-Webb, P. (2022). *Algorithms of Education: How datafication and artificial intelligence shape policy*. University of Minnesota Press. doi:10.5749/9781452968797

Halaweh, M. (2023). ChatGPT in education: Strategies for responsible implementation. *Contemporary Educational Technology*, *15*(2), ep421. doi:10.30935/cedtech/13036

Haleem, A., Javaid, M., Qadri, M. A., & Suman, R. (2022). Understanding the role of digital technologies in education: A review. *Sustainable Operations and Computers*, *3*, 275–285. doi:10.1016/j.susoc.2022.05.004

Haman, M., & Školník, M. (2023). Using ChatGPT to conduct a literature review [Letter to the editor]. *Accountability in Research*, 1–3. doi:10.1080/08989621.2023.2185514 PMID:36879536

Hamari, J., Koivisto, J., & Sarsa, H. (2014a). Does gamification work?–a literature review of empirical studies on gamification. In *2014 47th Hawaii international conference on system sciences (HICSS)* (pp. 3025–3034). IEEE.

Hamari, J., Shernoff, D. J., Rowe, E., Coller, B., Asbell-Clarke, J., & Edwards, T. (2014b). Challenging games help students learn: An empirical study on engagement, flow, and immersion in game-based learning. *Computers in Human Behavior*, *54*, 170–179. doi:10.1016/j.chb.2015.07.045

Hampel, R. (2015). *Developing online language teaching: Research-based pedagogies and reflective practices*. Springer. doi:10.1057/9781137412263

Hang, Y., Khan, S., Alharbi, A., & Nazir, S. (2022). Assessing English teaching linguistic and artificial intelligence for efficient learning using analytical hierarchy process and Technique for Order of Preference by Similarity to Ideal Solution. *Journal of Software (Malden, MA)*, 2462. doi:10.1002mr.2462

Hanks, J. (2019). From research-as-practice to exploratory practice-as-research in language teaching and beyond. *Language Teaching*, *52*(2), 143–187. doi:10.1017/S0261444819000016

Haristiani, N. (2019). Artificial Intelligence (AI) Chatbot as Language Learning Medium: An inquiry. *Journal of Physics: Conference Series*, *1387*(1), 012020. doi:10.1088/1742-6596/1387/1/012020

Hattie, J., & Timperley, H. (2007). The power of feedback. *Review of Educational Research*, *77*(1), 81–112. doi:10.3102/003465430298487

He, L. & Smith, J., (2018) Pronunciation in Second Language Learning and Teaching Proceedings. *Immerse Me, 10*(1).

Heift, T., & Schulze, M. (2007). *Errors and intelligence in computer-assisted language learning: Parsers and pedagogues*. Routledge. doi:10.4324/9780203012215

Heitmann, S., Grund, A., Berthold, K., Fries, S., & Roelle, J. (2018). Testing is more desirable when it is adaptive and still desirable when compared to note-taking. *Frontiers in Psychology*, *9*, 2596. doi:10.3389/fpsyg.2018.02596 PMID:30619005

Hellmich, E. A. (2019). Language teacher beliefs about technology: Expanding the ecology. *International Journal of Computer-Assisted Language Learning and Teaching*, *9*(4), 1–17. doi:10.4018/IJCALLT.2019100101

Heritage, M. (2021). *Formative assessment: Making it happen in the classroom*. Corwin Press.

Hernández-Leo, D., Martinez-Maldonado, R., Pardo, A., Muñoz-Cristóbal, J. A., & Rodríguez-Triana, M. J. (2019). Analytics for learning design: A layered framework and tools. *British Journal of Educational Technology*, *50*(1), 139–152. doi:10.1111/bjet.12645

Herodotou, C., Rienties, B., Boroowa, A., Zdrahal, Z., & Hlosta, M. (2019). A large-scale implementation of predictive learning analytics in higher education: Lessons learned and challenges ahead. *Educational Technology Research and Development*, *67*(5), 1273–1302. doi:10.100711423-019-09685-0

Herrington, J., & Oliver, R. (2000). An instructional design framework for authentic learning environments. *Educational Technology Research and Development*, *48*(3), 23–48. doi:10.1007/BF02319856

Higgs, T. V., & Krashen, S. D. (1983). Principles and Practice in Second Language Acquisition. *Modern Language Journal*, *67*(2), 168. doi:10.2307/328293

Hockley, N. (2023). Artificial Intelligence in English Language Teaching: The Good, the Bad and the Ugly. *RELC Journal*, *0*(0). doi:10.1177/00336882231168504

Hockly, N. (2012). Digital literacies. *ELT Journal*, *66*(1), 108–112. doi:10.1093/elt/ccr077

Holmes, W., Persson, J., Chounta, I. J., Wasson, B., & Dimitrova, V. (2022). *Artificial intelligence and education: A critical view through the lens of human rights, democracy and rule of law*.

Holmes, W., Bialik, M., & Fadel, C. (2019). *Artificial Intelligence in Education: Promises and Implications for Teaching and Learning*. The Center for Curriculum Redesign.

Holstein, K., McLaren, B. M., & Aleven, V. (2019). Intelligent tutors as teachers' aides: Exploring teacher needs for real-time analytics in blended classrooms. In *Proceedings of the Seventh International Learning Analytics & Knowledge Conference* (pp. 257-266).

Hong, W. C. H. (2023). The impact of ChatGPT on foreign language teaching and learning: Opportunities in education and research. *Journal of Educational Technology and Innovation*, *5*(1), 37–45. https://jeti.thewsu.org/index.php/cieti/article/view/103

Hooper, L., Livingstone, S., & Pothong, K. (2022). Problems with data governance in UK schools: The cases of Google Classroom and ClassDojo. London: Digital Futures Commission. 5Rights Foundation.

Hossein, D., & Dehganzadeh, H. (2020). Investigating effects of digital gamification-based language learning: A systematic review. *Journal of English Language Teaching and Learning*, *12*, 53–93.

Hosseini, M., Rasmussen, L. M., & Resnik, D. B. (2023). Using AI to write scholarly publications. *Accountability in Research*, 1–9. doi:10.1080/08989621.2023.2168535 PMID:36697395

Hsu, M.-H., Chan, T.-M., & Yu, C.-S. (2023). Termbot: A chatbot-based crossword game for gamified medical terminology learning. *International Journal of Environmental Research and Public Health*, *20*(5), 4185. doi:10.3390/ijerph20054185 PMID:36901193

Hu Au, E., & Lee, J. J. (2017). Virtual reality in education: A tool for learning in the experience age. *International Journal of Innovation in Education*, *4*(4), 215. doi:10.1504/IJIIE.2017.091481

Huang, J., Saleh, S., & Liu, Y. (2021a). A review on artificial intelligence in education. *Academic Journal of Interdisciplinary Studies*, *10*(3), 206–206. doi:10.36941/ajis-2021-0077

Huang, W., Hew, K. F., & Fryer, L. K. (2022). Chatbots for language learning—Are they really useful? A systematic review of chatbot-supported language learning. *Journal of Computer Assisted Learning*, *38*(1), 237–257. doi:10.1111/jcal.12610

Huang, X., Zou, D., Cheng, G., & Xie, H. (2021b). A systematic review of AR and VR enhanced language learning. *Sustainability (Basel)*, *13*(9), 4639. doi:10.3390u13094639

Huang, Y.-H., & Chuang, T.-Y. (2016). Technology-assisted sheltered instruction: Instructional streaming video in an EFL multi-purpose computer course. *Computer Assisted Language Learning*, *29*(3), 618–637. doi:10.1080/09588221.2014.1000933

Hussein, M. A., Hassan, H., & Nassef, M. (2019). Automated language essay scoring systems: A literature review. *PeerJ. Computer Science*, *5*, e208. doi:10.7717/peerj-cs.208 PMID:33816861

Ifeanyi, U. (2020). Language Teaching Methods: A Conceptual Approach. *Research Gate*, *9*(January 2015).

Ikonta, N. R., & Ugonna, N. C. (2015). The effect of Rosetta Stone (computer-assisted language learning) software on English as second language students' proficiency in English language. *American Educational Research Journal*, *3*(1), 69–79.

International Committee of Medical Journal Editors (ICMJE). (n.d.). Defining the Role of Authors and Contributors. ICMJE. https://www.icmje.org/recommendations/browse/roles-and-responsibilities/defining-the-role-of-authors-and-contributors.html

Jaelani, A., & Sutari, D. R. (2020). Students' Perception of Using Duolingo Application As a Media in Learning Vocabulary. *The 2nd Bogor English and Teacher (BEST) Conference.*

Jaiswal, A., & Arun, C. J. (2021). Potential of artificial intelligence for transformation of education system in India. *International Journal of Education and Development Using Information and Communication Technology*, *17*(1), 142–158.

Jang, J. (2021). A study on a Korean speaking class based on metaverse: Using Gather. town. *Journal of Korean Language Education*, *32*, 279–301.

Janssen, D., Tummel, C., Richert, A., & Isenhardt, I. (2016). Virtual Environments in Higher Education – Immersion as a Key Construct for Learning 4.0. [IJAC]. *International Journal of Advanced Corporate Learning*, *9*(2), 20. doi:10.3991/ijac.v9i2.6000

Jauregi, K., De Graaff, R., Van den Bergh, H., & Kriz, M. (2012). Native/non-native speaker interactions through video-web communication: A clue for enhancing motivation? *Computer Assisted Language Learning*, *25*(1), 1–19. doi:10.1080/09588221.2011.582587

Jebahi, K. (2022). Approaches and Methods in Language Teaching and Learning over Time. *Language and Literature*, *24*(3), 88–106. doi:10.20360/langandlit29595

Jeon, J. (2021). Chatbot-assisted dynamic assessment (CA-DA) for L2 vocabulary learning and diagnosis. *Computer Assisted Language Learning*, 1–27. doi:10.1080/09588221.2021.1987272

Jeon, J. H. (2021). A Study on the principle of metaverse composition with a focus on Roblox. *Korean Association for Visual Culture*, *38*, 257–279. doi:10.21299/jovc.2021.38.10

Jolley, J. R., & Maimone, L. (2015). Free online machine translation: Use and perceptions by Spanish students and instructors. In A. K. Moeller (Ed.), *Learn language, explore cultures, transform lives* (pp. 181–200). University of Nebraska-Lincoln.

Jolley, J. R., & Maimone, L. (2022). Thirty years of machine translation in language teaching and learning: A review of the literature. *Journal of Linguistics and Language Teaching*, *14*(1), 26–44. doi:10.5070/L214151760

Kaeophanuek, S., Na-Songkhla, J., & Nilsook, P. (2019). A Learning Process Model To Enhance Digital Literacy Using Critical Inquiry Through Digital Storytelling (Cidst). *International Journal of Emerging Technologies in Learning*, *03*(14), 22. doi:10.3991/ijet.v14i03.8326

Kaharuddin, A. (2021). Assessing the effect of using artificial intelligence on the writing skill of Indonesian learners of English. *Linguistics and Culture Review, 5*(1).

Kaharuddin. (2022). E-Learning During the COVID-19 Outbreak: The Effect of the Grammar Translation Method and the Direct Method on Students' English Competence. *Journal of Language Teaching and Research, 13*(2). doi:10.17507/jltr.1302.06

Kampermann, A., Opdenakker, R., Heijden, B. V. D., & Bücker, J. (2021). Intercultural competencies for fostering technology-mediated collaboration in developing countries. *Sustainability (Basel), 13*(14), 7790. doi:10.3390u13147790

Kannan, J., & Munday, P. (2018). New Trends in Second Language Learning and Teaching through the lens of ICT, Networked Learning, and Artificial Intelligence. In *Fernandez Juncal C.* Hernández. doi:10.5209/CLAC.62495

Kapp, K. M. (2012). *The gamification of learning and instruction: Game-based methods and strategies for training and education.* John Wiley & Sons.

Karakaş, A. (forthcoming). Supporting the teaching of GELT through VOKI. *RELC Journal*, 0-0.

Karakaş, A. (2017). English voices in text-to-speech tools representation of English users and their varieties from a World Englishes perspective. *Advances in Language and Literary Studies, 8*(5), 108–119. doi:10.7575/aiac.alls.v.8n.5p.108

Kartal, G. (2023). Contemporary language teaching and learning with ChatGPT. *Contemporary Research in Language and Linguistics, 1*(1), 59-70. http://crlljournal.org/index.php/crll/article/view/10

Kartal, G. (2023). Contemporary Language Teaching and Learning with ChatGPT. *Contemporary Research in Language and Linguistics, 1*(1). 59-70. http://crlljournal.org/index.php/crll/article/view/10/9

Kartal, G. (2022). Evaluating a mobile instant messaging tool for efficient large-class speaking instruction. *Computer Assisted Language Learning*, 1–29. doi:10.1080/09588221.2022.2074463

Kartal, G. (2023). Contemporary language teaching and learning with ChatGPT. *Contemporary Research in Language and Linguistics, 1*(1), 59–70.

Kartal, G., & Balçikanli, C. (2018). Willingness to communicate and communication anxiety of EFL learners in a virtual world. *I-manager's Journal of Educational Technology, 15*(3), 7–25.

Kasneci, E., Seßler, K., Küchemann, S., Bannert, M., Dementieva, D., Fischer, F., Gasser, U., Groh, G., Günnemann, S., Hüllermeier, E., Krusche, S., Kutyniok, G., Michaeli, T., Nerdel, C., Pfeffer, J., Poquet, O., Sailer, M., Schmidt, A., Seidel, T., & Kasneci, G. (2023). ChatGPT for good? On opportunities and challenges of large language models for education. *Learning and Individual Differences, 103*, 102274. doi:10.1016/j.lindif.2023.102274

Kato, Y., & Hanks, J. (2021). Learner-initiated exploratory practice: Revisiting curiosity. *ELT Journal.*

Keerthiwansha, N. (2018). Artificial intelligence education (AIEd) in English as a second language (ESL) classroom in Sri Lanka. *Artificial Intelligence*, *6*(1), 31–36.

Kemp, R. (2020). Lessons in self-betrayal: On the pitfalls of transformative education. *Educational Theory*, *70*(5), 603–616. doi:10.1111/edth.12446

Kern, R., Ware, P., & Warschauer, M. (2016). Computer-mediated communication and language learning. In G. Hall (Ed.), *The Routledge handbook of English languageteaching* (pp. 542–555). Routledge. doi:10.4324/9781315676203-45

Kessler, G. (2018). Technology and the future of language teaching. *Foreign Language Annals*, *51*(1), 205–218. doi:10.1111/flan.12318

Kieseier, T., Thoma, D., Vogelbacher, M., & Holger, H. (2022). Differential effects of metalinguistic awareness components in early foreign language acquisition of English vocabulary and grammar. *Language Awareness*, *31*(4), 495–514. doi:10.1080/09658416.2022.2093888

Kılıçkaya, F. & Kıc-Drgas, J. (2023). *Misuse of AI (Artificial Intelligence) in assignments.*

Kim, N. Y., Cha, Y., & Kim, H. S. (2019). Future English learning: Chatbots and artificial intelligence. *Multimedia-Assisted Language Learning, 22*(3).

Kim, N.-Y., Cha, Y., & Kim, H.-S. (2019). Future english learning: Chatbots and artificial intelligence. *Multimedia-Assisted Language Learning, 22*(3).

Kim, J. S., & Lee, J. H. (2021). Overcoming barriers to cross-cultural cooperation in AI ethics and governance. *Philosophy & Technology*, *34*(2), 321–327. doi:10.100713347-020-00402-x

Kim, M., Sim, J., & Ryu, S. (2022). A Study on Foreign Students' Perception of Metaverse-Based Korean Language Course as General Education. *The Korean Association of General Education*, *16*(6), 183–195. Advance online publication. doi:10.46392/kjge.2022.16.6.183

Kim, N.-Y. (2017). Effects of different types of chatbots on EFL learners' speaking competence and learner perception. *Cross-Cultural Studies*, *48*, 223–252. doi:10.21049/ccs.2017.48..223

Kim, N.-Y. (2018a). A study on chatbots for developing Korean college students' English listening and reading skills. *Journal of Digital Convergence*, *16*(8), 19–26. doi:10.14400/JDC.2018.16.8.019

Kim, N.-Y. (2018b). Chatbots and Korean EFL students' English vocabulary learning. *Journal of Digital Convergence*, *16*(2), 1–7. doi:10.14400/JDC.2018.16.2.001

Kim, S., Song, K., Lockee, B., & Burton, J. (2018). *Gamification in Learning and Education.* Springer International Publishing., doi:10.1007/978-3-319-47283-6

Kite-Powell, J. (2017). The Role of Artificial Intelligence and Language. *Forbes*. https://www.forbes.com/sites/jenniferhicks/2017/12/30/the-role-of-artificial-intelligence-and- language/

Knewton. (n.d.). Adaptive learning for all. Retrieved from https://www.knewton.com/

Knox, J. (2020). Artificial intelligence and education in China. *Learning, Media and Technology, 45*(3), 298–311. doi:10.1080/17439884.2020.1754236

Koedinger, K. R., Anderson, J. R., Hadley, W. H., & Mark, M. A. (1997). Intelligent tutoring goes to school in the big city. *International Journal of Artificial Intelligence in Education, 8*(1), 30–43.

Kohnke, L. (2022). A pedagogical chatbot: A supplemental language learning tool. *RELC Journal, 0*(0). Advance online publication. doi:10.1177/00336882211067054

Kohnke, L. (2023). L2 learners' perceptions of a chatbot as a potential independent language learning tool. *International Journal of Mobile Learning and Organisation, 17*(1-2), 214–226. doi:10.1504/IJMLO.2023.128339

Kohnke, L., Moorhouse, B. L., & Zou, D. (2023). ChatGPT for language teaching and learning. *RELC Journal*, 00336882231162868.

Kohnke, L., Moorhouse, B. L., & Zou, D. (2023). ChatGPT for Language Teaching and Learning. *RELC Journal.* Advance online publication. doi:10.1177/00336882231162868

Koml, J. (2021). The rise of education rentiers: Digital platforms, digital data and rents. *Learning, Media and Technology, 46*(3), 320–332.

Koohang, A., Nord, J. H., Ooi, K.-B., Tan, G. W.-H., Al-Emran, M., Aw, E. C.-X., Baabdullah, A. M., Buhalis, D., Cham, T.-H., Dennis, C., Dutot, V., Dwivedi, Y. K., Hughes, L., Mogaji, E., Pandey, N., Phau, I., Raman, R., Sharma, A., Sigala, M., & Wong, L.-W. (2023). Shaping the Metaverse into Reality: A Holistic Multidisciplinary Understanding of Opportunities, Challenges, and Avenues for Future Investigation. *Journal of Computer Information Systems, 63*(3), 1–31. doi:10.1080/08874417.2023.2165197

Kooli, C. (2023). Chatbots in education and research: A critical examination of ethical implications and solutions. *Sustainability (Basel), 15*(7), 5614. doi:10.3390u15075614

Koraishi, O. (2023). Teaching English in the age of AI: Embracing ChatGPT to optimize EFL materials and assessment. *Language Education and Technology, 3*(1), 55-72. https://langedutech.com/letjournal/index.php/let/article/view/48

Koraishi, O. (2023). Teaching English in the age of AI: Embracing ChatGPT to optimize EFL materials and assessment. *Language Education and Technology, 3*(1). 55-72. https://langedutech.com/letjournal/index.php/let/article/view/48

Koraishi, O. (2023). Teaching English in the age of AI: Embracing ChatGPT to optimize EFL materials and assessment. [LET Journal]. *Language Education & Technology, 3*(1), 55–72.

Koraishi, O. (2023). *Teaching English in the age of AI: Embracing ChatGPT to optimize EFL materials and assessment.* Language Education & Technology.

Kose, U., Arslan, A., & Campus, A. K. (2015). E-learning experience with artificial intelligence supported software: An international application on English language courses. *GLOKALde, 1*(3), 61–75.

Kovačević, D. (2023). Use of ChatGPT in ESP teaching process. *22nd International Symposium INFOTEH-JAHORINA (INFOTEH),* (pp. 1–5). 10.1109/INFOTEH57020.2023.10094133

Krogh, A. (2008). What are artificial neural networks? *Nature Biotechnology*, *26*(2), 195–197. doi:10.1038/nbt1386 PMID:18259176

Kuddus, K. (2022). Artificial intelligence in language learning: Practices and prospects. *Advanced Analytics and Deep Learning Models*, 1-17.

Kuhail, M. A., Elsayary, A., Farooq, S., & Alghamdi, A. (2022). Exploring Immersive Learning Experiences: A Survey. In Informatics, 9(4). doi:10.3390/informatics9040075

Kukulska-Hulme, A., & Shield, L. (2008). An overview of mobile assisted language learning: From content delivery to supported collaboration and interaction. *ReCALL*, *20*(3), 271–289. doi:10.1017/S0958344008000335

Kumar, D. N. (2019). Implementation of artificial intelligence in imparting education and evaluating student performance. *Journal of Artificial Intelligence and Capsule Networks*, *1*(1), 1–9. doi:10.36548/jaicn.2019.1.001

Kurniawan, D., Bunau, E., & Wardah, W. (2021). The use of Rosetta Stone language learning software in teaching listening: Documentary research. *Journal of English Education Program*, 2(2), 97–103. doi:10.26418/jeep.v2i2.45516

Lai, V. D., Ngo, N. T., Veyseh, A. P. B., Man, H., Dernoncourt, F., Bui, T., & Nguyen, T. H. (2023). Chatgpt beyond english: Towards a comprehensive evaluation of large language models in multilingual learning. *arXiv preprint arXiv:2304.05613.*

Landa-Blanco, M., Flores, M., & Mercado, M. (2023). *Human vs. AI Authorship: Does it Matter in Evaluating Creative Writing? A Pilot Study Using ChatGPT*: psyarxiv.com. https://doi.org/doi:10.31234/osf.io/wjsm3osf.io/wjsm3

Landers, R. N. (2014). Developing a theory of gamified learning: Linking serious games and gamification of learning. *Simulation & Gaming*, *45*(6), 752–768. doi:10.1177/1046878114563660

Lankshear, C., & Knobel, M. (2006). Digital Literacy and Digital Literacies: - Policy, Pedagogy and Research Considerations for Education. *Nordic Journal of Digital Literacy*, *1*, 8–20.

Lan, Y. J. (2020a). Immersion into virtual reality for language learning. *Psychology of Learning and Motivation*, *72*, 1–26. doi:10.1016/bs.plm.2020.03.001

Lan, Y. J. (2020b). Immersion, interaction and experience-oriented learning: Bringing VR into FL learning. *Language Learning & Technology*, *24*(1), 1–15.

Lan, Y. J., Sung, Y. T., & Chang, K. E. (2007). A mobile-device-supported peer-assisted learning system for collaborative early EFL reading. *Language Learning & Technology, 11*(3), 130–151.

Laufer, B. (1992). How much lexis is necessary for reading comprehension? In P. J. L. Arnaud & H. Be'joint (Eds.), *Vocabulary and Applied Linguistics* (pp. 126–132). Macmillan. doi:10.1007/978-1-349-12396-4_12

Laufer, B. (1994). The lexical profile of second language writing: Does it change over time? *RELC Journal, 25*(2), 21–33. doi:10.1177/003368829402500202

LeCun, Y., Bengio, Y., & Hinton, G. (2015). Deep learning. *Nature, 521*(7553), 436–444. doi:10.1038/nature14539 PMID:26017442

Lee, I., Ali, S., Zhang, H., DiPaola, D., & Breazeal, C. (2021, March). Developing middle school students' AI literacy. In *Proceedings of the 52nd ACM technical symposium on computer science education* (pp. 191-197). ACM. 10.1145/3408877.3432513

Lee, J. (1999). Effectiveness of computer-based instructional simulation: A Meta-analysis. *International Journal of Instructional Media, 26*(1), 71–85.

Lee, J. (2020). Problem-based gaming via an augmented reality mobile game and a printed game in foreign language education. *Education and Information Technologies, 27*(1), 743–771. doi:10.100710639-020-10391-1

Lee, J. Y. (2023). Can an artificial intelligence chatbot be the author of a scholarly article? *Journal of Educational Evaluation for Health Professions, 20*, 1–6. doi:10.3352/jeehp.2023.20.6 PMID:36842449

Lee, J., & Yoo-kyung, J. (2022). Effects of Video Conferencing and Metaverse Platforms on Korean EFL University Learners' Self-assessed L2 Speaking, Interaction, Immersion, and Affective Factors. *Journal of Research in Curriculum Instruction, 26*(4).

Lee, S. M. (2020). The impact of using machine translation on EFL students' writing. *Computer Assisted Language Learning, 33*(3), 157–175. doi:10.1080/09588221.2018.1553186

Lee, S. M. (2022). Different effects of machine translation on L2 revisions across students' L2 writing proficiency levels. *Language Learning & Technology, 26*(1), 1–21.

Lee, S. M. (2023). The effectiveness of machine translation in foreign language education: A systematic review and meta-analysis. *Computer Assisted Language Learning, 36*(1-2), 103–125. doi:10.1080/09588221.2021.1901745

Lesia Viktorivna, K., Andrii Oleksandrovych, V., Iryna Oleksandrivna, K., & Nadia Oleksandrivna, K. (2022). *Artificial Intelligence in Language Learning: What Are We Afraid Of.* Arab World English Journal.

Leung, C., Harris, R., & Rampton, B. (1997). The Idealised Native speaker, Reified Ethnicities, and Classroom Realities. *TESOL Quarterly, 3*(31), 543. doi:10.2307/3587837

Lew, S., Gul, T., & Pecore, J. L. (2021). ESOL pre-service teachers' culturally and linguistically responsive teaching in mixed-reality simulations. *Information and Learning Sciences*, *122*(1/2), 45–67. doi:10.1108/ILS-01-2020-0012

Li, X. (2017). *The construction of Intelligent Teaching Model based on Artificial Intelligence*. https://doi.org/ doi:10.3991/ijet.v12.i12.7963

Lin, S. Y., Chen, M. P., Wang, L. C., Kao, Y. T., Zou, D., & Xie, H. (2019). Enhancing low achievers EFL learning with interactive digital technologies. In C. Maiga, S. Hyo-Jeong, W. Lung-Hsiang, Y. Fu-Yun, S. Ju-Ling, & B. Ivica (Eds.), *Proceedings of the ICCE 2019 - 27th International Conference on Computers in Education*. (pp. 617–623). Kenting: Asia-Pacific Society for Computers in Education.

Lin, T. J., & Lan, Y. J. (2015). Language learning in virtual reality environments: Past, present, and future. *Journal of Educational Technology & Society*, *18*(4), 486–497.

Liu, M. (2023). Exploring the Application of Artificial Intelligence in Foreign Language Teaching: Challenges and Future Development. In *SHS Web of Conferences* (*Vol. 168*). EDP Sciences.

Liu, Y., & Liu, M. (2019). Research on college English teaching under the background of artificial intelligence. Journal of Physics: Conference Series. doi:10.1089/big.2018.0151

Li, X. (2019). The application and feasibility of artificial intelligence in college English teaching. In *Proceedings of the 9th International Conference on Education and Social Science* (pp. 1627–1631). Francis Academic Press. https://webofproceedings.org/proceedings_series/ESSP/ICESS%202019/ICESS19312.pd

Li, Z., & Hegelheimer, V. (2013). Mobile-assisted grammar exercises: Effects on self-editing in L2 writing. *Language Learning & Technology*, *17*(3), 135–156.

Loewen, S., Crowther, D., Isbell, D., Kim, K., Maloney, J., & Rawal, H. (2019). Mobile-assisted Language Learning: A Duolingo Case Study. *ReCALL*, *3*(31), 293–311. doi:10.1017/S0958344019000065

Loewen, S., Isbell, D. R., & Sporn, Z. (2020). The effectiveness of app-based language instruction for developing receptive linguistic knowledge and oral communicative ability. *Foreign Language Annals*, *53*(2), 209–233. doi:10.1111/flan.12454

Lord, G. (2016). Rosetta Stone for language learning: An exploratory study. *IALLT Journal of Language Learning Technologies*, *46*(1), 1–35. doi:10.17161/iallt.v46i1.8552

Love, R., Dembry, C., Hardie, A., Brezina, V., & McEnery, T. (2017). The Spoken BNC2014: And building a spoken corpus of everyday conversations. *International Journal of Corpus Linguistics*, *22*(3), 319–344. doi:10.1075/ijcl.22.3.02lov

Luckin, R., & Holmes, W. (2016) Intelligence Unleashed: An argument for AI in Education. *UCL Knowledge Lab*. London, UK. https://discovery.ucl.ac.uk/id/eprint/1475756

Luo, H., Li, G., Feng, Q., Yang, Y., & Zuo, M. (2021). Virtual reality in K-12 and higher education: A systematic review of the literature from 2000 to 2019. *Journal of Computer Assisted Learning*, *37*(3), 887–901. doi:10.1111/jcal.12538

Lyu, B., & Lai, C. (2022). Analysing learner engagement with native speaker feedback on an educational social networking site: An ecological perspective. *Computer Assisted Language Learning*, 1–35. doi:10.1080/09588221.2022.2030364

Macedo, D. (2006). Literacies of power: What Americans are not allowed to know (Expanded ed.). Boulder, CO: Westview Press.

Machover, C., & Tice, S. E. (1994). Virtual reality. *IEEE Computer Graphics and Applications*, *14*(1), 15–16. doi:10.1109/38.250913

MacPhail, A., Tannehill, D., Leirhaug, P. E., & Borghouts, L. (2023). Promoting instructional alignment in physical education teacher education. *Physical Education and Sport Pedagogy*, *28*(2), 153–164. doi:10.1080/17408989.2021.1958177

Mageira, K., Pittou, D., Papasalouros, A., Kotis, K., Zangogianni, P., & Daradoumis, A. (2022). Educational AI chatbots for content and language integrated learning. *Applied Sciences (Basel, Switzerland)*, *12*(3239), 1–16. doi:10.3390/app12073239

Maguire, M., & Delahunt, B. (2017). Doing a thematic analysis: A practical, step-by-step guide for learning and teaching scholars. AISHE-J. *The All Ireland Journal of Teaching and Learning in Higher Education*, *9*(3), 3351–33514.

Majid, S. N. A., & Salam, A. R. (2021). A systematic review of augmented reality applications in language learning. *International Journal of Emerging Technologies in Learning*, *16*(10), 18–34. doi:10.3991/ijet.v16i10.17273

Makarova, I., Duarte, J., & Huilcán, M. I. (2023). Experts' views on the contribution of language awareness and translanguaging for minority language education. *Language Awareness*, *32*(1), 74–93. Advance online publication. doi:10.1080/09658416.2021.1963976

Mallik, S., & Gangopadhyay, A. (2023). Proactive and reactive engagement of artificial intelligence methods for education: A review. *Frontiers in Artificial Intelligence*, *6*, 1151391. doi:10.3389/frai.2023.1151391 PMID:37215064

Mansory, M. (2020). The Significance of Non-traditional and Alternative Assessment in English Language Teaching: Evidence From Literature. *International Journal of Linguistics*, *12*(5), 210. doi:10.5296/ijl.v12i5.17782

Marr, B. (2018). *What is artificial intelligence and how will it change our world?* Bernard Marr. https://www.bernardmarr.com/default.asp?contentID=963

Mauranen, A. (2004). Spoken corpus for an ordinary learner. In J. Sinclair (Ed.), *How to use corpora in language teaching* (pp. 89–105). John Benjamins Publishing Company. doi:10.1075cl.12.09mau

Mayfield, E., Madaio, M., Prabhumoye, S., Gerritsen, D., McLaughlin, B., Dixon-Román, E., & Black, A. W. (2019, August). Equity beyond bias in language technologies for education. In *Proceedings of the Fourteenth Workshop on Innovative Use of NLP for Building Educational Applications* (pp. 444-460). 10.18653/v1/W19-4446

McQuillan, D. (2022). *Resisting AI: An Anti-Fascist Approach to Artificial Intelligence.* Bristol University Press.

Mei, Y. (2018). Comments on the audiolingual method. *International Journal of Arts and Commerce*, *7*(4).

Mendes de Oliveira, M., Sporn, Z., Kliemann, L., Borschke, A., & Meyering, M. (2021). Online language learning and workplace communication: a study on Babbel's virtual-classroom solution. In Computer Assisted Language Learning. doi:10.1080/09588221.2021.2002364

Meng-yue, C., Dan, L., & Jun, W. (2020). A study of college English culture Intelligence-Aided Teaching System and Teaching Pattern. *English Language Teaching, 13*(3). Published by Canadian Center of Science and Education.

Meurers, D. (2015). Learner corpora and natural language processing. In S. Granger, G. Gilquin, & F. Meunier (Eds.), *The Cambridge handbook of learner corpus research* (pp. 537–566). Cambridge University Press., doi:10.1017/CBO9781139649414.024

Meurers, D. (2020). Natural language processing and language learning. In C. A. Chapelle (Ed.), *The Concise Encyclopedia of Applied Linguistics* (pp. 817–831). John Wiley & Sons Inc.

Meurers, D., & Dickinson, M. (2017). Evidence and interpretation in language learning research: Opportunities for collaboration with computational linguistics. *Language Learning*, *67*(1), 66–95. doi:10.1111/lang.12233

MhlangaD. (2023). Open AI in education, the responsible and ethical use of ChatGPT towards lifelong learning. *Education, the Responsible and Ethical Use of ChatGPT Towards Lifelong Learning,* doi:10.2139/ssrn.4354422

Mikeladze, T. (2023). Creating teaching materials with ChatGPT. *13th International Research Conference on Education, Language and Literature*.

Mills, K. A. (2022). Potentials and Challenges of Extended Reality Technologies for Language Learning. *Anglistik: International Journal of English Studies, 33*(1), 147–163. www.tcpdf.org

Mishra, P., & Koehler, M. J. (2006). Technological pedagogical content knowledge: A new framework for teacher knowledge. *Teachers College Record, 108*(6), 1017–1054. doi:10.1111/j.1467-9620.2006.00684.x

Mislevy, R. J., Almond, R. G., & Lukas, J. F. (2003). *A Brief Introduction to Evidence-Centered Design.* Educational Testing Service. doi:10.1002/j.2333-8504.2003.tb01908.x

Mkansi, M., & Mkalipi, N. (2023). Natural language processing and machine learning approach to teaching and learning research philosophies and paradigms. *Electronic Journal of Business Research Methods, 21*(1), 14–30. doi:10.34190/ejbrm.21.1.2627

Modha, D. S., Ananthanarayanan, R., Esser, S. K., Ndirango, A., Sherbondy, A. J., & Singh, R. (2011). Cognitive computing. *Communications of the ACM, 54*(8), 62–71. https://doi.acm.org/10.1145/1978542.1978559. doi:10.1145/1978542.1978559

Moeller, A. K., & Nugent, K. (2014). Building intercultural competence in the language classroom. *Faculty Publications: Department of Teaching, Learning and Teacher Education, 161*, 1-18. https://digitalcommons.unl.edu/teachlearnfacpub/161

Mohamed, A. M. (2023). Exploring the potential of an AI-based Chatbot (ChatGPT) in enhancing English as a Foreign Language (EFL) teaching: Perceptions of EFL Faculty Members. *Education and Information Technologies*, 1–23. doi:10.100710639-023-11917-z

Napper, V. S. (2012). Alignment of Learning, Teaching, and Assessment. In Encyclopedia of the Sciences of Learning. doi:10.1007/978-1-4419-1428-6_1847

Nation, I. (2012). *Learning vocabulary in another language*. Cambridge University Press. doi:10.1017/CBO9781139524759

Nesi, H., & Thompson, P. (2006). *The British academic spoken English corpus manual*. University of Warwick.

Ng, D. T. K., Leung, J. K. L., Chu, S. K. W., & Qiao, M. S. (2021). Conceptualizing AI literacy: An exploratory review. Computers and Education. *Artificial Intelligence, 2*, 100041.

Ng, L. K., & Lo, C. K. (2022). Flipped Classroom and Gamification Approach: Its Impact on Performance and Academic Commitment on Sustainable Learning in Education. *Sustainability (Basel), 14*(9), 5428. doi:10.3390u14095428

Nguwi, Y. Y. (2023). Technologies for Education: From Gamification to AI-enabled Learning. *International Journal of Multidisciplinary Perspectives in Higher Education, 8*(1), 111–132.

Nguyen, A., Ngo, H. N., Hong, Y., Dang, B., & Nguyen, B. P. T. (2023). Ethical principles for artificial intelligence in education. *Education and Information Technologies, 28*(4), 4221–4241. doi:10.100710639-022-11316-w PMID:36254344

Nichols, T. P., & Garcia, A. (2022). Platform studies in Education. *Harvard Educational Review, 92*(2), 209–230. doi:10.17763/1943-5045-92.2.209

Nicol, D. J., & Macfarlane-Dick, D. (2006). Formative assessment and self-regulated learning: A model and seven principles of good feedback practice. *Studies in Higher Education, 31*(2), 199–218. doi:10.1080/03075070600572090

Nielsen, J. (1994). *Usability engineering*. Morgan Kaufmann.

Nielson, K. B. (2011). Self-study with language learning software in the workplace: What happens?
Passey, D. (2019). Computer science (CS) or information and communication technologies (ICT): The curriculum needs both. *Education and Information Technologies*, *24*(2), 1039–1058.

Nikitina, L. (2001). Creating an authentic learning environment in the foreign language classroom. *International Journal of Instruction*, *4*(1), 33–46.

Niño, A. (2008). Evaluating the use of machine translation post-editing in the foreign language class. *Computer Assisted Language Learning*, *21*(1), 29–49. doi:10.1080/09588220701865482

Niño, A. (2009). Machine translation in foreign language learning: Language learners' and tutors' perceptions of its advantages and disadvantages. *ReCALL*, *21*(2), 241–258. doi:10.1017/S0958344009000172

Niño, A. (2020). Exploring the use of online machine translation for independent language learning. *Research in Learning Technology*, *28*(0), 1–32. doi:10.25304/rlt.v28.2402

Nunan, D. (1989). *Understanding language classrooms*. Prentice Hall International (UK).

Nykon, Y. (2023). How AI Helps Crack a New Language? *Intellias*. https://intellias.com/how-ai-helps-crack-a-new-language/

O'Connor, S.ChatGPT. (2022). Open artificial intelligence platforms in nursing education: Tools for academic progress or abuse? *Nurse Education in Practice*, *66*, 103537–103537. doi:10.1016/j.nepr.2022.103537 PMID:36549229

O'Flaherty, M. (2022.). *Bias in Algorithms –Artificial Intelligence and Discrimination Report of European UnionAgency for Fundamental rights*. FRA. https://fra.europa.eu/sites/default/files/fra_uploads/fra-2022-bias-in-algorithms_en.pdf

O'Neill, E. M. (2019). Training students to use online translators and dictionaries: The impact on second language writing scores. *International Journal of Research Studies in Language Learning*, *8*(2), 47–65. doi:10.5861/ijrsll.2019.4002

Office of English Language Programs. (2019). *The Monster Book of Language Teaching Activities*. American English. www.americanenglish.state.gov

OparaE.Mfon-Ette TheresaA.AdukeT. C. (2023). ChatGPT for teaching, learning and research: Prospects and challenges. *Global Academy Journal of Humanities and Social Sciences, 5 (2)*. 33-40. https://ssrn.com/abstract=4375470

Open A. I. (2023). *ChatGPT (July 12 version)* [Large language model]. https://chat.openai.com/chat

Open to Debate Staff. (2019). What is the oxford style of debate? *Open to debate*. https://opentodebate.org/what-is-the-oxford-style-debate-format/

Oxford, R. (1999). Relationship between second language learning strategies and language proficiency in the context of learner autonomy and self-regulation. *Revista Canaria de Estudios Ingleses*, *38*, 109–126.

Parmaxi, A. (2023). Virtual reality in language learning: A systematic review and implications for research and practice. *Interactive Learning Environments*, *31*(1), 172–184. doi:10.1080/10494820.2020.1765392

Paterson, K. (2023). Machine translation in higher education: Perceptions, policy, and pedagogy. *TESOL Journal*, *14*(2), e690. doi:10.1002/tesj.690

Pedro, F., Subosa, M., Rivas, A., & Valverde, P. (2019). *Artificial Intelligence in Education: Challenges and opportunities for sustainable development.* UNESCO, 2019. https://unesdoc.unesco.org/ark:/48223/pf0000366994?pos

Perkins, M. (2023). Academic Integrity considerations of AI Large Language Models in the post-pandemic era: ChatGPT and beyond. *Journal of University Teaching & Learning Practice, 20*(2), 07.

Perrotta, C., Selwyn, N., & Ewin, C. (2022). *Artificial intelligence and the affective labour of understanding: The intimate moderation of a language model.* New Media & Society. . doi:10.1177/14614448221075296

Phakamach, P., Senarith, P., & Wachirawongpaisarn, S. (2022). The Metaverse in Education: The Future of Immersive Teaching & Learning. *RICE Journal of Creative Entrepreneurship and Management*, *3*(2), 75–88.

Pinherio, A., Barbosa, A., Carvalho, R., Freitas, F., Tsai, Y. S., Gasevic, D., & Ferreira, R. (2021). Automatic feedback in online learning environments: A systematic literature review. *Computers and Education Artificial Intelligence*, *2*, 1–17. doi:10.1016/j.caeai.2021.100027

Pinto, R. D., Peixoto, B., Melo, M., Cabral, L., & Bessa, M. (2021). Foreign language learning gamification using virtual reality—A systematic review of empirical research. *Education Sciences*, *11*(5), 222. Advance online publication. doi:10.3390/educsci11050222

Poersch, J. M. (2005). A new paradigm for learning language: Connectionist artificial intelligence. *Linguagem & ensino, 8*(1), 161-183.

Polizzi, G. (2020). Digital literacy and the national curriculum for England: Learning from how the experts engage with and evaluate online content. *Computers & Education*, *152*, 103859. doi:10.1016/j.compedu.2020.103859

Polyzi, P., & Moussiades, L. (2023). An artificial vocabulary learning assistant. *Education and Information Technologies*. doi:10.100710639-023-11810-9

Popenici, S. A., & Kerr, S. (2017). Exploring the impact of artifcial intelligence on teaching and learning in higher education. *Research and Practice in Technology Enhanced Learning*, *12*(1), 1–13. doi:10.118641039-017-0062-8 PMID:30613250

Qasem, F., Ghaleb, M., Mahdi, H. S., Al Khateeb, A., & Al Fadda, H. (2023). Dialog chatbot as an interactive online tool in enhancing ESP vocabulary learning. *Saudi Journal of Language Studies*, *3*(2), 76–86. doi:10.1108/SJLS-10-2022-0072

Qian, K., Shea, R., Li, Y., Fryer, L. K., & Yu, Z. (2023). User Adaptive Language Learning Chatbots with a Curriculum. In N. Wang, G. Rebolledo-Mendez, V. Dimitrova, N. Matsuda, & O. C. Santos (Eds.), *Artificial Intelligence in Education. Posters and Late Breaking Results, Workshops and Tutorials, Industry and Innovation Tracks, Practitioners, Doctoral Consortium and Blue Sky. AIED 2023. Communications in Computer and Information Science* (Vol. 1831). Springer. doi:10.1007/978-3-031-36336-8_48

Qiu, X., Chiu, C.-K., Zhao, L.-L., Sun, C.-F., & Chen, S. (2021). Trends in VR/AR technology-supporting language learning from 2008 to 2019: A research perspective. *Interactive Learning Environments*. Advance online publication. doi:10.1080/10494820.2021.1874999

Quansah, F. (2018). Traditional or Performance Assessment: What is the Right Way to Assessing Learners? *Research on Humanities and Social Sciences, 8*(1).

Quinlan, T., Higgins, D., & Wolff, S. (2012). Evaluating the construct coverage of the e-rater® scoring engine. *ETS Research Report Series*, *2012*(1), 1–21.

Radford, A., Wu, J., Child, R., Luan, D., Amodei, D., & Sutskever, I. (2019). Language models are unsupervised multitask learners. *OpenAI blog, 1*(8), 9.

Radianti, J., Majchrzak, T. A., Fromm, J., & Wohlgenannt, I. (2020). A systematic review of immersive virtual reality applications for higher education: Design elements, lessons learned, and research agenda. *Computers & Education*, *147*, 1–29. doi:10.1016/j.compedu.2019.103778

Raina, V., & Gales, M. (2022). Multiple-Choice Question Generation: Towards an Automated Assessment Framework. *arXiv preprint arXiv:2209.11830.* https://doi.org//arXiv.2209.11830 doi:10.48550

Rainie, L., & Anderson, J. (2017). *Code-dependent: Pros and cons of the algorithm age*. Pew Research Center.

Rashidi, N., & Khosravi, N. (2010). Assessing the role of depth and breadth of vocabulary knowledge in reading comprehension of Iranian EFL learners. *Journal of Pan-Pacific Association of Applied Linguistics*, *14*(1), 81–108.

Reddy, P., Chaudhary, K., Sharma, B., Chand, R. (2020). *Digital Literacy: a Catalyst For The 21st Century Education.* doi:10.1109/CSDE50874.2020.9411548

Rehm, G., Marheinecke, K., Hegele, S., Piperidis, S., Bontcheva, K., Hajič, J., & Yvon, F. (2020). The European language technology landscape in 2020: Language-centric and human-centric AI for cross-cultural communication in multilingual Europe. *Proceedings of the 12th Language Resources and Evaluation Conference (LREC 2020)* (pp. 3315-3325), European Language Resources Association (ELRA), Marseille, France.

Reich, J., & Ruipérez-Valiente, J. A. (2019). The MOOC pivot. *Science, 363*(6423), 130–131. doi:10.1126cience.aav7958 PMID:30630920

Reinhardt, J., & Thorne, S. (2016). Metaphors for digital games and language learning. In F. Farr & L. Murray (Eds.), *Routledge handbook of language learning and technology* (pp. 415–430). Routledge.

Richardson, M., & Clesham, R. (2021). Rise of the machines? The evolving role of Artificial Intelligence (AI) technologies in high stakes assessment. *London Review of Education, 19*(1), 1–13. doi:10.14324/LRE.19.1.09

Riloff, E., & Thelen, M. (2000). A rule-based question answering system for reading comprehension tests. In *Proceedings of the 2000 ANLP/NAACL Workshop on Reading comprehension tests as evaluation for computer-based language understanding sytems*. Association for Computational Linguistics, USA, 13–19. https://doi.org/10.3115/1117595.1117598

Ritonga, M., Febriani, S. R., Kustati, M., Khaef, E., Ritonga, A. W., & Yasmar, R. (2022). Duolingo: An Arabic Speaking Skills' Learning Platform for Andragogy Education. *Education Research International, 2022*, 1–9. doi:10.1155/2022/7090752

Ro, C. (2023). Students switch to AI to learn languages. *BBC news*.

Rodriguez-Torrealba, R., Garcia-Lopez, E., & Garcia-Cabot, A. (2022). End-to-End generation of Multiple-Choice questions using Text-to-Text transfer Transformer models. *Expert Systems with Applications, 208*, 118258. doi:10.1016/j.eswa.2022.118258

Rogers, Y., Sharp, H., & Preece, J. (2011). *Interaction design: Beyond human-computer interaction* (3rd ed.). John Wiley & Sons.

Roll, I., & Wylie, R. (2016). Evolution and Revolution In artificial intelligence In Education. *International Journal of Artificial Intelligence in Education, 2*(26), 582–599. doi:10.100740593-016-0110-3

Rosell-Aguilar, F. (2018). Autonomous language learning through a mobile application: A user evaluation of the busuu app. *Computer Assisted Language Learning, 31*(8), 854–881. doi:10.1080/09588221.2018.1456465

Rusmiyanto, R., Huriati, N., Fitriani, N., Tyas, N. K., Rofi'i, A., & Sari, M. N. (2023). The Role of Artificial Intelligence (AI) In Developing English Language Learner's Communication Skills. *Journal of Education, 6*(1), 750–757.

Russell, S. J. (2010). *Artificial intelligence a modern approach*. Pearson Education, Inc.

Russell, S. J., & Norvig, P. (2010). *Artificial intelligence: A modern approach*. Pearson Education.

Ryan, R. M., & Deci, E. L. (2000). Intrinsic and extrinsic motivations: Classic definitions and new directions. *Contemporary Educational Psychology, 25*(1), 54–67. doi:10.1006/ceps.1999.1020 PMID:10620381

Sailer, M., Hense, J. U., Mayr, S. K., & Mandl, H. (2017). How gamification motivates: An experimental study of the effects of specific game design elements on psychological need satisfaction. *Computers in Human Behavior*, *69*, 371–380. doi:10.1016/j.chb.2016.12.033

Sakai, N. (2023). *Investigating the Feasibility of ChatGPT for Personalized English Language Learning: A Case Study on its Applicability to Japanese Students*. https://osf.io/cv9f2/download

Salas-Pilco, S. Z., Xiao, K., & Oshima, J. (2022). Artificial intelligence and new technologies in inclusive education for minority students: A systematic review. *Sustainability (Basel)*, *14*(20), 13572. doi:10.3390u142013572

Sartre, J. (2013). We have only this life to live: The selected essays of Jean-Paul Sartre 1939-1975 (A. Van Den Hoven, Trans.). Aronson, R. & Van Den Hoven, A. (Ed.s). New York, NY: New York Review of Books.

Sartre, J. (1948). *What is literature? And other essays* (S. Ungar, Trans.). Harvard University Press.

Sartre, J. (1956). *Being and nothingness: An essay on phenomenological ontology* (H. Barnes, Trans.). Washington Square Press.

Sartre, J. (1963). *Search for a method* (H. Barnes, Trans.). Alfred A. Knopf.

Sartre, J. (2021). *Being and nothingness: The principal text of modern existentialism* (S. Richmond, Trans.). Washington Square Press.

Schank, R. C., & Childers, P. (1984). *The cognitive computer on language, learning, and artificial intelligence*.

Schmidt, T., & Strasser, T. (2022). Artificial intelligence in foreign language learning and teaching. Anglistik. *International Journal of English Studies*, *33*(1), 165–184. doi:10.33675/ANGL/2022/1/14

Schmidt, T., & Strasser, T. (2022). Artificial intelligence in foreign language learning and teaching: A CALL for intelligent practice. Anglistik. *International Journal of English Studies*, *33*(1), 165–184.

Schmitt, N. (2010). *Researching vocabulary: A vocabulary research manual*. Palgrave Macmillan. doi:10.1057/9780230293977

Schwartz, R., Vassilev, A., Greene, K., Perine, L., Burt, A., & Hall, P. (2022). Towards a standard for identifying and managing bias in artificial intelligence. NIST special publication, 1270. doi:10.6028/NIST.SP.1270

Sclater, N., Peasgood, A., & Mullan, J. (2016). *Learning Analytics in Higher Education: A Review of UK and International Practice*. Jisc.

Scrivner, O., Madewell, J., Buckley, C., & Perez, N. (2019). Best Practices in the Use of Augmented and Virtual Reality Technologies for SLA: Design, Implementation, and Feedback. In M. Carrió-Pastor (Ed.), *Teaching Language and Teaching Literature in Virtual Environments* (pp. 55–72). Springer Nature. doi:10.1007/978-981-13-1358-5_4Shortt, M., Tilak, S., Kuznetcova, I., Martens, B., & Akinkuolie, B. (2021). Gamification in mobile-assisted language learning: A systematic review of Duolingo literature from public release of 2012 to early 2020. *Computer Assisted Language Learning*. doi:10.1080/09588221.2021.1933540

Selwyn, N. (2019). *Should Robots Replace Teachers?* AI and the Future of Education. Polity.

Selwyn, N., & Jandrić, P. (2020). Postdigital living in the age of Covid-19: Unsettling what we see as possible. *Postdigital Science and Education, 2*(3), 233–238. doi:10.100742438-020-00166-9

Sethi, A., & Singh, K. (2022, March). Natural language processing based automated essay scoring with parameter-efficient transformer approach. In *2022 6th International Conference on Computing Methodologies and Communication (ICCMC)* (pp. 749-756). IEEE. 10.1109/ICCMC53470.2022.9753760

Settles, B., & Meeder, B. (2016). A trainable spaced repetition model for language learning. In *Proceedings of the 54th Annual Meeting of the Association for Computational Linguistics* (Volume 1: Long Papers) (pp. 1848–1858). Berlin, Germany: Association for Computational Linguistics. 10.18653/v1/P16-1174

Shadiev, R., Hwang, W. Y., & Huang, Y. M. (2017). Review of research on mobile language learning in authentic environments. *Computer Assisted Language Learning, 30*(3–4), 284–303. doi:10.1080/09588221.2017.1308383

Shadiev, R., Wang, X., & Huang, Y. M. (2021). Cross-cultural learning in virtual reality environment: Facilitating cross-cultural understanding, trait emotional intelligence, and sense of presence. *Educational Technology Research and Development, 69*(5), 2917–2936. doi:10.100711423-021-10044-1

Sharadgah, T. A., & Sa'di, R. A. (2022). A Systematic Review of Research on the Use of Artificial Intelligence in English Language Teaching and Learning (2015-2021): What are the Current Effects? *Journal of Information Technology Education, 21*, 333–377. doi:10.28945/4999

Shermis, M. D., & Burstein, J. (Eds.). (2013). *Handbook of Automated Essay Evaluation: Current Applications and New Directions*. Routledge. doi:10.4324/9780203122761

Shin, M. H. (2018). How to use artificial intelligence in the English language learning classroom. *Indian Journal of Public Health Research & Development, 9*(9), 557–561. doi:10.5958/0976-5506.2018.01058.6

Shohamy, E. (2020). *The power of tests: A critical perspective on the uses of language tests*. Routledge. doi:10.4324/9781003062318

Shortt, M., Tilak, S., Kuznetcova, I., Martens, B., & Akinkuolie, B. (2021). Gamification In Mobile-assisted Language Learning: A Systematic Review Of Duolingo Literature From Public Release Of 2012 To Early 2020. *Computer Assisted Language Learning, 3*(36), 517–554. doi:10.1080/09588221.2021.1933540

Shute, V. J., & Ventura, M. (2013). *Stealth Assessment: Measuring and Supporting Learning in Video Games*. MIT Press. doi:10.7551/mitpress/9589.001.0001

Shute, V., & Rahimi, S. (2017). Review of computer-based assessment for learning in elementary and secondary education. *Journal of Computer Assisted Learning, 33*(1), 1–19. doi:10.1111/jcal.12172

Siegerink, B., Pet, L. A., Rosendaal, F. R., & Schoones, J. W. (2023). ChatGPT as an author of academic papers is wrong and highlights the concepts of accountability and contributorship. *Nurse Education in Practice, 68*, 103599. doi:10.1016/j.nepr.2023.103599 PMID:36898252

Siemens, G. (2013). Learning analytics: The emergence of a discipline. *The American Behavioral Scientist, 57*(10), 1380–1400. doi:10.1177/0002764213498851

Siemens, G., & Long, P. (2011). Penetrating the fog: Analytics in learning and education. *EDUCAUSE Review, 46*(5), 30.

Sindermann, C., Sha, P., Zhou, M., Wernicke, J., Schmitt, H. S., Li, M., Sariyska, R., Stavrou, M., Becker, B., & Montag, C. (2021). Assessing the attitude towards artificial intelligence: Introduction of a short measure in German, Chinese, and English language. *KI-Künstliche intelligenz, 35,* 109-118.

Singh, G., Kaur, G., & Thaemphan, L. (2021). Artificial intelligence in ESL–A survey on school students and teachers in Ubon Ratchathani Thailand. *The Eleventh Annual International Symposium of Foreign Language Learning (AISOFOLL).*

Smutny, P., & Schreiberova, P. (2020). Chatbot for learning: A review of educational chatbots for the Facebook messenger. *Computers & Education, 151*, 111. doi:10.1016/j.compedu.2020.103862

Socher, R. (2018). AI's Next Great Challenge: Understanding the Nuances of Language *Hardward Business Review* [Online]. https://hbr.org/2018/07/ais-next-great-challenge-understanding-the-nuances-of-language

Somers, H., Gaspari, F., & Niño, A. (2006). Detecting inappropriate use of free online machine translation by language students. A special case of plagiarism detection. In *Proceedings of the 11th Annual conference of the European Association for Machine Translation.*

Soni, M. (2022). Implications of Artificial Intelligence in English Language Teaching. *International Journal of English: Literature, Language & Skills.* www.ijells.com

Soto, J. B., Ocampo, D. T., Colon, L. B., & Oropesa, A. V. (2020). Perceptions of ImmerseMe virtual reality platform to improve English communicative skills in higher education. *International Journal of Interactive Mobile Technologies, 14*(7), 4–19. doi:10.3991/ijim.v14i07.12181

Sottilare, R. A., Graesser, A. C., Hu, X., & Sinatra, A. M. (2018). Design recommendations for intelligent tutoring systems: Volume 6 - affect and learning. US Army Research Laboratory. https://doi.org/ doi:10.21236/ada600864

Spector, J. M., Lockee, B. B., Childress, M. D., & Magliaro, S. G. (Eds.). (2016). *Learning, Design, and Technology*. Springer.

Sporn, Z., Chanter, J., & Meehan, D. (2020). Babbel Language Learning Podcasts. [IJAC]. *International Journal of Advanced Corporate Learning, 13*(3), 43. doi:10.3991/ijac.v13i3.17025

Springer Nature. (2023a). *Editorial: Tools such as ChatGPT threaten transparent science; here are our ground rules for their use*, 613. Springer. doi:10.1038/d41586-023-00191-1

Springer Nature. (2023b). Artificial intelligence (AI) (Online). Spinger. https://www.nature.com/nature-portfolio/editorial-policies/ai

Stæhr, L. S. (2008). Vocabulary size and the skills of listening, reading and writing. *Language Learning Journal, 36*(2), 139–152. doi:10.1080/09571730802389975

Stæhr, L. S. (2009). Vocabulary knowledge and advanced listening comprehension in English as a foreign language. *Studies in Second Language Acquisition, 31*(4), 577–607. doi:10.1017/S0272263109990039

Stephens, G. E., & Roberts, K. L. (2017). Facilitating collaboration in online groups. *The Journal of Educators Online, 14*(1).

Stokel-Walker, C. (2022). *AI bot ChatGPT writes smart essays: Should academics worry?* doi:10.1038/d41586-022-04397-7

Stokel-Walker, C. (2023). *ChatGPT listed as author on research papers: many scientists disapprove* (613). doi:10.1038/d41586-023-00107-z

Strange Loop Games. (n.d.). *Eco*. Strange Loop Games. https://play.eco/

Sujatha, A., & Menon, S. A. (2021). First Steps in Online Gamification: Tips for the Language Classroom. *Gedrag en Organisatie, 34*(4), 227–241.

Sullivan, S. C. (2015). Shifting Educational Paradigms: From Traditional to Competency-Based Education for Diverse Learners. *American Secondary Education, 43*(3).

Sumakul, D. T. Y., Hamied, F. A., & Sukyadi, D. (2022). Artificial intelligence in EFL classrooms: Friend or foe? *LEARN Journal: Language Education and Acquisition Research Network, 15*(1), 232-256. https://files.eric.ed.gov/fulltext/EJ1336138.pdf

Sumakul, D. T. Y., Hamied, F. A., & Sukyadi, D. (2022). Artificial intelligence in EFL classrooms: Friend or foe? *LEARN Journal: Language Education and Acquisition Research Network, 15*(1), 232–256.

Sun, X. (2022). Ten years later: Reexamining the TESOL Technology Standards for Language Teachers. *TESOL Journal, 13*(4), 1–15. doi:10.1002/tesj.684

Sun, Z., Anbarasan, M., & Kumar, D. P. (2020). Design of online intelligent English teaching platforms based on artificial intelligence techniques. *Computational Intelligence, 37*(3), 1166–1180. doi:10.1111/coin.12351

Sur, E. (2022). Okuryazarlık Kavramı ve Türkiye'deki Okuryazarlık Araştırmaları Üzerine Bir İnceleme *Ahmet Keleşoğlu Eğitim Fakültesi Dergisi (AKEF). Dergisi, 4*(2), 445–467. doi:10.38151/akef.2022.27

Sutton, R. S., & Barto, A. G. (2018). *Reinforcement learning: An introduction.* MIT Press.

Swiecki, Z., Khosravi, H., Chen, G., Martinez-Maldonado, R., Lodge, J. M., Milligan, S., Selwyn, N., & Gašević, D. (2022). Assessment in the age of artificial intelligence. *Computers and Education: Artificial Intelligence, 3*, 100075. doi:10.1016/j.caeai.2022.100075

Syafrizal, S., & Septiawati, T. (2022). Enhancing listening skills of EFL Indonesian learners through Busuu application. *International Journal of English Language and Literature Studies, 11*(3), 147–154. Advance online publication. doi:10.55493/5019.v11i3.4615

Takacs, Z. K., & Bus, A. G. (2016). Benefits of motion in animated storybooks for children's visual attention and story comprehension. An eye-tracking study. *Frontiers in Psychology, 7*, 1–12. doi:10.3389/fpsyg.2016.01591 PMID:27790183

Tao, J., & Gao, X. (2022). Teaching and learning languages online: Challenges and responses. *System, 107*, 107. doi:10.1016/j.system.2022.102819

Tariq, K. (2014) *Siri, Google Now, Cortana: The Ultimate Digital Voice Assistant?* WCCFTech.com. http://wccftech.com/digital-voice-assistant/#ixzz3lcDQvCrq

Teixeira da Silva, T. J. A. (2021). Outsourced English revision, editing, publication consultation, and integrity services should be acknowledged in an academic paper. *Journal of Nanoparticle Research, 23*(81), 81. doi:10.100711051-021-05199-0

Teixeira da Silva, T. J. A. (2023). Is ChatGPT a valid author? *Nurse Education in Practice, 68*(103600), 103600. doi:10.1016/j.nepr.2023.103600 PMID:36906947

Teng, F. (2014). Assessing the depth and breadth of vocabulary knowledge with listening comprehension. *PASAA, 48*, 29–56.

Teubner, T., Flath, C. M., Weinhardt, C., Aalst, W., & Hinz, O. (2023). Welcome to the Era of ChatGPT et al. *Business & Information Systems Engineering, 65*(2), 95–101. doi:10.100712599-023-00795-x

The impact of AI on language learning and teaching. (n.d.). *TalkPal AI*. https://talkpal.ai/the-impact-of-ai-on-language-learning-and-teaching/

Thompson, P., & Nesi, H. (2001). The British Academic Spoken English (BASE) Corpus Project. *Language Teaching Research*, *5*(3), 263–264. doi:10.1177/136216880100500305

Thorp, H. (2023). ChatGPT is fun, but not an author. *Science*, *379*(6630), 313. Advance online publication. doi:10.1126cience.adg7879 PMID:36701446

Tias, I. W. U., Izzatika, A., & Perdana, R. (2022). Empowerment of Critical and Creative Thinking (CCT) Skills Through Student Worksheets Based on Inquiry Social Complexity (ISC). *WSEAS Transactions on Environment and Development*, *18*, 865–872. doi:10.37394/232015.2022.18.81

Tomei, L. A. (2010). Learning Theories and Pedagogy: Teaching the Traditional Learner. *Designing Instruction for the Traditional, Adult, and Distance Learner: A New Engine for Technology-Based Teaching*.

Topal, M., & Karaca, O. (2022). Gamification in E-Learning. In *Research Anthology on Developments in Gamification and Game-Based Learning* (pp. 1–20). IGI Global., doi:10.4018/978-1-6684-3710-0.ch001

Torfi, A., Shirvani, R. A., Keneshloo, Y., Tavaf, N., & Fox, E. A. (2020). Natural language processing advancements by deep learning. *Survey (London, England)*. Advance online publication. doi:10.48550/arXiv.2003.01200

Tsai, S. C. (2019). Using google translate in EFL drafts: A preliminary investigation. *Computer Assisted Language Learning*, *32*(5-6), 5–6, 510–526. doi:10.1080/09588221.2018.1527361

Tsai, S. C. (2022). Chinese students' perceptions of using Google Translate as a translingual CALL tool in EFL writing. *Computer Assisted Language Learning*, *35*(5-6), 1250–1272. doi:10.1080/09588221.2020.1799412

Tularam, G. (2018). Traditional vs Non-Traditional Teaching and Learning Strategies: The Case of E-Learning. *International Journal for Mathematics Teaching and Learning*, *19*(1), 129–158. doi:10.4256/ijmtl.v19i1.21

Turan, Z., & Karabey, S. C. (2023). The use of immersive technologies in distance education: A systematic review. *Education and Information Technologies*. doi:10.100710639-023-11849-8 PMID:37361798

Turing, A. M. (1950). Computing machinery and intelligence. *Mind*, *59*(236), 433–460. doi:10.1093/mind/LIX.236.433

Ur, P. (2019, September 6). *Penny Ur - My Top 30 teaching Tips (plus some extras!)* [Video]. YouTube. https://youtu.be/ddOudlhnjPE?t=1274

Urlaub, P., & Dessein, E. (2022). Machine translation and foreign language education. *Frontiers*, *1-5*, 936111. Advance online publication. doi:10.3389/frai.2022.936111 PMID:35937139

Ur, P. (2022). *Penny Ur's 77 tips for teaching vocabulary*. Cambridge University Press., doi:10.1017/9781009072892

Utamachant, P., Anutariya, C., & Pongnumkul, S. (2023). i-Ntervene: Applying an evidence-based learning analytics intervention to support computer programming instruction. *Smart Learning Environments, 10*(1), 37. doi:10.118640561-023-00257-7

Vaidya, T., Zhang, Y., Sherr, M., & Shields, C. (2015, August). Cocaine noodles: exploiting the gap between human and machine speech recognition. In *Proceedings of the 9th USENIX Conference.*

Valenti, S., Neri, F., & Cucchiarelli, A. (2003). An Overview of Current Research on Automated Essay Grading. *Journal of Information Technology Education*, *2*(1), 319–330. doi:10.28945/331

Van der Kleij, F. M., Feskens, R. C., & Eggen, T. J. (2015). Effects of feedback in a computer-based learning environment on students' learning outcomes: A meta-analysis. *Review of Educational Research*, *85*(4), 475–511. doi:10.3102/0034654314564881

van Lieshout, C., & Cardoso, W. (2022). Google Translate as a tool for self-directed language learning. *Language Learning & Technology*, *26*(1), 1–19.

VanLehn, K. (2011). The relative effectiveness of human tutoring, intelligent tutoring systems, and other tutoring systems. *Educational Psychologist*, *46*(4), 197–221. doi:10.1080/00461520.2011.611369

Vázquez-Cano, E. (2021). Artificial intelligence and education: A pedagogical challenge for the 21st century. *Educational Process: international journal, 10*(3), 7-12.

Verbert, K., Duval, E., Klerkx, J., Govaerts, S., & Santos, J. L. (2013). Learning analytics dashboard applications. *The American Behavioral Scientist*, *57*(10), 1500–1509. doi:10.1177/0002764213479363

Vesin, B., Mangaroska, K., & Giannakos, M. (2018). Learning in smart environments: User-centered design and analytics of an adaptive learning system. *Smart Learning Environments*, *5*(1), 1–21. doi:10.118640561-018-0071-0

von Kleist, H. (1951). On the Gradual Construction of Thoughts during Speech (M. Hamburger, Trans.). *German Life and Letters*, *5*(1), 42–46. doi:10.1111/j.1468-0483.1951.tb01029.x

Voskoglou, M. (2023). *Artificial Intelligence and Digital Technologies in the Future Education.* Qeios. doi:10.32388/07VE29

Wang, R. (2019). Research on artificial intelligence promoting English learning change. *3rd international conference on economics and management, education, humanities and social sciences (EMEHSS 2019)*.

Wang, Q., Madaio, M., Kane, S., Kapania, S., Terry, M., & Wilcox, L. (2023). Designing Responsible AI: Adaptations of UX Practice to Meet Responsible AI Challenges. In *Proceedings of the 2023 CHI Conference on Human Factors in Computing Systems* (pp. 1-16). 10.1145/3544548.3581278

Wang, Y. C. (2023). Gamification in a News English Course. *Education Sciences*, *13*(1), 90. Advance online publication. doi:10.3390/educsci13010090

Wang, Y. F., & Petrina, S. (2013). Using learning analytics to understand the design of an intelligent language tutor – Chatbot Lucy. *International Journal of Advanced Computer Science and Applications*, *4*(11), 124–131. doi:10.14569/IJACSA.2013.041117

Wardat, Y., Tashtoush, M. A., AlAli, R., & Jarrah, A. M. (2023). ChatGPT: A revolutionary tool for teaching and learning mathematics. *Eurasia Journal of Mathematics, Science and Technology Education*, *19*(7), em2286. doi:10.29333/ejmste/13272

Warschauer, M. (2004). *Technology and social inclusion: Rethinking the digital divide*. MIT.

Warschauer, M., & Ware, P. (2006). Automated writing evaluation: Defining the classroom research agenda. *Language Teaching Research*, *10*(2), 157–180. doi:10.1191/1362168806lr190oa

Wilkins, D. A. (1972). *Linguistics in language teaching*. Arnold.

Witt, S. M. (2012, June). Automatic error detection in pronunciation training: Where we are and where we need to go. In *International Symposium on Automatic Detection on Errors in Pronunciation Training* (Vol. 1).

Xiao, Y., & Hu, J. (2019). Assessment of optimal pedagogical factors for Canadian ESL learners' reading literacy through artificial intelligence algorithms. *International Journal of English Linguistics*, *9*(4), 1–14. doi:10.5539/ijel.v9n4p1

Xie, Y., Ryder, L., & Chen, Y. (2019). Using interactive virtual reality tools in an advanced Chinese language class: A case study. *TechTrends*, *63*(3), 251–259. doi:10.100711528-019-00389-z

Xin, Y. (2022). Influence of Learning Engagement on Learning Effect under a Virtual Reality (VR) Environment. *International Journal of Emerging Technologies in Learning*, *17*(5), 226–237. doi:10.3991/ijet.v17i05.29451

Xi, X. (2010). Automated scoring and feedback systems: Where are we and where are we heading? *Language Testing*, *27*(3), 291–300. doi:10.1177/0265532210364643

Xu, W. (2023). AI in HCI Design and User Experience. arXiv preprint arXiv:2301.00987.

Xu, W., Meng, J., Raja, S. K. S., Priya, M. P., & Kiruthiga Devi, M. (2023). Artificial intelligence in constructing personalized and accurate feedback systems for students. *International Journal of Modeling, Simulation, and Scientific Computing*, *14*(01), 2341001. doi:10.1142/S1793962323410015

Yan, D. (2023). Impact of ChatGPT on learners in a L2 writing practicum: An exploratory investigation. *Education and Information Technologies*, 1–25. doi:10.100710639-023-11742-4

Yang, P., & Liu, Z. (2022). The influence of Immersive Virtual Reality (IVR) on skill transfer of learners: The moderating effects of learning engagement. *International Journal of Emerging Technologies in Learning*, *17*(10), 62–73. doi:10.3991/ijet.v17i10.30923

Yanhua, Z. (2020). The application of artificial intelligence in foreign language teaching. *ICAIE*, *40-42*, 40–42. doi:10.1109/ICAIE50891.2020.00017

Yeo-Teh, N., & Tang, B. (2023). Letter to Editor: NLP systems such as ChatGPT cannot be listed as an author because these cannot fulfill widely adopted authorship criteria. Accountability in Research. 1–3. doi:10.1080/08989621.2023.2177160

Yu, H. (2023). Reflection on whether Chat GPT should be banned by academia from the perspective of education and teaching. *Frontiers in Psychology*, *14*, 1181712. doi:10.3389/fpsyg.2023.1181712 PMID:37325766

Zain, F. M., Sailin, S. N., Kasim, M., Abdul Karim, A. M., & Zameri, N. N. (2022). Developing an Augmented Reality Immersive Learning Design (AILeaD) Framework: A Fuzzy Delphi Approach. [IJIM]. *International Journal of Interactive Mobile Technologies*, *16*(11), 65–90. doi:10.3991/ijim.v16i11.30063

Zawacki-Richter, O., Marín, V. I., Bond, M., & Gouverneur, F. (2019). Systematic review of research on artificial intelligence applications in higher education–where are the educators? *International Journal of Educational Technology in Higher Education*, *16*(1), 1–27. doi:10.118641239-019-0171-0

Zeichner, K., & Noffke, S. (2001). Practitioner research. In V. Richardson (Ed.), *Handbook of research on teaching* (4th ed., pp. 298–330). American Educational Research Association.

Zeide, E. (2017). The structural consequences of big data-driven education. *Big Data*, *5*(2), 164–172. doi:10.1089/big.2016.0061

Zerogpt.net. (2023). *ZeroGPT*. Zero GPT. https://zerogpt.net/

Zhang, H., & Torres-Hostench, O. (2022). Training in machine translation post-editing for foreign language students. *Language Learning & Technology*, *26*(1), 1–17.

Zhang, R., & Zou, D. (2020). Types, purposes, and effectiveness of state-of-the-art technologies for second and foreign language learning. *Computer Assisted Language Learning*, 1–47.

Zhang, Y. (2022). Construction of English language autonomous learning center system based on artificial intelligence technology. *Mathematical Problems in Engineering*, *2022*, 1–12. doi:10.1155/2022/7900493

Zhao, L., Wu, X., & Luo, H. (2022). Developing AI literacy for primary and middle school teachers in China: Based on a structural equation modeling analysis. *Sustainability (Basel)*, *14*(21), 14549. doi:10.3390u142114549

Zhavoronkov, A. (2022). Rapamycin in the context of Pascal's Wager: Generative pre-trained transformer perspective. *Oncoscience*, *9*, 82–84. doi:10.18632/oncoscience.571 PMID:36589923

Zheng, J. M., Chan, K. W., & Gibson, I. (1998). Virtual reality. *IEEE Potentials*, *17*(2), 20–23. doi:10.1109/45.666641 PMID:9699075

Zhou, Y. (2021b). Artificial neural network-based smart aerogel glazing in low-energy buildings: A state-of-the-art review. *iScience*, *24*(12), 103420. doi:10.1016/j.isci.2021.103420 PMID:34849473

Zhou, Z. H. (2021a). *Machine learning*. Springer Nature. doi:10.1007/978-981-15-1967-3

Zichermann, G., & Cunningham, C. (2011). *Gamification by design: Implementing game mechanics in web and mobile apps*. O'Reilly Media.

Zimmerman, B. J. (2008). Investigating self-regulation and motivation: Historical background, methodological developments, and future prospects. *American Educational Research Journal*, *45*(1), 166–183. doi:10.3102/0002831207312909

Zou, J., & Schiebinger, L. (2018). AI can be sexist and racist — It's time to make it fair. [Shermis]. *Nature*, *559*(7714), 324–326. doi:10.1038/d41586-018-05707-8 PMID:30018439

Zou, S. (2017). Designing and practice of a college English teaching platform based on artificial intelligence. *Journal of Computational and Theoretical Nanoscience*, *14*(1), 104–108. doi:10.1166/jctn.2017.6133

Žukauskas, P., Vveinhardt, J., & Andriukaitienė, R. (2018). Philosophy and Paradigm of Scientific Research. In *Management Culture and Corporate Social Responsibility*. IntechOpen., doi:10.5772/intechopen.70628

About the Contributors

Galip Kartal is an accomplished Associate Professor in the Department of English Language Teaching at Necmettin Erbakan University in Konya, Turkey. He holds a BA, MA, and PhD in English Language Teaching, reflecting his extensive expertise in the field.Dr. Kartal's research interests span teaching vocabulary, innovative language learning and teaching techniques, and second language teacher education with a focus on professional development. In recent years, he has also explored the potential of AI-supported language teaching to transform traditional instructional methods and improve student outcomes. As a dedicated educator and researcher, Dr. Kartal continues to make significant contributions to the field of English Language Teaching, shaping the future of language education for teachers and learners alike.

***

Arif Bakla is a lecturer at Translation and Interpretation Department, Ankara Yıldırım Beyazıt University, Ankara, Turkey. He holds a PhD degree in ELT. Among his research interests are vocabulary instruction, CALL, feedback in L2 writing. He has recently published in various international journals, including Language Learning & Technology, ReCALL, Computers & Education, Qualitative Research, Instructional Science and Australian Journal of Education. He is the author of the book *Putting Pen to Paper: Academic Paragraph Writing*.

Mavis Chamboko-Mpotaringa is a holder of a Ph.D, a Master of Management Sciences and a Bachelor of Commerce (Hons) degrees in Tourism and Hospitality Management. She also holds a Post Graduate Certificate in Education (PGCE) and Teaching English as a Foreign Language (TEFL) certification. She has over ten years of experience in education and tourism. Dr. Chamboko-Mpotaringa is a multidiscipline researcher who has published journal articles and presented her research findings at local and international conferences. As she completes this project, she focuses on her next research project on the metaverse.

Chad C. Davidson has a master's in philosophy and master's in language education. He combined these two passions when he attained his Ph.D. from Kansas State University. His dissertation is entitled, "Exploring multiple language learning from an existential perspective: An applied philosophical inquiry of self-cultivation and aspiration in language learning." This underscores his main research interest: an applied philosophy of language education with the goal of higher-order value incorporation and harmonization throughout all areas of language education.

Ayşenur Hoşoğlu is an MA student in Applied Linguistics program at Karadeniz Technical University. She holds her BA degree with high honours at the same university's English Language and Literature department. Her main research areas include Corpus Linguistics, Learner Corpora, Data-Driven Learning, English for Specific Purposes, English for Academic Purposes, Translation Studies, Academic Writing, and Critical Discourse Analysis. Hoşoğlu is currently working at Avrasya University as a research assistant

Matti Ibrahim is a doctoral candidate of international relations and school leadership. She has published and presented on a range of topics from international relations, gun control, and education. Mrs. Ibrahim holds a bachelor's degree in cultural and geospatial studies, a master's degree in Teaching English to Speakers of Other Languages, and teaches English at Necmettin Erbakan University.

Mohamed Ibrahim is a Professor of Curriculum and Instruction and Director of the Master of Education in Instructional Design & Technology program at Arkansas Tech University's College of Education. He received his Ph.D. in Educational Technology from Oklahoma State University. Dr. Ibrahim has over 20 years of experience teaching graduate and undergraduate courses in educational technology, instructional design, curriculum development, and research methods. His areas of expertise include online learning, multimedia design, flipped classroom strategies, project-based learning, and integrating emerging technologies into teaching. Dr. Ibrahim is actively engaged in research on enhancing student learning outcomes and motivation through technology integration, metacognition, and multimedia design. He has presented his scholarly work at major conferences including AERA, SITE, EdMedia, ASEE and ISEC. His research has been published in peer-reviewed journals such as Learning, Media and Technology; Journal of Computing Sciences in Colleges; and International Journal of E-Learning. At Arkansas Tech, Dr. Ibrahim serves on several university committees focused on curriculum, faculty development, and student success initiatives. He mentors undergraduate researchers and is the academic advisor for student organizations. Dr. Ibrahim has secured internal and external grant funding to support his research and professional development activities. He is also an active member of leading education organizations such as AERA, ASEE, and ArATE. Through his diverse academic roles, he aims to empower educators and students to leverage technology for impactful teaching and learning.

Ali Karakaş is an associate professor of Applied Linguistics in the Department of Foreign Language Education, Burdur Mehmet Akif Ersoy University, Burdur, Turkey. He's also a postdoctoral member of the Centre for Global Englishes, Southampton University, UK. His main research interests include Global Englishes, English as a lingua franca, World Englishes, Language policy and planning, and language teacher education. He also serves on the editorial boards of several national and international journals, including *Asian EFL Journal* and *The Journal of English as an International Language*. He is the co-editor of the book, *English as the Medium of Instruction in Turkish Higher Education* published by Springer. Currently, he is interested in research on translanguaging practices in EMI classrooms in the Turkish higher education context.

Blandina Manditereza is a Lecturer in the Department of Childhood Education,Faculty of Education, at the University of The Free State, Bloemfontein, South Africa. She received a Diploma in Primary Education from Nyadire Teachers College,a BTech Education Management Degree from Tshwane University of Technology, an Honors in Education Degree from Central University of Technology, a Masters in Education Degree from Central University of Technology as well, and a PhD in Philosophy (Curriculum Studies) from the University of the Free State.

Zoe Marlowe is an Assistant Professor in the English Language Teacher Education department at Biruni University, Istanbul. Dr. Marlowe's research focus is primarily on improving English language learning and teaching in the Turkish university setting. As a native English speaking American teacher, her primary areas of focus and interest include linguistics, listening, critical reading and writing, and sociolinguistics.

Ali Şükrü Özbay holds his BA in English Language and Literature from Ankara University and MA from KTU, Applied Linguistics Program and PhD from the English Language and Literature department of KTU. His main areas of interest include Corpus Linguistics and Learner Corpora, translation studies, Pragmatics, Sociolinguistics, Academic Writing and error analysis, and Phraseology. He has published research articles and book chapters on corpus linguistics, phraseology, data-driven learning, meta-discourse, semantic prosody and lexical priming. Associated Professor Dr. Özbay is currently the Departmental Coordinator of Erasmus Exchange Programs, and a faculty member at Karadeniz Technical University, Turkey.

Sibel Özdemir-Çağatay earned her undergraduate degree in ELT from Boğaziçi University, Turkey in 2007 and completed the international teaching certificate of In-service Training in English Language teaching (ICELT) delivered by Cambridge University in 2009. She did her master's in MA TEFL program at Bilkent University in 2012, and completed her PhD in English Language Teaching at Hacettepe University in 2018. She worked as a lecturer at Bilkent University between the years 2007 and 2009 and since 2009, she has been working as a lecturer (PhD) at Middle East Technical University (METU), Turkey. In addition to her own research studies, she is currently working as the coordinator of the Research & Development Unit (R&D) of Foreign Languages Department at METU, conducting research to improve the implementations at the department. She has also delivered EAP classes such as academic writing for publishing purposes for academics working in different universities and second language acquisition courses for pre-service English teachers. Her professional interests lie in attributions, L2 Motivational Self System (L2MSS), English Medium Instruction (EMI), motivation, teacher education & identity, and culture in language teaching. She has several publications in journals indexed in Scopus, ESCI, ERIC and also in some international books.

Ercüment Öztürk graduated from the department of Computer Engineering at Pamukkale University in 2012 and then joined the department of Computer Engineering of Artvin Çoruh University in 2014. Recieved his M.Sc. degree from Karadeniz Technical University and now is a Ph.D. candidate at the same department where he still works as a research assistant. His main research areas of interest include Machine Learning, Heuristic Algorithms, Optimization Problems, Artificial Intelligence, Deep Learning, and AI Applications.

Reena Satpute holds B. E. (Information Technology, 2007) and M. Tech. (Computer Science & Engineering, 2014) from R.T.M. Nagpur University, Nagpur. Currently, she is a research Scholar of Shri. Ramdeobaba College of Engineering & Management, Nagpur. At present, she is working as an Assistant Professor in faculty of Science and Technology and CDOE at Datta Meghe Institute of Higher Education & Research (DU), Sawangi (M). She is having overall 16 Years of experience including teaching and industry. She has proficiency in Artificial intelligence, Natural Language Processing, Java Programming, Database management System, Data Warehousing, Data Mining and Software Testing etc. Recently Ms. Reena has been awarded with YOUNG RESEARCHER AWARD - 2023 by Institute of Scholars. She has been honoured with "BEST TEACHER AWARD as well. Also, she has been appreciated by Ministry of Education Affairs (MEA) for her outstanding teaching and monitoring of international students studying under Centre of Distance and Online Education. Apart from this, she is an author of two books "Core PHP -

For the Web" and "Artificial Intelligence - An Predictable Evolution". In addition to this, her 3 book chapters will be published soon in IGI Global publisher. Out of 04, she has credit of 02 copyrights in her account. She has associated with diverse Professional Bodies of Engineering and Technology. She is vigorous Member of International Association of Engineers (IAENG). She is Associate Member (UACEE) of Institute of Research Engineers & Doctors (IRED). She had been a Graduate Student Member of Institute of Electrical & Electronics Engineers (IEEE), Bombay Section. She has attended around 20 workshops, 10 FDP, 03 Short Term Training Programmes (STTP) and seminars organized and conducted by greatly renowned councils such as DTE, UGC, Dale CARNEGIE, IIT Bombay and ISTE chapters etc. She has published around 15 research papers in National and International Journals with significant ISSN approved Number and conferences. Few research articles are published in Scopus indexed journal also. Author is actively involved in various social activities.

Ümran Üstünbaş, PhD. is currently working as an assistant professor at Zonguldak Bülent Ecevit University, Ereğli Faculty of Education, English Language Teaching Department, Türkiye. She completed her BA degree in English Language Teaching (ELT) at Anadolu University, Türkiye, MA degree in TEFL at Bilkent University, Türkiye and PhD. degree in ELT at Hacettepe University, Türkiye. Her research interests are teacher education and training, educational technologies, L2 writing andpragmatics and educational policies.

Buse Uzuner holds her BA degree in English Language and Literature with high honours degree from Karadeniz Technical University and MA degree in Applied Linguistics with high honours degree from the same university. Her main areas of interest include corpus linguistics, learner corpora, academic writing, data-driven learning.

Sabahattin Yeşilçınar, PhD, holds an MA in English language literature from Van Yüzüncü Yıl University and a PhD in English language teaching from Gazi University. He is Assistant Professor in the Department of English Language Teaching at Muş Alparslan University. His research interests include teacher education, teacher assessment, technology in language teaching and learning, and language testing. He teaches English speaking, listening and writing, and Learning and Teaching Approaches in English at the undergraduate level.

Yusuf Emre Yesilyurt, Deparment of Foreign Languages Education, Burdur Mehmet Akif Ersoy University, Turkiye He graduated from English Language Teaching Department of Gazi University, Turkiye in 2009. He worked as an English language teacher at a state high school in İstanbul for a year. He then earned his MA degree in TESOL from Bristol University, UK in 2013. Following his MA graduation, he started working as a research assistant at Burdur Mehmet Akif Ersoy University. In order to obtain his PhD degree, he started working as a research assistant at Gazi University. Upon his graduation in 2021, he came back to Burdur Mehmet Akif Ersoy University. Now, he is working as an assistant professor at the English Language Teaching Department of this university. His main research interests include academic writing, teaching and researching writing, automated writing evaluation, artificial intelligence and education, and conversation analysis in language teaching and learning.

Mustafa Yildiz holds a PhD from the department of English Language Teaching of Anadolu University. He is currently working as an English instructor at Samsun University, Türkiye. His research interests include vocabulary acquisition/teaching.

Index

F

G

H

I

L

M

N

O

P

S

T

V

W

www.ingramcontent.com/pod-product-compliance
Lightning Source LLC
LaVergne TN
LVHW080557300926
849162LV00005B/974